PowerShell Core for Linux Administrators Cookbook

Use PowerShell Core 6.x on Linux to automate complex, repetitive, and time-consuming tasks

Prashanth Jayaram
Ram Iyer

BIRMINGHAM - MUMBAI

PowerShell Core for Linux Administrators Cookbook

Commissioning Editor: Vijin Boricha
Acquisition Editor: Rohit Rajkumar
Content Development Editor: Deepti Thore
Technical Editor: Rudolph Almeida
Copy Editor: Safis Editing
Project Coordinator: Jagdish Prabhu
Proofreader: Safis Editing
Indexer: Rekha Nair
Graphics: Jisha Chirayil
Production Coordinator: Arvindkumar Gupta

First published: November 2018

Production reference: 1291118

Published by Packt Publishing Ltd.
Livery Place
35 Livery Street
Birmingham
B3 2PB, UK.

ISBN 978-1-78913-723-1

www.packtpub.com

To all my respected teachers; my loving wife Ambika, my sole daughters, Pravitha and Prarthana; my caring brothers, Balu and Gopinath; my dearest friend, Adarsh; the precious gift of my life, my Mom, Indira and my Dad, Jayaram; and my entire family. Thank you for all the support and for everything you have done so far. It is difficult to express my gratitude in words.

– Prasanth Jayaram

To Mum and Dad.

– Ram Iyer

`mapt.io`

Mapt is an online digital library that gives you full access to over 5,000 books and videos, as well as industry leading tools to help you plan your personal development and advance your career. For more information, please visit our website.

Why subscribe?

- Spend less time learning and more time coding with practical eBooks and Videos from over 4,000 industry professionals

- Improve your learning with Skill Plans built especially for you

- Get a free eBook or video every month

- Mapt is fully searchable

- Copy and paste, print, and bookmark content

Packt.com

Did you know that Packt offers eBook versions of every book published, with PDF and ePub files available? You can upgrade to the eBook version at `www.packt.com` and as a print book customer, you are entitled to a discount on the eBook copy. Get in touch with us at `customercare@packtpub.com` for more details.

At `www.packt.com`, you can also read a collection of free technical articles, sign up for a range of free newsletters, and receive exclusive discounts and offers on Packt books and eBooks.

Contributors

About the authors

Prashanth Jayaram is a product design and automation expert in database technology with 12 years of rich, extensive, hands-on experience in designing database solutions with next-gen database technologies. He was awarded as the second-best SQL author of 2017 for his contribution to the SQL Server technology space. He has written over 200 articles about SQL, NoSQL, PowerShell, Python, SQL on Linux, SQL on Azure, and SQL on AWS.

Ram Iyer is an automation and application performance management specialist with about eight years of experience in enterprise IT. While ensuring that the environment in his enterprise performs optimally is his primary role, he is passionate about automation using PowerShell, and has contributed to over 60 enterprise-grade automation solutions in Windows, Microsoft Exchange, Microsoft Active Directory, Microsoft System Center, Citrix XenApp, VMware PowerCLI, and Microsoft Azure, using PowerShell. He gives back to the community by conducting training sessions in PowerShell and blogging about administration using PowerShell.

About the reviewers

Cathal Mullane has worked in the build, release and DevOps area for the past four years. After graduating from Limerick Institute of Technology with a first class honors degree in software development, he began to work with Hewlett Packard. In 2016, he joined Fleetmatics (now Verizon Connect) as a build engineer. His main duties were the building, packaging, and deployment of the platform components to all the environments. He was involved in introducing new continuous integration and continuous deployment pipelines that were used to break up the existing monolith solution into small components that could be deployed at any time. This was achieved using PowerShell scripts along with tools from the Atlassian Stack and Octopus Deploy.

Jose Angel Muñoz is a systems engineer with more than 20 years of experience in Linux and Windows systems administration. He is currently working for RAET, where he has discovered the magic of automation and infrastructure as code. Jose Angel is also collaborating with the Ansible, creating new Python and PowerShell modules.

Jose Angel use to collaborate with the Linux Magazine, where he published several technical articles about different topics such as monitoring, security, virtualization, or development.

Mohit Goyal is a budding technical expert with 10 years of experience as an IT professional. He has worked on varied range of technologies, chiefly in infrastructure services and automation, from cloud-based to on-premises systems. He has a knack for maximizing the potential of product teams and automating software delivery processes. He currently works at Johnson Controls, Inc. as a Senior DevOps engineer. He has been involved in the DevOps and PowerShell community and also maintains a popular blog where he contributes posts related to his research and everyday technical realizations.

Vic Perdana has over 13 years of experience with broad knowledge and consulting skills in cloud technology, DevOps, and automation. He has lead teams and managed large-scale application and infrastructure deployment projects, specifically to do with hybrid-infrastructure migration. Vic's current focus is on the development, implementation, and architecture of Azure solutions, resolving a broad range of business and technical challenges faced by many customers.

Vic holds a Master of IT degree from the University of Melbourne and currently works as a Senior Consultant at Dimension Data.

Packt is searching for authors like you

If you're interested in becoming an author for Packt, please visit `authors.packtpub.com` and apply today. We have worked with thousands of developers and tech professionals, just like you, to help them share their insight with the global tech community. You can make a general application, apply for a specific hot topic that we are recruiting an author for, or submit your own idea.

Table of Contents

Preface

PowerShell Core is an implementation of .NET Core. .NET Core is a cross-platform open source management framework that adheres to the POSIX standards and provides API calls that work well with all of the major operating systems: Windows, Linux, and macOS.

.NET Core for Linux has been a success because of its adherence to standards, and because of its lightweight implementation. PowerShell extends the capabilities toward the management of Linux servers, cloud infrastructure, and the utilization of Docker containers.

PowerShell Core for Linux Administrators Cookbook takes readers through a complete tour of understanding PowerShell Core on .NET Core in general, and PowerShell on Linux for management and automation, as well as advanced concepts, such as creating cmdlet-like functions, through to using PowerShell to manage remote machines using OpenSSH, automatic job scheduler, Docker containers, Azure and AWS Cloud, and Microsoft SQL databases.

Who this book is for

This book is for you if you are a Linux administrator who's open to other scripting frameworks, a system administrator who manages Linux as well as Windows workloads, and is looking to unify management, a Linux administrator who wants a framework that easily handles structured data, a Windows administrator who is new to PowerShell and wants to learn PowerShell scripting, or if you are a system administrator who is just generally curious.

Bash is, without a doubt, a great shell. While Windows PowerShell uses many Linux commands as convenience aliases, PowerShell Core on Linux is unobtrusive. PowerShell Core on Linux treats Linux commands as Linux commands (and not as convenience aliases) and calls the respective application, such as ls or grep. This way, PowerShell Core sits well in the Linux framework, and provides system administrators with a flexible, quickly-evolving toolset that enables them to write a script once and run the script everywhere—on Linux or Windows.

PowerShell is perhaps the only framework in Linux that works well with structured data. Structured data and the object model simplify automation, by packaging related data and functions within the object. Access to these members of the objects improve efficiency, thereby making automation smoother.

This book understands that an object-oriented shell has mostly been unheard of (OS/2 Workspace Shell, anybody?), and takes the reader through the concept of an object-oriented shell. Therefore, this book assumes some very basic knowledge on the reader's part, with respect to how an operating system is structured and how to use the command-line interface to work with the operating system. No experience in PowerShell is assumed.

In this book, you will learn the following topics:

- The fundamentals of .NET Core and PowerShell Core
- How to work with .NET (and, by extension, PowerShell) objects, understanding how they are structured and how they work
- The different constructs, and how to create scripts, functions, and simple script modules, all with best practices in mind
- The administration of computers locally as well as remotely, including scheduling remote jobs and retrieving their output
- How to work with the cloud (Amazon Web Services has been touched upon, while Azure has been covered in more detail)

What this book covers

Chapter 1, *Introducing PowerShell Core*, introduces PowerShell Core. The chapter covers the installation of PowerShell and the basic setup, along with an introduction to objects.

Chapter 2, *Preparing for Administration Using PowerShell*, helps to understand how PowerShell behaves, how to efficiently write commands by reducing keystrokes, and how redirection works.

Chapter 3, *First Steps in Administration Using PowerShell*, introduces the basic utilities, such as finding and working with processes running in the system.

Chapter 4, *Passing Data through the Pipelines*, demonstrates how the pipeline works, and how to leverage it to work with the returned objects.

Chapter 5, *Using Variables and Objects*, focuses on the built-in variables, the environment, and working with objects, including extending existing objects and creating custom ones.

Chapter 6, *Working with Strings*, introduces the string as an object, and walks through string manipulation using operators as well as the methods built into the string objects.

Chapter 7, *Flow Control Using Branches and Loops*, walks through using branching and looping constructs to control the flow of scripts and functions.

Chapter 8, *Performing Calculations*, briefly demonstrates how to work with numbers by performing arithmetic operations, calculations, and conversions, along with introducing the administrative constants.

Chapter 9, *Using Arrays and Hashtables*, explains how arrays and hash tables are created, used, and manipulated in PowerShell.

Chapter 10, *Handling Files and Directories*, focuses on file and directory operations, such as sending and retrieving content to and from a file, searching for content, and working with structured as well as unstructured files.

Chapter 11, *Building Scripts and Functions*, begins with creating a simple script and then proceeds to writing functions that accept arguments.

Chapter 12, *Advanced Concepts of Functions*, extends the knowledge gained in the previous chapters and introduces the concepts of parameters, parameter aliases and sets, working with dependencies, adding help, and so on, in order to create functions that behave like cmdlets.

Chapter 13, *Debugging and Error Handling*, shows how to work with, and handle, errors and warnings, and walks through how to use the debug tab of Visual Studio Code.

Chapter 14, *Enterprise Administration Using PowerShell*, covers how to set up PowerShell for remote access and enterprise administration. It explains the use of PowerShell across Windows and Linux environments.

Chapter 15, *PowerShell and Cloud Operations*, aims at getting started with cloud administration using PowerShell. This chapter introduces the use of PowerShell on Azure and AWS cloud services.

Chapter 16, *Using PowerShell for SQL Database Management*, introduces PowerShell for SQL database management, starting from the installation of the SQL Server module through to integrating Python with PowerShell for database management.

Chapter 17, *Using PowerShell with Docker*, explains the implementation of Docker management using PowerShell. Coupled with the understanding gained in Chapter 1, *Introducing PowerShell Core*, this chapter explains how to use the Docker module, as well as using the Docker API with .NET Core.

To get the most out of this book

Before you begin, you need to have some basic knowledge of how Linux works. That is to say, you need to know what a desktop environment is, or how to work with a package manager. You also need to know how to troubleshoot basic errors. Knowing the very basics of what a `for` loop is, or what `Switch-Case` is, would help you learn faster.

Also, if you are new to PowerShell, reading the first chapter is recommended. This chapter contains a couple of important guidelines for working efficiently with PowerShell.

The book also assumes that you are working on either Ubuntu or CentOS. While PowerShell constructs themselves do not behave differently with different Linux flavors (or even different platforms), the installation—and sometimes the configuration—may be different on different flavors of Linux.

Download the example code files

You can download the example code files for this book from your account at `www.packt.com`. If you purchased this book elsewhere, you can visit `www.packt.com/support` and register to have the files emailed directly to you.

You can download the code files by following these steps:

1. Log in or register at `www.packt.com`.
2. Select the **SUPPORT** tab.
3. Click on **Code Downloads & Errata**.
4. Enter the name of the book in the **Search** box and follow the on-screen instructions.

Once the file is downloaded, please make sure that you unzip or extract the folder using the latest version of:

- WinRAR/7-Zip for Windows
- Zipeg/iZip/UnRarX for Mac
- 7-Zip/PeaZip for Linux

The code bundle for the book is also hosted on GitHub at `https://github.com/PacktPublishing/PowerShell-Core-Linux-Administrators-Cookbook`. In case there is an update to the code, it will be updated on the existing GitHub repository.

We also have other code bundles from our rich catalogue of books and videos available at `https://github.com/PacktPublishing/`. Check them out!

Download the color images

We also provide a PDF file that has colour images of the screenshots/diagrams used in this book. You can download it here: `https://www.packtpub.com/sites/default/files/downloads/9781789137231_ColorImages.pdf`.

Conventions used

There are a number of text conventions used throughout this book.

`CodeInText`: Indicates code words in text, database table names, folder names, filenames, file extensions, path names, dummy URLs, user input, and Twitter handles. Here is an example: "Create a file called simply `script.ps1`."

A block of code is set as follows:

```
Get-Date
hostname
Write-Output "Hello, $env:username!"
```

When we wish to draw your attention to a particular part of a code block, the relevant lines or items are set in bold:

```
$Date = Get-Date
if ($Date.DayOfWeek –in 'Saturday', 'Sunday') {
    Write-Host 'It is a weekend!'
}
else {
    Write-Host 'It is a weekday.'
}
```

Any command-line input or output is written as follows:

```
PS> Get-Process dconf-editor
PS> Stop-Process -Id 20608
```

Bold: Indicates a new term, an important word, or words that you see on screen. For example, words in menus or dialog boxes appear in the text like this. Here is an example: "Click the Cloud Shell icon in the top navigation bar of the Azure portal; select either **Bash** or **PowerShell**."

Warnings or important notes appear like this.

 Tips and tricks appear like this.

Sections

In this book, you will find several headings that appear frequently (*Getting ready, How to do it..., How it works..., There's more...*, and *See also*).

To give clear instructions on how to complete a recipe, use these sections as follows:

Getting ready

This section tells you what to expect in the recipe and describes how to set up any software or any preliminary settings required for the recipe.

How to do it...

This section contains the steps required to follow the recipe.

How it works...

This section usually consists of a detailed explanation of what happened in the previous section.

There's more...

This section consists of additional information about the recipe in order to increase your knowledgeable of it.

See also

This section provides helpful links to other useful information for the recipe.

Get in touch

Feedback from our readers is always welcome.

General feedback: If you have questions about any aspect of this book, mention the book title in the subject of your message and email us at customercare@packtpub.com.

Errata: Although we have taken every care to ensure the accuracy of our content, mistakes do happen. If you have found a mistake in this book, we would be grateful if you would report this to us. Please visit www.packt.com/submit-errata, selecting your book, clicking on the Errata Submission Form link, and entering the details.

Piracy: If you come across any illegal copies of our works in any form on the internet, we would be grateful if you would provide us with the location address or website name. Please contact us at copyright@packt.com with a link to the material.

If you are interested in becoming an author: If there is a topic that you have expertise in, and you are interested in either writing or contributing to a book, please visit authors.packtpub.com.

Reviews

Please leave a review. Once you have read and used this book, why not leave a review on the site that you purchased it from? Potential readers can then see and use your unbiased opinion to make purchase decisions, we at Packt can understand what you think about our products, and our authors can see your feedback on their book. Thank you!

For more information about Packt, please visit packt.com.

Introducing PowerShell Core

1

In this chapter, we will cover the following recipes:

- Installing PowerShell
- Updating and using Help
- Exploring the `about_` topics
- Discovering cmdlets
- Finding and installing PowerShell modules
- Listing the various providers in PowerShell
- Understanding objects
- Parsing input from text to object
- Comparing the outputs of Bash and PowerShell
- Comparing Windows PowerShell and PowerShell Core
- Working with aliases
- Dissecting a .NET Core Object
- Listing the execution policies and setting a suitable one

Introduction

Carl Sagan once said the following:

> *If you are skeptical, then no new ideas will make it through to you. You will never learn anything new. You become a crotchety old person convinced that nonsense is ruling the world. (There is, of course, much data to support you.) But every now and then, maybe once in a hundred cases, a new idea turns out to be on the mark, valid, and wonderful. If you are too much in the habit of being skeptical about everything, you are going to miss or resent it, and ... you will be standing in the way of understanding and progress.*

Us system administrators start building our arsenal of administration tools from the very first day. Usually, we do not think of adding tools to do something that our favorite already does—this would be like adding a redundant weapon. However, these alternate tools turn out to be great. PowerShell, to me, was one such tool.

There is a good chance that you are reading this page at a bookstore—digital or physical—and there is a good chance that the question in your mind is, Is this book for me?

The answer is probably yes, if you are any of the following:

- A Linux administrator, open to other scripting frameworks
- A system administrator who manages Linux as well as Windows workloads, looking to unify management
- A Linux administrator who wants a framework that handles—and aces in—structured data (as a side note, PowerShell is probably the only framework in Linux that works well with structured data)
- A Windows Administrator, new to PowerShell, wanting to learn PowerShell scripting
- A generally curious system administrator

A brief note on .NET Core

Microsoft's announcement of open sourcing .NET in 2014 almost stirred a storm. Many rushed to the stands (so to speak) to read about the unbelievable—how could Microsoft possibly open source the core of their operating system? Some were cynical, while others rejoiced. Then came the announcement—a little louder and clearer—that **.NET Core** was open source, not the **.NET Framework**. Many said that .NET Core was a subset of .NET Framework.

.NET was first announced in 2000, as a new platform based on internet standards. Along with it, by the end of the year, Microsoft published the **Common Language Infrastructure** as a standard, so that anyone who wanted could write their own .NET framework based on those standards. .NET Framework has been the basis of Windows since the noughties.

Windows PowerShell was released to the general market in 2006, as an implementation of .NET Framework, and focused on system administrators (or sysadmins), enabling them to better manage their workloads or daily activities and automate them. PowerShell 1.0 was leaps and bounds ahead of the hitherto rulers of automation Windows: Batch and VBScript.

In June, 2016, Microsoft released a collaboratively refactored, more modern and efficient .NET. The .NET Core was officially born. While .NET Framework continues to rule the Windows arena, .NET Core, which is open source and cross-platform, has picked up great momentum and grows every day. .NET Core seems to be the way forward.

PowerShell Core is based on .NET Core, and therefore is open source, with the same vision as .NET Core: to be cross-platform.

The assumptions

This book assumes no experience in PowerShell, and so sticks to the basic and intermediate levels. That is to say, we will not create complex PowerShell modules in this book. We will start by installing PowerShell, understanding the object model, working through scripting by understanding PowerShell constructs, creating functions, creating simple script modules, and so on, as system administrators (and not as programmers). We will also learn how to manage Docker and cloud workloads using PowerShell.

How to read this book

You may skip recipes or even chapters. Whenever there is a need for something we created in a recipe that you have skipped, we will mention the recipe in the prerequisites. For example, we will state something similar to the following: follow the *How to do it...* section of the skipped recipe to fulfill this prerequisite.

An important note

There are two editions of PowerShell available today:

1. Windows PowerShell (up to v5.1, proprietary; `powershell`)
2. PowerShell Core (6.0+, open source; `pwsh`)

Windows PowerShell is based on .NET Framework, which is Microsoft's proprietary framework that Windows is built on. PowerShell began at 1.0, and was considered feature-complete at 5.1. Microsoft has stopped developing Windows PowerShell; going forward, it will only receive bug fixes.

The open source PowerShell Core 6.0 is based on the open source .NET Core. This book is about open source PowerShell. Windows PowerShell and PowerShell Core are two different entities, with two different code bases.

While PowerShell to a Windows administrator has so far meant Windows PowerShell, officially, PowerShell now means the open source PowerShell Core. In this book, we follow this convention: going forward, every mention of PowerShell points to the open source PowerShell Core 6. Windows PowerShell is referred to as Windows PowerShell.

Writing the cmdlets (Linux admins note)

If you are a Linux administrator, chances are, you do not like long commands—verbosity, to be specific. We will try to make the commands as short as possible, but in the interest of readability (which is an important convention in PowerShell), we will also mention the full commands.

 Tab completion comes in handy for reducing keystrokes. PowerShell tab-completes cmdlets, parameters, and in many cases, even parameter values. We will learn about this in the *Running cmdlets with minimal keystrokes* section of `Chapter 2`, *Preparing for Administration Using PowerShell*.

In general, we split scripting from running cmdlets on the console in the following ways:

- By using aliases (carefully) and short parameter names at the Terminal to save keystrokes and time
- By being verbose in scripts, so that everyone using them can read and understand them

Off we go

This is where it all starts: with the installation of PowerShell on your system. The installation of PowerShell is simple and straightforward. Since PowerShell is open source, its source code is available on GitHub. At the moment, Windows, Debian (and Ubuntu), Red Hat Linux (and CentOS), Fedora, OpenSUSE, and macOS are officially supported by the PowerShell project. Arch Linux and Kali Linux are supported by the community, as indicated in the README project. Community support is also available for the Snapcraft edition of PowerShell, which can be used on many of the modern-day Linux distributions.

PowerShell 6, at the time of writing this book, is experimentally available for Raspbian Stretch as well as the ARM edition of Windows (`https://github.com/PowerShell/PowerShell/blob/master/README.md`).

Installing PowerShell

In this book, we will focus on installing PowerShell on Ubuntu (16.04 and 18.04) and CentOS 7, since Ubuntu and CentOS were among the first to be supported by the PowerShell project.

PowerShell is available in two releases: stable and preview. The stable releases are suitable for a production environment since they are more reliable. The preview releases are for test environments where the administrators are allowed to feel a little adventurous. The expectation from the administrators is to report bugs they come across, along with providing feedback on the capabilities of it.

 As of the Preview 4 release of PowerShell 6.1, `pwsh` (stable) and `pwsh-preview` (preview) can be installed side by side, without the worry of interference.

Getting ready

Linux administrators will already know how to do this. If you are new to Linux, getting ready to install PowerShell on your computer is simple. You simply need a working Linux computer that you have administrator privileges on. Depending on what mode you pick to install PowerShell, you may or may not need a package manager. Chances are, your Linux distribution already has a package manager available.

Also, many of the future recipes will require a desktop environment so that you can work with tools such as Visual Studio Code.

Ubuntu does not ship with `curl`. Install `curl` by running the following command:

```
$ sudo apt install curl
```

How to do it...

As we have already discussed, we will look at the procedure of installing PowerShell on Ubuntu (and its derivatives) as well as CentOS (and its derivatives).

Installation on Ubuntu

There really are many ways to install PowerShell on your computer. Since we are installing PowerShell on Ubuntu, we will look at two ways of doing so. The first is by adding Microsoft's key, registering the repository, and then using the **Advanced Package Tool** (**APT**) to install PowerShell. The second method is by doing so directly, using the `.deb` package from GitHub.

Installing from the repository

Ubuntu 16.04 and Ubuntu 18.04 have the stable release of PowerShell available. Follow these steps if you wish to install PowerShell on Ubuntu:

1. Download the GPG keys for the Microsoft repository:

   ```
   $ # On Ubuntu 16.04
   $ wget -q
   https://packages.microsoft.com/config/ubuntu/16.04/packages-microso
   ft-prod.deb

   $ # On Ubuntu 18.04
   $ wget -q
   https://packages.microsoft.com/config/ubuntu/18.04/packages-microso
   ft-prod.deb
   ```

2. Register the GPG keys:

   ```
   $ sudo dpkg -i packages-microsoft-prod.deb
   ```

3. Update the package list using the following command:

   ```
   $ sudo apt update
   ```

4. Install PowerShell using `apt-get`:

   ```
   $ # To install PowerShell (stable)
   $ sudo apt install -y powershell

   $ # To install PowerShell (preview)
   $ sudo apt install -y powershell-preview
   ```

5. Run PowerShell using the following command:

```
$ # If you installed PowerShell (stable)
$ pwsh

$ # If you installed PowerShell (preview)
$ pwsh-preview
```

Installing via direct download

Follow these steps to install PowerShell on Ubuntu:

1. Go to `https://github.com/powershell/powershell`.
2. Scroll down to the table that contains the list of Linux distributions officially supported by the PowerShell team.
3. Click on the relevant link, that is, `.deb` under **Downloads (stable)** or **Downloads (preview)**.
4. Read the installation instructions if you need additional information.
5. Use `dpkg` to install the package:

```
$ sudo dpkg -i powershell-version-os-osversion_architecture.deb
$ sudo apt install -f
```

Installation on CentOS

The installation of PowerShell on CentOS 7 (or Red Hat 7) also has two methods: the repository and a direct download. The process is similar to that of installation on Ubuntu Linux. While it is recommended that PowerShell is installed from the repository, use the second method—the direct download method—should you choose otherwise.

Installing from the repository

To begin the installation, follow these steps:

1. First, register the Microsoft repository:

```
$ curl https://packages.microsoft.com/config/rhel/7/prod.repo |
sudo tee /etc/yum.repos.d/microsoft.repo
```

2. Next, install PowerShell using `yum`:

```
$ sudo yum install -y powershell
```

Installing via direct download

Follow these steps to install PowerShell on CentOS:

1. Go to `https://github.com/powershell/powershell`.
2. Scroll down to the table that contains the list of Linux distributions officially supported by the PowerShell team.
3. Click on the relevant link, that is, `.rpm` under **Downloads (stable)**—we will stick to the stable release.
4. Read the installation instructions if you need additional information.
5. Install the RPM package using the following command (assuming your download is at `~/Downloads` and your `pwd` is `~/Downloads`):

```
$ sudo yum install <the-downloaded-file.rpm>
```

Using the Snapcraft package

If your distribution supports the installation of Snapcraft (snap) packages, you can install PowerShell using the `snap` command:

1. Install `snapd` if you do not already have it. Here is how you do this on Ubuntu:

```
$ sudo apt install snapd
```

2. Next, install the PowerShell Snapcraft package:

```
$ snap install powershell --classic
```

3. You may be prompted for your credentials. Enter your credentials at the prompt.
4. Launch PowerShell:

```
$ pwsh
```

Using the binary archives

If your package manager does not have PowerShell, use the binary archives:

1. Install the dependencies based on your operating system. Here are the dependencies required in the case of Ubuntu 16.04, Ubuntu 18.04, and CentOS:

Operating System	Dependencies
Ubuntu 16.04	libc6, libgcc1, libgssapi-krb5-2, liblttng-ust0, libstdc++6, libcurl3, libunwind8, libuuid1, zlib1g, libssl1.0.0, libicu52
Ubuntu 18.04	libc6, libgcc1, libgssapi-krb5-2, liblttng-ust0, libstdc++6, libcurl3, libunwind8, libuuid1, zlib1g, libssl1.0.0, libicu60
CentOS7	libunwind, libcurl, openssl-libs, libicu

2. Use `curl` to get the archived file:

```
$ curl -L -o /tmp/powershell.tar.gz
https://github.com/PowerShell/PowerShell/releases/download/v6.1.0/p
owershell-6.1.0-linux-x64.tar.gz
```

3. Create the directory where PowerShell will be installed:

```
$ sudo mkdir -p /opt/microsoft/powershell/6.1.0
```

4. Unpack the binaries into the directory you just created:

```
$ sudo tar zxf /tmp/powershell.tar.gz -C
/opt/microsoft/powershell/6.1.0
```

5. Add execute permissions to the file:

```
$ sudo chmod +x /opt/microsoft/powershell/6.1.0/pwsh
```

6. Create a symbolic link to point to `pwsh`:

```
$ sudo ln -s /opt/microsoft/powershell/6.1.0/pwsh /usr/bin/pwsh
```

Bonus– using the Install-PowerShell script (including on macOS)

The official PowerShell repository has a script that detects your operating system and installs PowerShell based on the operating system and the distribution.

Your computer must have the following:

- The Bash shell
- sed
- A native package manager

We need the Visual Studio Code IDE so that we can follow the exercises in this book. Run the following command to commence the installation:

```
$ bash <(wget -O -
https://raw.githubusercontent.com/PowerShell/PowerShell/master/tool
s/install-powershell.sh) -includeide
```

 If you do not have a desktop environment on your computer, you will not be able to install Visual Studio Code. Either install a desktop environment or omit the -includeide switch.

For more information, go through the README file at https://github.com/PowerShell/PowerShell/blob/master/tools/install-powershell-readme.md.

How it works...

The package manager installs the package with all of its dependencies and makes the relevant commands available for use.

Starting with Snap 2.20, you can install Snapcraft packages with relaxed security boundaries using the --classic switch. Snaps usually run in a sandboxed environment, meaning that they are separated from the host, so to speak. However, PowerShell, being a shell, needs access to all of the host resources so that it can function as desired, hence the --classic install. Also note that this is not supported on systems such as Ubuntu Core.

See also

- The *Comparing Windows PowerShell and PowerShell Core* recipe

Updating and using Help

Help documentation is very important in PowerShell, regardless of whether a certain cmdlet is packaged by providers such as Microsoft, VMware, or Citrix, or community-created. Help is not a switch in PowerShell. PowerShell uses the `Get-Help` cmdlet (pronounced command-let) to fetch the Help information enclosed within cmdlets.

By default, PowerShell is installed with minimal Help information, which contains only the description and the parameters. In this recipe, we will update Help and learn to get Help by using cmdlets, specific parameters, or certain keywords.

Getting ready

To go through this recipe, you must have PowerShell 6 installed on your computer, and you must have administrator privileges available. To install PowerShell, refer the *Installing PowerShell* recipe in this chapter.

How to do it...

To update the Help files for the locally installed PowerShell modules, follow these steps:

1. Type `exit` to exit PowerShell. This is so that you can relaunch PowerShell with elevated privileges. This is required for some of the modules, based on the permissions used to install them.
2. Enter `sudo pwsh` (or `sudo pwsh-preview`) to launch PowerShell as a superuser.
3. At the **PS>** prompt, run `Update-Help`.

4. Wait for the update progress bar to appear. The bar will fill as the Help files download onto your computer:

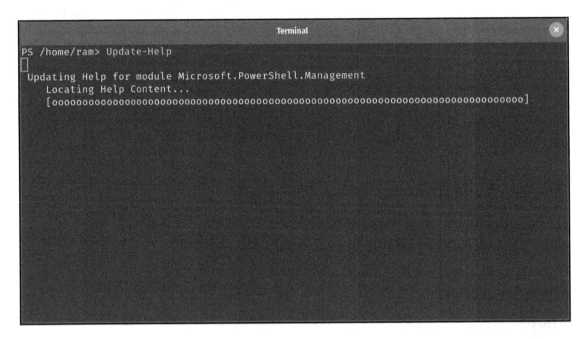

5. Use `exit` to exit PowerShell as a superuser, and launch PowerShell as a regular user.

We can now proceed and fetch Help information for other cmdlets.

6. At the command prompt, enter the following command:

```
PS> Get-Help Write-Host
```

You will get an output similar to the following:

```
                                  Terminal                                    ✕
PS /home/ram> Get-Help Write-Host

NAME
    Write-Host

SYNOPSIS
    Writes customized output to a host.

SYNTAX
    Write-Host [[-Object] <Object>] [-BackgroundColor {Black | DarkBlue | DarkGreen |
    DarkCyan | DarkRed | DarkMagenta | DarkYellow | Gray | DarkGray | Blue | Green |
    Cyan | Red | Magenta | Yellow | White}] [-ForegroundColor {Black | DarkBlue |
    DarkGreen | DarkCyan | DarkRed | DarkMagenta | DarkYellow | Gray | DarkGray | Blue |
    Green | Cyan | Red | Magenta | Yellow | White}] [-NoNewline] [-Separator <Object>]
    [<CommonParameters>]


DESCRIPTION
    The `Write-Host` cmdlet customizes output. You can specify the color of text by

RELATED LINKS
    Clear-Host
    Out-Host
```

7. Next, gather different levels of Help information by using the following commands:

    ```
    PS> Get-Help Write-Host -Full

    PS> Get-Help Write-Host -Examples

    PS> Get-Help Write-Host -Online
    ```

8. Pass a different cmdlet as a parameter to Get-Help. Note the two groups of parameters:

    ```
    PS> Get-Help Get-Command
    ```

9. Compare the outputs of the different commands you ran.

10. Now, look for Help information for the specific parameter of Write-Host (the second command in the following code is for reference; this states what the first command means to PowerShell):

    ```
    PS> get-help write-host -par foregroundcolor
    PS> # Verbose version: Get-Help -Name Write-Host -Parameter
    ForegroundColor
    ```

Now let's look for a certain keyword within the Help information:

1. Convert the output of Get-Help Get-Command into text, one string at a time, rather than putting in the entirety of the Help information as a single string:

```
PS> get-help get-command | out-string -s
PS> # Verbose version: Get-Help Get-Command | Out-String -Stream
```

2. Pipe this to the Select-String cmdlet to perform a grep-like operation:

```
PS> get-help get-command | out-string -s | select-string 'wildcard'
PS> # Verbose version: Get-Help -Name Get-Command | Out-String -
Stream | Select-String -Pattern 'wildcard'
```

3. This gives you an output of a line that contains wildcard:

```
Terminal                                                                    _  ✕

PS /home/ram> Get-Help Get-Command | Out-String -Stream | Select-String -Pattern 'wildcard'


    `Get-Command` that uses the exact name of the command, without wildcard characters,
automatically imports the module that contains the command so that you can use the
command immediately. To enable, disable, and configure automatic importing of modules,
use the `$PSModuleAutoLoadingPreference` preference variable. For more information, see
about_Preference_Variables (About/about_Preference_Variables.md).


PS /home/ram> ▯
```

How it works...

It is inconvenient to leave your Terminal to read Help online. We would prefer to have all of the Help available locally. PowerShell can potentially work on low-memory devices such as Raspberry, but saving all of the Help in the limited space we have is not advisable. This is one of the reasons PowerShell comes with minimal Help by default. The reason updating Help requires elevated privileges is that the Help information is stored within the shell. Therefore, non-administrators may not be able to update Help without administrator intervention.

As a general practice, cmdlets come pre-packaged with Help information, and Get-Help works like the man command in Linux. The output of Get-Help has the name of the cmdlet, the syntax to use with the cmdlet, the alias(es) available for the cmdlet and more online Help if required. -Full and -Examples are (mutually exclusive) switches that tell PowerShell about the level of Help you need.

The groups of parameters, as seen in the case of Get-Command, under SYNTAX, are called parameter sets. They tell us which parameters can be used together. Parameters not appearing in the same parameter set cannot be used together. For example, you cannot use -Noun and -Name with Get-Command at the same time; it wouldn't be logical to do so.

If the Help information seems elaborate, and you would like to learn about a specific parameter of a cmdlet, you can specify that parameter, and the Help will be filtered accordingly. Since the output of most PowerShell cmdlets is objects, it is easy to select the necessary object and discard the rest from the output. Also note that this is the recommended approach to fetch Help that's specific to a certain parameter.

 PowerShell, in general, is case-insensitive. Therefore, Noun and noun, or Parameter and parameter, mean the same thing to it. The use of CamelCase is the general convention in PowerShell. With the almost ubiquitous tab completion, this is a cakewalk.

Next, let's talk about searching Help for specific keywords. PowerShell outputs objects. However, at the end, when the content comes to the host, the content can be processed by Linux commands such as grep. Therefore, to search Help for specific keywords, you could always pipe the output to grep. If you would like to go the PowerShell way (especially if you go by the write once, run everywhere philosophy), this requires minor modifications. First, we fetch the Help; the output is an object (so that it can be processed further if needed). We convert this into a string using Out-String, since search is nothing but string matching.

PowerShell cmdlets output single or multiple instances of objects (we will discuss objects in more detail in the *Understanding objects* recipe). Out-String waits for all of the Get-Help commands to be processed and converts the output into a single concatenated string. To break the string into chunks, we use the -Stream switch, which instructs Out-String to not concatenate the output. This way, each paragraph is processed separately. Next, we use the Select-String cmdlet, along with the search keyword to perform keyword matching. The output of this is the chunk (paragraph, in this case) with the keyword.

See also

- The *Working with aliases* recipe
- The *Updating and using Help* recipe
- The *Running cmdlets with minimal keystrokes* recipe in Chapter 2, *Preparing for Administration using PowerShell*

Exploring about_ topics

Documentation is one of the key strengths of PowerShell. While not all modules have complete documentation, all of the modules written by Microsoft, along with the well-done third-party ones, do. By default, PowerShell itself has exhaustive documentation built within it. In this recipe, we will look at about_ topics, pick one of the topics from the output, and read more about the subject we picked.

Getting ready

A prerequisite to be able to fetch any output in this recipe is to update the local copy of PowerShell Help documentation. Follow the *Updating and using Help* recipe to update the local PowerShell Help documentation.

How to do it...

Let's begin by listing all of the about_* Help files:

1. List all the about_ topics:

   ```
   PS> get-help about_*
   ```

2. Display the documentation about PowerShell modules:

   ```
   PS> get-help about_modules
   ```

How it works...

Get-Help gives you information about cmdlets if the cmdlet is passed as an argument. In cases where you know only a part of the name of the cmdlet, you can use a combination of characters and wildcards to list out cmdlets that match the search string (about_*, in our case).

Now, we can pick the topic we would like to read about and enter that specific about_ topic. Get-Help shows the complete documentation about the topic.

Discovering cmdlets

So far, we have seen how we can get Help on cmdlets. We used the Get-Command cmdlet as an example argument. Now, we are going to use Get-Command to discover cmdlets in PowerShell. Get-Help and Get-Command become the two most important cmdlets when you need any Help information in PowerShell.

PowerShell is like plain English—PowerShell follows the Verb-Noun format in cmdlet naming, which makes the cmdlets sound like plain English commands. It is a convention in PowerShell to use approved verbs, which ensures that verbs are limited in order to facilitate discovery. The nouns, on the other hand, can be arbitrary.

> Thinking in the scripting/programming language of your choice, along with muscle memory, is key to speed and efficiency. PowerShell's English-like structure helps in this regard; it is easy to think in PowerShell. For instance, if you would like to know the current date, all you have to say is Get-Date, and PowerShell will print the date and time on the screen for you.

How to do it...

Get-Command can help determine the best cmdlet for a task. To find cmdlets, follow these steps:

1. Enter Get-Command to get a list of all of the available cmdlets in PowerShell. The number of cmdlets returned will change based on when you last updated PowerShell and the modules you have loaded:

```
PS> Get-Command
```

This may not be particularly useful—what would you do with a list of commands if you were looking for something to do with processes?

2. The lazy way of doing this is by using the following command:

```
PS> Get-Command *proc*
```

3. To be specific and look for a command that deals with processes, use the following code:

```
PS> get-command -no process
PS> # Verbose version: Get-Command -Noun 'Process'
```

In PowerShell, the convention is to always have the noun in the singular form. Therefore, it is always `Process`, `Service`, `Computer`, and so on, and never Processes, Services, Computers, and so on.

4. To look for cmdlets that help you export objects, use the following code:

```
PS> get-command -v export
PS> # Verbose version: Get-Command -Verb 'Export'
```

PowerShell has a standard set of verbs. This is to ensure the discoverability of cmdlets. If you use a nonstandard verb when creating your cmdlets, PowerShell will warn you that your cmdlet may not be discoverable. To get a list of approved verbs, run the `Get-Verb` cmdlet.

5. The `-Noun` and `-Verb` parameters also accept wildcards:

```
PS> get-command -no proc*
```

6. Imagine that you just installed a PowerShell module (more on that later) and would like to look for cmdlets packaged in the module. For this example, we will use the `SqlServer` module:

```
PS> get-command -v get -m sqlserver
PS> # Verbose version: Get-Command -Verb 'Get' -Module 'SqlServer'
```

How it works...

PowerShell cmdlets are in the Verb-Noun form. The word appearing before the hyphen is the verb, and the one after is the noun. When cmdlets are loaded from modules, PowerShell identifies the verbs and the nouns in them. The search promptly returns the cmdlets based on the search specifications. Filters based on the name of the verb, noun, or even the module restrict the search accordingly.

Finding and installing PowerShell modules

Loosely coupling the components is one of the keys to the success of a framework. PowerShell follows this principle as well. All cmdlets are packaged within PowerShell modules. The modules can be first-party provided, created by you, or created by other software vendors.

Initially, extending PowerShell capabilities was done using snap-ins. With PowerShell 2.0, PowerShell modules were introduced. One other place that Microsoft has gotten it right is advocating the use of modules over snap-ins. The installation of PowerShell modules, which could have been a hassle in the past, has been streamlined today. PowerShell now comes pre-packaged with a package manager called `PowerShellGet`, which connects to the official Microsoft PowerShell Gallery (`https://www.powershellgallery.com`). The PowerShell Gallery is an online repository that contains modules, scripts, and other utilities that have been created by providers—as well as the community—that administrators can download and install to extend PowerShell's capabilities.

While it is possible to download PowerShell modules from third-party sites, our focus in this book will be on the PowerShell Repository.

How to do it...

We will start by finding cmdlets that work with modules, and proceed to work with these modules:

1. Launch PowerShell by running `pwsh` on the Terminal.
2. Look for commands that work with modules:

```
PS> get-command -no module PS> # Verbose version: Get-Command -Noun
'Module'
```

The output should look something like this:

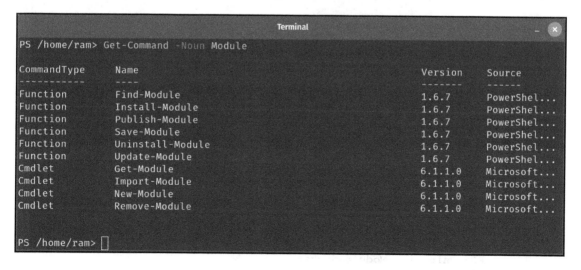

Pick `Find-Module` for this task. If you would like to, use the `Get-Help` cmdlet to learn about what `Find-Module` does.

3. Search for a module to help you work with `Docker` containers:

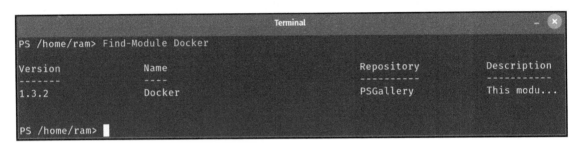

4. Now, install the module. You will need to use superuser privileges to install the Docker module. Use the following command to install Docker without having to exit the current PowerShell session:

```
PS> sudo pwsh -c install-module docker
```

If you would rather use a new session and call the `Install-Module` cmdlet from within it, terminate the current PowerShell session and launch a new one with `sudo`:

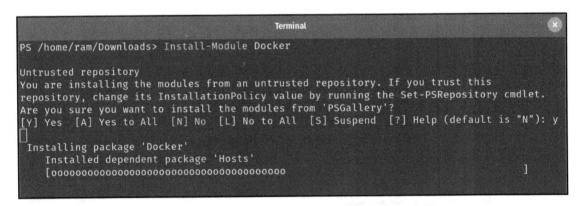

5. To update a module, use the `Update-Module` cmdlet:

```
PS> Update-Module docker
```

6. To uninstall a module from the machine, use the `Uninstall-Module` cmdlet:

```
PS> Uninstall-Module docker
```

7. To load a certain module into the current session, use the `Import-Module` cmdlet. You do not need elevated privileges to load or unload a module to or from the session:

```
PS> Import-Module docker
```

8. To remove a module from the session, use the `Remove-Module` cmdlet:

```
PS> Remove-Module docker
```

How it works...

Hundreds of modules, scripts, and Desired State Configuration resources have been registered with the `PSGallery` repository. Microsoft now recommends using this repository for module management. Using the `Find-Module` cmdlet, PowerShell makes a connection to the repository and gets a list of all available modules. Then, it runs a search on the returned results based on the criteria you mention.

In PowerShell, `Find` usually means working with the internet, and `Get` is usually used to get objects from the local machine.

You can also find scripts that can perform repetitive tasks. To find scripts, use the `Find-Script` cmdlet. It works similar to the `Find-Module` cmdlet, except that it finds individual scripts rather than modules.

Installation of modules is a simple process of pulling the modules down from the repository, similar to `npm` or `chocolatey`. These tasks are taken care of by the `PowerShellGet` module, which ships with PowerShell. Installing, updating, and uninstalling PowerShell modules may require elevated privileges.

To load the capabilities of a module into the PowerShell session, use `Import-Module`. PowerShell modules have members such as cmdlets, functions, aliases, and so on for sessions. `Import-Module` loads these members into the session. By default, the sessions are unloaded when exiting the session. However, if you would like to manually unload them, use the `Remove-Module` cmdlet. `Remove-Module` does not remove the entire module; it just unloads it.

The modules are installed in one of the `$env:PsModulePath` directories. You don't need to specify the path to modules that are installed this way. If the module files are saved elsewhere, you will need to specify the path to the module's `psd1` or `psm1` file when calling `Import-Module`. Also, some modules enable automated loading. Just call a cmdlet from the module, and the module will auto-import.

`Import-Module` has parameters such as `-Prefix` and `-NoClobber`. The `-Prefix` parameter adds the specified prefix to the nouns of all of the cmdlets in the module. For instance, `Import-Module docker -pre dm` will import the Docker cmdlets as `Invoke-dmDockerCommand` instead of `Invoke-DockerCommand`. The `-NoClobber` switch helps in cases where there may be cmdlet name conflicts; it prevents the already loaded cmdlets from being replaced by the ones from the module being imported.

There's more...

Try installing the module in portable mode, by first saving the module using `Save-Module` and then calling `Import-Module` with the path to the module file as the parameter.

You can also get the list of directories from which PowerShell discovers modules. At the prompt, type the following and press the *Enter* key:

```
PS> $env:PSModulePath
```

See also

- The *Writing a script module* recipe in Chapter 12, Advanced Concepts of Functions
- The *Calling a PowerShell script* recipe in Chapter 2, *Preparing for Administration using PowerShell*

Listing the various providers in PowerShell

Before we start preparing for administration using PowerShell, it would be helpful to understand the concept of providers.

How to do it...

To list the providers in PowerShell, follow these steps:

1. Run `pwsh` to load PowerShell on the Terminal.
2. Run the following command:

   ```
   PS> Get-PsProvider
   ```

   You will get something that looks like this:

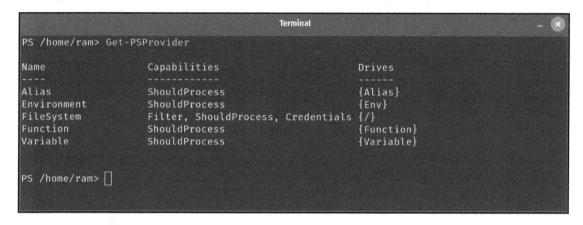

   Note the providers that are available in PowerShell, and the drives and capabilities found within these providers.

3. Navigate to the `Alias:` drive:

   ```
   PS> Set-Location Alias:
   PS> Get-ChildItem
   ```

Note how the prompt is now Alias:

Note the preceding colon after the drive name (`Alias:` and not `Alias`). This is necessary for you to indicate to PowerShell that you are switching drives. Without the colon, PowerShell would simply try to look for a directory called Alias in your present working directory.

How it works...

On Linux, PowerShell support is limited (at the time of writing this book). Discussion on the issues pertaining to providers on Linux indicates that further development is highly likely, especially regarding cross-provider support.

A provider is a program that logically represents non-filesystem drives as though they are drives. For instance, on Windows, the Registry is a database of configuration information. In PowerShell 6 on Windows and on Windows PowerShell, the Registry is a provider; this way, administrators can use PowerShell to navigate and manipulate Registry keys in the same way that we work with files. This capability is available on Linux as well, however, there aren't as many providers as there are on Windows.

 If you are interested in programming, providers in PowerShell are a great example of the concept of overloading in object-oriented programming.

The Name column gives the names of the providers. Each provider may have one or more drives. For instance, the FileSystem provider in Windows shows all of the partitions (C:, D:, E:, and so on) present on the computer. A `Set-Location` operation is performed on these drives within the providers, and not the providers themselves. To indicate to PowerShell that you are connecting to a drive and not a subdirectory, the name of the drive must be followed by a colon.

See also

- The *Adding safety switches to functions* recipe from `Chapter 12`, *Advanced Concepts of Functions*

Understanding objects

PowerShell is object-oriented, text being an object too. An object in PowerShell contains entities within it, which are called members. These members can be referred to using what is called the member access operator, which is nothing but a dot (.). In this recipe, we will look at picking members from within objects.

Since we are going to be dealing with members of objects, we will now look at one of the most important cmdlets in PowerShell: Get-Member.

How to do it...

1. We will start by gathering the properties of our home directory. The path to this is stored in the automatic variable known as $HOME:

   ```
   PS> Get-Item $HOME | Get-Member
   ```

   Note the TypeName of the object—the very first line—as well as the MemberType column in the table.

2. Next, check when the home directory was last written to:

   ```
   PS> (Get-Item $HOME).LastWriteTime
   ```

3. Can we find out when the parent of your $HOME was created?

   ```
   PS> (Get-Item $HOME).Parent | Get-Member
   PS> (Get-Item $HOME).Parent.CreationTime
   ```

   To reiterate, PowerShell is not case-sensitive. However, to improve readability, we have stuck to the PowerShell convention of using camel case.

4. What are the members of this object?

   ```
   PS> (Get-Item $HOME).Parent.CreationTime | Get-Member
   ```

5. Pick out the year:

   ```
   PS> (Get-Item $HOME).Parent.CreationTime.Year
   ```

6. Next, let's use a method from within the returned object and convert it into plain text. We saw that `CreationTime` is a `DateTime` object. Let's convert that into a plain string:

```
PS> (Get-Item $HOME).Parent.CreationTime.ToString()
```

7. Find the type of object returned by the previous command. Press the up arrow key to bring back the previous command and pipe its output to `Get-Member`. Compare the output of `Get-Member` without `.ToString()`:

```
PS> (Get-Item $HOME).Parent.CreationTime.ToString() | Get-Member

PS> (Get-Item $HOME).Parent.CreationTime | Get-Member
```

How it works...

This recipe is only here to show you that PowerShell outputs objects, and what an object looks like. We will look at leveraging the `TypeName` much later, when we modify the returned objects.

For now, we will stick to properties as the first step for understanding the object model of PowerShell. To demonstrate that methods are also available for use, we will use one that's among the simplest of them, the `ToString()` method; it's simple because it does not need any arguments—only empty parentheses.

The `Get-Member` cmdlet is very important in PowerShell because it lets you peek into the object that a certain cmdlet returned. It shows the type of the object returned (`TypeName`), and shows the properties and methods available. The properties and methods are of different data types themselves, which can be seen in the `Definition` column. As you get comfortable with objects, you will start to leverage these data types to simplify your tasks.

There's more...

Just because you can (and not because this is the way to do so), create a subdirectory within your home directory using the `CreateSubdirectory()` method from the object returned by `Get-Item`:

```
PS> (Get-Item $HOME).CreateSubdirectory('test-directory')
```

```
                              Terminal                                    _  (x)
PS /home/ram> (Get-Item $HOME).CreateSubdirectory('test-directory')

Mode                LastWriteTime          Length Name
----                -------------          ------ ----
d-----        11/14/18   9:40 AM                  test-directory


PS /home/ram> []
```

This should show you the new directory that you just created:

```
PS> Get-ChildItem $HOME # To list the contents of your home directory
```

See also

- The *Selecting columns from the output* recipe from `Chapter 4`, *Passing Data Through the Pipeline*

Parsing input from text to object

Moving to the object model from text could seem a little daunting at first. However, with PowerShell, it is not very hard to switch to the new model, especially given that PowerShell can convert text into objects given the right tools. In this recipe, we will look at two of the ways that PowerShell converts textual data into objects.

Getting ready

Before we dive into the recipe, let's give ourselves a little introduction to how text-to-object parsing is handled. One way is to use .NET's built-in functionality, and the second way involves using a cmdlet to perform the conversion based on a delimiter.

The basic requirement for this recipe is simple: you simply need PowerShell installed on your computer. We will edit the file within PowerShell. If you would be more comfortable using a text editor instead, that works as well. Most Linux distributions pack a text editor. If not, use your package manager to install Vim, Nano, Gedit, Visual Studio Code, Atom, or any other text/code editor.

How to do it...

First, we will look at converting text into an object from a plain text input at the Terminal. This involves using what is known as a PowerShell Type Accelerator. A PowerShell Type Accelerator is an alias for .NET classes. Using these, we can call .NET classes and use many of their functionalities within PowerShell:

1. Let's take plain text as input and convert the text into a date object. To check what sort of object your input is, use the Get-Member cmdlet:

   PS> '21 June 2018' | Get-Member

 Enclosing any text within single quotes defines the text as a non-expanding literal string. No explicit definition is required in this case.

2. The TypeName says System.String. This confirms that what we entered was plain text. Now, let's use a Type Accelerator (or, more specifically, a cast operator) and convert this text into a DateTime object. The accelerator for this purpose is [DateTime]; place this accelerator before the literal string:

   PS> [DateTime]'21 June 2018'

   ```
   Thursday, 21 June 2018 00:00:00
   ```

3. Next, find the TypeName of the object that was returned:

   PS> [DateTime]'21 June 2018' | Get-Member

   ```
   TypeName: System.DateTime
   ```

   Voila, the string has been successfully parsed into date and time!

4. It is also possible to achieve the same result with the Get-Date cmdlet when it is called with the text argument:

   PS> Get-Date '21 June 2018'

   ```
   Thursday, 21 June 2018 00:00:00
   ```

5. Similarly, the TypeName would be as follows:

   PS> Get-Date '21 June 2018' | Get-Member

   ```
   TypeName: System.DateTime
   ```

6. Just like we did in the previous recipe, we can now manipulate the object to show information in a more meaningful way. For instance, if you care only about the year, you would write the following:

```
PS> (Get-Date '21 June 2018').Year
2018
```

The other way of converting text into an object is to use cmdlets that perform such tasks. PowerShell packs a few converter cmdlets, one of which is Import-Csv. You may have noticed that PowerShell usually generates output in a tabular format. This is a simple representation of objects. The Import-Csv cmdlet converts data in a delimited row-and-column structure into objects, where each row is an instance of the object itself, and each column is a property of the object:

1. To demonstrate this, let's create a CSV file with the following content in it. At the PowerShell prompt, type/paste in the following:

```
PS> @'
WS,CPU,Id,SI,ProcessName
161226752,23.42,1914,1566,io.elementary.a
199598080,77.84,1050,1040,gnome-shell
216113152,0.67,19250,1566,atom
474685440,619.05,1568,1566,Xorg
1387864064,1890.29,15720,1566,firefox
'@ | Out-File sample.csv
```

You could perform the same operation using the touch command and the text editor of your choice. The goal is to get the content into the sample file.

2. Next, read the contents of the file using PowerShell:

```
PS> Get-Content ./sample.csv
```

3. That looks like simple text. Let's look at the type name of the object to confirm that this is indeed plain text. Type in the following:

```
PS> Get-Content ./sample.csv | Get-Member
```

```
    TypeName: System.String
```

4. That is a plain and simple string. Now, let's convert the content into a simple object. This is done using Import-Csv:

```
PS> Import-Csv ./sample.csv
```

That should give you a list-like output, like so:

```
                                     Terminal                                          ⊗
PS /home/ram> Import-Csv ./sample.csv


WS            : 161226752
CPU           : 23.42
Id            : 1914
SI            : 1566
ProcessName   : io.elementary.a

WS            : 199598080
CPU           : 77.84
Id            : 1050
SI            : 1040
ProcessName   : gnome-shell

WS            : 216113152
CPU           : 0.67
Id            : 19250
SI            : 1566
ProcessName   : atom

WS            : 474685440
CPU           : 619.05
Id            : 1568
SI            : 1566
ProcessName   : Xorg

WS            : 1387864064
CPU           : 1890.29
Id            : 15720
```

5. To confirm that the output is objects, list out its members:

```
                                     Terminal                                      _  ⊗
PS /home/ram> Import-Csv ./sample.csv | Get-Member


    TypeName: System.Management.Automation.PSCustomObject

Name        MemberType   Definition
----        ----------   ----------
Equals      Method       bool Equals(System.Object obj)
GetHashCode Method       int GetHashCode()
GetType     Method       type GetType()
ToString    Method       string ToString()
CPU         NoteProperty string CPU=23.42
Id          NoteProperty string Id=1914
ProcessName NoteProperty string ProcessName=io.elementary.a
SI          NoteProperty string SI=1566
WS          NoteProperty string WS=161226752


PS /home/ram>
```

In general, the content is a custom object, which is denoted by `PSCustomObject`. The columns we had in the CSV are of type `NoteProperty`, as shown by `MemberType`.

A `NoteProperty` is a generic property whose characteristics are similar to those of a string. While most properties are inherited from .NET, `NoteProperty` is custom-created within PowerShell as a name-value pair.

6. If you would rather look at the content as a table, format the content as a table. You can do this by using the following command:

```
PS> Import-Csv ./sample.csv | Format-Table
```

```
Terminal                                                      _  ⊗

PS /home/ram> Import-Csv ./sample.csv | Format-Table

WS          CPU      Id     SI    ProcessName
--          ---      --     --    -----------
161226752   23.42    1914   1566  io.elementary.a
199598080   77.84    1050   1040  gnome-shell
216113152   0.67     19250  1566  atom
474685440   619.05   1568   1566  Xorg
1387864064  1890.29  15720  1566  firefox


PS /home/ram> []
```

We have successfully converted text into an object. However, note that this is just a simple conversion, and that the output of `Import-Csv` is still string-like. Although all of the content is now string-based objects, these are easier to handle in PowerShell.

Also note that `Format-Table` and other `Format-*` cmdlets output strings. These are among the handful of PowerShell cmdlets that do not generate a .NET object. Therefore, do not use any of these format cmdlets if you would like to process an object further. The format cmdlets should only be used at the end of the pipeline.

How it works...

Type accelerators are another form of encapsulation of .NET code in PowerShell. Recall the first recipe in this chapter, wherein we created a .NET object within PowerShell. We used the PowerShell command `New-Object -TypeName System.IO.DirectoryInfo -ArgumentList '/home/ram'` to get information on a home directory: we created a new instance of `System.IO.DirectoryInfo` and passed an argument to it. That was a lot of code to write. To accelerate this process, we could use `[IO.DirectoryInfo]'/home/ram'` (`System` is the default namespace; PowerShell will understand it without us explicitly mentioning it when calling accelerators), which outputs the same object as the former command.

With `Import-Csv`, on the other hand, the process is a simple conversion of data from text into name-value pairs. This is similar to using `ConvertFrom-Text` with a `Delimiter` parameter. This way, we instruct PowerShell to convert each row of text into instances of the object: the first row in the row-column structure is taken as the property name, and the rest of the rows are data. The cells are separated using a delimiter, which was a comma in the case of the CSV file.

There's more...

Look for more conversion cmdlets that are built into PowerShell. This can be done using the `Get-Command -Verb ConvertFrom` command.

See also

- More about type accelerators in the Hey, Scripting Guy! Blog (`https://blogs.technet.microsoft.com/heyscriptingguy/2013/07/08/use-powershell-to-find-powershell-type-accelerators/`)
- The *Understanding Here-Strings* recipe from `Chapter 6`, *Working with Strings*
- The different kinds of members (`https://docs.microsoft.com/en-us/dotnet/api/system.management.automation.psmembertypes?view=pscore-6.0.0`) in PowerShell

Comparing the outputs of Bash and PowerShell

PowerShell and Bash are both shells, and are capable of interacting with the kernel. Just like Bash can run on Windows, PowerShell can now run on Linux. While almost all of the aspects of which shell is better than the other is debatable, and the choice of shell is simply a matter of personal preference today, it is true that PowerShell is as powerful as .NET Core can get.

The primary difference between the two shells is that PowerShell outputs objects, while Bash returns text. Manipulation of the output in Bash involves manipulating text first, and then running further commands on the manipulated text to fetch the desired output. PowerShell, on the other hand, handles content as objects and, by design, requires comparatively less manipulation.

Structured data, as noted by Jeffrey Snover (the inventor of Windows PowerShell), is getting more popular as days pass, and structured data is where PowerShell shines the most.

Getting ready

In this recipe, we are going to pick one example to show you how simple and efficient it is to handle file metadata using PowerShell, primarily since the output is an object. We will list the files and folders within our home directory, along with the date and time of modification using both `ls` in Bash and `Get-ChildItem` in PowerShell.

We will use PowerShell to run the Linux commands as well.

How to do it...

1. At the Bash prompt, enter `ls -l` to list all of the files, along with the metadata that the command shows by default:

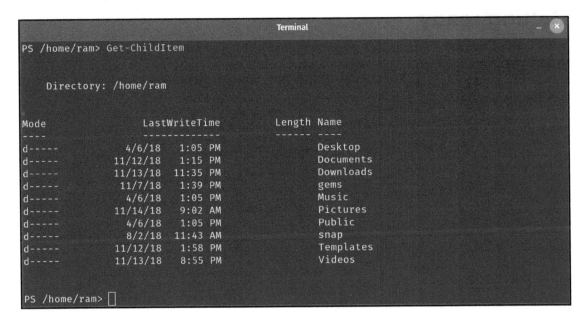

```
                                    Terminal                        -  x
PS /home/ram> ls -l
total 40
drwxr-xr-x  2 ram ram 4096 Apr  6  2018 Desktop
drwxr-xr-x  8 ram ram 4096 Nov 12 13:15 Documents
drwxr-xr-x  5 ram ram 4096 Nov 13 23:35 Downloads
drwxr-xr-x  9 ram ram 4096 Nov  7 13:39 gems
drwxr-xr-x  2 ram ram 4096 Apr  6  2018 Music
drwxr-xr-x 19 ram ram 4096 Nov 14 09:01 Pictures
drwxr-xr-x  2 ram ram 4096 Apr  6  2018 Public
drwxr-xr-x  4 ram ram 4096 Aug  2 11:43 snap
drwxr-xr-x  2 ram ram 4096 Nov 12 13:58 Templates
drwxr-xr-x  2 ram ram 4096 Nov 13 20:55 Videos
PS /home/ram> 
```

2. Go to the Terminal that has PowerShell running and type in `Get-ChildItem` at the prompt:

```
                                    Terminal                        -  x
PS /home/ram> Get-ChildItem


    Directory: /home/ram


Mode                 LastWriteTime         Length Name
----                 -------------         ------ ----
d-----          4/6/18     1:05 PM                Desktop
d-----        11/12/18     1:15 PM                Documents
d-----        11/13/18    11:35 PM                Downloads
d-----         11/7/18     1:39 PM                gems
d-----          4/6/18     1:05 PM                Music
d-----        11/14/18     9:02 AM                Pictures
d-----          4/6/18     1:05 PM                Public
d-----          8/2/18    11:43 AM                snap
d-----        11/12/18     1:58 PM                Templates
d-----        11/13/18     8:55 PM                Videos


PS /home/ram> 
```

3. Now, let's pick only the name of the folders and the last modified date and time. This is done in Bash by passing the output of `ls -l` to `awk`:

```
ls -l | awk '{print $6, $7, $8, $9}'
```

```
PS /home/ram> ls -l | awk '{print $6, $7, $8, $9}'

Apr 6 2018 Desktop
Nov 12 13:15 Documents
Nov 13 23:35 Downloads
Nov 7 13:39 gems
Apr 6 2018 Music
Nov 14 09:02 Pictures
Apr 6 2018 Public
Aug 2 11:43 snap
Nov 12 13:58 Templates
Nov 13 20:55 Videos
PS /home/ram>
```

4. Next, let's pick the same information on PowerShell as well:

```
Get-ChildItem | select LastWriteTime, Name
```

```
PS /home/ram> Get-ChildItem | Select-Object LastWriteTime, Name

LastWriteTime           Name
-------------           ----
4/6/18 1:05:23 PM       Desktop
11/12/18 1:15:35 PM     Documents
11/13/18 11:35:10 PM    Downloads
11/7/18 1:39:37 PM      gems
4/6/18 1:05:23 PM       Music
11/14/18 9:04:35 AM     Pictures
4/6/18 1:05:23 PM       Public
8/2/18 11:43:35 AM      snap
11/12/18 1:58:13 PM     Templates
11/14/18 9:04:27 AM     test subdirectory
11/13/18 8:55:55 PM     Videos

PS /home/ram>
```

As you may have noticed, the output is very similar in both cases. However, with PowerShell, you can see the names of the columns as well, which means that you do not have to look for further documentation. Also, the selection of columns is simpler in PowerShell; no text manipulation is required. On the other hand, in Bash, we can use the `awk` command to manipulate the text output.

5. Let's go one step further and create a subdirectory with a space in the name:

```
$ mkdir 'test subdirectory'
$ ls -l | awk '{print $6, $7, $8, $9}'
```

```
Terminal                                                    _  ✕
PS /home/ram> mkdir 'test subdirectory'
PS /home/ram> ls -l | awk '{print $6, $7, $8, $9}'

Apr  6 2018 Desktop
Nov 12 13:15 Documents
Nov 13 23:35 Downloads
Nov  7 13:39 gems
Apr  6 2018 Music
Nov 14 09:04 Pictures
Apr  6 2018 Public
Aug  2 11:43 snap
Nov 12 13:58 Templates
Nov 14 09:04 test
Nov 13 20:55 Videos
PS /home/ram>
```

Note that what should have been **test subdirectory** appears as **test**. Compare this with the output from PowerShell:

```
Terminal                                                    _  ✕
PS /home/ram> Get-ChildItem | Select-Object LastWriteTime, Name

LastWriteTime          Name
-------------          ----
4/6/18 1:05:23 PM      Desktop
11/12/18 1:15:35 PM    Documents
11/13/18 11:35:10 PM   Downloads
11/7/18 1:39:37 PM     gems
4/6/18 1:05:23 PM      Music
11/14/18 9:04:35 AM    Pictures
4/6/18 1:05:23 PM      Public
8/2/18 11:43:35 AM     snap
11/12/18 1:58:13 PM    Templates
11/14/18 9:04:27 AM    test subdirectory
11/13/18 8:55:55 PM    Videos

PS /home/ram>
```

How it works...

PowerShell reads content from the filesystem as objects, not as text. Therefore, you perform a selection of the desired columns (or, as we shall later see, properties) directly. Bash, on the other hand, outputs text, columns from which are manipulated using a delimiter.

To demonstrate that this is the case, we created a new subdirectory with a space in its name, and we performed the column selection just like we did before, only in this case we did not get the complete name of the new subdirectory. This is because the name contained a whitespace, which is a delimiter in awk.

 Comparing Bash and PowerShell is like comparing apples and oranges—in more ways than one. However, understanding the differences helps us leverage each of the tools to our benefit.

See also

- The *Selecting columns from the output* recipe from Chapter 4, *Passing Data Through the Pipeline*

Comparing Windows PowerShell and PowerShell Core

Windows PowerShell and PowerShell Core are two different implementations. The former is based on a larger framework, the .NET Framework. The latter, on the other hand, is a more modern framework, the .NET Core. PowerShell Core is cross-platform since its parent is. Windows PowerShell, on the other hand, is Windows-only, but has more capabilities than PowerShell at the time of writing this book.

The PowerShell that this book talks about is the cross-platform PowerShell Core. This is referred to as PowerShell. The PowerShell that is Windows-specific is referred to as Windows PowerShell.

Windows PowerShell leverages the internal components and the architectural model of Windows, with its capabilities enhanced by WinRM as well as Windows Management Instrumentation. In fact, most of the differences exist because of the inherent differences between Windows and Unix-like operating systems.

Support for snap-ins

PowerShell will not support the legacy version of modules, also known as **snap-ins**. Many of the snap-ins of old have been repackaged to be binary modules. Therefore, the unavailability of snap-ins should not be of much concern. Future development of these binary modules should, in theory, work on either PowerShell, provided that the host supports the API calls that are part of the binaries. For example, let's imagine that the Windows Active Directory module was repackaged into a binary PowerShell module. This module would run on Windows PowerShell as well as PowerShell on Windows. However, since Windows Active Directory does not run on Linux, the module would not work with PowerShell on Linux.

Convenience aliases

One important point to note is that commands such as `ls` and `mkdir` are aliases in Windows PowerShell, which means that running `ls` on Windows PowerShell would run `Get-ChildItem` in the background (this is also true for PowerShell on Windows). In Linux, however, running `ls` from within PowerShell would run the actual `ls` command; `ls` is not an alias in PowerShell on Linux—it is the command itself, whose output would be plain text. You can validate this by running `ls | Get-Member` on PowerShell on Linux, and comparing it with PowerShell on Windows as well as Windows PowerShell (it is, therefore, good to stick to the best practice of not using aliases in scripts):

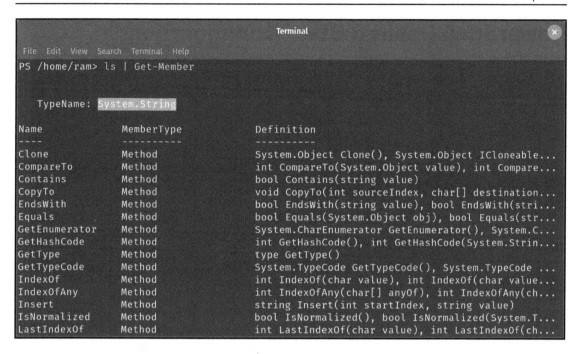

```
                                    Terminal                                   ⊗
 File  Edit  View  Search  Terminal  Help
PS /home/ram> ls | Get-Member


   TypeName: System.String

Name                MemberType       Definition
----                ----------       ----------
Clone               Method           System.Object Clone(), System.Object ICloneable...
CompareTo           Method           int CompareTo(System.Object value), int Compare...
Contains            Method           bool Contains(string value)
CopyTo              Method           void CopyTo(int sourceIndex, char[] destination...
EndsWith            Method           bool EndsWith(string value), bool EndsWith(stri...
Equals              Method           bool Equals(System.Object obj), bool Equals(str...
GetEnumerator       Method           System.CharEnumerator GetEnumerator(), System.C...
GetHashCode         Method           int GetHashCode(), int GetHashCode(System.Strin...
GetType             Method           type GetType()
GetTypeCode         Method           System.TypeCode GetTypeCode(), System.TypeCode ...
IndexOf             Method           int IndexOf(char value), int IndexOf(char value...
IndexOfAny          Method           int IndexOfAny(char[] anyOf), int IndexOfAny(ch...
Insert              Method           string Insert(int startIndex, string value)
IsNormalized        Method           bool IsNormalized(), bool IsNormalized(System.T...
LastIndexOf         Method           int LastIndexOf(char value), int LastIndexOf(ch...
```

 PowerShell knows whether it is running on Linux, Windows, or macOS by means of the values of the automatic variables IsLinux, IsWindows, and IsMacOS. On any system, only one of these variables has the value True. When PowerShell sees that IsLinux is True, it would run Linux commands instead of the convenience aliases that were initially created to facilitate Linux administrators. For more information on these automatic variables, read the *Configuring built-in variables* recipe.

PowerShell Workflows

Windows administrators who are used to PowerShell Workflows in Windows PowerShell need to note that they are absent in PowerShell. PowerShell Workflows were a little advanced (to put it nicely) and were used in specific scenarios where multiple cmdlets were to be run in parallel, or activities had to, say, survive a reboot. Workflows work on the Windows Workflow Foundation, which is not cross-platform. Therefore, PowerShell Workflows will not run on PowerShell. However, the unavailability of PowerShell Workflows is no deal-breaker. Workflows were not used much either.

PowerShell Desired State Configuration

Desired State Configuration (**DSC**) is a work in progress at the time of writing this book. As of now, there are two code bases of DSC resources: LCM for Linux, which is managed by Microsoft's Unix team, and DSC Resources for Windows PowerShell, which was written by the PowerShell team. It could be some time before the DSC code base becomes cross-platform.

Working with aliases

An alias, as the meaning goes, is an alternative name for cmdlet. They serve two purposes:

- To reduce the number of keystrokes
- To make the transition to PowerShell smoother

Traditionally, aliases were created in PowerShell so that Windows and Linux administrators did not find the new framework intimidating to work with. Regardless, aliases are best used only on the command line, and not in scripts, because some aliases are not aliases in Linux, and, in general, aliases affect readability. (For instance, it would take conscious effort to realize that gbp stands for Get-PSBreakPoint.)

How to do it...

As we have already mentioned, it is simple to think in PowerShell. When we know that the verb to fetch any information locally is Get, and the noun in this case would be Alias, the cmdlet should be Get-Alias:

1. Run Get-Help to understand how to use the cmdlet:

   ```
   PS> Get-Help Get-Alias
   ```

   If you're unsure about any command, or you would like to reduce keystrokes without involving aliases, use tab-completion. Write a part of the cmdlet or parameter and press the *Tab* key. PowerShell will complete the command for you, or show you suggestions, based on which platform you're doing this on.

2. According to the help documentation, all of the parameters for Get-Alias are optional (they are all enclosed in [ ]). Therefore, simply running Get-Alias will give us a list of all of the aliases that are available in the current instance of PowerShell:

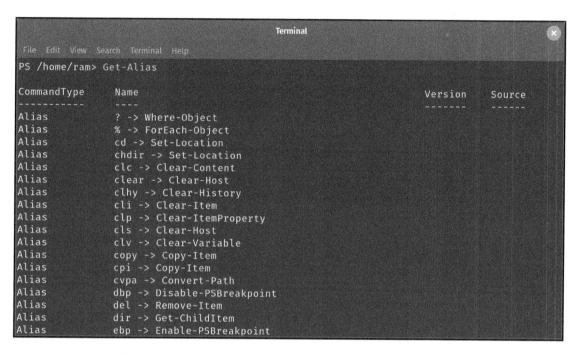

3. Now, let's try to resolve the gbp alias to the PowerShell cmdlet that it actually runs in:

```
PS> Get-Alias gbp
```

4. Now, do the opposite: get the alias for a certain cmdlet. The Definition in the second parameter set of the help documentation should be used. The output shows the actual PowerShell cmdlet that runs when an alias is called:

```
PS /home/ram> Get-Alias -Definition Get-ChildItem
```

5. We can see two aliases as output, both of which run Get-ChildItem under the hood. Now, let's run dir as well as Get-ChildItem and compare their outputs:

```
PS> dir
```

```
PS> Get-ChildItem
```

6. The two outputs are identical. Now, let's look at what type of object the commands return:

```
PS> /home/ram> dir | Get-Member
```

```
PS> /home/ram> Get-ChildItem | Get-Member
```

They returned the same object as well.

Now, let's create an alias:

1. First, identify a word that you'd like to use as the alias. For example, let's consider listdir.
2. Run listdir on PowerShell to ensure that such a cmdlet (or a Linux command) does not already exist.
3. List out the cmdlets that deal with aliases by running the following command:

```
PS> Get-Command *alias
```

4. New-Alias is the cmdlet we are looking for, since it creates a new alias.

> In PowerShell, the Set verb is used to modify something. Therefore, Set-Alias is used to modify an alias that already exists.

5. Read the help documentation for New-Alias by running the following command:

```
PS> Get-Help New-Alias
```

The help document indicates that only the Name and the Value parameters are mandatory. We will only use these two to create this simple alias.

6. Run the following command to create the custom alias:

```
PS> New-Alias listdir Get-ChildItem
```

7. Check whether the alias was created as desired or not:

```
PS> Get-Alias listdir
```

8. Next, run the alias to see what output it gives:

```
PS /home/ram> listdir
```

That is the output that we are familiar with—the output of Get-ChildItem.

 Aliases are ephemeral by default. They exist only as long as your PowerShell session exists. To use custom aliases without having to recreate them each time, export these aliases (the instructions for which are in the next recipe) and import them using your PowerShell profile. We will look at profiles in Chapter 2, *Preparing for Administration using PowerShell*.

Since aliases are ephemeral, let's export the alias we created. The output of Get-Command a few steps ago showed Export-Alias. Get-Help for the cmdlet shows that there are two ways to export the aliases: as a comma-separated values file, and as a script.

Export the aliases as a CSV file:

```
PS> Export-Alias aliases.csv
```

Export the aliases as a script as well:

```
PS> Export-Alias aliases.ps1 -As Script
```

View the contents of both files either using cat or Get-Content.

Optionally, edit the file to remove all of the aliases except the ones you created. The custom aliases can be found at the bottom of the list.

Next, import the aliases into your PowerShell session:

1. Restart PowerShell.
2. Check if the listdir alias that you created exists:

```
PS> Get-Alias listdir
```

3. Now, import either of the alias exports:

```
PS> Import-Alias ./aliases.csv
PS> # Or, simply call the script, ./aliases.ps1
```

If you did not remove the pre-existing aliases, you may receive several errors, each saying that the new alias could not be created. There are two ways to handle this: the first way is to remove the default aliases from the export file (which is recommended), and the second way is to use the – `Force` parameter (this may still result in errors, but there would be significantly fewer).

If you would like to add these aliases to your session, follow the *Enabling automated execution of commands for each load* recipe in `Chapter 2`, *Preparing for Administration Using PowerShell*.

How it works...

Aliases are nothing but mappings that are done within PowerShell. The short words are mapped to PowerShell cmdlets; the cmdlets are recorded as `Definition` in each of the aliases. Aliases also support the same parameters as the cmdlet as well, since aliases are merely pointers to the right cmdlet. When you run anything on PowerShell, PowerShell checks its list of cmdlets and aliases (among other definitions) to understand what you are asking for. When PowerShell encounters an alias, it looks for which cmdlet it points to, and runs the cmdlet.

Using `New-Alias`, you can create a pointer with a custom name that points to the desired PowerShell cmdlet. When the custom cmdlets are exported as a script, the contents show `New-Alias` for each of the aliases available in the session.

Exporting aliases as CSV makes it easier to extend within a text editor if needed. The `Import-Alias` cmdlet understands that the first column in the CSV is the name of the alias, and that the second is its definition.

There's more...

Add more content to your aliases, such as descriptions. Refer to the help documentation for `Get-Alias` to see what more you can do with aliases.

If you have a Windows computer, try running `Get-Alias` against Linux commands such as `ls`.

See also

1. The *Understanding cmdlets and parameters* recipe from `Chapter 2`, *Preparing for Administration Using PowerShell*
2. The *Enabling automated execution of commands for each load* recipe from `Chapter 2`, *Preparing for Administration Using PowerShell*

Dissecting a .NET Core object

This is a tangential recipe, in case you are interested in seeing how PowerShell has been implemented.

.NET Core works on a cross-platform standard Common Language Infrastructure. Therefore, it has been possible to encapsulate the internal workings of Linux using .NET Core. As we will see in future chapters, PowerShell is object-oriented, just like .NET Core. For this demonstration, we will pick a simple system class called `System.IO.DirectoryInfo` to show information about a certain directory. We will also compare the output of the .NET Core object to the output of a PowerShell cmdlet, which also shows information about a certain directory.

 You do not have to remember the names of the .NET Core classes or methods, or their syntax to work with PowerShell; that is the whole point of the existence of PowerShell. However, if you need information on the .NET libraries and the classes, extensive help documentation is available online ().

Getting ready

Every object has members—properties and methods. In case you're new to the concepts of object-oriented programming, properties are qualities of an object (what the object has), and methods are the capabilities of an object (what the object can do). Therefore, to quote (arguably) the most overused example of properties and methods: if a car is an object, its height, its color, and so on would be its properties, while accelerating, braking, and so on would be the methods that the object supports.

How to do it...

1. With PowerShell, .NET Core is also installed as a dependency. Let's create an object in PowerShell that will call a .NET class and its default constructor. This constructor requires an argument:

```
PS> New-Object -TypeName System.IO.DirectoryInfo -ArgumentList
$HOME
```

Here, /home/ram is my home directory. Replace this path with yours.

2. Use the Get-Item cmdlet with the same argument as before, and see what you get:

```
PS> Get-Item $HOME
```

3. Close! Now, let's look at the members of the output object we just received by using Get-Member:

```
PS> Get-Item $HOME | Get-Member
```

This will list a series of members (properties, methods) that are part of the output. We're primarily concerned about the very first line for now.

How it works...

Note the very first line of the output, TypeName: System.IO.DirectoryInfo. That is the exact type name we used when we created the .NET object:

```
                                        Terminal                                    ⊗
 File  Edit  View  Search  Terminal  Help
 PS /home/ram> Get-Item '/home/ram' | Get-Member

 TypeName: System.IO.DirectoryInfo

 Name                          MemberType     Definition
 ----                          ----------     ----------
 LinkType                      CodeProperty   System.String LinkType{get=GetLinkType;}
 Mode                          CodeProperty   System.String Mode{get=Mode;}
 Target                        CodeProperty   System.Collections.Generic.IEnumerable`1[[System.String, System.Privat...
 Create                        Method         void Create()
 CreateSubdirectory            Method         System.IO.DirectoryInfo CreateSubdirectory(string path)
 Delete                        Method         void Delete(), void Delete(bool recursive)
 EnumerateDirectories          Method         System.Collections.Generic.IEnumerable[System.IO.DirectoryInfo] Enumer...
 EnumerateFiles                Method         System.Collections.Generic.IEnumerable[System.IO.FileInfo] EnumerateFi...
 EnumerateFileSystemInfos      Method         System.Collections.Generic.IEnumerable[System.IO.FileSystemInfo] Enume...
 Equals                        Method         bool Equals(System.Object obj)
 GetDirectories                Method         System.IO.DirectoryInfo[] GetDirectories(), System.IO.DirectoryInfo[] ...
 GetFiles                      Method         System.IO.FileInfo[] GetFiles(string searchPattern), System.IO.FileInf...
 GetFileSystemInfos            Method         System.IO.FileSystemInfo[] GetFileSystemInfos(string searchPattern), S...
 GetHashCode                   Method         int GetHashCode()
 GetLifetimeService            Method         System.Object GetLifetimeService()
 GetObjectData                 Method         void GetObjectData(System.Runtime.Serialization.SerializationInfo info...
 GetType                       Method         type GetType()
 InitializeLifetimeService     Method         System.Object InitializeLifetimeService()
 MoveTo                        Method         void MoveTo(string destDirName)
 Refresh                       Method         void Refresh()
 ToString                      Method         string ToString()
 PSChildName                   NoteProperty   string PSChildName=ram
 PSDrive                       NoteProperty   PSDriveInfo PSDrive=/
```

This proves that the same task of showing information on the current working directory can be achieved by either calling a .NET constructor or by running a PowerShell cmdlet, the implication being that PowerShell cmdlets are simply encapsulated .NET code. In essence, Get-Item calls the System.IO.DirectoryInfo class under the hood, with the arguments passed along with the cmdlet.

Like they say: "If the C# guys can do it, so can you."

See also

- The System.IO.DirectoryInfo .NET class (https://docs.microsoft.com/en-us/dotnet/api/system.io.directoryinfo?redirectedfrom=MSDNview=netframework-4.7.2)

Listing out the execution policies and setting a suitable one

This is a Windows-only recipe. Skip this if you never plan to work on Windows.

There was a time when running scripts on Windows computers was a cakewalk. Windows computers were highly prone to remote script executions. With PowerShell, Microsoft added a safety belt that allowed the user some control over how PowerShell scripts were loaded. Some specific models of script executions got restricted, which plugged some holes in the system.

 It is important to remember that execution policies are not a security feature. There are ways to circumvent this fence. Execution policies are in place only to ensure that users don't accidentally run scripts without awareness.

PowerShell Core on Windows and Windows PowerShell contain this feature. Running PowerShell scripts on Windows is still restricted by default. On PowerShell Core on Linux, execution policies do not work at the moment, and, based on the interactions in the community, it is uncertain whether this feature will ever make it to PowerShell on Linux. Regardless, if you are reading this book, you are more than capable of understanding the perils of scripts from unknown sources.

An execution policy determines what type of scripts can be executed. Here are the six execution policies (excluding Default):

1. `AllSigned`
2. `RemoteSigned`
3. `Restricted`
4. `Unrestricted`
5. `Bypass`
6. `Undefined`

There are three scopes as well:

1. `Process`
2. `CurrentUser`
3. `LocalMachine`

A combination of an execution policy and a scope are what determine the condition that scripts can be loaded under. Microsoft has documented in detail what each of the policies is. In general, `AllSigned` requires that all of the scripts that run on the computer are signed using a code-signing certificate by a trusted certification authority. If this policy is set, PowerShell will not run unsigned scripts, even if you were the one to create them.

`Restricted` is the default policy: commands can be run, but not scripts. `RemoteSigned` allows scripts that have been created on your own computer to run. Scripts that have been downloaded from the internet cannot be run.

`Bypass` is similar to `Unrestricted`, however, it is used in specific scenarios, such as when PowerShell forms the basis of a certain application, and the application has its own security implementation.

`Unrestricted` means that all scripts and commands can run after a simple confirmation. `Undefined` means that no policy has been defined for a particular scope. Follow the recipe to find the execution policy that is effective on the session, and change it to suit your needs.

Getting ready

This recipe can only be run on Windows. If you're running a pure Linux environment, you cannot work with this recipe. You may run the commands, but you will see the Unrestricted policy set at all levels.

If you have a Windows computer to work with, you can proceed with this recipe, regardless of whether it has PowerShell or Windows PowerShell.

How to do it...

Open a PowerShell window by running `pwsh` or `powershell`. The `pwsh` command calls PowerShell, and `powershell` calls Windows PowerShell.

Windows PowerShell comes preinstalled on all modern Windows operating systems; PowerShell, on the other hand, has to be installed. Note that all of the current PowerShell cmdlets will run on Windows PowerShell as well:

1. First, run the `Get-Command` cmdlet to find out how to work with execution policies:

   PS> Get-Command -Noun Execution*

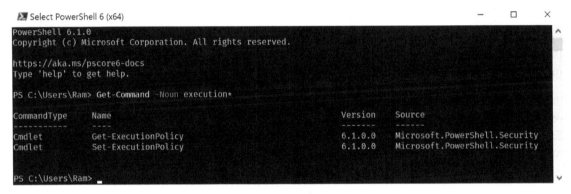

2. Now, let's get help on running the cmdlet:

   PS> Get-Help Get-ExecutionPolicy

3. We want to know the execution policy set on the machine. Therefore, we will run the following code:

   PS> Get-ExecutionPolicy

This shows that the execution policy is currently effective on the current PowerShell session.

4. To list out the policies set at various scopes, run the following command:

   PS> Get-ExecutionPolicy -List

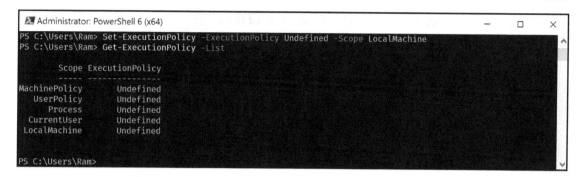

We can see that the policy is only set at the `LocalMachine` level, and that it is set as `RemoteSigned`, which is the same as what is reflected in the previous step. The policy at the `LocalUser` and the `Process` scopes is `Undefined`, which made the session pick the execution policy from `LocalMachine`.

Now, let's set the execution policy for the local machine to be `Undefined` and see what our session picks up.

5. For this to work, close the current PowerShell session and open a new session as the administrator.
6. Next, run the following command:

```
PS> Get-Help Set-ExecutionPolicy
```

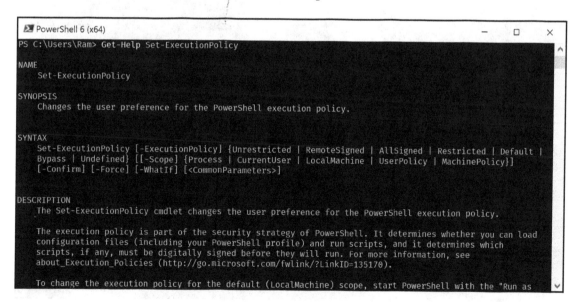

7. The help document shows that the value of the `ExecutionPolicy` parameter is mandatory, and that `Undefined` is one of the valid values it will accept. We want to set the policy at the `LocalMachine` scope, and so we will use the following code:

 You will need to launch PowerShell (either Core or Windows) with elevated privileges to set the policy at the `LocalMachine` level.

```
PS> Set-ExecutionPolicy -ExecutionPolicy Undefined -Scope
LocalMachine
```

8. Now, list the execution policies at the various scopes:

```
PS> Get-ExecutionPolicy -List
```

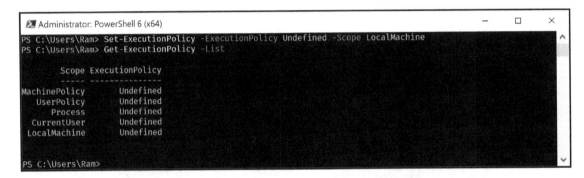

9. Now, let's check the currently effective execution policy:

```
PS> Get-ExecutionPolicy
```

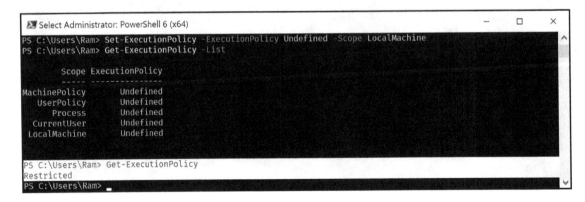

10. Finally, let's set the execution policy back to how it was before we began the recipe. You may want to change the policy to suit your needs, based on what authority you have on the computer:

```
PS> Set-ExecutionPolicy RemoteSigned -Scope LocalMachine
```

How it works...

Execution policies are nothing but conditions that are set on the system to avoid accidental script runs. They work at different scopes.

There are three scopes in PowerShell, as we have already stated. The `LocalSystem` scope is at the end of the chain. Right above it is the `CurrentUser` scope. At the top is the `Process` scope. The level of precedence is `Process` > `CurrentUser` > `LocalMachine`. Therefore, if any policy other than `Undefined` is set at the `Process` scope, the session will use the policy that's currently set on the process. In case it is `Undefined`, it will look for the policy set on the `CurrentUser` scope. If `CurrentUser` has the policy marked as `Undefined` as well, the session will apply the policy that was applied at the `LocalMachine` level. If `LocalMachine` has `Undefined` set, the session will pick the `Default` policy, which is based on what PowerShell has defined as the policy, which may vary based on the version of your operating system. On Windows 2016, for instance, the default policy is `RemoteSigned`.

The policies set at the `CurrentUser` and `LocalMachine` levels are stored in the Windows Registry. The policy set on the Process scope is stored in the ephemeral environment variable, that is, `$env:PSExecutionPolicyPreference`.

See also

- About_Execution_Policies (https://docs.microsoft.com/en-us/powershell/module/microsoft.powershell.core/about/about_execution_policies?view=powershell-6)

Preparing for Administration Using PowerShell

2

In this chapter, we will cover the following topics:

- Installing Visual Studio Code
- Configuring automatic variables
- Changing the shell behavior using variables
- Enabling automated execution of commands for each load
- Customizing the Terminal prompt
- Understanding standard redirection in PowerShell
- Calling native Linux commands from PowerShell
- Understanding cmdlets and parameters
- Running cmdlets with minimal keystrokes
- Finding parameter aliases
- Calling a PowerShell script
- Dot-sourcing a PowerShell script
- Calling a PowerShell cmdlet from outside of PowerShell
- Recording the cmdlets run on the PowerShell console

Introduction

It is a common notion that the more you use the Terminal (as opposed to the GUI), the more efficient you are. Typing out commands is much easier and faster than clicking around the screen. However, to someone who has just begun using the Terminal, it may not be so. Over time, as administrators grow more and more comfortable with the Terminal, they learn to configure it for speed and efficiency, much like training a horse. Further, most efficient administrators like automating several parts of their workflow—customizing .bashrc and Vim scripts are examples of this. In this chapter, we will familiarize ourselves with the different consoles and tools that work with PowerShell, and will also look at a few simple recipes that would help customize our workspace, so that we can be more efficient.

Installing Visual Studio Code

Scripting can happen on the console itself, with Vim. It is also possible to use other editors, such as Gedit or even Atom, to write PowerShell scripts. It is, however, recommended to use Microsoft's open source code editor, called Visual Studio Code (or vscode). In this recipe, we will look at installing Visual Studio Code and configuring it to work with PowerShell.

Getting ready

We will look at the steps to install vscode on Ubuntu. Today, most repositories contain Visual Studio Code. You can check in the software store of your distribution to install vscode. If not, the easiest way to install vscode is to download the .deb (or the .rpm package if you are on CentOS) and run it to install the package on your computer.

How to do it...

Installing **Visual Studio Code (VS Code)** is simple:

1. If your Linux distribution has a software store, search the store for Visual Studio Code.
2. If you find Visual Studio Code, install the package from there. If not, proceed with the next step.

3. The package name for Visual Studio Code is `code`. Use your package manager to search for the package in the repository. On Ubuntu, the command would be:

```
$ sudo apt-cache pkgnames code
```

4. If you are able to find the package in your repository, install Visual Studio Code like you would any other package:

```
$ sudo apt install code
```

5. If you are unable to find the package, go to `https://code.visualstudio.com/Download` and download the right `code` package for your distribution.

6. To install Visual Studio Code, call your package manager with the path to the downloaded package:

```
$ sudo apt install ./code_<version>_<architecture>.deb
```

7. If you would rather install Visual Studio Code in portable mode, download the Visual Studio Code tarball and extract its contents to a convenient location to run Visual Studio Code. However, remember that updates to Visual Studio Code will be handled by Visual Studio Code itself in this case.

Visual Studio Code is a powerful code editor in itself. However, it may not fully support PowerShell right out of the box. You would need to install the extension that packs capabilities that help write and run PowerShell scripts.

Follow these steps to install the PowerShell extension for Visual Studio Code:

1. Launch Visual Studio Code either using the application launcher or by entering `code` at the Terminal
2. Click on the Extensions icon or press *Ctrl + Shift + X* to go to the Extensions pane
3. In the search bar, enter `powershell publisher:Microsoft` and hit *Enter* to search for the PowerShell package
4. Click on **Install** in the resulting package—the PowerShell package should be on top
5. Once the installation completes, click on the **Reload** button on the extensions page to reload Visual Studio Code with PowerShell capabilities

You are now ready to develop PowerShell scripts using a friendly editor that supports almost all of the capabilities that the Windows PowerShell **Integrated Scripting Environment** (**ISE**) has and more!

How it works...

Windows PowerShell ISE was the de facto environment to develop PowerShell scripts. We even used this to write full-fledged applications in PowerShell. Then came Adam Driscoll's PowerShell extension to Microsoft Visual Studio, which integrated PowerShell into the integrated development environment.

Over time, the .NET Foundation was formed, and Microsoft started working on a lightweight code editor called Visual Studio Code that packed many of the great features of Visual Studio, without all of the load of the language libraries. Visual Studio Code is just the core and contains an extension manager and an extension repository that contains the PowerShell extension. This extension installs the integrated PowerShell Terminal, IntelliSense suggestions, the PowerShell grammar, snippets, and so on, to help PowerShell script writers create and run PowerShell scripts and modules.

Using a package manager to install Visual Studio Code ensures that all of the dependencies are met. Also, this method of installation ensures that the signing key is added to the system. This way, updates to Visual Studio Code can be installed through the system, such as by running `sudo apt upgrade`.

See also

- Installing VS Code on Linux (`https://code.visualstudio.com/docs/setup/linux`)

Configuring automatic variables

Perhaps nothing contributes to efficiency like configurability. Configuring a system is a way of tuning it to your taste. You are the only one who knows what works best for you. Therefore, the more configurable a system is, the better it can be tweaked to your preference. Automatic variables in PowerShell are one of the first steps to customization in PowerShell (profiles are the other; we shall look into them shortly). In this recipe, we will list out all of the automatic variables and configure some of them to our requirements.

Getting ready

Read the *Listing the various providers in PowerShell* recipe of Chapter 1, *Introducing PowerShell Core,* to learn how to use the various providers in PowerShell.

How to do it...

Let's first list out the variables we have. This can be done in two ways:

- Using a cmdlet
- Using a provider

Let us first look at using the cmdlet to list out the variables built into PowerShell:

1. Open a Terminal window. If you have one open, restart PowerShell.
2. Find the cmdlet that works with variables:

   ```
   PS> Get-Command -Noun Variable
   ```

   Remember that the noun in a cmdlet is always singular. Therefore, it would be Variable and not Variables.

3. There are five cmdlets that deal with variables. We want to fetch a list of all variables already existing in a new session of PowerShell. Let us pick Get-Variable and fetch help information for it:

   ```
   PS> Get-Help Get-Variable
   ```

4. This is the cmdlet that we need to list out all of the variables predefined in the current scope:

   ```
   PS> Get-Variable
   ```

Any variables you define would be listed here. Hence, it is important that you start a fresh session of PowerShell to see what variables have been predefined.

Let's now use a PowerShell provider to list out the variables defined in the current scope:

1. List out the PowerShell providers. We looked at providers in Chapter 1, *Introducing PowerShell Core*:

   ```
   PS> Get-PsProvider
   ```

2. Change the location to the Variable: drive of the Variable provider. This is done using Set-Location:

   ```
   PS> Set-Location Variable:
   ```

3. Now, let us list out all of the available child items of the `Variable:` drive:

```
PS> Get-ChildItem
```

The output of this was identical to that of `Get-Variable`, called without an argument.

How it works...

PowerShell is built with some variables that control its behavior, and administrators are allowed to modify some of them to suit their needs. Some variables, however, cannot be modified; they are contextual and add some amount of flexibility (or modularity, as the case might be) to the shell.

One such example would be `$PWD`, which contains the path of the present directory. This variable changes itself based on the execution of `Set-Location`. Values cannot be explicitly assigned to such variables; setting values explicitly would have no effect on the behavior of the shell.

Some variables, on the other hand, accept values and let us control the execution of commands and scripts. We shall look at an example in the next recipe.

Changing shell behavior using variables

In the previous recipe, we took a look at the existing variables. In this recipe, we will change the value of one of the variables to control the behavior of PowerShell. Again, remember that the change in the value is ephemeral; the values would be reset once the PowerShell process is restarted.

Getting ready

Read the previous recipe to understand the automatic variables that come predefined. Also, start Visual Studio Code. Perform the following steps to start Visual Studio Code:

1. Open applications (I use the GNOME desktop environment, which shows all applications with *Super* + *A*).
2. Type in `code`.
3. Press *Ctrl* + ` to launch the Terminal.
4. Click on **New File** on the welcome screen (or press *Ctrl* + *N*).

5. At the bottom right of the Visual Studio Code window, you will see the file type set to **Plain Text**. Click on it; you will be taken to the command bar on top.

6. Type in `powershell` in the command bar. The **PowerShell Integrated Console** will open at the bottom:

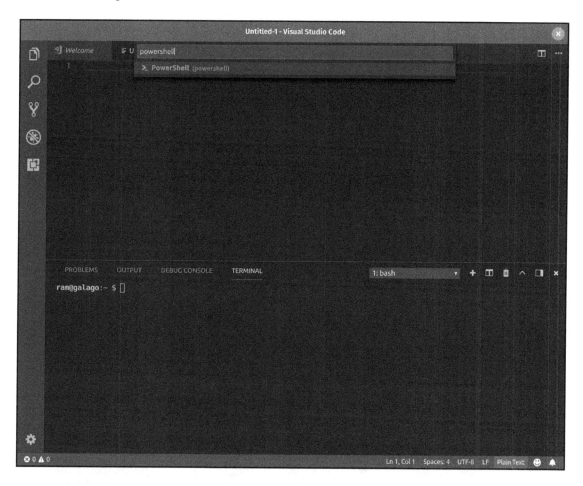

We are all set for the recipe now.

How to do it...

1. Let's run a command that will result in an error. For now, let us not focus on the syntax of the command; our only goal for now is to generate an error. At the first line of the script window, type in the following:

```
PS> Get-ChildItem /home/ram/random-directory
PS> Write-Host "Hello world!"
```

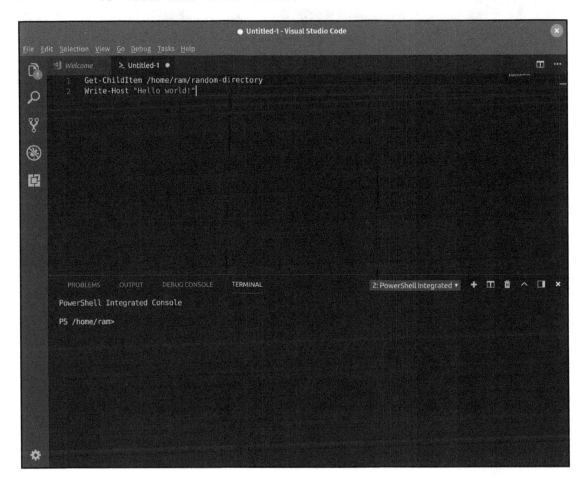

2. Run the two-liner script using the *F5* key:

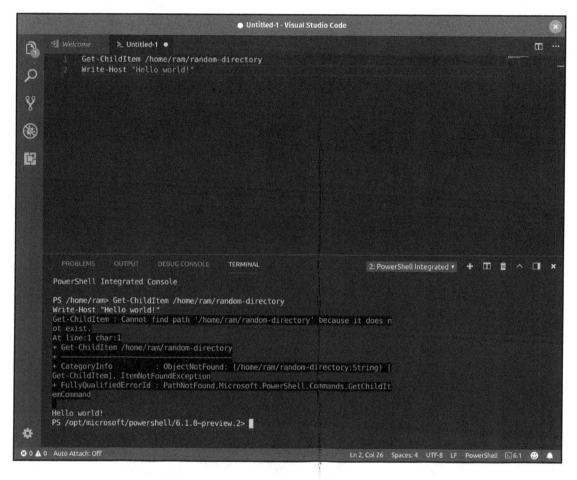

PowerShell is prompt to show an error. It also displays the `Hello world!` string.

3. Let's set the error action preference, using the variable, `ErrorActionPreference`. We know there's such a variable from the previous recipe. First, though, restart PowerShell. The easiest way is to click on the little bin icon at the top of the integrated console window. When Visual Studio Code asks if you would like to restart the session, click on **Yes**:

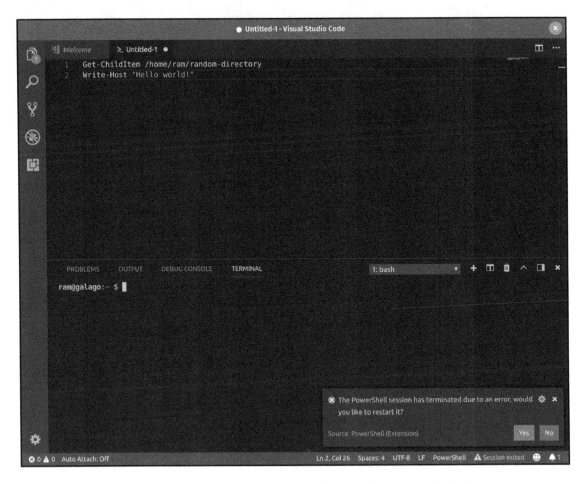

4. Set the `ErrorActionPreference` variable. At the **PowerShell Integrated Console**, enter the following:

```
PS> Set-Variable ErrorActionPreference SilentlyContinue
```

5. Run the two-liner script again.There is no error this time. And we see `Hello world!` at the console.

If you do not want the entire script appear at the prompt, make the first line of the script `Clear-Host`; this will clear the screen before showing the output.

6. What if you were to check whether an error was generated at all? We check the value of the automatic variable, `Error`:

PS> Get-Variable Error

7. The `Value` column contains some text. Let's select and expand the contents of `Value`:

```
PS> Get-Variable Error | Select-Object -ExpandProperty Value
```

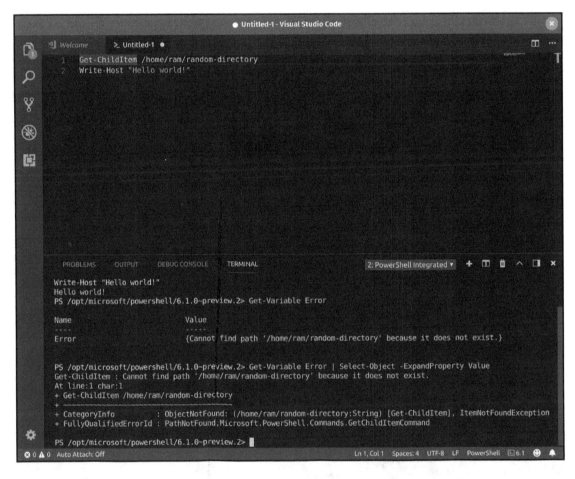

The output text is the same as what we received before we set the error action preference.

> You can also simply call the `Error` variable to read all of the errors that occurred in the current session.

How it works…

By default, the error action preference is `Continue`, which means that PowerShell would display the error and continue with the execution of the rest of the script (this effect is not noticeable when running individual commands; hence, the creation of the two-liner, or three-liner if you added `Clear-Host` at the top). By setting `ErrorActionPreference` to `SilentlyContinue`, we instruct PowerShell to record the error but not show it on the screen and, at the same time, to go on with executing the rest of the script.

See also

- `about_Preference_Variables`, `$ErrorActionPreference` (https://docs. microsoft.com/en-us/powershell/module/microsoft.powershell.core/about/ about_preference_variables?view=powershell-6#erroractionpreference)

Enabling automated execution of commands for each load

As we saw in the previous recipes, these changes are ephemeral; they remain as long as the session is active. There might be situations where administrators might require running a few commands or loading modules to enable them to work faster. For instance, I tend to load a series of modules that help me manage Microsoft Exchange, Active Directory, VMware vSphere infrastructure, Citrix XenApp, Microsoft System Center, and other environments using PowerShell.

All of these products require different ways of loading the modules, snap-ins, and scripts, and many of them require a certain configuration every time you load the modules (such as connecting to VM servers with administrator credentials). These can be done using the PowerShell profile.

Getting ready

PowerShell, by default, does not create a profile during installation. It simply runs with its default configuration. Any override to this configuration would require creating and modifying the profile:

1. Open a PowerShell console. (You could either run `pwsh` at the Terminal or use the Visual Studio Code console. This recipe uses the Terminal.)

2. Reveal the path of your profile. To do this, simply call the automatic variable:

   ```
   PS> $PROFILE
   ```

3. Check if your profile exists:

   ```
   PS> Test-Path $PROFILE
   ```

4. If you get `True` as the response, you can proceed with the recipe. If the response is `False`, which is most likely the case, run the following:

   ```
   PS> New-Item $PROFILE -ItemType File
   ```

5. You may receive an error, saying a part of the path was not found. This is because your `~/.config/` directory does not, by default, contain a `powershell` directory. Adding `-Force` to the command creates this directory and creates your profile file at the location:

   ```
   PS> New-Item $PROFILE -ItemType File -Force
   ```

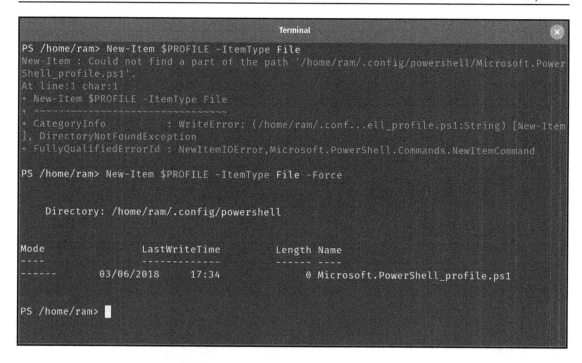

6. We will now edit the profile in Visual Studio Code. At the Terminal, type the following:

```
PS> code $PROFILE
```

How to do it...

You should have the profile open now. It would currently be empty. Let us now customize PowerShell's error action behavior. Remember that we said that setting ErrorActionPreference to SilentlyContinue at the Terminal was temporary. Let us now ensure that ErrorActionPreference is permanently set to SilentlyContinue every time we launch PowerShell:

1. Switch to the Terminal window. If you have the window open since the last recipe, restart PowerShell.

2. Let us see what the error action preference is at the moment:

```
PS> Get-Variable ErrorActionPreference
Continue
```

3. Switch to Visual Studio Code. The profile should already be open for edits.

4. At the very first line, type in the following:

```
PS> Set-Variable ErrorActionPreference SilentlyContinue
```

5. Save the profile and close the file.

6. At the Terminal, type `exit` to exit from PowerShell. Start PowerShell again.

7. Let us now check what the value is for `ErrorActionPreference`. At the prompt, type the following:

```
PS> $ErrorActionPreference
SilentlyContinue
```

8. To ensure the preference is indeed in place, type the following:

```
PS> Get-ChildItem /home/ram/random-directory
```

```
Terminal                                                            ⊗

ram@galago:~ $ pwsh
PowerShell v6.1.0-preview.2
Copyright (c) Microsoft Corporation. All rights reserved.

https://aka.ms/pscore6-docs
Type 'help' to get help.

PS /home/ram> $ErrorActionPreference
Continue
PS /home/ram> vim $PROFILE
PS /home/ram> exit
ram@galago:~ $ pwsh
PowerShell v6.1.0-preview.2
Copyright (c) Microsoft Corporation. All rights reserved.

https://aka.ms/pscore6-docs
Type 'help' to get help.

PS /home/ram> $ErrorActionPreference
SilentlyContinue
PS /home/ram> Get-ChildItem /home/ram/random-directory
PS /home/ram> ▯
```

The cursor simply returned to the prompt at the next line without throwing an error.

How it works...

Long story short, the PowerShell profile executes every time a PowerShell session is loaded. This profile is a PowerShell script file that can contain a series of commands and functions, which would be executed just like any other script.

One important point to remember is that there is a different profile for each host. For instance, there is a separate profile for PowerShell loaded on the Terminal and a different one for the integrated terminal on Visual Studio Code. This is because each of the terminals has a different nature.

> Execution policies have not been implemented in PowerShell on Linux. In case PowerShell on Linux gains the safety belt in the future, the execution policy should be set to allow execution of scripts in order for the profile to load.

There's more...

It is bad practice to set a global action preference. Empty the profile to remove the error action preference. Since the profile has nothing else, you could even delete the profile using the following command:

```
PS> Remove-Item $PROFILE
```

Read the best practices for more information.

Customizing the Terminal prompt

In the previous recipe, we customized the error action preference using the profile. We used an already-demonstrated command to show that commands that can be run on the PowerShell console can be added to the profile as well, and this was a way to automate running a certain set of commands which could be used to increase productivity.

Now, we will take the next step and customize our console prompt. The options are theoretically endless; this recipe is just another demonstration of how flexible PowerShell is.

Getting ready

You need Visual Studio Code for this recipe. If you did not follow along with the last recipe, follow the steps in the *Getting ready* section of the last recipe to create a PowerShell profile; only this time, run the commands at the **PowerShell Integrated Console** of Visual Studio Code.

How to do it...

Ensure that the profile is empty. If you just created the profile, you can simply proceed further. If not, clear all contents in the profile. If the error action preference is set in the profile, it will become hard to troubleshoot scripts that you create in the future:

1. Enter the following in the main window:

```
function prompt {
  $Location = (Get-Location).Path.ToString()
  switch -Wildcard ($Location) {
      "/home/$env:USERNAME" { $Location = '~'; break }
      "/home/$env:USERNAME/Documents" { $Location = 'Documents';
break }
      "/home/$env:USERNAME/Downloads" { $Location = 'Downloads';
break }
      "/home/$env:USERNAME/Pictures" { $Location = 'Pictures'; break
}
      "/home/$env:USERNAME/Videos" { $Location = 'Videos'; break }
      "/home/$env:USERNAME/Music" { $Location = 'Music'; break }
      "/home/$env:USERNAME/Documents/code" { $Location = 'Code';
break }
      "/home/$env:USERNAME/*" { $Location =
$Location.Replace("/home/$env:USERNAME/", '~/'); break }
      Default { }
    }
  Write-Host "PS " -NoNewline
  Write-Host `
    ($($env:USERNAME) + "@" +
"$([System.Net.Dns]::GetHostByName((hostname)).HostName) ") `
    -NoNewLine -ForegroundColor Cyan
  Write-Host "$Location" -NoNewline -ForegroundColor Green
  Write-Host ("`n> ") -NoNewline
  return " "
}
```

2. Save the profile script file.
3. Click on the little bin icon at the top of the integrated console to kill the current PowerShell session.
4. When Visual Studio Code prompts you whether you would like to restart the session, click **Yes**.

Your prompt should look like the one shown in the following screenshot:

How it works...

The prompt is controlled by a function called `prompt`. To demonstrate this, we could use the following:

```
PS> Get-Command prompt
```

The output shows that there is indeed such a command, which is of the `Function` type. To know the contents of the `prompt` function, enter the following:

```
PS> (Get-Command prompt).ScriptBlock
```

The output shows you the entire function you just wrote. This is, however, the function that overrode the default `prompt` function. If you clear your profile, restart the PowerShell session, and type in the preceding command; you would see a simple three-liner output, which is the default `prompt` function.

The function we wrote replaces the default script block with our custom code. Here is what you did:

First, you declare the function you are about to write. This is done using the keyword, `function`, followed by the name of the function. Since we want to work with the prompt, we use the existing function name so as to override the default functionality. The next thing that follows is the script block, which starts with a {.

We want the location to appear at the prompt. This is must-have information, for obvious reasons.

If you notice, PowerShell shows the complete `home` path at the prompt. While this works, we are used to the tilde for `home`. Also, I know that `Documents`, `Music`, and other folders reside within my `home` folder, and I would rather have just the name of the folder appear at the prompt. This would mean some text manipulation. Therefore, I assign the current location to a variable, `$Location`.

Next, we perform a switch-case operation and arrive at the value for what needs to be displayed at the prompt. Do not worry about the syntax for now; we will look at it in the chapters that follow.

Later, we use a few `Write-Host` statements to construct the prompt text. The `-NoNewLine` parameter ensures that the contents of each statement do not go to the next line. When we need a line break, we explicitly add `` `n ``.

If you want to break a long-running line in a script, use the backtick (`` ` ``) character at the point where you would like to break the line and press *Enter* to break the line after the backtick. PowerShell would treat the line with the backtick, as well as the line that follows, as the same line. Similarly, if you would like to write two statements in the same line, use the semicolon (;) at the end of the first statement and continue with the second after a space. PowerShell will treat both the clauses as separate statements, just like plain English.

Since `Write-Host` just sends text to the host and does not return anything, we add a return statement to the function with merely an empty space.

When we reload the **PowerShell Integrated Console**, the profile is loaded and, this time, the custom `prompt` function in the profile overrides the default `prompt` function and presents us with a nice prompt, formatted just the way we defined it.

There's more...

Play around with the sequences and the contents of the `Write-Host` statements for now to customize your prompt. Once we are comfortable with the syntax in PowerShell, we should be able to customize the profile further.

See also

- about_Prompts (https://docs.microsoft.com/en-us/powershell/module/microsoft.powershell.core/about/about_prompts?view=powershell-6)

Understanding standard redirection in PowerShell

During the process of learning to use Bash or sh, we learn to use the redirection operators, such as <, >, and >>. PowerShell works on redirection as well. However, the implementation of redirection is different in PowerShell.

Redirection in PowerShell mainly relies on streams, which are covered in a different chapter. For this recipe, we stick with the default stream, which is `Success`. This recipe covers different, simple redirections to help with basic administration.

Before we begin, let us understand that PowerShell is very different from Bash in terms of redirection, although it packs some minor similarities; similarities enough to make you not go away, but rather appreciate the flexibility of the object model and the uniformity of use.

How to do it...

We shall perform four activities in this recipe:

1. Redirect output to a file
2. Append another output to the same file
3. Send the output of a command to the console as well as a file
4. Accept the input of one command into another

Apart from the operators that we use in the first two activities, we will also look at the cmdlet equivalents to those operators:

1. List out all of the processes running on your computer at the moment:

    ```
    PS> Get-Process
    ```

2. The output was shown on the console. Now, let us redirect the contents into a file:

    ```
    PS> Get-Process > processes.txt
    ```

3. List out the contents of the file:

    ```
    PS> Get-Content ./processes.txt
    ```

4. Let us now append the file with the date and timestamp:

    ```
    PS> Get-Date >> ./processes.txt
    ```

5. Read the contents of the file now:

    ```
    PS> Get-Content ./processes.txt
    ```

You can see that the file now contains a list of all of the processes running in the system, as well as the timestamp. The timestamp got appended to the file.

In PowerShell, the same results can be accomplished using the `Out-File` cmdlet. (`Out-File` has more features, such as setting the encoding and new line control.) Let us accomplish the same tasks using the `Out-File` cmdlet. You may want to delete `processes.txt` before proceeding:

1. List out the currently-running processes again and send the output to a file using `Out-File`:

   PS> Get-Process | Out-File processes.txt

2. Append the timestamp to the file:

   PS> Get-Date | Out-File processes.txt -Append

   If you notice, the output of `Get-Process` and `Get-Date` went directly to the file; nothing got displayed on the host.

If we want to display the output on the console as well as send the content to a file, we simply use `Tee-Object` instead of `Out-File`. If you would like, delete the file, `processes.txt`, again:

1. Run the following command:

   PS> Get-Process | Tee-Object ./processes.txt

   The list of running processes should be shown at the Terminal.

2. Check the contents of the file, `processes.txt`:

   PS /home/ram> Get-Content ./processes.txt

As you can see, the list of processes appears in the text file as well.

Let us now proceed with learning to make cmdlets accept input from files. Linux administrators are used to making commands accept input from a file, like so:

$ command < input_file.txt

The command accepts input from `input_file.txt` and performs operations on the input content.

In PowerShell, this is handled using `Get-Content` and the pipe (`|`). The PowerShell equivalent of a command accepting input from a file would be as follows:

PS> Get-Content input_file.txt | command

This might seem the other way around to most of those who are not used to PowerShell. Let us break down the process into pieces and try to understand it better. For instance, let us say you have a list of files in a text file called input.txt:

1. Reveal the contents of the text file:

   PS> Get-Content input.txt

   The contents of input.txt are as follows:

2. List out the contents of the current directory:

   $ ls

   We have five test files in the current directory, four of which are in the list (the input file). Let us say that you would like to delete the files listed in the input file, from the directory.

3. Pass the output of Get-Content to the command, Remove-Item, through the pipe:

   PS> Get-Content input.txt | Remove-Item

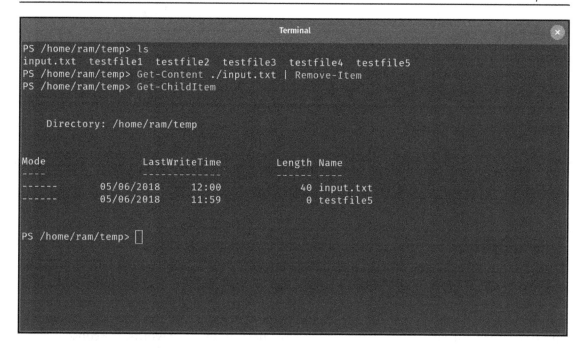

```
                              Terminal                              ⊗
PS /home/ram/temp> ls
input.txt  testfile1  testfile2  testfile3  testfile4  testfile5
PS /home/ram/temp> Get-Content ./input.txt | Remove-Item
PS /home/ram/temp> Get-ChildItem


    Directory: /home/ram/temp


Mode                 LastWriteTime           Length Name
----                 -------------           ------ ----
------          05/06/2018    12:00              40 input.txt
------          05/06/2018    11:59               0 testfile5


PS /home/ram/temp> []
```

4. List out the files currently present in the directory:

   `PS> Get-ChildItem`

If you compare the output of `ls` (before) and `Get-ChildItem` (after), the files that were listed in the text file are no more.

How it works...

In this recipe, we set out to understand the similarities between Bash and PowerShell. In spite of being fundamentally different from Bash, PowerShell does have some similarities to Bash. Two of the similarities, as we saw, are passing content to files and appending content to the files.

We looked at three cmdlets in this recipe, one of which was used twice.

Out-File

Those comfortable with Bash use the > for sending the output to a file, and >> to append the output to an existing file. In PowerShell, we use the Out-File cmdlet. We run a command that sends output to the standard output and, through the pipe, redirects the output to Out-File, which handles writing the output to a file. Usually, Out-File is used to send content to a text file.

When there is a need to append the content to a file, we use the -Append switch with Out-File. This way, if the file that is being written to already contains content, the content isn't overwritten (overwriting content is the default behavior of Out-File).

Tee-Object

There are situations where you need to send content to a file, as well as display the content on the console. This is handled using a simple call of Tee-Object. Tee-Object works like the letter T; apart from sending content to a file or a variable, it also sends the content down the pipeline. If Tee-Object is the last cmdlet in the statement, the pipeline output is sent out to standard output, which in most cases is the host (or in other words, the console by default).

In our recipe, we sent the first output to the file, processes.txt, and the second output was not sent down the pipeline. Therefore, Tee-Object picked the standard output.

Accepting input from a file

This process is significantly different in PowerShell, compared to Bash. In Bash, we call the command first, and then ask it to accept input from a file. In PowerShell, we make PowerShell read the contents of the input file first and then send the output to the command that accepts input through the pipeline.

In our recipe, we read the contents of the file, input.txt, which contained a list of four filenames. We used Get-Content to read the content from the file. Get-Content sent the output to the standard output at first, thereby showing us the contents of the file. We then added a pipe to tell PowerShell that we need further processing, and then added Remove-Item to the command chain. (Remove-Item deletes items, which could be directories, files, or links.)

As we will see later in this chapter, the first parameter (positional parameter, position 1) of `Remove-Item` is `Path`, which is also the parameter that accepts input through the pipeline. For more information, run the following command and read about the `Path` parameter of `Remove-Item`:

```
PS> Get-Help Remove-Item -Parameter Path
```

```
Terminal                                                                    ⊗

PS /home/ram> Get-Help Remove-Item -Parameter Path

-Path <String[]>
    Specifies a path of the items being removed. Wildcard characters are permitted.

    Required?                    true
    Position?                    1
    Default value                None
    Accept pipeline input?       True (ByPropertyName, ByValue)
    Accept wildcard characters?  false


PS /home/ram> █
```

There's more...

Clean up the contents that we created for this recipe if you are the type that likes directories clean! If we need more files or directories in later recipes, we will create them as needed.

See also

- The *Understanding cmdlets and parameters* recipe

Calling native Linux commands from PowerShell

In Chapter 1, *Introducing PowerShell Core*, we saw how native Linux commands were not convenience aliases in PowerShell on Linux, but the commands themselves. In this recipe, we will demonstrate using Linux commands at the PowerShell prompt. Remember, we used a Bash Terminal to run the `ls -l` and `awk` commands to list the contents of a directory and separate the columns in the output in the recipe, *Comparing the outputs of Bash and PowerShell* in Chapter 1, *Introducing PowerShell Core*. We will perform the same operation on the `home` directory, from within PowerShell, without using any of the PowerShell cmdlets.

Getting started

It is recommended that you have a Windows PC with PowerShell installed on it (Windows PowerShell would also do) in order to compare the output and see if we encounter any errors.

How to do it...

1. At the PowerShell prompt, type in the following command to list the contents of the directory:

   ```
   PS> ls -l
   ```

   You see the familiar output (albeit without any of the colors if your Terminal emulator uses colors for filenames).

2. Let us now look at the .NET type name of the output. For this, we need to use the `Get-Member` cmdlet:

   ```
   PS> ls -l | Get-Member
   ```

   PowerShell displays `TypeName: System.String`, which is consistent with what we saw in the aforementioned recipe.

3. If you have a Windows PC with PowerShell (or Windows PowerShell), run the same command on it:

   ```
   PS> ls -l | Get-Member
   ```

Notice the .NET type name here; it is `System.IO.DirectoryInfo` and, if you scroll down the console a little, you will also see `System.IO.FileInfo`.

4. At the PowerShell on Windows (or Windows PowerShell) prompt, type the following:

```
PS> ls -l
```

You will receive an error, stating that there was no value given to the parameter, `LiteralPath`:

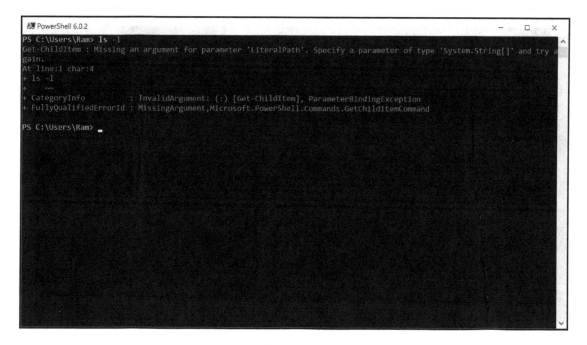

5. At the PowerShell prompt on the Windows PC, enter the following and press the *Tab* key on your keyboard, instead of *Enter*:

```
PS> ls -l
```

You will see that the parameter name was completed to `LiteralPath`.

6. Press the *Esc* key to clear the command line.
7. Come back to Linux and, at the PowerShell prompt, type in the following and press the *Tab* key:

```
PS> ls -l
```

8. Nothing happens. Now, enter the following and press the *Tab* key:

```
PS> Get-ChildItem -l
```

The parameter name was completed to `-LiteralPath`. Let us take one more step and conclude this recipe.

9. At the PowerShell prompt on Windows, run the following command:

```
PS> Get-Alias ls
```

10. Switch back to Linux and run the same command:

```
PS> Get-Alias ls
```

You receive an error stating that there is no such alias:

```
                                    Terminal                                    ⊗
PS /home/ram> Get-Alias ls
Get-Alias : This command cannot find a matching alias because an alias with the name 'ls'
does not exist.
At line:1 char:1
+ Get-Alias ls
+ ~~~~~~~~~~~~
+ CategoryInfo          : ObjectNotFound: (ls:String) [Get-Alias], ItemNotFoundException
+ FullyQualifiedErrorId : ItemNotFoundException,Microsoft.PowerShell.Commands.GetAliasComm
and

PS /home/ram> []
```

How it works...

When we run any of the Linux commands on PowerShell on Linux, PowerShell does not
call the convenience aliases that were created for the benefit of Linux administrators, when
Windows PowerShell was launched; these convenience aliases have not been included in
PowerShell on Linux. PowerShell, instead, runs the actual Linux commands and shows the
output on the console. Piping the output to other Linux commands work the same way as
they do on Bash, when running them on PowerShell on Linux.

The first point to note is that ls -l is an actual command in Linux, and it returns the list of
files and directories in the current directory, in a table format. When the same command is
run on PowerShell on Windows, we receive an error, since PowerShell on Windows
interprets ls as Get-ChildItem and -l as the incomplete but definitive call to -
LiteralPath and returns an error that the literal path was not specified.

When we run Get-Alias on ls on both operating systems, PowerShell on Linux returns
an error, while PowerShell on Windows shows the underlying PowerShell cmdlet.

The other point that pins down this fact is that the output of `ls` is a string, as opposed to a system object, when the same `ls` is run on PowerShell on Windows. On Windows, PowerShell calls `Get-ChildItem` under the hood and the output shown is that of `Get-ChildItem`. This is supported by the type name in the output of `Get-Member`, which is from the `System.IO` namespace. On the other hand, on Linux, running `Get-Member` on the output of `ls` simply returns `System.String`.

See also

- about_Aliases (`https://docs.microsoft.com/en-us/powershell/module/microsoft.powershell.core/about/about_aliases?view=powershell-6`)

Understanding cmdlets and parameters

Most of our scripting and administration is going to revolve around running cmdlets and chaining them. In some situations, we run a cmdlet expecting it to work a certain way, only to find out that the cmdlet threw an error, or worse, did something undesirable.

The key to getting cmdlets to do what we want them to do is to eliminate ambiguity. In this recipe, we will learn to construct commands contextually and effectively.

Getting ready

Read the Help section of `Chapter 1`, *Introducing PowerShell Core*. Let us understand the notifications used in the help information that `Get-Help` shows.

While this may not be an exhaustive guide to using the help information, it should cover most of your daily help document reading needs. The idea is to show you the notations. These notations may appear in several combinations (parameter values in curly braces, surrounded by square brackets, for example):

Notation	Meaning
-Parameter <DataType>	No square brackets: Mandatory parameter, named. The parameter must be called by name and a value of `DataType` must be specified.
[-Parameter <DataType>]	Square brackets around the parameter-data-type-pair: Optional parameter, although it must be called by name, and a value of `DataType` must be passed.

[-Parameter] <DataType>	Square brackets around the parameter name: Positional parameter. You can simply pass a value of DataType to the cmdlet, as long as the value is at the position shown by the parameter in the help text. The parameter need not be called by name as long as the position is right.
[[-Parameter] <DataType>]	Square brackets around the parameter name, and another pair of square brackets around the parameter-data-type-pair: Positional parameter, which is optional.
-Parameter <DataType[]>	Square brackets after DataType: Multi-valued parameter. This parameter accepts multiple values as input, each pair of values separated by a comma.
-Parameter	No data type: Switch parameter. Calling the parameter makes the switch $true, and not calling it uses the default value for the switch. To disable the switch, set it to false, such as -Parameter:$false.
-Parameter {Value1 | Value2 | Value3}	Values surrounded by curly braces: Parameter that accepts predefined values as input. In this case, you would call the parameter -Parameter Value1, or -Parameter Value2. In other words, this parameter does not accept arbitrary values.

Bash champions take note: PowerShell needs a comma separating the values in a multi-valued parameter. Therefore, if you would like to call Remove-Item on three files, you would enter Remove-Item file1, file2, file3. If only a space separates the values (like Bash's input), PowerShell will consider the three values as values to three positional parameters and would either throw an error or do something you did not want it to, based on the cmdlet you call. In general, use of named parameters is recommended.

In general, anything surrounded by square brackets is optional. Anything surrounded by curly braces indicates predefined parameter values (the pipe separates each value). The data type followed by an empty pair of square brackets indicates an array of that data type. And the position of the parameter is to be noted.

Notice the combination: Required is false, there is a default value as shown in the text below the parameter name, and the position is 1. This means that you can simply call the cmdlet, and it would run itself against the default value for its first parameter. The example used here is Get-ChildItem.

How to do it...

That was a long *Getting ready* section. Let us now put this knowledge to use:

1. Run a command to get a list of files and directories in the current location:

   ```
   PS> Get-ChildItem
   ```

2. Let us now add a . to indicate the current location:

   ```
   PS> Get-ChildItem .
   ```

3. Compare the output of the last two commands.
4. Let us go with the following:

   ```
   PS> Get-ChildItem -Path .
   ```

   Is the output the same as that of the last two commands?

5. Run the following and note the values for each of the keys:

   ```
   PS> Get-Help Get-ChildItem -Parameter Path
   ```

   ```
   -Path <String[]>
       Specifies a path to one or more locations. Wildcards are
   permitted. The default location is the current directory (`.`).
       Required?                 false
       Position?                 1
       Default value             Current directory
       Accept pipeline input?    True (ByPropertyName, ByValue)
       Accept wildcard characters? true
   ```

6. Create a file in the current location, called `file1` by calling the parameter by name:

   ```
   PS> Get-Help New-Item

   .

   .
   SYNTAX
       New-Item [[-Path] <String[]>] [-Confirm] [-Credential
   <PSCredential>] [-Force] [-ItemType <String>] -Name <String> [-
   UseTransaction] [-Value <Object>] [-WhatIf] [<CommonParameters>]

       New-Item [-Path] <String[]> [-Confirm] [-Credential
   <PSCredential>] [-Force] [-ItemType <String>] [-UseTransaction] [-
   Value <Object>] [-WhatIf] [<CommonParameters>]
   ```

7. We have two possibilities: Path and Name. Look for information on Path:

```
PS> Get-Help New-Item -Parameter Path
```

```
-Path <String[]>
    Specifies the path of the location of the new item. Wildcard
characters are permitted.

    You can specify the name of the new item in Name , or include
it in Path .

    Required?                      true
    Position?                      0
    Default value                  None
    Accept pipeline input?         True (ByPropertyName)
    Accept wildcard characters?    false
```

If we use Name, we have to call it by name (no pun intended). If not, we can specify the name as part of Path (no alliteration intended either).

8. Let us use Path first. -Path need not be written, since it is a positional parameter:

```
PS> New-Item file1
```

9. Try the same operation with Name. This time, mention the parameter name:

```
PS> New-Item -Name file2
```

10. If you would like, create a third file, by calling Path by name:

```
PS> New-Item -Path file3
```

11. List out the contents of the current location:

```
PS> Get-ChildItem -Path .
```

The files are present.

12. Let us now delete the files:

```
PS> Get-Help Remove-Item
```

13. Mention the filenames as paths:

```
PS> Remove-Item file1
```

14. List the contents of the directory:

    ```
    PS> Get-ChildItem -Path .
    ```

15. Let us delete multiple files in one shot. And this time, let us call the parameter by name:

    ```
    PS> Remove-Item -Path file2, file3
    ```

16. Let us now create a directory. We need to use a parameter called ItemType, which has predefined values, based on the provider (we are using FileSystem):

    ```
    PS> New-Item -Path test-dir -ItemType Directory
    ```

17. Create three new files, like so:

    ```
    PS> New-Item test-dir/file1, test-dir/file2 -ItemType File
    PS> New-Item test-dir/child-dir -ItemType Directory
    PS> New-Item test-dir/child-dir/file3 -ItemType File
    ```

18. Now, let us delete the contents. Wait for a confirmation prompt to appear after running the command:

    ```
    PS> Remove-Item -Path test-dir
    ```

19. Read the prompt. It says something about the Recurse parameter.
20. Choose L and press *Enter* to abort the process.
21. Enter the following command:

    ```
    PS> Remove-Item -Path test-dir -Recurse
    ```

22. That was quiet! List out the contents of the current directory to ensure test-dir is gone:

    ```
    PS> Get-ChildItem
    ```

The directory is indeed gone.

How it works...

Working with cmdlets is simple. There are two kinds of parameters: named and positional.

Positional parameters work based on the position. They are programmed in such a way that PowerShell understands their logical sequence and performs its actions. For instance, when moving items, the general way of working is to call the command and pass the source first and then the destination.

Therefore, the following would mean that you want to move the `GitHub` directory to `Code`:

```
PS> Move-Item /home/ram/Documents/GitHub /home/ram/Documents/Code/
```

Many PowerShell cmdlets are programmed to understand this.

Named parameters, on the other hand, are to be called by name. Help text shows them without any brackets surrounding them. Calling the positional parameters by name is optional—you are allowed to simply pass the values. However, be careful with what position or sequence you mention them in.

The best practice is to always pass parameter values, calling them by name when writing scripts. When running quick commands, on the other hand, you may omit calling positional parameters by name in the interest of speed.

Some parameters have predefined value validation added to them. These parameters accept only those values that have been defined in them. For instance, `ItemType` only accepts `File`, `Directory`, `SymbolicLink`, `Junction`, and `HardLink` as values, at the time of writing this section.

And then, there are switch parameters. `Recurse` is an example. When you call these parameters with no value, the parameters assume `True` in most cases. When you have to set them to `False`, you mention `-Parameter:$false` (for example, `-Confirm:$false`). If you do not call the switch parameter, the parameter goes with the default value specified in the cmdlet.

There's more...

If you would like to create the files and directories again, don't run four commands. Run the following two:

```
PS> New-Item test-dir/child-dir -ItemType Directory -Force
PS> New-Item ./test-dir/file1, ./test-dir/file2, ./test-dir/child-dir/file3
```

The parameter, `Force`, creates `test-dir` when creating `child-dir`.

Go ahead and delete the entire directory if you want to, without the `Recurse` parameter. At the confirmation prompt, press *Enter* (`Y` is the default response).

Running cmdlets with minimal keystrokes

Commands have been made to be short, historically. However, the situation turned into a dilemma over time, since shorter commands meant that they had to be remembered and longer commands meant more keystrokes.

PowerShell has long commands; however, it deals with them in two ways:

- Aliases, which tend to be shorter
- Tab completion, which require more keystrokes than aliases, but doesn't require remembering much

The first way necessitates using our memory to recall command names as required. The second, on the other hand, solves the keystroke issue efficiently.

Bash users are used to getting a list of matches laid out in a nice tabular format when the *Tab* key matches more than one string in the context. On the other hand, the matches cycle at the cursor in Windows (which most Bash users find weird).

Be that as it may, tab completion is a boon, and this recipe makes complete use of tab completion and simple string matching to significantly reduce keystrokes when using PowerShell cmdlets.

Getting ready

We use the GNOME Terminal emulator for this recipe. Tab completion on PowerShell on Linux on Gnome Terminal behaves exactly the same way that it works on Bash on GNOME Terminal:

- If only one word matches the string before the tab, the word is completed
- If multiple words match the string before the tab, all possible options are listed

If you are using Visual Studio Code for this recipe, or a different Terminal emulator, its behavior may be different.

How to do it...

Let us get right to it!

Say we would like to get the list of files and directories within the current directory:

1. The right way of doing this, as per best practices, would be as follows:

    ```
    PS> Get-ChildItem -Path .
    ```

2. However, as we've seen before, the easy way of doing this would be as follows:

    ```
    PS> gci
    ```

    We would use the former way when including the cmdlet in a script. This avoids ambiguity in most contexts that the script would run in. This usually means minimal bugs. The latter, on the other hand, is the short way of running the same cmdlet, by leveraging the user-friendly features of it, combined with the awareness of the environment as an intelligent human. This approach significantly reduces keystrokes—three characters, as opposed to 21.

    Although, if you are writing a script and would like to reduce keystrokes, you could still do it, without having to remember things such as `gpv` means `Get-ItemPropertyValue`.

    Enter: tab completion.

3. Follow the keystrokes mentioned here:

    ```
    PS> get-ch<Tab><Space>.
    ```

    Those were ten keystrokes including `<Enter>`.

    There may be situations where you would need to call a named parameter. And the named parameter might be long.

4. Find a command that has `ComputerName` as a parameter:

```
PS> get-comm<Tab><Space>-param<Tab><Space>computername<Enter>
```

This completes to the following:

```
PS> Get-Command -Parameter computername
```

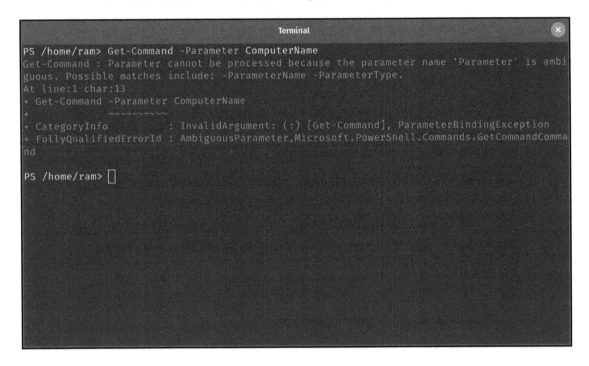

```
PS /home/ram> Get-Command -Parameter ComputerName
Get-Command : Parameter cannot be processed because the parameter name 'Parameter' is ambi
guous. Possible matches include: -ParameterName -ParameterType.
At line:1 char:13
+ Get-Command -Parameter ComputerName
+             ~~~~~~~~~~
+ CategoryInfo          : InvalidArgument: (:) [Get-Command], ParameterBindingException
+ FullyQualifiedErrorId : AmbiguousParameter,Microsoft.PowerShell.Commands.GetCommandComma
nd

PS /home/ram> []
```

But it throws an error. The error says, `Possible matches include: -ParameterName -ParameterType`. This is the caveat in PowerShell on Linux. Let us try again:

```
PS> get-comm<Tab><Space>-param<Tab><Tab>
```

```
                                    Terminal                              ⊗
PS /home/ram> Get-Command -Parameter ComputerName
Get-Command : Parameter cannot be processed because the parameter name 'Parameter' is ambi
guous. Possible matches include: -ParameterName -ParameterType.
At line:1 char:13
+ Get-Command -Parameter ComputerName
+             ~~~~~~~~~~
+ CategoryInfo          : InvalidArgument: (:) [Get-Command], ParameterBindingException
+ FullyQualifiedErrorId : AmbiguousParameter,Microsoft.PowerShell.Commands.GetCommandComma
nd

PS /home/ram> Get-Command -Parameter
ParameterName  ParameterType
PS /home/ram> Get-Command -ParameterName ComputerName

CommandType     Name                                           Version    Source
-----------     ----                                           -------    ------
Cmdlet          Enter-PSSession                                6.1.0.0    Microsof...
Cmdlet          Get-PSSession                                  6.1.0.0    Microsof...
Cmdlet          Invoke-Command                                 6.1.0.0    Microsof...
Cmdlet          New-PSSession                                  6.1.0.0    Microsof...
Cmdlet          Receive-Job                                    6.1.0.0    Microsof...
Cmdlet          Remove-PSSession                               6.1.0.0    Microsof...
Cmdlet          Send-MailMessage                               3.1.0.0    Microsof...
Cmdlet          Test-Connection                                3.1.0.0    Microsof...
```

5. Read the list of possibilities and select `ParameterName`:

   ```
   PS> get-comm<Tab><Space>-param<Tab>n<Tab><Space>computername<Enter>
   ```

6. The complete resolution of that would be as follows:

   ```
   PS> Get-Command -ParameterName computername
   ```

   And it worked.

   Next, let us suspend the activity in our session for, say, five seconds. The cmdlet for this would be `Start-Sleep`.

7. Let us first get help on the cmdlet:

   ```
   PS> Get-Help Start-Sleep
   ```

   The help text says that the parameter at position one, which need not be named, is `Seconds` (square brackets around `Seconds` in the second parameter set), and it accepts integer values.

8. Therefore, to suspend the session for 5 seconds, we would use the following:

   ```
   PS> Start-Sleep 5
   ```

9. If we wanted the session (or script) suspended for 100 milliseconds, we would need to use the named `Milliseconds` parameter. With tab completion, it would be as follows:

```
PS> start-s<Tab><Space>-mi<Tab>100
```

This would resolve to the following:

```
PS> Start-Sleep -Milliseconds 100
```

10. You can, in fact, reduce the number of tabs when using parameter names. Just type enough for PowerShell to uniquely identify the parameter name:

```
PS> start-s<Tab><Space>-m<Space>100
```

This would resolve to the following:

```
PS> Start-Sleep -m 100
```

If the delay was not noticeable, feel free to increase the number a little (say, to 3000).

How it works...

We have already seen how to use aliases. Aliases work just like normal cmdlets, including the syntax of their parameters. The only catch is that we have to remember the aliases. Custom aliases, as we shall see in the *Best practices* section, are a bad idea given that the aliases have to be imported everywhere we want to run scripts that have custom aliases.

Tab completion on the other hand, reduces the number of keystrokes, but requires muscle memory. It requires some level of practice, given which significantly improves productivity.

Tab completion works when writing cmdlets, writing parameter names, as well as when passing pre-defined values to parameters, such as the following:

```
PS> set-exec<Tab><Space>-exec<Tab><Space>unre<Tab>
```

This completes to the following:

```
PS> Set-ExecutionPolicy -ExecutionPolicy Unrestricted
```

In many situations, it is not necessary to use tab completion at all, for instance, in the case of `Start-Sleep`. There is no parameter that starts with m in the case of cmdlets. Therefore, using -m was sufficient for PowerShell to uniquely identify -`Milliseconds`. That saved us the <Tab> keystroke as well.

Productivity with respect to writing scripts in PowerShell is a skill that comes with practice. While aliases sure are a shortcut to speed, they have their perils. On the other hand, using the keyboard to write scripts helps with muscle memory, which not only helps us think in PowerShell, it also helps in speeding up tab completion, which works equally well when running commands at the console or writing scripts.

Using short parameter names is generally not a good practice while scripting; use these with a similar caution as aliases. Short parameter names affect readability and might break scripts at some point in the future. For instance, you call a certain cmdlet in a script with a short parameter name, `-comp`, which at the time of the creation of the script, stood only for `ComputerName`. Later, imagine the cmdlet receives an update with an added parameter, `-CompatibilityMode`; this would break the script that you wrote.

There's more...

Try to type the most commonly used cmdlets along with the parameters to practice tab completion.

Get familiar with Visual Studio Code by typing the cmdlets in the script pane. Notice how cmdlet, parameter, and parameter value completion work in Visual Studio Code. If you prefer completion to work the same way as at the console, refer to my custom settings JSON in the book's GitHub repository.

Finding parameter aliases

We worked with aliases for cmdlets, we saw how to uniquely identify parameter names without having to type the entire parameter name, and we looked at leveraging the power of tab completion.

To complete the cycle, let's also look at parameter aliases.

As you may have guessed, parameter aliases work very similar to cmdlet aliases. The primary goal of these aliases is to reduce keystrokes.

Parameter aliases are not documented in a friendly way, but they can be easily found thanks to the object-oriented model of PowerShell. In this recipe, we will look at how to fetch parameter aliases.

Getting ready

Find all of the commands that take in `ComputerName` as a parameter, with minimal keystrokes:

```
PS> get-comm<Tab>-parametern<Tab>Cn
```

This resolves to the following:

```
PS> Get-Command -ParameterName Cn
```

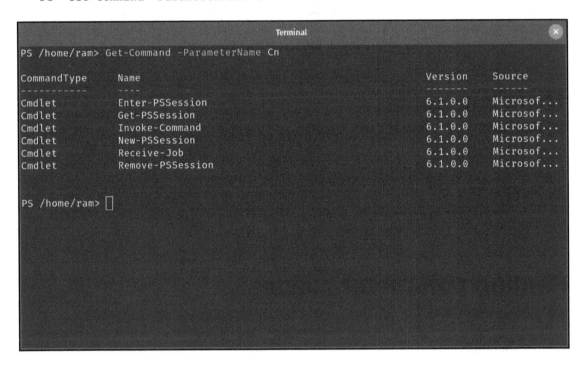

The output was the same as that we ran a while ago:

```
PS> Get-Command -ParameterName ComputerName
```

How did PowerShell know that `Cn` stands for `ComputerName`?

How to do it...

Parameters are part of cmdlets, and `Get-Command` is the cmdlet that fetches information about cmdlets:

1. For this example, let us pick the cmdlet, `Invoke-Command`:

   ```
   PS> Get-Command Invoke-Command
   ```

2. Examine the object that this command outputs:

   ```
   PS> Get-Command Invoke-Command | Get-Member
   ```

3. The output shows a member called `Parameters`. Use the member access operator to pick the member:

   ```
   PS> (Get-Command Invoke-Command).Parameters
   ```

4. See what members this member contains:

   ```
   PS> (Get-Command Invoke-Command).Parameters | Get-Member
   ```

5. Would `Values` show us the information we need? Try the following:

   ```
   PS> (Get-Command Invoke-Command).Parameters.Values
   ```

6. Yes, that does give us something, but there is too much output. We need only the parameter names and their aliases:

   ```
   PS> (Get-Command Invoke-Command).Parameters.Values | select Name,
   Aliases
   ```

There you go.

How it works...

We saw while reading about the Core and its capabilities, that PowerShell, most of the time, returns objects. And every object can have objects within itself. Going by the same path as that of .NET, a member access operator can be used to select the members (which could be properties or methods). Properties are addressed by simply using the property names, while methods need arguments passed to them (an empty pair of parentheses is still needed if no argument is being passed).

The parameters of a cmdlet are objects of the output that the `Get-Command` cmdlet returns. Therefore, calling `Get-Command` with the cmdlet, `Invoke-Command`, returns data about `Invoke-Command` as the output object. This can be further broken down to several other objects (members), among which, there is `Parameters`.

`Parameters` itself can be further broken down into other members, `Values` being one of them—`Values` contains the names of the parameters, as revealed by running `Get-Member`. We select two objects from within `Values`, called `Name` and `Aliases`. These parameter aliases can be used in place of parameters themselves.

There are two caveats with parameter aliases:

- They are case-sensitive, which means reaching for the *Shift* key

- They have to be remembered, even though they have a pattern to them, just like cmdlet aliases do (`ip` for `Import` and `g` for `Get`, for instance)

Calling a PowerShell script

PowerShell scripts are nothing but a series of PowerShell cmdlets, each in a line of a `ps1` file. These instructions are executed one after the other, similar to the good old shell script. Using Visual Studio Code makes running PowerShell scripts simpler, in that you simply have to run the script to make the script work its magic.

However, running PowerShell scripts on Visual Studio Code is not the usual way of automation for obvious reasons. Also, there are many ways to run a PowerShell script. We shall look at a very simple way of running the script in this recipe; as we progress in this book, we will also add more features to our scripts and, further, will package them into modules for future use.

Getting ready

This recipe uses Visual Studio Code to write the script. While any text or code editor would work for the script, we use Visual Studio Code because, in my experience, it is the friendliest editor for PowerShell scripting:

1. Open Visual Studio Code and create a new file
2. Create a new directory at a convenient location (`~/Code`, perhaps?)
3. Save the empty file as `hello-world.ps1` within the directory you just created
4. Observe the bottom right of Visual Studio Code; it should now say, **PowerShell**
5. Press *Ctrl + `* to close the console at the bottom to reduce distraction

If everything is as shown in the following screenshot, you are good to go (ignore the color of the status bar at the bottom, as well as the Git status at the bottom-left for now):

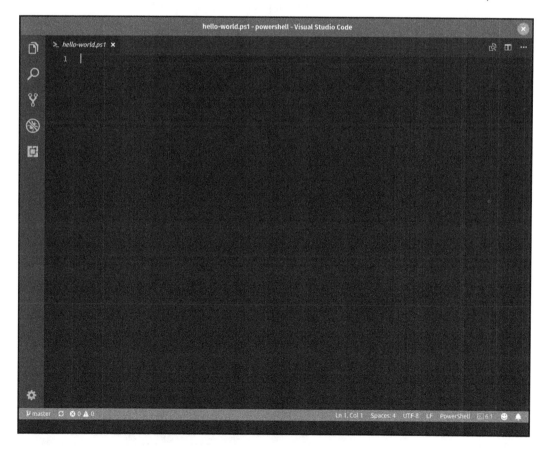

How to do it...

1. At the script pane, type in the following:

   ```
   PS> Write-Host "Hello, World!"
   ```

2. Save the script (**File** > **Save** or *Ctrl + S*).
3. Click on Debug on the left. Alternatively, press *Ctrl + Shift + D*. This opens the Debug pane.
4. Press the green Start debugging button. The console should pop out and display `Hello, World!`.
5. Let us run the script one more time. This time, we will not open the Debug pane or press buttons on the screen. Simply, press *F5*.

   `Hello, World!` should again be displayed in the console:

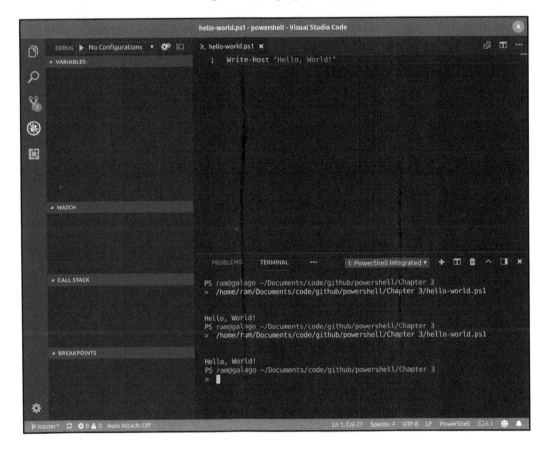

Let us now call the script without using the debug controls:

1. Close the file (*Ctrl + W*).
2. At the prompt on the console, type in the following:

   ```
   PS> ./hello-world.ps1
   ```

   You should see Hello, World! appear.

3. Navigate to home.
4. Type &, add a space, ./, and start typing the path to where you stored the script. Use tab completion just like you would do on Bash.
5. When you reach the location of the script file, press *Enter* to call the file:

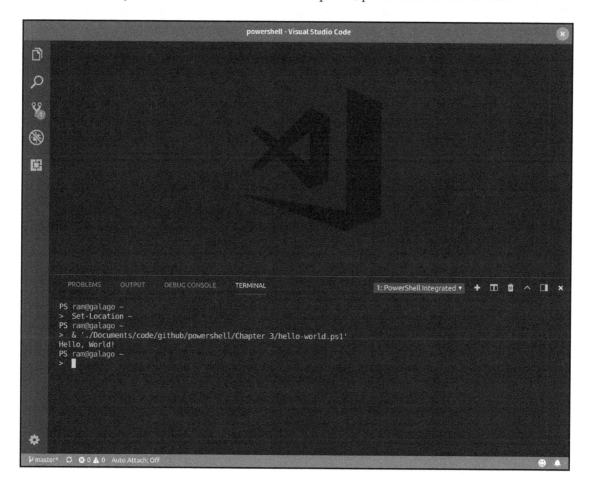

How it works...

The simplest way to run a PowerShell script is to debug it at the ISE. We use Visual Studio Code as our IDE of choice in this case. The other two ways of calling the script described in this recipe are from the PowerShell console. You may use the integrated console in Visual Studio Code or a PowerShell console called at the Terminal for this purpose.

When the script is located at the present working directory, PowerShell just calls the `ps1` file and executes it. Another way of calling PowerShell scripts is to use & (or the call operator): type & followed by a space, followed by the path to the script file. This way of calling handles spaces in the path well.

If the path to the script contains spaces, the path would need to be surrounded by quotes. This would make PowerShell think that you are simply giving it a string value. PowerShell would, then, simply display the path as text the moment you press *Enter*.

When you use the & call operator, you tell PowerShell that you want to run a script (or a command).

Another way of calling scripts is to use . (or the dot operator), which we shall look at in the next recipe.

Dot-sourcing a PowerShell script

In the previous recipe, we saw how to call PowerShell scripts from outside of the IDE. We gave PowerShell the path and explicitly mentioned that we would like it to run the script, by using a call operator.

This way is ideal if you would just like the script to perform its task and not leave anything behind, such as variable values. However, there are situations where we would like to run a script and, say, retain values of the variables we declared and assigned in them or use the functions we declared in them.

In such situations where we would like the functions, variables, and even aliases retained in the current session, we use dot-sourcing.

How to do it...

If you deleted the file after the previous recipe, restore it or recreate it using the steps in the previous recipe. Then, perform the following steps:

1. Open the script file that you created in the previous recipe. At the second line, type the following:

    ```
    PS> $Message = "I was dot-sourced!"
    ```

2. Save the script. Do not run it yet.
3. Place your cursor at the integrated console, and call the script using the call operator:

    ```
    PS> & ./hello-world
    ```

4. We declared $Message and assigned a string value to it. Call the variable to see what value it contains:

    ```
    PS> $Message
    ```

    It contains nothing.

5. Dot-source the script (there are two dots; one is the operator, and the other after the space is reference to the current directory):

    ```
    PS> . ./hello-world.ps1
    ```

6. Call the $Message variable again:

```
PS> $Message
```

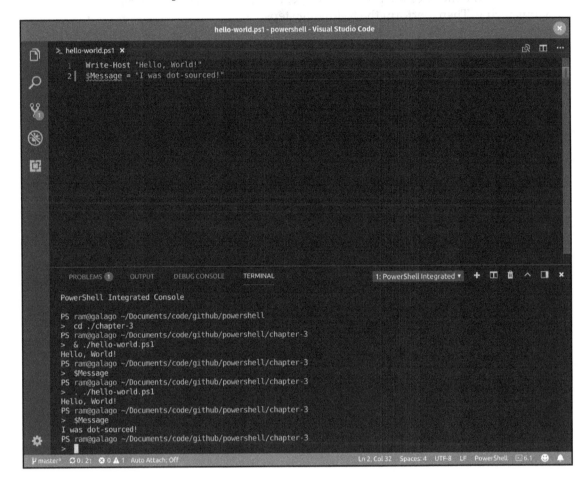

How it works...

When a script or a command is called using the call operator, the script or command is simply run without the current session (or technically, the scope) being modified. The command or script runs and exits without changing anything pertaining to the session, including changes to built-in/automatic variables.

When changes to the scope are desired, the script or command must be dot-sourced. This way, whatever variables, functions, or aliases are defined in it are retained in the current scope.

There's more...

Create a new alias using `New-Alias` within the `hello-world.ps1` script. Try to get the value of the alias after first calling the script (using the debug control, as well as using the call operator), and then by dot-sourcing the script. Observe the outcomes.

Calling a PowerShell cmdlet from outside of PowerShell

So far we have learned how to call cmdlets from the console, run scripts at the IDE, and call scripts in two modes. In this very short recipe, we shall learn how to call a PowerShell cmdlet from outside of PowerShell.

How to do it...

1. Open a Terminal window.
2. At the prompt, type the following:

   ```
   $ pwsh -h
   ```

3. Read the syntax for the command.

4. At the prompt, type the following:

```
$ pwsh -c Get-ChildItem
```

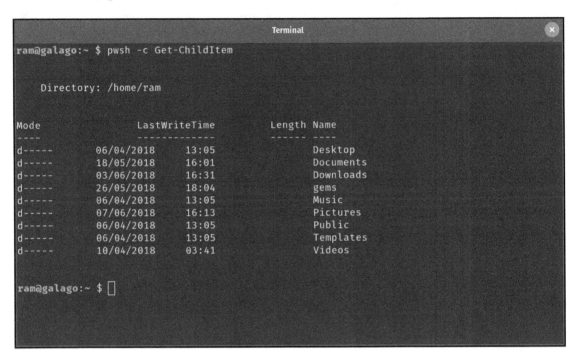

5. Let us now run the `hello-world.ps1` script:

```
$ pwsh -f ./Documents/code/github/powershell/chapter-3/hello-world.ps1
```

```
Terminal                                                          ⊗
ram@galago:~ $ pwsh -f ./Documents/code/github/powershell/chapter-3/hello-world.ps1
Hello, World!
ram@galago:~ $ ▯
```

How it works...

PowerShell is not an application that runs on top of Bash. PowerShell is a shell itself.
However, it can be called from Bash just like another application. Like applications, the
pwsh command takes in arguments, which are then processed by PowerShell.

The two main ways we may want to use PowerShell from within Bash is to run a single
command or call a script file. You can even call a script block; however, this must be done
from within PowerShell. In most cases, running single cmdlets or calling a script should
suffice.

In general, when calling pwsh with cmdlets, make –Command (or –c) the last parameter,
since anything that comes after the cmdlet itself is considered a cmdlet argument. The same
goes for –File as well.

When a script is designed to accept arguments, the script arguments can be passed after the
script name, just like with cmdlets.

Recording the cmdlets run on the PowerShell console

Often, there are situations in which you perform a series of tasks on your PowerShell console and, after quite some trial and error, come across a solution. And then you wish you had recorded everything you did on the console. You could still copy content from the console, so you try to scroll up. But you can only go so far. Your command history (a little like Bash history) can help you, but sometimes, that feels limited as well.

A few months ago, we were troubleshooting a sync issue between two of their software update distribution systems, which were supposed to work in sync. After some of us were done beating around the GUI, we decided to pick PowerShell to fix the issue. We ran a series of commands and, after a few hours of fighting with the systems, they yielded and we were back up and running.

Our managers asked for all of the steps that we took to achieve this, so that they could be documented for future use. Of course, I cannot tell you all of the steps that we took—because of the scope of this book and the agreements with our clients—but I can tell you what can help in such situations.

How to do it...

Start PowerShell at the Terminal or use the **PowerShell Integrated Console** on Visual Studio Code:

1. Run the following command:

   ```
   PS> Start-Transcript -Path ./command-transcript.txt
   ```

2. You can also simply run the cmdlet without any arguments; it would automatically create a text file with an auto-generated filename. Get the current system date and time:

   ```
   PS> Get-Date
   ```

3. List out all of the files and directories in the current location:

```
PS> Get-ChildItem .
```

4. Create a new directory:

```
PS> New-Item test-transcript -ItemType Directory
```

5. Create a new file within the directory:

```
PS> New-Item -Path test-transcript/testing-transcript.txt -ItemType
File
```

6. Add content to the file:

```
PS> @'
In publishing and graphic design, lorem ipsum is a placeholder text
commonly used to demonstrate the visual form of a document without
relying on meaningful content (also called greeking).
Replacing the actual content with placeholder text allows designers
to design the form of the content before the content itself has
been produced.
—Wikipedia
'@ | Out-File ./test-transcript/testing-transcript.txt -Append
```

7. Delete the directory:

```
PS> Remove-Item -Path ./test-transcript -Recurse
```

8. Stop recording what you did:

```
PS> Stop-Transcript
```

9. You should have now received the location of the transcript file. Read the contents of the file:

```
PS> Get-Content -Path ./command-transcript.txt
```

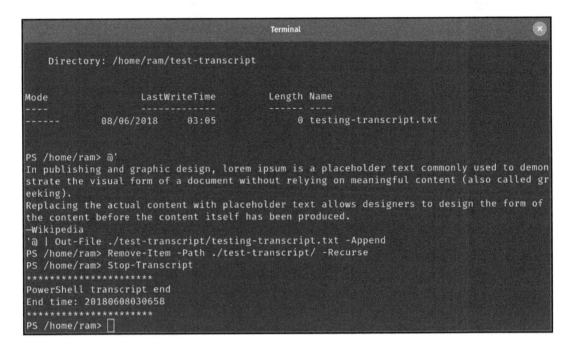

How it works...

A transcript created by running `Start-Transcript` stores all of your actions and the console output of all of the commands you ran in a text file. The transcript also contains some other useful information pertaining to the context the commands were run in.

A transcript file is a little more than a history file, in that the former contains the output of the commands, apart from the commands themselves.

The `Start-Transcript` cmdlet does not require any argument at all; it can create a text file at the user's home, with a unique name to ensure that no other transcript is rewritten. In other words, `Path` is an optional parameter.

This concludes this chapter about preparing for administration using PowerShell. It's time to crack your knuckles and refill your coffee mug. Did I tell you coffee speeds up thinking in PowerShell? It is a placebo, you say? Let's not get into an argument right now.

3
First Steps in Administration Using PowerShell

In this chapter, we will cover the following topics:

- Working with date properties
- Working with date and time methods
- Working with a currently-running process to measure resource consumption
- Launching and stopping a process
- Finding the owner of a process
- Invoking an application based on the file type
- Installing the CronTab PowerShell module
- Scheduling jobs in PowerShell
- Removing scheduled jobs in PowerShell

Introduction

As per the *Harvard Business Review*, a way to effectively learn is to cycle between information feasting and information fasting. Given that we have familiarized ourselves (and perhaps been a little overwhelmed by the volume of the last chapter), we will take a lighter approach to our first steps to administration using PowerShell.

So far, we have seen how to run cmdlets, what their parameters are, how to set and use aliases, and so on. In this chapter, we will learn how to use some basic utilities, work with processes, and call applications.

Also, even though the title of this book says Linux, most of the recipes in this book should work on Windows as well; minor modifications may be required, such as using the backslash in paths.

Working with date properties

PowerShell is best learned by starting with simple cmdlets. And `Get-Date` is one of the simplest, yet not completely leveraged cmdlets present in PowerShell. In this recipe, we will play with dates and see how they can be used in different scenarios. As always, the possibilities with PowerShell are quite more than a book can cover. In the interest of brevity, we will look at just enough to enable you to launch yourself gracefully into the world of PowerShell automation; the rest, you should be able to handle by yourself.

Getting ready

If you followed along with the previous chapters and performed all of the exercises mentioned in them, you should be good to go. Otherwise, go to `Chapter 1`, *Introducing PowerShell Core,* and get yourself a copy of PowerShell. Come back here to continue. This recipe uses only the Terminal, so there is no need for anything else.

How to do it...

Before we start working with dates, let's make a simple call for the date:

1. Display the current date and time:

   ```
   PS> Get-Date

   Saturday, 16 June 2018 12:14:07
   ```

2. Find out what members this returned object has:

   ```
   PS> Get-Date | Get-Member
   ```

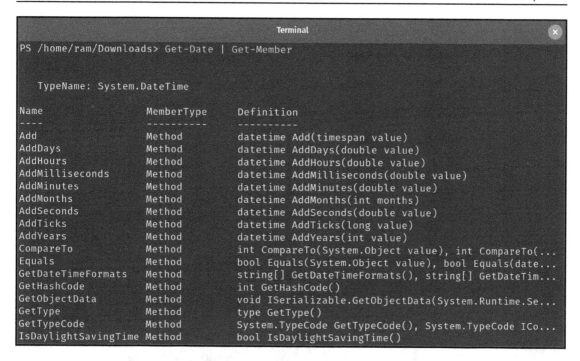

```
                              Terminal                              ⊗
PS /home/ram/Downloads> Get-Date | Get-Member


    TypeName: System.DateTime

Name                    MemberType    Definition
----                    ----------    ----------
Add                     Method        datetime Add(timespan value)
AddDays                 Method        datetime AddDays(double value)
AddHours                Method        datetime AddHours(double value)
AddMilliseconds         Method        datetime AddMilliseconds(double value)
AddMinutes              Method        datetime AddMinutes(double value)
AddMonths               Method        datetime AddMonths(int months)
AddSeconds              Method        datetime AddSeconds(double value)
AddTicks                Method        datetime AddTicks(long value)
AddYears                Method        datetime AddYears(int value)
CompareTo               Method        int CompareTo(System.Object value), int CompareTo(...
Equals                  Method        bool Equals(System.Object value), bool Equals(date...
GetDateTimeFormats      Method        string[] GetDateTimeFormats(), string[] GetDateTim...
GetHashCode             Method        int GetHashCode()
GetObjectData           Method        void ISerializable.GetObjectData(System.Runtime.Se...
GetType                 Method        type GetType()
GetTypeCode             Method        System.TypeCode GetTypeCode(), System.TypeCode ICo...
IsDaylightSavingTime    Method        bool IsDaylightSavingTime()
```

There is a whole bunch of properties and methods.

3. Attempt to display the date using the format 16/06/2018:

```
                              Terminal                            —  ⊗
PS /home/ram> $Date = Get-Date
PS /home/ram> $Date.Day
Day        DayOfWeek   DayOfYear
PS /home/ram> "$Date.Day/$Date.Month/$Date.Year"
```

The colors do not look right.

4. Change the command as follows. The syntax should look better now, based on your Terminal theme (Don't worry about why the change works for now; we shall look at this when dealing with variables at a later point.):

```
PS> "$($Date.Day)/$($Date.Month)/$($Date.Year)"
16/6/2018
```

But that was a lot of work. Is there an easier way?

5. Look in Help to see what parameters you get:

   PS> Get-Help Get-Date

   The Help text shows that there is a `Format` parameter.

6. Type the following to get the short date:

   PS> Get-Date -Format d

   Try the following as the values for `Format`: g, U,
   yyyy/MM/dd and yyyyMMddhhmmss.

```
Terminal                                                        _  ⊗
PS /home/ram> Get-Date -Format d
11/14/18
PS /home/ram> Get-Date -Format g
11/14/18 9:09 AM
PS /home/ram> Get-Date -Format U
Wednesday, November 14, 2018 3:39:21 AM
PS /home/ram> Get-Date -Format yyyy/MM/dd
2018/11/14
PS /home/ram> Get-Date -Format yyyyMMddhhmmss
20181114090941
PS /home/ram> []
```

7. If you're more comfortable with the UNIX formatting of date, use the `Uformat` parameter:

   PS> Get-Date -Uformat %d/%m/%Y

   Let's take one more step to pass a custom date to the system and fetch a little information from it, leveraging the members of the object that is output by `Get-Date`.

8. Find what day Halloween falls on in 2018:

   PS> (Get-Date -Day 31 -Month 10 -Year 2018).DayOfWeek
   Wednesday

9. If you know how the date in your locale works, pass the date as follows and get the same information:

   PS> (Get-Date 31/10/2018).DayOfWeek

10. If you remember the concept of cast operators, use it to get the information you need:

 Remember to use the YMD or MDY format when calling the `DateTime` accelerator, in order to avoid errors.

```
PS> ([datetime]'10/31/2018').DayOfWeek
```

To avoid ambiguity, spell out the month:

```
PS> ([datetime]'31 October 2018').DayOfWeek
```

How it works...

The `System.DateTime` class in .NET packs a good enough amount of properties and methods. The `Get-Date` cmdlet leverages these properties and methods by means of encapsulation. The `Get-Date` cmdlet, by default, pulls the current date and time of the system and allows you to pick child objects from it, or quickly tie them together as formats.

Besides these operations, the cmdlet also allows you to pass a simple string format such as date and time and converts the input string into the `DateTime` object.

While `Get-Date` takes into account your current locale, the type accelerator, `DateTime`, works on the YMD—or the MDY-formatted date-time.

See also

- The `DateTimeFormatInfo` Class | Remarks (https://docs.microsoft.com/en-us/dotnet/api/system.globalization.datetimeformatinfo?redirectedfrom= MSDNview=netframework-4.7.2#Remarks)
- The *Parsing input from text to object* recipe from Chapter 1, *Introducing PowerShell Core*

Working with date and time methods

In the previous recipe, *Working with date properties*, we focused on the properties that the DateTime object has. The parameters we saw for Get-Date also worked on these properties. In this recipe, we shall look at methods within the DateTime object and learn to use them to our benefit. The main idea behind this recipe, though, is to make you comfortable using methods that are part of the output objects.

How to do it...

Let's first start with converting local time into UTC:

1. At the prompt, type in Get-Date and list out the members of the output object:

   ```
   PS> Get-Date | Get-Member
   ```

2. Call the ToUniversalTime method:

   Reduce keystrokes by using tab-completion.

   ```
   PS> (Get-Date).ToUniversalTime()
   ```

   Compare the output to your local time.

3. Let's see what day it would be, exactly 35 days from today:

   ```
   PS> (Get-Date).AddDays(35)
   ```

4. If you would like to see what time it would be after 3 hours and 18 minutes, type the following:

   ```
   PS> (Get-Date).AddHours(3).AddMinutes(18)
   ```

5. Find out how many days have passed since the World Environment Day, 2016. Enter the command as shown in the following screenshot:

```
                                    Terminal                          _ ⊗
PS /home/ram> (Get-Date).Subtract((Get-Date '5 June 2016'))


Days               : 892
Hours              : 9
Minutes            : 10
Seconds            : 30
Milliseconds       : 807
Ticks              : 771018308076507
TotalDays          : 892.382301014476
TotalHours         : 21417.1752243474
TotalMinutes       : 1285030.51346084
TotalSeconds       : 77101830.8076507
TotalMilliseconds  : 77101830807.6507


PS /home/ram> []
```

How it works...

The object that is returned by `Get-Date` has several methods just as it has properties. In this recipe, we use the methods to manipulate the date the way we need it. Methods are called with arguments. When you do not want to specify any argument, make sure to still call the methods with an empty pair of parentheses.

Methods can be chained in the way we did when adding hours as well as minutes. As long as the output object does not change, in most cases, you should be able to call methods pertaining to the object by chaining them. If, for instance, you convert the date object into a string at the first method, the second method should be a string input-enabled method. When in doubt, use the `Get-Member` cmdlet on the output to see what methods it would support.

When you look at `Get-Member` run against the `DateTime` object, you see that the `Subtract` method accepts `DateTime` as its argument. Hence, the use of `Get-Date` within the argument. Passing a cmdlet output as an argument to a method requires the cmdlet, along with the parameters that are passed, to be enclosed within an additional pair of parentheses :`Subtract((Get-Date '5 June 2016'))`, as opposed to `Subtract(Get-Date '5 June 2016')`. This is so that the inner command is executed first to get a value and then passed to the method.

Working with currently-running processes to measure resource consumption

A good chunk of administration involves working with processes on a given computer. PowerShell contains cmdlets that enable you to work with processes on a computer. In this recipe, we will list out all of the processes running in the system and fetch the amount of resources the processes are collectively consuming.

In Chapter 4, *Passing Data Through Pipelines*, we will look at other options, such as filtration, using what we learn in this recipe.

How to do it...

As we have already discussed, our goal here is to work with processes:

1. List out the cmdlets that help you work with processes:

   ```
   PS> Get-Command -Noun Process
   ```

   Remember that PowerShell uses only singular nouns.

   We get five cmdlets. What we initially need is Get-Process.

2. Run the cmdlet to see what it shows:

   ```
   PS> Get-Process
   ```

   The output is a long table of processes, the memory they are consuming, the CPU time they are using, and so on.

3. Get the total count of processes currently running in the system:

   ```
   PS> (Get-Process).Count
   ```

4. Fetch the average of the pages of memory used by the processes. The term for this is Working Set, denoted as WS:

   ```
   PS> Get-Process | Measure-Object -Property WS -Average
   ```

5. There are other fields in the hash table as well. Let's get all of that information:

```
PS> Get-Process | Measure-Object –Property WS –Average –Sum –
Minimum –Maximum
```

6. Get the average, sum, minimum, and maximum for both the working sets as well as the CPU with the help of the command shown in the following screenshot:

```
                                   Terminal                              – ⊗
PS /home/ram> Get-Process | Measure-Object -Property WS, CPU -Average -Sum -Minimum -Maximum


Count            : 286
Average          : 19055895.2727273
Sum              : 5449986048
Maximum          : 634781696
Minimum          : 0
StandardDeviation :
Property         : WS

Count            : 286
Average          : 1.23545454545454
Sum              : 353.34
Maximum          : 82.44
Minimum          : 0
StandardDeviation :
Property         : CPU


PS /home/ram> ▯
```

How it works...

The cmdlet, Get-Process, gives out an entire table of all of the processes running in the system. Think of each row as an individual object and the entire table as an array of these rows. Count (or in other words, length) is, logically, a property of an array. Therefore, we call the cmdlet and, on the object that is output, we run a counting operation. This gives us how many processes are running in the system at the moment.

The next cmdlet we see is an important one, as well: Measure-Object. This cmdlet is designed to perform measurements on the objects that are output. In our case, we pick the WS property to perform measurements on. If no property is specified, PowerShell will pick the property based on its definition in the output object.

`Measure-Object` is capable of performing some neat arithmetic calculations on the output object. We use this capability of the cmdlet to fetch the average first and then the sum, the minimum value, and the maximum value as well. The `Property` parameter accepts a string array as input (`Get-Help Measure-Object -Parameter Property`). Therefore, we specify `WS` as well as `CPU` (separated by commas) in the cmdlet and then perform the measurement operation.

Launching and stopping a process

All pro-terminal administrators launch and stop processes from the Terminal all of the time. This usually happens at the Terminal prompt on Bash. With PowerShell, the process is not very different. This recipe will show you how to work the processes. And by the way, this recipe is where you go on a full information fast.

Getting ready

Open Visual Studio Code. If the status bar at the bottom is blue, chances are that a folder is open in Visual Studio Code. Visual Studio Code saves the location it is open at, so even if you start a session of Visual Studio Code after a fresh reboot, you would still see a folder open. We need the folder closed. To do this, press *Ctrl + Shift + N* (or go to **File > New Window**). Close the window where a folder is open.

How to do it...

If you listed out the commands in the previous recipe, scroll up to find what cmdlets might help you with this recipe:

1. At the prompt, type in the following to start Visual Studio Code:

   ```
   PS> Start-Process code
   ```

   Ensure that the status bar at the bottom is not blue. If it is blue, read the *Getting ready* section of this recipe. Press *Ctrl + Shift + E* or click on the Explorer icon on the left sidebar of Visual Studio Code. There should not be any directory open there.

2. Open Visual Studio Code in the directory where you created the `hello-world` script:

```
PS> Start-Process code -ArgumentList
/home/ram/Documents/code/github/powershell/
```

Press *Ctrl* + *Shift* + *E* or click on the Explorer icon on the left sidebar of Visual Studio Code. Do you see the directory open?

Now, let's stop the Visual Studio Code process.

3. List out the processes running in the system and see if anything matches `code`:

```
PS> Get-Process | grep code
```

4. If you want the PowerShell way of doing it, run the following command and note the name in the `ProcessName` column:

```
PS> Get-Process *code*
```

5. PowerShell deals with objects; `grep` outputs text. Therefore, now that we know that the exact name of the process is `code`, we directly get details on the process:

```
PS> Get-Process code
```

That gives us a valid output.

6. Stop all of the `code` processes:

```
PS> Stop-Process code
```

That would not work; the cmdlet accepts a `System.Diagnostics.Process` object as input.

7. Enclose `Get-Process` within parentheses and pass the input to `Stop-Process`:

```
PS> Stop-Process (Get-Process code)
```

8. See if there is a `code` process running any more:

```
PS> Get-Process code
```

```
                                    Terminal                                 ⊗

PS /home/ram> Stop-Process code
Stop-Process : Cannot bind parameter 'InputObject'. Cannot convert the "code" value of typ
e "System.String" to type "System.Diagnostics.Process".
At line:1 char:14
+ Stop-Process code
+
+ CategoryInfo          : InvalidArgument: (:) [Stop-Process], ParameterBindingException
+ FullyQualifiedErrorId : CannotConvertArgumentNoMessage,Microsoft.PowerShell.Commands.Sto
pProcessCommand

PS /home/ram> Stop-Process (Get-Process code)
PS /home/ram> Get-Process code
Get-Process : Cannot find a process with the name "code". Verify the process name and call
 the cmdlet again.
At line:1 char:1
+ Get-Process code
+ ~~~~~~~~~~~~~~~~~
+ CategoryInfo          : ObjectNotFound: (code:String) [Get-Process], ProcessCommandExcep
tion
+ FullyQualifiedErrorId : NoProcessFoundForGivenName,Microsoft.PowerShell.Commands.GetProc
essCommand

PS /home/ram> ▯
```

The best way of stopping a process is by using its ID.

9. I am running `dconf-editor` on my PC right now and would like to close it. You may choose any process to stop; play safe, though:

```
PS> Get-Process dconf-editor
PS> Stop-Process -Id 20608
```

How it works...

The cmdlet, `Start-Process`, works with paths. In the case of `code`, though, Linux knows the path where the package is installed. Therefore, simply calling the package by command is sufficient.

The Visual Studio Code process accepts the directory/file location as input. Therefore, we add the `ArgumentList` parameter and pass the path to the process as an argument. This opens that directory in Visual Studio Code.

Stopping a process requires a .NET object as input by default; `Stop-Process` would not accept a string as the default input. Therefore, we enclose the `Get-Process` cmdlet within parentheses, so that it gets executed first and outputs a `System.Diagnostics.Process` object, which is then processed by `Stop-Process`.

In order to be exact with respect to which process we would like to stop, we use the process ID and pass it as the argument to `Stop-Process`.

Finding the owner of a process

In the recipe, *Working with currently-running processes to measure resource consumption, covered in this chapter,* we listed out the processes running in the system. The table did not show us the process owner. In this recipe, we look at working with processes started by a certain owner.

How to do it...

The `Get-Process` cmdlet can fetch us this information:

1. At the prompt, type the following to get all of the parameters that the `Get-Process` cmdlet accepts:

   ```
   PS> Get-Help Get-Process
   ```

2. We see a parameter, `IncludeUserName` (the name suggests it is a switch parameter). Get more information on it:

```
PS> Get-Help Get-Process –Parameter IncludeUserName
```

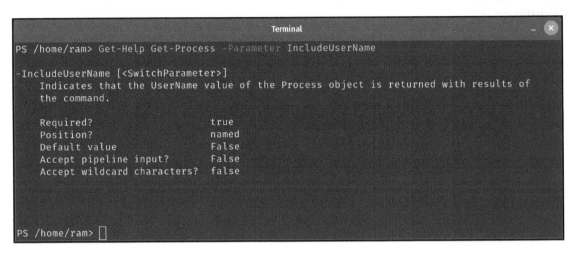

```
PS /home/ram> Get-Help Get-Process -Parameter IncludeUserName

-IncludeUserName [<SwitchParameter>]
    Indicates that the UserName value of the Process object is returned with results of
    the command.

    Required?                    true
    Position?                    named
    Default value                False
    Accept pipeline input?       False
    Accept wildcard characters?  false

PS /home/ram>
```

3. Run the following command:

```
PS> Get-Process –IncludeUserName
```

4. Filter out the processes started by you. We will use `grep` for this operation until we learn how to filter in PowerShell. You can replace `$env:USER` with your username, if you would like:

```
PS> Get-Process –IncludeUserName | grep $env:USER
```

5. Count the number of processes running under your name:

```
PS> (Get-Process –IncludeUserName | grep $env:USER).Count
```

6. If you would like to use the `Measure-Object` cmdlet, you can:

```
PS> Get-Process –IncludeUserName | grep $env:USER | Measure-Object
```

7. See what amount of working set all of the processes started by you consume:

```
PS> Get-Process –IncludeUserName | grep $env:USER | Measure-Object
–Property WS –Sum
```

```
Terminal                                                    _  ⊗
PS /home/ram> Get-Process -IncludeUserName | grep ram | Measure-Object -Property WS -Sum
Measure-Object : Cannot process argument because the value of argument "Property" is not v
alid. Change the value of the "Property" argument and run the operation again.
At line:1 char:43
+ ... rocess -IncludeUserName | grep ram | Measure-Object -Property WS -Sum
+                                                         ~~~~~~~~~~~~~~~~~~~~~~~~~~~~~~~~~~~~
+ CategoryInfo          : InvalidArgument: (:) [Measure-Object], PSArgumentException
+ FullyQualifiedErrorId : GenericMeasurePropertyNotFound,Microsoft.PowerShell.Commands.Mea
sureObjectCommand

PS /home/ram> []
```

There is an error. Try the following instead:

```
PS> Get-Process -incl | Where-Object UserName -eq $env:USER | Measure-
Object ws -sum
PS> # Verbose version: Get-Process -IncludeUserName | Where-Object UserName
-eq $env:USER | Measure-Object -Property WS -Sum
```

You get the details this time:

```
Terminal                                                    _  ⊗
PS /home/ram> Get-Process -IncludeUserName | Where-Object UserName -eq $env:USER | Measure
-Object -Property WS -Sum


Count           : 89
Average         :
Sum             : 4979838976
Maximum         :
Minimum         :
StandardDeviation :
Property        : WS



PS /home/ram> []
```

How it works...

Get-Process does not show you the process owner information by default. In some
situations, it may be necessary to have this information. In this simple recipe, we use the
help documentation to get all of the parameters and use the IncludeUserName switch
parameter to get the process owner information.

In the next step, we filter out the processes started by a certain user and then count the number of processes. We do the same using `Measure-Object` as well and notice that the output is the same. `Measure-Object` has object in its name, but worked on text that was output by `grep`. At the same time, it said at the next step that the value of `Property` is invalid.

The answer to why `Measure-Object` worked when counting is in the step that precedes it. We know that if an array is output, PowerShell can count the number of elements in the array. `Measure-Object` is also capable of the same: measuring what can be measured in string arrays—`Count` works on string arrays.

However, when we tried to fetch the total working set, `Measure-Object` could not get us that. The reason is that the output of `grep`, as we have seen before, is plain text:

```
PS> Get-Process -IncludeUserName | grep $env:USER | Get-Member
```

There's more...

This is something that's perhaps a few steps ahead, but what if we wanted to get that working set information anyway, from the output of `grep`? Simple challenge, accepted:

```
PS> Get-Process -IncludeUserName | grep $env:USER | awk '{print $1}' |
ForEach-Object {[Double]$_} | Measure-Object -Sum
```

```
                                        Terminal                          _  ⊗
PS /home/ram> Get-Process -IncludeUserName | grep ram | awk '{print $1}' | ForEach-Object
{[Double]$_} | Measure-Object -Sum


Count             : 85
Average           :
Sum               : 4272.34
Maximum           :
Minimum           :
StandardDeviation :
Property          :


PS /home/ram> TADAA!
```

Do not worry too much about how that works, for now. Once we read and understand looping through available elements, we will have a better understanding of how we got this to work. For now, understand that we converted each of the returned strings into `double` values using the `Double` cast operator. Then, we did `Measure-Object` and found the sum.

Of course, with only PowerShell, this process is much simpler since we would be dealing with the objects straight away. The alternative using `Where-Object` demonstrates that.

See also

- The *Comparing the outputs of Bash and PowerShell* recipe in `Chapter 1`, *Introducing PowerShell Core*

Invoking an application based on the file type

So far, we have seen how to use `Start-Process` to start an application. That involves, in many cases, launching the application and, from the application, opening a file that you want to work on using the application. In this recipe, we will leverage the concept of file association and a proper calling cmdlet to launch an application. In fact, we will go a little further than that.

How to do it...

Download a few images from the web to work with this recipe. They could be anything; just ensure that all of them are of the same file type:

1. Navigate to the location where you saved the image files.
2. At the prompt, type in the following command to open your image viewer and the files in it:

```
PS> Invoke-Item -Path *.png
```

3. Create a text file in the same location:

```
PS> New-Item file-1.txt -ItemType File
```

4. Invoke all of the files in their respective applications:

```
PS> Invoke-Item *
```

How it works...

In the recipe, *Calling a PowerShell cmdlet from outside of PowerShell* in Chapter 2, *Preparing for Administration using PowerShell*, we called a PowerShell script from Bash by first invoking PowerShell and then passing the path to the script as an argument to the pwsh command. The process is very similar in PowerShell as well, as seen in the recipe, *Launching and stopping a process*. However, in the aforementioned recipes, we call the applications first and then pass the file as an argument. Therefore, we do not rely on file associations.

The Invoke-Item cmdlet relies on the internal file association to open the files. The real use of Invoke-Item is when opening multiple files, whether of the same kind, or different kinds of files within the same path using the respective applications that handle them.

Installing the CronTab PowerShell module

In this recipe, we will discuss the installation details of a PowerShell module to manage Cron jobs using PowerShell on a Linux machine.

There are times when there is a need for performing administrative tasks or scheduling a script to execute automatically at a given time. Linux distributions, by default, come with a scheduling utility, called CronTab, which allows any given tasks to be run automatically in the background at a given time. Cron is a time-based scheduler program. It generates events based on the definition in the crontab file.

How to do it...

The PowerShell crontab wrapper module is not available in the PowerShell repository as yet. You must download the files manually to install the module. The simplest way is to clone the PowerShell repository and install the module from within its demos directory.

If you would rather only install the CronTab module alone, download the `<repo>/demos/crontab` directory manually. Then, start PowerShell as a super-user and navigate to `crontab`. Continue from step 4, running the `Import-Module` cmdlet to import the `CronTab` module.

1. Clone the PowerShell repository on to your computer:

   ```
   $ mkdir ~/code
   $ cd ./code/
   $ git clone https://github.com/PowerShell/PowerShell.git
   ```

2. Start `pwsh` as a super-user.

3. Go to the `demos/crontab/CronTab` directory within the repository. This is where the module manifest is placed:

   ```
   PS> Set-Location ~/code/PowerShell/demos/crontab
   ```

4. Use the `Import-Module` cmdlet on the module manifest to import the module:

   ```
   PS> Import-Module -Name ./CronTab/CronTab.psd1
   ```

5. To list the components of the `CronTab` module, use the `Get-Module` cmdlet:

   ```
   PS> Get-Module -Name CronTab | Format-List
   ```

```
Terminal                                                              _  ⊗
PS /home/ram/code/PowerShell/demos/crontab> Get-Module -Name CronTab | Format-List


Name              : CronTab
Path              : /home/ram/code/PowerShell/demos/crontab/CronTab/CronTab.psm1
Description       : Sample module for managing CronTab
ModuleType        : Script
Version           : 0.1.0.0
NestedModules     : {}
ExportedFunctions : {Get-CronJob, Get-CronTabUser, New-CronJob, Remove-CronJob}
ExportedCmdlets   :
ExportedVariables :
ExportedAliases   :


PS /home/ram/code/PowerShell/demos/crontab> []
```

6. To list the available command types of the `CronTab` module, use the `Get-Command` cmdlet:

```
PS> Get-Command -Module CronTab
```

```
Terminal                                                              –  ✕
PS /home/ram/code/PowerShell/demos/crontab> Get-Command -Module CronTab

CommandType     Name                                    Version   Source
-----------     ----                                    -------   ------
Function        Get-CronJob                             0.1.0.0   CronTab
Function        Get-CronTabUser                         0.1.0.0   CronTab
Function        New-CronJob                             0.1.0.0   CronTab
Function        Remove-CronJob                          0.1.0.0   CronTab

PS /home/ram/code/PowerShell/demos/crontab> []
```

How it works...

When you download the CronTab module, the following files get copied to the CronTab folder from the URL mentioned in the recipe and these files contain the module data:

- `onTCrab.ps1xml`
- `CronTab.psd1`
- `CronTab.psm1`

The `Import-Module` cmdlet registers the cmdlets available in the module into the PowerShell session and makes the module ready for use. The `Import-Module` cmdlet is run against the module manifest, which is the `psd1` file.

When you run the `Get-Command` cmdlet, you get a list of all of the cmdlets available in the module.

Scheduling jobs in PowerShell

In this recipe, we will see how to schedule a job using PowerShell cmdlets.

Getting ready

This recipe may involve some of the capabilities that work well only with super-user privileges. Therefore, perform the following steps:

1. Log in to the Terminal using super-user privileges.
2. Open a PowerShell console using the `pwsh` command.
3. Import the module (refer to the recipe, *Installing the CronTab PowerShell module*).

How to do it...

You need a script that needs to be scheduled. If you don't have a script, use a simple command:

1. First, check the existence of the command or script that you want to schedule from the Terminal:

   ```
   $ pwsh -f "/tmp/DataLoading.PS1;"
   ```

   The `DataLoading.PS1` script is from the `Chapter 16`, *Using PowerShell for SQL Database Management*, the *Data formatting examples with PowerShell* recipe. This is just for the demo. You can use any of the scripts of your choice to run the code.

2. To run the script based on a schedule, use the `New-CronJob` cmdlet:

   ```
   PS> New-CronJob -Command 'pwsh -f "/tmp/DataLoading.PS1;"' -Minute
   0,15,30,45 | Out-Host

   PS> New-CronJob -Command 'pwsh -f "/tmp/DataLoading.PS1;"' -Minute
   */15 | Out-Host

   PS> New-CronJob -Command 'pwsh -f "/tmp/DataLoading.PS1;"' -Minute
   */15 -Hour 10-12 | Out-Host

   PS> New-CronJob -Command 'rm -rf /tmp/clr*' -Minute 15 -Hour 1 |
   Out-Host

   PS> New-CronJob -Command 'pwsh -f "/tmp/DataLoading.PS1;"' -Minute
   */15 -Hour 10-12 -DayOfWeek sun,tue,fri -Month Jan,Mar,Jun,Sep,Dec
   | Out-Host
   ```

3. To get the list of currently scheduled jobs, run the Get-CronJob cmdlet:

```
PS /> Get-CronJob |Format-Table -AutoSize
Minute Hour DayOfMonth Month DayOfWeek Command
------ ---- ---------- ----- --------- -------
2 * * * * python ./pythonexmaple.py
5 1 * * * rm -rf /tmp/clr*.*
15 * * * * /usr/bin/pwsh -c "cd /tmp/; ./DataLoading.PS1;"
*/15 * * * * /usr/bin/pwsh -c "cd /tmp/; ./DataLoading.PS1;"
0,15,30,45 * * * * /usr/bin/pwsh -c "cd /tmp/; ./DataLoading.PS1;"
*/15 10-12 * * * /usr/bin/pwsh -c "cd /tmp/; ./DataLoading.PS1;"
*/15 10-12 * Jan,Mar sun,tue,fri /usr/bin/pwsh -c "cd /tmp/;
./DataLoading.PS1;"
```

4. To view the contents of scheduled jobs in the crontab configuration file, use Get-CronJob:

```
PS > Get-CronJob
2 * * * * python ./pythonexmaple.py
5 1 * * * rm -rf /tmp/clr*.*
*/15 * * * * /usr/bin/pwsh -c "cd /tmp/; ./DataLoading.PS1;"
0,15,30,45 * * * * /usr/bin/pwsh -c "cd /tmp/; ./DataLoading.PS1;"
*/15 10-12 * * * /usr/bin/pwsh -c "cd /tmp/; ./DataLoading.PS1;"
*/15 10-12 * Jan, Mar, Jun, Sep, Dec sun, tue, fri /usr/bin/pwsh -c
"cd /tmp/; ./DataLoading.PS1;"
```

How it works...

The PowerShell implementation of crontab is technically a wrapper, which encapsulates the crontab commands that work in Linux. Why use PowerShell to schedule jobs if the underlying functions are that of crontab? The reason would be the uniformity of usage, the consistency, and the object-oriented approach. If you know how to use PowerShell, that is all you need in order to be able to use crontab as well. That is the goal.

The New-CronTab cmdlet is used to define new tasks. The parameters available define the frequency with which the tasks are to be executed. The Cron jobs are executed with the same privileges as with which the New-CronTab cmdlet was executed. In other words, if you launched PowerShell as a super-user and ran New-CronTab to define a schedule, the commands that would be run on the specified schedule would be run with super-user privileges.

In the steps, the command to run is listed using the `-Command` parameter.

Let us also look briefly at what input the `New-CronTab` accepts. There are two ways to run a command every 15 minutes: The first is where each minute is specified:

```
0,15,30,45 * * * * /path/command
```

Alternatively, you can simplify the same to `*/15`:

```
*/15 * * * * /path/command
```

A range can also be specified for scheduling a job. In our example, the job runs at 10 A.M., 11 A.M., and 12 P.M., using the range option:

```
*/15 10-12 * * * /path/command
```

In the last example (the `Names` format), the job is scheduled to run using the `DayOfweek` (`sun`, `tue`, `fri`) and `Month` (`Jan`, `Mar`) parameters:

```
*/15      10-12 *           Jan,Mar sun,tue,fri /usr/bin/pwsh -c "cd /tmp/;
./DataLoading.PS1;"
```

The Cron table configuration is read using the `Get-CronTab` cmdlet. Each line represents a record of metadata about the scheduled job; it specifies the frequency and the command/script that should be executed.

The caveat as of now is that, if you set up Cron jobs incorrectly, they appear to silently fail. Cron has its own reserved `syslog` facility, so you should have a look at the `/etc/syslog.conf` file (or the equivalent file in your Linux distribution) to see where the messages from `cron` are sent. Common destinations include `/var/log/cron`, `/var/log/messages`, and `/var/log/syslog`.

Removing scheduled jobs in PowerShell

In this recipe, we're going to see the steps to remove the entries from the CronTab file.

How to do it...

Now that we have created entries into the cron configuration file, let's attempt to remove those entries:

1. List the jobs using the Get-CronJob cmdlet. This will get you the list of jobs that are created by reading the CronTab file:

   ```
   PS> Get-CronJob | Format-Table -AutoSize
   ```

2. Apply a conditional logic to segregate the required job entries using the Where-Object clause. You will read more about this in Chapter 4, *Passing Data Through Pipelines*:

   ```
   PS > Get-CronJob | Where-Object {$_.Month -match 'Jan'} | Format-Table -AutoSize

   Minute Hour DayOfMonth Month DayOfWeek Command
   ------ ---- ---------- ----- --------- -------
   */15 10-12 * Jan,Mar,Jun,Sep,Dec sun,tue,fri /usr/bin/pwsh -c "cd
   /tmp/; ./DataLoading.PS1;"
   */15 10-12 * Jan,Mar sun,tue,fri /usr/bin/pwsh -c "cd /tmp/;
   ./DataLoading.PS1;"
   ```

3. Remove the entries using Remove-CronJob:

   ```
   PS > Get-CronJob | Where-Object {$_.Month -match 'Jan'} | Remove-CronJob

   Confirm
   Are you sure you want to perform this action?
   Performing the operation "Remove" on target "/usr/bin/pwsh -c "cd
   /tmp/; ./DataLoading.PS1;"".
   [Y] Yes [A] Yes to All [N] No [L] No to All [S] Suspend [?] Help
   (default is "Y"): Y

   Confirm
   Are you sure you want to perform this action?
   Performing the operation "Remove" on target "/usr/bin/pwsh -c "cd
   /tmp/; ./DataLoading.PS1;"".
   [Y] Yes [A] Yes to All [N] No [L] No to All [S] Suspend [?] Help
   (default is "Y"): Y
   PS /home/PacktPub>
   ```

How it works...

When we would like to remove cron jobs, we list out the cron jobs and then pass the job objects via the pipeline to the cmdlet, `Remove-CronJob`, to remove the jobs from the configuration file.

There is a conditional logic mentioned in the recipe. This concept of conditional filtration is covered in the recipe, *Filtering objects*, in `Chapter 4`, *Passing Data through the Pipeline*. The concept of using `$_` is covered in the recipe, *Selecting columns from the output*, also of the aforementioned chapter.

See also

- The *Selecting columns from the output* recipe in `Chapter 4`, *Passing Data through the Pipeline*
- The *Filtering objects* recipe covered in `Chapter 4`, *Passing Data through the Pipeline*

4
Passing Data through the Pipeline

In this chapter, we will cover the following recipes:

- Selecting columns from the output
- Limiting the number of output objects
- Expanding the properties within properties
- Filtering objects
- Grouping the output
- Sorting the output
- Taking actions on the returned objects
- Understanding pipeline-enabled parameters
- Importing content into PowerShell

Introduction

It is time for some information feasting now. In `Chapter 3`, *First Steps in Administration using PowerShell*, we looked at a few simple concepts such as working with dates and processes. In doing so, we learned a thing or two about using PowerShell as well, such as using it for measuring output objects.

In this chapter, we will learn to use something that makes PowerShell highly efficient and friendly: the pipeline.

Most Linux administrators would have used the pipeline in their shell commands or shell scripts, and most administrators who use any form of shell scripting would be aware that the pipe sends the output of one command as input to the next. It is also true in the case of Bash (and its derivatives) that the pipe sends text from the preceding command to the succeeding one.

Most PowerShell cmdlets output objects, and the pipeline in PowerShell sends the output object to the next command. When we run a PowerShell command (and not a Linux command) in PowerShell, we get a table-like output in most cases. We may think that it is all of the output.

When we ask PowerShell to get any information, it pulls out the entire object in the background. This object (or a package that contains a lot of objects) is then processed using PowerShell's built-in formatting rules in order for it to be displayed on the host. To quote Microsoft:

> *What you see onscreen is a summary of information, and not a complete representation of the output object.*

Therefore, more often than not, what you see on the screen as the output of a certain command is just a tip of the iceberg! It's just that the submerged part was chosen not to be displayed based on the formatting rules. In this chapter, we will use the pipeline to get more from the objects than is displayed on the screen by default, and leverage the capability of the pipeline to get more out of PowerShell than meets the eye.

Selecting columns from the output

When my brother saw me exploring `awk`, he said, "Boy, have we overused this command!". Of course, not everything displayed on the screen is important—or even necessary. In this recipe, we will learn how to separate columns in PowerShell without using the Linux command `awk`.

Getting ready

Go to a directory that has some files that we can play with. If you do not have such a directory, create one and create some files in there. Let the files be of different extensions so that we can use them in future recipes as well.

If you have not already, clone the Git repository, which you can find at `https://github.com/PacktPublishing/PowerShell-6.0-Linux-Administration-Cookbook`. There is a quick-and-dirty script called `Initialize-PacktPs6CoreLinuxLab.ps1` under the `ch04` directory. Run the script to get the necessary files.

How to do it...

The awk command works with text, and, based on the delimiters in the output text, separates the output into columns. This separated output is displayed as columns again when you use the print function, like in C. PowerShell works a little differently.

Let's get started:

1. If you haven't create any files yet, please do so. Here are some commands you could use to create the files:

    ```
    PS> New-Item ./random/cities -ItemType Directory -Force
    PS> Set-Location ./random/
    PS> New-Item random-text.txt, himalayas.jpg, crunched-numbers.csv,
    bangalore.jpg, screenshot-001.png, screenshot-002.png,
    screenshot-003.png, demo.doc, my-plugin.rb, ./cities/mumbai.html,
    ./cities/nyc.html, ./cities/cairo.html, ./cities/dubai.html,
    ./cities/paris.html -ItemType File
    ```

2. You may also want to download some real multimedia content, just so we get the length (file size) property for future use. Just download any random images or media files.

3. Navigate to the location where you saved the files. I have them in a directory called random in my home directory. You would, too, if you used the Initialize-PacktPs6CoreLinuxLab.ps1 script:

    ```
    PS> Set-Location ./random/
    ```

     Use tab-completion to complete the cmdlet, as well as the path.

4. List out the contents in the current location:

    ```
    PS> Get-ChildItem -Path .
    ```

A sample output is shown in the following screenshot:

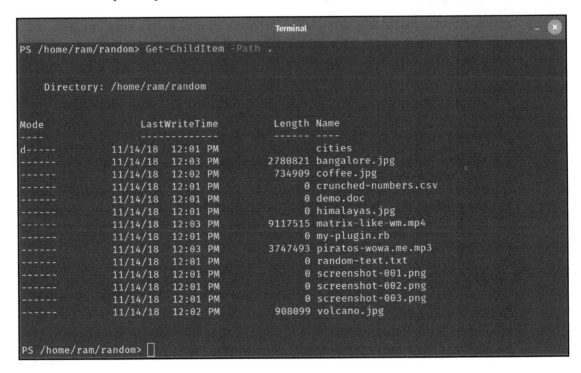

```
Terminal                                                                    _  ✕

PS /home/ram/random> Get-ChildItem -Path .


    Directory: /home/ram/random


Mode                LastWriteTime         Length Name
----                -------------         ------ ----
d-----        11/14/18   12:01 PM                cities
------        11/14/18   12:03 PM        2780821 bangalore.jpg
------        11/14/18   12:02 PM         734909 coffee.jpg
------        11/14/18   12:01 PM              0 crunched-numbers.csv
------        11/14/18   12:01 PM              0 demo.doc
------        11/14/18   12:01 PM              0 himalayas.jpg
------        11/14/18   12:03 PM        9117515 matrix-like-wm.mp4
------        11/14/18   12:01 PM              0 my-plugin.rb
------        11/14/18   12:03 PM        3747493 piratos-wowa.me.mp3
------        11/14/18   12:01 PM              0 random-text.txt
------        11/14/18   12:01 PM              0 screenshot-001.png
------        11/14/18   12:01 PM              0 screenshot-002.png
------        11/14/18   12:01 PM              0 screenshot-003.png
------        11/14/18   12:02 PM         908099 volcano.jpg

PS /home/ram/random> █
```

5. Let us say that you don't need the `Mode` column:

    ```
    PS> Get-ChildItem -Path . | Select-Object LastWriteTime, Length,
    Name
    ```

     It's important to note that, by using `Select-Object`, you are stripping the object of the properties that you did not call with `Select-Object`. Therefore, the object returned at the end of the preceding command would not have properties such as `CreationTime`, `FullName`, and so on, anymore.

Here is the output of the preceding command:

```
                                    Terminal                              _  ⊗
PS /home/ram/random> Get-ChildItem -Path . | Select-Object LastWriteTime, Length, Name

LastWriteTime           Length  Name
-------------           ------  ----
11/14/18 12:01:58 PM            cities
11/14/18 12:03:38 PM 2780821    bangalore.jpg
11/14/18 12:02:31 PM 734909     coffee.jpg
11/14/18 12:01:56 PM 0          crunched-numbers.csv
11/14/18 12:01:56 PM 0          demo.doc
11/14/18 12:01:56 PM 0          himalayas.jpg
11/14/18 12:03:26 PM 9117515    matrix-like-wm.mp4
11/14/18 12:01:56 PM 0          my-plugin.rb
11/14/18 12:03:29 PM 3747493    piratos-wowa.me.mp3
11/14/18 12:01:56 PM 0          random-text.txt
11/14/18 12:01:56 PM 0          screenshot-001.png
11/14/18 12:01:56 PM 0          screenshot-002.png
11/14/18 12:01:56 PM 0          screenshot-003.png
11/14/18 12:02:14 PM 908099     volcano.jpg

PS /home/ram/random> □
```

As you may have noticed, `Select-Object` does not follow the naming or capitalization convention that PowerShell uses. Why is that? Run `Get-Command select` to find out.

6. This sequence does not really make sense in the current context. Shuffle the columns:

```
PS> Get-ChildItem -Path . | Select-Object Name, Length,
LastWriteTime
```

Note how the output columns are rearranged compared to the previous output:

```
Terminal                                                              _  ✕
PS /home/ram/random> Get-ChildItem -Path . | Select-Object Name, Length, LastWriteTime

Name                    Length  LastWriteTime
----                    ------  -------------
cities                          11/14/18 12:01:58 PM
bangalore.jpg           2780821 11/14/18 12:03:38 PM
coffee.jpg              734909  11/14/18 12:02:31 PM
crunched-numbers.csv    0       11/14/18 12:01:56 PM
demo.doc                0       11/14/18 12:01:56 PM
himalayas.jpg           0       11/14/18 12:01:56 PM
matrix-like-wm.mp4      9117515 11/14/18 12:03:26 PM
my-plugin.rb            0       11/14/18 12:01:56 PM
piratos-wowa.me.mp3     3747493 11/14/18 12:03:29 PM
random-text.txt         0       11/14/18 12:01:56 PM
screenshot-001.png      0       11/14/18 12:01:56 PM
screenshot-002.png      0       11/14/18 12:01:56 PM
screenshot-003.png      0       11/14/18 12:01:56 PM
volcano.jpg             908099  11/14/18 12:02:14 PM

PS /home/ram/random> ▯
```

That looks much better.

7. Now, change the column name of `LastWriteTime` to `Modified`:

```
PS> Get-ChildItem -Path . | Select-Object Name, Length,
@{Name='Modified'; Expression={$_.LastWriteTime}}
```

Note the name of the last column now, and compare it with the previous output.

8. Now, pick just the year—not the entire date:

```
PS> Get-ChildItem -Path . | Select-Object Name, Length,
@{Name='Modified'; Expression={$_.LastWriteTime.Year}}
```

9. See how many days have passed since the last change:

```
PS> Get-ChildItem -Path . | select Name, Length,
@{Name='DaysSinceModification'; Expression={[math]::Round(((Get-
Date) - $_.LastWriteTime).TotalDays)}}
```

How it works...

If you ran `Get-Command select`, you would have understood by now that `select` is in fact an alias for `Select-Object`. As already established, PowerShell outputs objects. These objects are then formatted using built-in formatting rules that are shown on the screen in a certain way.

When we use `Select-Object`, we override the formatting rules by specifying which objects need to be shown to us. While the primary objective of `Select-Object` is to pick the columns we need, the cmdlet also allows us to sequence the output columns.

PowerShell also gives us the freedom to modify the name of the columns that are returned. In such a case, we use a hashtable to specify the name that we want, and what data we want shown under the column. You can even perform calculations on the data that's returned, and make this a calculated property. At the last step, we subtract the date of last modification from the current date, pick the total number of days that have passed since, and then use the `Round` method of the `[math]` accelerator to get a rounded figure of the number of days since the last modification.

There's more...

Try `Select-Object` with other cmdlets such as `Get-Command` to select only the columns that you need.

See also

- The *Creating a simple hash table* recipe in `Chapter 9`, *Using Arrays and and Hashtables*
- Read the recipe, *Filtering Objects*, to know more about the automatic variable, `$_`

Limiting the number of output objects

In the previous recipe, *Selecting columns from the output*, we saw how the `Select-Object` cmdlet can be used to select only the columns we want. In this recipe, we will learn how to limit the output of a cmdlet to a subset of the total items returned.

Getting ready

Ensure that you are at a location that has a few files. List out the contents of the current directory and count the number of items returned. If the number is less than 5, you may want to consider adding more items to the directory. Follow these steps to get started:

1. Enter the following command to count the number of files and directories at the current path:

   ```
   PS> (Get-ChildItem -Path .).Count
   ```

2. If you would like to reduce keystrokes, given that we are only running commands at the terminal, you could use the alias and the defaults of the cmdlet:

   ```
   PS> (gci).Count
   ```

 Those parentheses are required; the parentheses work similar to how they work in mathematics: the instruction within the parentheses is processed first. In this case, we want gci to be executed first, and then the Count property from within the returned object picked.

3. Get the list of parameters Select-Object has:

   ```
   PS> Get-Help Select-Object
   ```

We can see parameters such as First and Last, and they accept integer values.

How to do it...

Navigate to the directory where you have the files:

1. Select only the first five files and directories from the returned list by using the First parameter:

   ```
   PS> Get-ChildItem . | Select-Object -First 5
   ```

2. Let's say we would like to pick the last five elements:

   ```
   PS> Get-ChildItem . | Select-Object -Last 5
   ```

3. We are doing this so that we can skip the first three objects:

   ```
   PS> Get-ChildItem . | Select-Object -Skip 3
   ```

4. If you would like to skip the last two objects, you can use the following code:

```
PS> Get-ChildItem . | Select-Object -SkipLast 2
```

5. To pick the fourth element from the output, you can use the following code:

```
PS> Get-ChildItem . | Select-Object -Index 3
```

6. Now, combine it with what we learned in the previous recipe. Pick only the filenames and the last modified time of the first four elements:

```
PS> Get-ChildItem . | select -Property Name, LastWriteTime -First 4
```

How it works...

This is a simple recipe that helps you work with the number of items returned in the output. With `Select-Object` in PowerShell, we need not loop through output, while simultaneously counting to only get the number of elements that we want. The `Select-Object` cmdlet has that functionality built in.

The parameter names are self-explanatory, except perhaps the `Index` parameter, which works exactly how the numbering of array elements works with most programming languages: it starts with zero. Therefore, the fourth element in the array would have an index of 3, and not 4.

The `Property` and `First` parameters can be combined together since they both feature in the same parameter set in the help documentation for `Select-Object`.

Expanding the properties within properties

So far, from what we have seen, two things are clear to us:

1. An object output feels richer and makes using the object easier
2. An object can have more objects within it

We have handled the first point using the `Select-Object` cmdlet, wherein we picked only the object's properties that we needed, and omitted the rest. This recipe is designed to break down the second point for better understanding.

Let us step into this recipe with one thing in mind: objects can contain objects within them, which in turn can contain more objects within them. To demonstrate this, we will use the `Get-Process` cmdlet.

How to do it...

Let's begin with listing out the processes; we will look at all of the properties that the `Get-Process` cmdlet gives us and look for complex ones:

1. Select all of the properties that are part of the output of the `Get-Process` cmdlet. Pick only the first object so that your console is not filled with content:

   ```
   PS> Get-Process | Select-Object -Property * -First 1
   ```

   Observe the `Threads` property.

2. Select the name of the process, the ID, and the threads:

   ```
   PS> Get-Process | Select-Object -Property Name, Id, Threads
   ```

3. List out all of the threads for the `pwsh` process:

   ```
   PS> Get-Process pwsh | Select-Object -ExpandProperty Threads
   ```

4. A lot of content is given as output. Say we want just the ID, the priority, and the start time of the resultant output:

   ```
   PS> Get-Process pwsh | Select-Object -ExpandProperty Threads |
   Select-Object -Property Id, PriorityLevel, StartTime
   ```

   This gave us the ID, the priority level, and the start time of all of the threads that are running under `pwsh`.

5. What if we use `ExpandProperty` on the ID?

   ```
   PS> Get-Process pwsh | Select-Object -ExpandProperty Threads |
   Select-Object -ExpandProperty Id
   ```

Some partial output of the preceding command is shown in the following screenshot:

```
Terminal                                               –   ✕
PS /home/ram/random> Get-Process pwsh | Select-Object -ExpandProperty Threads | Select-Obj
ect -ExpandProperty Id
4563
4564
4565
4568
4569
4570
4571
4577
4578
4579
4588
4589
4593
8119
8121
8122
8123
8124
8125
8126
```

How it works...

The default parameter for Select-Object, as we have seen, is Property. It accepts property names and shows their values in the output. This parameter can be used to fetch values of multiple properties (Name, Id, Threads).

However, some properties have more complex objects within them, as we saw in the case of the Threads property of the object returned by Get-Process. A simple way to identify complex objects is to see if they are enclosed in curly braces.

The ExpandProperty parameter accepts only a single property name as input and expands the property to show its objects. This can again be piped to Select-Object (or any other relevant cmdlet) for further processing.

In cases where the object is not complex, ExpandProperty simply shows the output without its header. As you may have noticed from the output of ExpandProperty, it does not contain the name of the expanded object itself (Threads, in our case); it contains only the value. The value, in turn, has multiple properties within it.

In the case of simple properties, using `ExpandProperty` simply strips off the property name from the output.

Filtering objects

In the *Limiting the number of output objects* recipe, we saw how to restrict the output content based on a number. In this recipe, we will look at filtering the output based on a certain criterion, and not a number.

Getting ready

Read the *Working with date properties* recipe in `Chapter 3`, *First Steps in Administration Using PowerShell*, if you have not read it already. This recipe uses one of the properties from the date object to filter content. While it is not critical to understand the filtration of objects, it still demonstrates the simplicity of filtration based on object properties.

How to do it...

Navigate to the location where you created files for use with this book:

1. List out the contents of this directory to see what content you have (if you are like me, you would have even forgotten where you created this directory, and what content you put in):

    ```
    PS> Set-Location ~/random
    PS> Get-ChildItem -Path .
    ```

    Note the names of the properties you got.

2. Now, pick only those files that are larger than 0 bytes:

    ```
    PS> Get-ChildItem -Path . | Where-Object -Property Length -GT -Value 0
    ```

3. Pick out all of the JPG files from the lot. To do this, add another condition to the existing condition. However, this time, use the `FilterScript` parameter instead of `Property`:

    ```
    PS> Get-ChildItem -Path . | Where-Object -FilterScript {$_.Length -GT 0 -and $_.Extension -EQ '.jpg'}
    ```

4. Add a condition to get only those files whose names start with `c`:

```
PS> Get-ChildItem -Path . | Where-Object -FilterScript {$_.Length -
GT 0 -and $_.Extension -EQ '.jpg' -and $_.Name -CMatch '^c'}
```

5. Now, choose the files that were created before the 30th minute of any hour:

```
PS> Get-ChildItem -Path . | Where-Object -FilterScript {$_.Length -
GT 0 -and $_.Extension -EQ '.jpg' -and $_.Name -CMatch '^c' -and
$_.LastWriteTime.Minute -LT 30}
```

There is only one file in the lab directory like this:

```
Terminal                                                          – ✕
PS /home/ram/random> Get-ChildItem -Path . | Where-Object -FilterScript {$_.Length -GT 0 -
and $_.Extension -EQ '.jpg' -and $_.Name -CMatch '^c' -and $_.LastWriteTime.Minute -LT 30}


    Directory: /home/ram/random


Mode                 LastWriteTime         Length Name
----                 -------------         ------ ----
------          11/14/18   12:02 PM        734909 coffee.jpg


PS /home/ram/random> []
```

How it works...

Filtration of the output is very simple in PowerShell. Given that the content output is an object, we could simply use the properties from within the object for the filtration.

This recipe shows two modes of filtration:

1. Using one property and comparing its value to the input
2. Using a filter script that uses multiple values and multiple conditions

The `Property` parameter accepts only one property. A conditional operator and a value for comparison are added to the statement to filter the output.

The `FilterScript` parameter, on the other hand, can handle more complex filtration, for example, when we need the output to meet several conditions.

A significant difference between using `Property` and `FilterScript` is the use of the automatic variable, `$_`. This variable contains the current object in the pipeline. For example, in this recipe, we pass the object from `Get-ChildItem` to `Where-Object` through the pipeline. The automatic variable, `$_`, contains the object returned by `Get-ChildItem`, so that `Where-Object` can process it. `$_.LastWriteTime`, in this case, picks the `LastWriteTime` property from the object returned by `Get-ChildItem`.

Also, the `LastWriteTime` object is of type `System.DateTime` or `DateTime`. (Run `(Get-ChildItem .).LastWriteTime | Get-Member` to find out more.) Therefore, it is possible to break it down further into days, hours, minutes, and so on, which is the reason why `$_.LastWriteTime.Minute` could be used for filtration.

There's more...

Try out the `Where-Object` cmdlet on other outputs, such as that of `Get-Process`.

Grouping the output

There are situations where we could group the objects that were given as output so that we could handle each group better, or simply so that we get a more organized output. In this recipe, we will look at passing the output of one cmdlet through the pipeline to `Group-Object` and group the output based on a property.

How to do it...

To group objects based on a property, we will use the `Get-ChildItem` cmdlet on the files that we created for use in this book:

1. Navigate to the location where you created or downloaded the files:

   ```
   PS> Set-Location ~/random
   ```

2. List out only the files (exclude the directories):

   ```
   PS> Get-ChildItem -Path . -File
   ```

   Alternatively, you can use the shorthand version:

   ```
   PS> gci -File
   ```

3. Group the objects based on the extension:

```
PS> Get-ChildItem . -File | Group-Object Extension
```

The shorthand version of this would be as follows:

```
PS> gci -File | group Extension
```

Here are all of the files, grouped by their extensions:

```
                                                Terminal                                    –  ⊗
PS /home/ram/random> Get-ChildItem -File | Group-Object Extension

Count Name                    Group
----- ----                    -----
    1 .csv                    {/home/ram/random/crunched-numbers.csv}
    1 .doc                    {/home/ram/random/demo.doc}
    4 .jpg                    {/home/ram/random/bangalore.jpg, /home/ram/random/coff...
    1 .mp3                    {/home/ram/random/piratos-wowa.me.mp3}
    1 .mp4                    {/home/ram/random/matrix-like-wm.mp4}
    3 .png                    {/home/ram/random/screenshot-001.png, /home/ram/random...
    1 .rb                     {/home/ram/random/my-plugin.rb}
    1 .txt                    {/home/ram/random/random-text.txt}

PS /home/ram/random> []
```

4. Use the `Select-Object` cmdlet to only show the extension and the number of files in each extension:

```
PS> Get-ChildItem -Path . -File | Group-Object -Property Extension
| Select-Object -Property Name, Count
```

5. Is there a simpler way to do this? Of course:

```
PS> Get-ChildItem -Path . -File | Group-Object -Property Extension
-NoElement
```

6. Now that we know how to handle grouping and expanded property selection, let's pick only the JPG files from the lot:

```
PS> Get-ChildItem -Path . -File | Group-Object -Property Extension
| Where-Object Name -EQ .jpg | Select-Object -ExpandProperty Group
```

Here is the output of the preceding command:

```
Terminal                                                                              _ ⊗
PS /home/ram/random> Get-ChildItem -Path . -File | Group-Object -Property Extension | Wher
e-Object Name -EQ .jpg | Select-Object -ExpandProperty Group


    Directory: /home/ram/random


Mode                 LastWriteTime         Length Name
----                 -------------         ------ ----
------        11/14/18  12:03 PM          2780821 bangalore.jpg
------        11/14/18  12:02 PM           734909 coffee.jpg
------        11/14/18  12:01 PM                0 himalayas.jpg
------        11/14/18  12:02 PM           908099 volcano.jpg


PS /home/ram/random> []
```

How it works...

What we did in this recipe was certainly non-intuitive, considering that we could use just `Where-Object` along with `Get-ChildItem`. However, the intention of this recipe was to demonstrate the use of `Group-Object`. The `Group-Object` cmdlet creates groups based on the criteria we specify, and names the groups on the criteria. In our case, the criteria for grouping was the extension, and so the names of the groups were the extensions.

Each of these groups contains its elements, which are objects in themselves. If we simply want the count and the names of the groups, we use the `NoElement` parameter. If we want only the elements, we use the `ExpandProperty` parameter of the `Select-Object` cmdlet and expand all of the elements. The elements that are expanded are the objects of the cmdlet preceding the `Group-Object` cmdlet (`Get-ChildItem`, in our case).

If `Where-Object` and other cmdlets could do what `Group-Object` could in a complicated way, why have it in the first place? Read on until the *Taking actions on the returned objects* recipe to find out more.

There's more...

If you have gotten the hang of tab-completion, you need not even select the properties that are not shown by default. All you have to do is type `Group-Object` after the pipe, add a space, and press the *Tab* key; PowerShell will show you what objects are available to use for grouping. Try it out with the following command:

```
PS> Get-ChildItem . -File | Group-Object<Space><Tab>
```

See also

- The *Taking actions on the returned objects* recipe

Sorting the output

It is time for another simple cmdlet, which will build toward the *Taking actions on the returned objects* recipe. In this recipe, we will sort the output objects to meet our requirements.

How to do it...

We will continue using the directory and the files we created for this book. If all of your files are of size zero bytes, download a few files with content. The file type does not matter:

1. List out the files in the directory:

   ```
   PS> Get-ChildItem -Path .
   ```

2. Filter the output so that you have only files:

   ```
   PS> Get-ChildItem -Path . -File
   ```

3. Pipe the object to the `Sort-Object` cmdlet to sort the output based on the file size:

   ```
   PS> Get-ChildItem -Path . -File | Sort-Object -Property Length
   ```

4. The shorthand for this expression would be as follows:

   ```
   PS> gci . -File | sort Length
   ```

5. Sort the files, from the largest file to the smallest file:

```
PS> Get-ChildItem -Path . -File | Sort-Object -Property Length -
Descending
```

6. Pick the largest three files in the lot:

```
PS> Get-ChildItem -Path . -File | Sort-Object -Property Length -
Descending -Top 3
```

7. Create two files, and, using a text editor, add some content to both of them (or use the following script block to create some random text):

```
PS> $($i = 0; while ($i -lt 520) {(-join ((65..90) + (97..122) |
Get-Random -Count 8 | ForEach-Object {[char]$_})).ToString();
$i++}) -join ' ' | Out-File ./random-text-1.txt; Start-Sleep -
Seconds 60; $($i = 0; while ($i -lt 500) {(-join ((65..90) +
(97..122) | Get-Random -Count 8 | ForEach-Object
{[char]$_})).ToString(); $i++}) -join ' ' | Out-File ./random-
text-2.txt
```

8. Now, sort the files in the directory, first by size, and then the name:

```
PS> Get-ChildItem -Path . -File | Sort-Object -Property Length,
Name
```

Observe the output that you get.

9. Sort the list in descending order:

```
PS> Get-ChildItem -Path . -File | Sort-Object -Property Length,
Name -Descending
```

Note the `Length` column:

```
                                   Terminal                              _  ⊗
PS /home/ram/random> Get-ChildItem -Path . -File | Sort-Object -Property Length, Name -Des
cending


       Directory: /home/ram/random


Mode                 LastWriteTime         Length Name
----                 -------------         ------ ----
------          11/14/18   12:03 PM        9117515 matrix-like-wm.mp4
------          11/14/18   12:03 PM        3747493 piratos-wowa.me.mp3
------          11/14/18   12:03 PM        2780821 bangalore.jpg
------          11/14/18   12:02 PM         908099 volcano.jpg
------          11/14/18   12:02 PM         734909 coffee.jpg
------          11/14/18   12:01 PM              0 screenshot-003.png
------          11/14/18   12:01 PM              0 screenshot-002.png
------          11/14/18   12:01 PM              0 screenshot-001.png
------          11/14/18   12:01 PM              0 random-text.txt
------          11/14/18   12:01 PM              0 my-plugin.rb
------          11/14/18   12:01 PM              0 himalayas.jpg
------          11/14/18   12:01 PM              0 demo.doc
------          11/14/18   12:01 PM              0 crunched-numbers.csv


PS /home/ram/random> ▯
```

How it works...

This recipe is another demonstration of passing objects through the pipeline. In the help documentation for `Sort-Object`, we can see a parameter called `InputObject`. This parameter is a generic term used in PowerShell for a parameter whose input comes through the pipeline.

`Sort-Object` accepts input from the pipeline, and sorts the content based on the property specified. If a property is not specified, the default property for the object output from the preceding command is used for sorting. If there are multiple properties being used as input, the sorting happens based on the order in which the properties are specified.

Sorting can happen in ascending order (default) or descending order.

Taking actions on the returned objects

We have been using the pipeline throughout this chapter to perform various activities on objects. We have been passing objects from one cmdlet to another and, in fact, taking actions on the objects being returned. This recipe, in the technical sense, is nothing new. However, to get ourselves more comfortable using the pipeline, and to show you that the pipeline is not just used for selection, filtration, and sorting, we will use the pipeline to also perform some deletions.

Getting ready

If you do not have files within the demo directory that we created, please go ahead and create some files. Make sure that some of the files have some content in them.

Let us say that you have been given a requirement. There is a certain team that would like the top two largest files of each type to be deleted from a directory. If there is only one file of a certain type, that file has to be left alone.

How to do it...

Here is an outline of the steps you will want to take:

1. Get all of the files at the path specified
2. Group all of the files by file type (extension)
3. Filter out those groups that contain more than one item
4. Expand each group, and sort the files by size (length)
5. Pick the two largest files in each group
6. Delete the files

While we are working on a sandbox directory, and since we are taking precautions so that we don't delete anything important, it is still better to only prototype the action using ShouldPerform (the WhatIf parameter). This way, the files won't actually be deleted, and PowerShell will only tell you what it would do if the command is run.

Let's get cracking:

1. List the contents of the current directory and group the output based on the extension:

   ```
   PS> Get-ChildItem -Path . -File | Group-Object -Property Extension
   ```

2. Filter to discard the lone files of each extension:

   ```
   PS> Get-ChildItem -Path . -File | Group-Object -Property Extension
   | Where-Object Count -GT 1
   ```

3. Now comes a loop construct. We will look at how this works in a future chapter. For now, just know that it works. The goal here is to only leverage the pipeline:

   ```
   PS> Get-ChildItem -Path . -File | Group-Object -Property Extension
   | Where-Object Count -GT 1 | ForEach-Object {$_.Group | Sort-Object
   Length -Bottom 2}
   ```

   Here is the output of the preceding command:

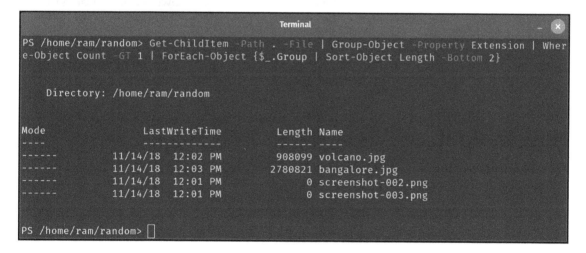

4. Delete these files using the `Remove-Item` cmdlet. Use the `WhatIf` switch if you do not want the files to be actually deleted:

   ```
   PS> Get-ChildItem -Path . -File | Group-Object -Property Extension
   | Where-Object Count -GT 1 | ForEach-Object {$_.Group | Sort-Object
   Length -Bottom 2} | Remove-Item -WhatIf
   ```

How it works...

When any cmdlet reads an object through the pipeline, it reads the entire contents of the object. Any cmdlet that is designed to accept input through the pipeline picks the right property from the object, and then takes actions on the objects. In the case of this recipe, it was the `Path` property that was picked in order to identify the files to delete.

To know if a certain cmdlet accepts input from the pipeline, run `Get-Help` on the cmdlet with the `Full` parameter, and see if the value for `Accept pipeline input?` is `true`. The `InputObject` parameter of `Where-Object` and the `Path` parameter of `Move-Item` are a couple of examples.

Understanding pipeline-enabled parameters

Understanding pipelines is not so much of a requirement if you plan to use PowerShell for only running commands on the console; it is well encapsulated, and the cmdlets are well designed to be able to handle passing objects between cmdlets. However, if you plan to create custom functions and modules, the concept of the pipeline is something you will want to understand well.

In this recipe, we will look into two ways cmdlets accept input. At the point where we create functions, we will look at how to enable pipeline input for parameters.

How to do it...

We will mostly use the help documentation to demonstrate the two different kinds of pipeline input. Follow these steps to get started:

1. At the prompt, type in the following command:

   ```
   PS> Get-Help Get-Item -Parameter Path
   ```

   The output says that the parameter accepts a string input, and accepts input by property name as well as by value:

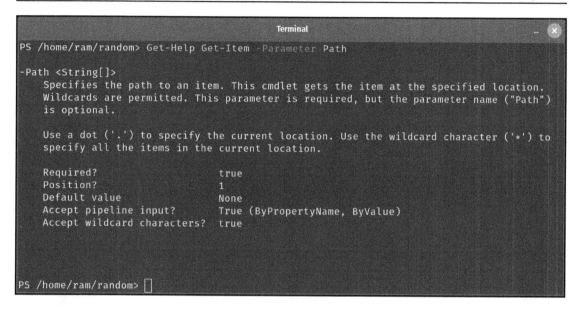

2. Type in the following code to see if a valid string is accepted:

```
PS> "$HOME/random" | Get-Item
```

Of course, substitute the path with that of the lab directory in your setup:

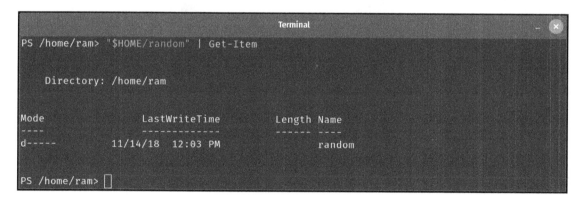

3. Let us try something similar with `Get-Date`:

```
PS> Get-Help Get-Date -Parameter *
```

The `Date` parameter accepts values through the pipeline. However, the type is `DateTime`, and not `string`.

4. Try sending a valid string through the pipeline to see if it gets converted into a date:

```
PS> '21 June 2018' | Get-Date
```

As we can see, it successfully converted the string into date and time:

```
                                    Terminal                                 _  ⊗
PS /home/ram> '21 June 2018' | Get-Date

Thursday, June 21, 2018 12:00:00 AM


PS /home/ram> Get-Help Get-Date -Parameter *

-Date <DateTime>
    Specifies a date and time. By default, `Get-Date` gets the current system date and
    time.

    Type the date in a format that is standard for the system locale, such as dd-MM-yyyy
    (German [Germany]) or MM/dd/yyyy (English [United States]).

    Required?                      false
    Position?                      0
    Default value                  Current date
    Accept pipeline input?         True (ByPropertyName, ByValue)
    Accept wildcard characters?    false


-Day <Int32>
    Specifies the day of the month that is displayed. Enter a value from 1 to 31. The
    default is the current day.
```

5. Now, let's go back to getting details of the current directory. This time, however, we will only pick the `FullName` property of the object:

```
PS> Get-Item . | Select-Object FullName
```

6. Pass this through the pipeline to the `Get-ChildItem` cmdlet:

```
PS> Get-Item . | Select-Object FullName | Get-ChildItem
```

As we can see, there is an error:

```
                              Terminal                              _  ⊗
PS /home/ram> Get-Item . | Select-Object FullName | Get-ChildItem
Get-ChildItem : Cannot find path '/home/ram/@{FullName=/home/ram}' because it does not exi
st.
At line:1 char:39
+ Get-Item . | Select-Object FullName | Get-ChildItem
+                                       ~~~~~~~~~~~~~~
+ CategoryInfo          : ObjectNotFound: (/home/ram/@{FullName=/home/ram}:String) [Get-Ch
ildItem], ItemNotFoundException
+ FullyQualifiedErrorId : PathNotFound,Microsoft.PowerShell.Commands.GetChildItemCommand

PS /home/ram> ▮
```

7. Change the property name to `LiteralPath`:

```
PS> Get-Item . | Select-Object @{Name = 'LiteralPath'; Expression =
{$_.FullName}}
```

8. Pass the object to `Get-ChildItem` through the pipeline:

```
PS> Get-Item . | Select-Object @{Name = 'LiteralPath'; Expression =
{$_.FullName}} | Get-ChildItem
```

That worked.

How it works...

There are two kinds of input through the pipeline:

- `ByPropertyName`
- `ByValue`

The `ByValue` type is perhaps the most common. If a parameter accepts input through the pipeline by value, it would look for the data type that matches the defined data type in the output, and pick the output as input for itself. In case the data type is not the same as what has been defined, but can be converted into the required type, the parameter would convert the value into the data type it takes in and process it. This happened in the case of `Get-Date`, where we sent the date as a string, and passed it through the pipeline to `Get-Date`.

In the case of `Get-Item`, the `Path` parameter accepted a string input and processed the command. In the case of `Get-Date`, the `Date` parameter converted the string into a `DateTime` object and processed the request.

`ByPropertyName`, compared to `ByValue`, looks for a property of the exact same name as the parameter. In our case, `LiteralPath` of `Get-ChildItem` threw an error when we passed the `FullName` property, even though it was essentially the literal path of the object, and a string value. The reason for this error was that the property was not called `LiteralPath`. When we changed the name of the property to `LiteralPath`, `Get-ChildItem` accepted the input through the pipeline and gave us the desired output.

Importing content into PowerShell

Administrators managing multiple computers need to have some sort of input fed into cmdlets so that they can automate tasks. While most Linux administrators are familiar with sending input to files, the important point with PowerShell is that, apart from taking file-based input (read: `Get-Content`), PowerShell is also capable of importing input. This imported input is a PowerShell object.

In this recipe, we will look at two kinds of import cmdlets and learn how to work with them.

How to do it...

In the *Parsing input from text to object* recipe in `Chapter 1`, *Introducing PowerShell Core*, we used `Import-Csv` to import a comma-separated values file to convert the data contained within to a PowerShell object. Let's recapitulate what we learned, but this time, now that we know how to work with objects, we will use the imported content in some way.

Before we import the content, let's first export some content into a CSV file. This way, we will have some relevant content to manipulate:

1. Navigate to the location where you created the files for this chapter. List the contents of the directory. While this book uses (and recommends) complete cmdlets even at the console (using tab-completion, of course), feel free to use aliases if you want:

   ```
   PS> Get-ChildItem -Path . | Select-Object Name, FullName,
   CreationTime, LastWriteTime, Extension, Length
   ```

2. Export the contents to a CSV file:

```
PS> Get-ChildItem -Path . | Select-Object Name, FullName,
CreationTime, LastWriteTime, Extension, Length | Export-Csv ./file-
list.csv
```

3. Open the file in a spreadsheet processor such as LibreOffice Calc, or even a text editor, to view its contents:

```
PS> Get-Content ./file-list.csv
```

That was a plain text representation of the object returned by Get-ChildItem.

4. Import the contents of the CSV file to convert this text into an object:

```
PS> Import-Csv ./file-list.csv
```

5. Find the type of the object returned by this command:

```
PS> Import-Csv ./file-list.csv | Get-Member
```

The object type is System.Management.Automation.PSCustomObject.

6. Check if this is the same as that returned by Get-ChildItem:

```
PS> Get-ChildItem . | Get-Member
```

7. The object returned by Import-Csv is different. Is it possible to treat it just like we do other objects? Get the CreationTime using the member access operator:

```
PS> (Import-Csv ./file-list.csv).CreationTime
```

8. Get just the year:

```
PS> (Import-Csv ./file-list.csv).CreationTime.Year
```

9. Find the type of object returned by the previous command:

```
PS> (Import-Csv ./file-list.csv).CreationTime | Get-Member
```

```
TypeName: System.String
```

10. Attempt to convert the LastWriteTime into a DateTime object. Pick just the first record, though:

```
PS> Get-Date (Import-Csv ./file-list.csv | Select-Object
CreationTime -First 1).CreationTime
```

11. What if we had to retain all of the objects within the object returned by `Get-ChildItem`, including their object types?

    ```
    PS> Get-ChildItem -Path . | Export-Clixml ./file-list.xml
    ```

12. Now, import the contents of the XML to the session:

    ```
    PS> Import-Clixml ./file-list.xml
    ```

13. Find out the type name of the object returned by the import command:

    ```
    PS> Import-Clixml ./file-list.xml | Get-Member
    ```

14. Pick the `CreationTime` property and find its type:

    ```
    PS> (Import-Clixml ./file-list.xml).CreationTime | Get-Member

        TypeName: System.DateTime
    ```

15. Pick just the year:

    ```
    PS> (Import-Clixml ./file-list.xml).CreationTime.Year
    ```

How it works...

Importing content from a CSV is a straightforward process. The columns in a CSV are separated by commas. PowerShell creates an object from the input content, with each column making a property of a PowerShell custom object. Operations that we perform on objects can be performed on the `PSCustomObject`, however, the only limitation with `Import-Csv` is that the properties cannot be multi-valued, nor can they have other sub-properties within them. There could be ways to achieve multi-valued properties with CSV, but they would involve some manipulation after the object is imported within PowerShell. One such way is to separate the values of the property with a delimiter, and then, after the import, split the delimited value.

On the other hand, a **CLIXML (Common Language Infrastructure XML)** is a complete .NET object. When a PowerShell object is exported to CLIXML, the object is retained as it is. That is, the CLIXML retains all of the properties (of theoretically any depth), and the methods that were part of the output object. In other words, it can be said that a CLIXML export is almost lossless in terms of the members of the object.

Using Variables and Objects

5

In this chapter, we will cover the following recipes:

- Using environment variables
- Storing the output of an instance of a .NET Core object
- Adding custom properties to an object
- Creating a custom object from a returned object
- Understanding the extension of type data
- Retaining object modifications across sessions
- Removing custom type data

Introduction

Variables are important to programming since they act as containers of information that are stored during the program's execution. Although piping makes PowerShell highly versatile, they still cannot replace variables, because objects passed through the pipeline must be consumed immediately, and not all scripts work that way, given our varied requirements.

We are all aware of the various data types: `int`, `double`, `string`, `char`, `array`, and so on. Two other important types of variables in PowerShell are hashtables and objects. A hashtable is a dictionary table that's formed with key-value pairs. An object, as we have seen, could be as complex and as simple as it can get in PowerShell, that is, holding values of different kinds.

In PowerShell, objects can be stored in variables. For instance, check out the following command:

```
PS> $Processes = Get-Process
```

Using this command would store all of the processes in the `$Processes` variable.

One more point to remember with variables is the scope. By default, variables have a local scope, meaning that they are valid within the function that they are specified in. Global variables are valid across the program. In general, it is best practice to use local variables, though.

Global variables are declared and used with the `$Global:` prefix, such as `$Global:MyVariable`.

Using environment variables

In this recipe, you will learn about environment variables. When interacting with the system through a shell session, there are many pieces of information that the shell requires in order to determine the program access, the available resources, default configuration, system properties, and so on. Some of these settings are configured within the system as variables, and these settings are commonly called environment variables.

While hardcoding this information during installation is one way to go, it makes the entire system a monolith that cannot be reconfigured without what is known as nuking-and-paving. With environment variables, another layer of flexibility is introduced.

How to do it...

Let's start working with an environment variable by using the following steps:

1. To display the environment variable, type in `Get-ChildItem env:` or `Get-Item env:` and press the *Enter* key:

   ```
   PS> Get-ChildItem env:
   PS> Get-Item env:
   ```

2. `Env:` is also a PowerShell provider, and works just like a filesystem. Therefore, you could also use `Set-Location` at `Env:` and use `Get-ChildItem .` to list the variables that are available in your system.

3. To display the value of the specified environment variable, run the following command:

   ```
   PS> Get-ChildItem Env:/PATH | Select-Object value | Format-Table -Wrap
   ```

After typing `Get-ChildItem Env:/`, you can use tab completion to populate all environment variables.

4. Use `Get-Member` on the `PATH` environment variable to find its type.
5. Before changing the environment variable, list the `PATH` variable using `$env:PATH | Get-Member`. It is a string. Save the contents someplace safe.
6. Now, update the `PATH` environment variable by adding the path of the `sqlcmd` tool executable to the `$env:PATH` variable. The operation is a simple addition of a string to the existing value:

```
PS> $env:PATH = $env:PATH + ':/opt/mssql-tools/bin'
PS /root> sqlcmd
```

You could add any location to `PATH`. If you insist on getting `sqlcmd`, head over to Microsoft Docs (`https://docs.microsoft.com/en-us/sql/linux/sql-server-linux-setup-tools?view=sql-server-linux-2017`) for SQL Server 2017 for instructions to get yourself a copy.

The output of the preceding code block is illustrated in the following screenshot:

```
PS /home/prashanth> sqlcmd
Microsoft (R) SQL Server Command Line Tool
Version 17.1.0000.1 Linux
Copyright (c) 2012 Microsoft. All rights reserved.

usage: sqlcmd            [-U login id]          [-P password]
  [-S server or Dsn if -D is provided]
  [-H hostname]          [-E trusted connection]
  [-N Encrypt Connection][-C Trust Server Certificate]
  [-d use database name] [-l login timeout]     [-t query timeout]
  [-h headers]           [-s colseparator]      [-w screen width]
  [-a packetsize]        [-e echo input]        [-I Enable Quoted Identifiers]
  [-c cmdend]
  [-q "cmdline query"]   [-Q "cmdline query" and exit]
  [-m errorlevel]        [-V severitylevel]     [-W remove trailing spaces]
  [-u unicode output]    [-r[0|1] msgs to stderr]
  [-i inputfile]         [-o outputfile]
  [-k[1|2] remove[replace] control characters]
  [-y variable length type display width]
  [-Y fixed length type display width]
  [-p[1] print statistics[colon format]]
  [-R use client regional setting]
  [-K application intent]
  [-M multisubnet failover]
  [-b On error batch abort]
  [-D Dsn flag, indicate -S is Dsn]
  [-X[1] disable commands, startup script, environment variables [and exit]]
  [-x disable variable substitution]
  [-? show syntax summary]
PS /home/prashanth>
```

7. Let's exit the session, launch a new session, check the `PATH` variable, and run the `sqlcmd` executable:

```
PS> sqlcmd

sqlcmd : The term 'sqlcmd' is not recognized as the name of a
cmdlet, function, script file, or operable program.
```

How it works...

As we saw in the *Listing the various providers in PowerShell* recipe in Chapter 1, *Introducing PowerShell Core*, `Env` is a provider that contains environment-specific configuration. Most of these configuration options are also exposed to us as environment variables. We are able to use the `Get-ChildItem` and `Get-Item` cmdlets to list the values of the available environment variables because `Env:` is a drive within the `Env` provider. Since environment variables do not have child items, `Get-Item` and `Get-ChildItem` return the same output.

Since these variables determine how your session behaves with you, changes made to these values are ephemeral. In other words, the value of `$env:PATH` is picked from the configuration on your Linux computer. The manual change made to `$env:PATH` that's made within a PowerShell session remains as long as the PowerShell session is alive. Changes made to `$env:PATH` do not change the value within the system itself.

If you would like to make a certain change permanent, edit the `.bashrc` or `~/.bash_profile` configuration files. If you would like to use PowerShell instead of Bash, make the change in your PowerShell profile. Instructions on how to do that can be found in the *Enabling automated execution of commands for each load* recipe in Chapter 2, *Preparing for Administration Using PowerShell*.

There's more...

You can also access environment variables by using a .NET type accelerator and its methods, like so:

```
PS> [environment]::GetEnvironmentVariable("PATH")
```

See also

- About environment variables: `Get-Help about_Environment_Variables`
- The *Listing the various providers in PowerShell* in `Chapter 1`, *Introducing PowerShell Core*
- The *Enabling the automated execution of commands for each load* recipe in `Chapter 2`, *Preparing for Administration Using PowerShell*

Storing the output of an instance of a .NET Core object

.NET is object-oriented, and works on classes and objects. PowerShell, being an extension of this framework, allows you to work with the .NET framework and COM interfaces so that you can perform many system administration tasks. This way, you are not limited to the tasks that can be performed using cmdlets.

In this recipe, we will define a simple class from within PowerShell.

Getting ready

We recommend using Visual Studio Code for this recipe. To find out how to install and configure it, visit the *Installing Visual Studio Code* recipe in `Chapter 2`, *Preparing for Administration Using PowerShell*.

How to do it...

Launch Visual Studio Code and address any immediate requirements it asks for. Then, follow these steps to get started:

1. Open a new file in Visual Studio Code and set the file type as PowerShell.
2. Type in the following in the script pane. The file does not have to be saved; execute it using the *F5* key to make it available in PowerShell:

```
class Person {
    [string]$Name
    [Int32]$Age
    [int32]$Salary
    Person () {}
```

```
        Person ([string]$Name, [int32]$Age) {
            $this.Name = $Name
            $this.Age = $Age
        }
        [int32] sal ([int32]$Salary, [int32]$Comm) {
            return $Salary * $Comm
        }
    }
```

2. To find the constructors of a class, call the static method `New`; type in the
   following at the prompt:

   PS> [Person]::New

3. This gives us two functions of the same name; these are overload definitions.
   Now, create a new object by passing in the parameters:

   PS> [Person]::New('Prashanth',34)

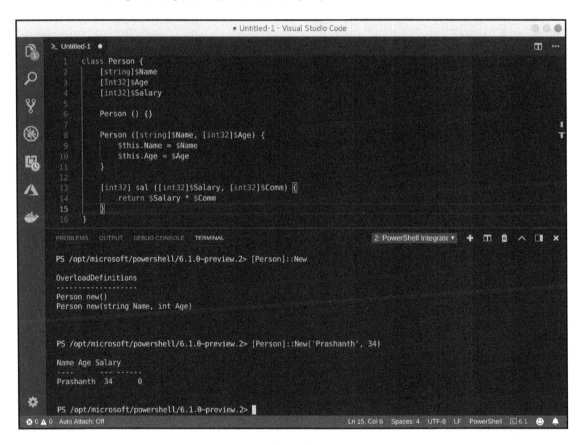

3. Now, let us invoke the constructor the PowerShell way, which in turn calls the .NET constructor. This creates an instance of the `Person` class (which, by definition, is an object):

```
PS> $Person = New-Object -TypeName Person -ArgumentList
'Prashanth', 34
```

4. To list the properties of the object (and by extension, the class), run the `Get-Member` cmdlet:

```
PS> $Person | Get-Member

PS> $Person | Select-Object Name, Age, Salary | Format-Table -
AutoSize

PS> $Person.sal(200,2)
```

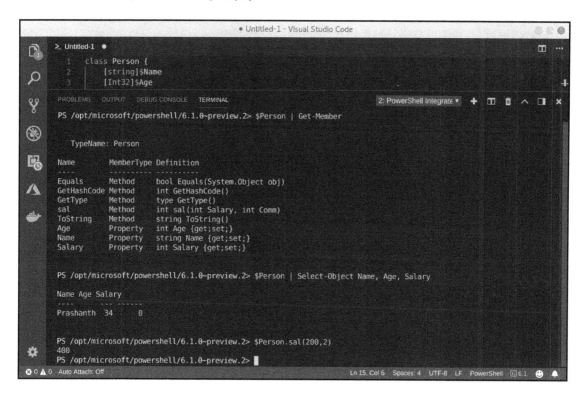

5. Next, let's take a look at the other samples. Let's use the `system-defined` class libraries:

```
PS> $MailClient = New-Object -TypeName System.Net.Mail.SmtpClient
'packtpub.smtpdomain.com'
PS> $Message = New-Object
System.Net.Mail.MailMessage('pjayaram@packtpub.com',
'pjayaram@packtpub.com', 'Subject', 'Welcome to Packt!')
PS> $MailClient.Send($Message)
```

6. Let's look at another example of password encryption by using `System.Management.Automation` class objects:

```
PS> $User = 'Prashanth'
PS> $Password = 'Y94b^E$85CBLU%at'
PS> $SecurePassword = ConvertTo-SecureString $Password -AsPlainText
-Force
PS> $Credentials = New-Object -TypeName
System.Management.Automation.PSCredential -ArgumentList $User,
$SecurePassword
PS> $Credentials | Get-Member
```

```
PS /home/prashanth> $User = 'Prashanth'
PS /home/prashanth> $Password = 'Y94b^E$85CBLU%at'
PS /home/prashanth> $SecurePassword = ConvertTo-SecureString $Password -AsPlainText -Force
PS /home/prashanth> $Credentials = New-Object -TypeName System.Management.Automation.PSCredential -ArgumentLis
t $User, $SecurePassword
PS /home/prashanth> $Credentials | Get-Member


   TypeName: System.Management.Automation.PSCredential

Name                 MemberType Definition
----                 ---------- ----------
Equals               Method     bool Equals(System.Object obj)
GetHashCode          Method     int GetHashCode()
GetNetworkCredential Method     System.Net.NetworkCredential GetNetworkCredential()
GetObjectData        Method     void GetObjectData(System.Runtime.Serialization.SerializationInfo info, Sy...
GetType              Method     type GetType()
ToString             Method     string ToString()
Password             Property   securestring Password {get;}
UserName             Property   string UserName {get;}

PS /home/prashanth>
```

How it works...

The goal of this recipe is to demonstrate how PowerShell works hand-in-hand with .NET, and to show you that objects that are created the .NET way can be called (and stored) easily in PowerShell. First, we declare a class with the `class` keyword. We then declare its parameters, and then create two constructors: one default and one that's parameterized.

We also create a method called `sal`. We define its return type as `int32`, and define two parameters. Within it, we define what needs to be returned.

Back at the PowerShell prompt, we call the static (method of the class, not of an object) `New` method. The syntax is to mention the class name, followed by two consecutive colons (`::`) to call it in the global namespace, followed by the name of the method.

If you follow these steps, you'll also see an example of using the two different system class libraries, `System.Net.Mail.SmtpClient` and `System.Net.Mail.MailMessage`, and the instantiation of a method by integrating the output of `mail-message` with the `SMTP-client` object.

Next, we use the system class library `System.Management.Automation.PSCredential`. In this example, we send some text to `ConvertTo-SecureString`, which takes input as plain text and converts it into a secure string. Then, we pass the encrypted string to the `PSCrendital` system class to store the username and the secure string in the `$Credentials` variable.

See also

- The *Installing Visual Studio Code* recipe in `Chapter 2`, *Preparing for Administration Using PowerShell*

Adding custom properties to an object

PowerShell cmdlets are capable of allowing administrators to work with most tasks. However, there are some situations where the returned objects don't satisfy the administrative needs of a certain script. In such situations, we may need to create our own custom objects based on the available .NET classes, or at least, add a custom property to the object.

While a string is an object of the `System.String` type, the `Get-Process` cmdlet returns an object of type `System.Diagnostics.Process`, `Get-ChildItem` returns an object with the type `System.IO.FileInfo`, and a custom-created object has the object type `PSCustomObject`.

How to do it...

Now, let's proceed and create a custom object:

1. To create a custom object, use the `New-Object` cmdlet:

   ```
   PS /home/PacktPub> New-Object -TypeName PSCustomObject
   ```

2. That was not of much use to us. Let's add a few properties into it, along with their values, and store these values in a variable:

   ```
   PS> $MyCustomObject = [pscustomobject]@{
     Name = 'Prashanth Jayaram'
     Title = 'PowerShell'
     Publisher = 'Packt'
   }

   PS> $MyCustomObject
   ```

4. To add properties to an object, use the `Add-Member` cmdlet:

   ```
   PS> $MyCustomObject | Add-Member -MemberType NoteProperty -Name
   'Location' -Value 'United States'
   PS> $MyCustomObject
   ```

5. To remove a property from an object, use the following command:

   ```
   PS> $MyCustomObject.PsObject.Properties.Remove('Location')

   PS> # To see if the property is still available, run:
   PS> $MyCustomObject.Location
   ```

6. To access properties, you can use the member access operator (.):

```
PS> $MyCustomObject.Name
Prashanth Jayaram

PS> $MyCustomObject.Title
PowerShell

PS> $MyCustomObject.Publisher
Packt
```

How it works...

Creating an object is straightforward. All you have to do is tell PowerShell that you are creating a custom object by calling the [psobject] accelerator and specifying the properties you would like to add to the object. After the accelerator is called, we specify the names of the properties, and assign values to them. Records are added one at a time using the hash literal notation (Name = 'Prashanth').

 It is easy to confuse a hashtable with a PSObject at this stage, given that we use the hash literal notation when creating the object. Remember that they are very different from each other. We will get into the details of what a hashtable is in Chapter 9, *Using Arrays and Hashtables*.

We mention three properties in the custom object we have created: Name, Title, and Publisher. If we would like to add additional properties in the future, we can simply use the Add-Member cmdlet, where we specify the object (we pass the object through the pipeline), and the name of the property, and assign a value to it.

Removing a property is a little more complex, since we do not have a Remove-Member cmdlet, nor are the members we use in the step easily discoverable. For instance, [PSCustomObject] | Get-Member does not reveal PsObject as being its member. We call the Remove method within the Properties object, which is within the PSObject object of the custom object we created. (So many objects!)

Accessing properties in an object is as simple as using the member access operator with the property name.

Remember, this object definition will exist as long as your PowerShell session is alive.

See also

- The *Creating and initializing a simple hashtable* recipe in `Chapter 9`, *Using Arrays and Hashtables*

Creating a custom object from a returned object

We now know how to create a custom object from scratch. In this recipe, we will use a returned object and modify the returned object to create a custom object. When we look at loops, we will extend this capability to create versatile custom objects; in production environments, this capability can be used to do more!

How to do it...

The first step to learning something is to simplify it. Therefore, we will select only one instance of an object and work with it. Follow these steps to get started:

1. Get all of the processes. Select only the name, ID, working set, and the start time, pick the fifth process in the list, and assign it to a variable:

```
PS> $Process = (Get-Process | Select-Object Name, Id, WS,
StartTime) [4]
```

2. Let's say that we did not like the names of the properties in the object. Let's change the names:

```
PS> $CustomProcess = New-Object -TypeName PSObject -Property @{
    ProcessName = $Process.Name
    ProcessId = $Process.Id
    WorkingSet = $Process.WS
    StartedAt = $Process.StartTime
}
PS> $CustomProcess
```

```
PS /home/prashanth> $Process = (Get-Process | Select-Object Name, Id, WS, StartTime)[4]
PS /home/prashanth> $CustomProcess = New-Object -TypeName PSObject -Property @{
>>    ProcessName = $Process.Name
>>    ProcessId = $Process.Id
>>    WorkingSet = $Process.WS
>>    StartedAt = $Process.StartTime
>> }
PS /home/prashanth> $CustomProcess

ProcessName      StartedAt ProcessId WorkingSet
-----------      --------- --------- ----------
accounts-daemon 11/07/18 1:54:15 pm       845    4235264

PS /home/prashanth>
```

3. However, that is not the sequence we specified. Let's get them in sequence:

```
PS> $CustomProcess = [ordered]@{
  ProcessName = $Process.Name
  ProcessId = $Process.Id
  WorkingSet = $Process.WS
  StartedAt = $Process.StartTime
}
PS> New-Object -TypeName PSObject -Property $CustomProcess
```

```
PS /home/prashanth> $CustomProcess = [ordered]@{
>>    ProcessName = $Process.Name
>>    ProcessId = $Process.Id
>>    WorkingSet = $Process.WS
>>    StartedAt = $Process.StartTime
>> }
PS /home/prashanth> New-Object -TypeName PSObject -Property $CustomProcess

ProcessName      ProcessId WorkingSet StartedAt
-----------      --------- ---------- ---------
accounts-daemon        845    4235264 11/07/18 1:54:15 pm

PS /home/prashanth>
```

4. Recreate the object with information regarding how long the process has been running for instead of when it was started:

```
PS> $CustomProcess = [ordered]@{
  ProcessName = $Process.Name
  ProcessId = $Process.Id
  WorkingSet = $Process.WS
  RunningMins = [math]::Floor(((Get-Date) -
$Process.StartTime).TotalMinutes)
  }
PS> New-Object -TypeName PsObject -Property $CustomProcess
```

```
PS /home/prashanth> $CustomProcess = [ordered]@{
>>     ProcessName = $Process.Name
>>     ProcessId = $Process.Id
>>     WorkingSet = $Process.WS
>>     RunningMins = [math]::Floor(((Get-Date) - $Process.StartTime).TotalMinutes)
>> }
PS /home/prashanth> New-Object -TypeName PsObject -Property $CustomProcess

ProcessName ProcessId WorkingSet RunningMins
----------- --------- ---------- -----------
accounts-daemon       845   4235264          14


PS /home/prashanth>
```

How it works...

In this recipe, we created a custom object ($CustomProcess) from an output object ($Process). The properties within $Process can be accessed using the member access operator. Values from $Process are treated as values for the properties in $CustomObject, however, the names in $CustomObject are different. In this recipe, we also used a calculated property, RunningMins.

An important point to note here is that the outcome of this recipe can also be achieved using calculated properties, along with Select-Object. However, in situations where object versatility is important and the number of instances of the objects is significantly larger, it is simpler to use a custom object. We will extend this capability in future chapters, after we learn how to use looping constructs.

The other point to note is the use of the `[ordered]` accelerator. More often than not, the properties of custom objects do not appear in the sequence we mention them in. In this recipe, we separate the hash literal notation from the creation of the custom object. First, we create an ordered hashtable with the property names, as well as the property values, and then we specify the created hashtable for the `Property` parameter of the `New-Object` cmdlet to create the custom object with the properties, which are shown in the sequence we want.

As with the previous recipe, the changes made to this object definition will exist as long as your PowerShell session is alive.

See also

- Creating .NET and COM Objects (`https://docs.microsoft.com/en-us/powershell/scripting/getting-started/cookbooks/creating-.net-and-com-objects--new-object-?view=powershell-6`)

Understanding the extension of type data

In the *Selecting columns from the output* recipe in `Chapter 4`, *Passing Data through the Pipeline*, we used a hashtable to set the name and the expression for a custom-named column. Later, we also used a small calculation within the `Select-Object` statement to get a calculated output. If you tried to select the column by the new name, that would have worked, too. Technically, you have already extended the object. But what is type data anyway? And why do we need a recipe to extend it when we can work with `Select-Object`?

Going too deep into what type data is and how to work with it, along with .NET classes and objects, could potentially make this concept an advanced one. Historically, most of us learners have put off learning advanced topics. Therefore, we will stick to the simple parts of it, and work only with PowerShell for now. This recipe will serve as a launchpad to help you understand what it is by making it simple and fun, keeping it away from anything advanced, in the interest of learning.

There are two options to extend the type data:

- Using PowerShell cmdlets (to understand how it all works)
- Using an XML file (for portability)

Getting ready

To understand what we are talking about, here, you need to have read the following recipes:

- *Selecting columns from the output* from `Chapter 4`, *Passing Data through the Pipeline*
- The *Creating a custom object from a returned object* recipe

Let's come back to the question at hand: why extend type data when we can use `Select-Object`?

Efficiency. While you could change the name, add a calculation, and reference the calculated property with the new name, that change would have existed only in that context. If you added it to a variable, as in the previous recipe, *Creating a custom object from a returned object,* where we made some nifty changes to the names and also created a custom `NoteProperty`, that would be a long way to go about it. This is where the extension of type data comes in.

The rule of the thumb is, if you do something repetitively, there's an issue: you haven't considered automating it. For example, if you run the following code:

```
PS> Get-ChildItem -Path . | select Name, Length, @{Name='Age';
Expression={[math]::Round(((Get-Date) - $_.LastWriteTime).TotalDays)}}
```

Instead of the following code:

```
PS> Get-ChildItem -Path . | select Name, Length, Age
```

If you do this 15 times a day, you should consider extending the object to give you what you care about.

How to do it...

Navigate to the location where you created files for lab usage:

1. Enter the following command:

```
PS> $FilesWithAge = Get-ChildItem . | Select-Object Name, Length,
LastWriteTime
```

2. Now, add a property to the `$FilesWithAge` variable; the property should be the age of each file, in days:

```
PS> $FilesWithAge | Add-Member -MemberType ScriptProperty -Name Age
-Value { [math]::Round(((Get-Date) -
$this.LastWriteTime).TotalDays) }
```

3. Add another property to it, called `ComputerName`, which is the name of your localhost:

```
PS> $ComputerName = hostname
PS> $FilesWithAge | Add-Member -MemberType NoteProperty -Name
ComputerName -Value $ComputerName
```

4. Add another property, as an alias to `LastWriteTime`, called `Modified`:

```
PS> $FilesWithAge | Add-Member -MemberType AliasProperty -Name
Modified -Value LastWriteTime
```

5. To format it so that it looks like a nice table, use the following code:

```
PS> $FilesWithAge | Format-Table -AutoSize
```

```
                                         Terminal                                    x
PS /home/ram/random> $FilesWithAge | Format-Table -AutoSize

Name                   Length  LastWriteTime        Age ComputerName Modified
----                   ------  -------------        --- ------------ --------
cities                         20/06/2018 13:15:14   20 galago       20/06/2018 13:15:14
bangalore.jpg          0       20/06/2018 13:15:14   20 galago       20/06/2018 13:15:14
coffee.jpg             211787  20/06/2018 13:24:47   20 galago       20/06/2018 13:24:47
crunched-numbers.csv   464     01/07/2018 19:59:04    9 galago       01/07/2018 19:59:04
demo.doc               0       20/06/2018 13:15:14   20 galago       20/06/2018 13:15:14
file-list.csv          1917    02/07/2018 12:14:26    8 galago       02/07/2018 12:14:26
file-list.xml          73088   02/07/2018 13:40:16    8 galago       02/07/2018 13:40:16
himalayas.jpg          0       20/06/2018 13:15:14   20 galago       20/06/2018 13:15:14
matrix-like-wm.mp4     5001938 20/06/2018 13:26:10   20 galago       20/06/2018 13:26:10
my-plugin.rb           0       20/06/2018 13:15:14   20 galago       20/06/2018 13:15:14
piratos-wowa.me.mp3    3747493 20/06/2018 13:28:42   20 galago       20/06/2018 13:28:42
random-text-1.txt      4680    01/07/2018 18:13:27    9 galago       01/07/2018 18:13:27
random-text-2.txt      4500    01/07/2018 18:14:28    9 galago       01/07/2018 18:14:28
screenshot-001.png     0       20/06/2018 13:15:14   20 galago       20/06/2018 13:15:14
screenshot-002.png     0       20/06/2018 13:15:14   20 galago       20/06/2018 13:15:14
screenshot-003.png     0       20/06/2018 13:15:14   20 galago       20/06/2018 13:15:14
volcano-copy.jpg       78954   30/06/2018 11:34:15   10 galago       30/06/2018 11:34:15
volcano.jpg            63538   20/06/2018 13:23:23   20 galago       20/06/2018 13:23:23
```

6. Now, delete the variable, and query the files within the current directory (because that is what the variable actually held):

```
PS> Remove-Variable FilesWithAge
PS> Get-ChildItem .
```

You cannot see the Age, the ComputerName, or the Modified properties. Try Get-Member, if you want.

Next, we will look at how we can extend the type data itself so that every time you run Get-ChildItem, you also get the three properties we added to the variable.

7. Let's see what object is returned when you run Get-ChildItem:

```
PS> Get-ChildItem | Get-Member
```

8. You get System.IO.DirectoryInfo, as well as System.IO.FileInfo. Now, we will pick System.IO.FileInfo. Run the following commands:

```
PS> $ComputerName = hostname

PS> Update-TypeData -TypeName System.IO.FileInfo -MemberType
NoteProperty -MemberName ComputerName -Value $ComputerName

PS> Update-TypeData -TypeName System.IO.FileInfo -MemberType
AliasProperty -MemberName Modified -Value LastWriteTime

PS> Update-TypeData -TypeName System.IO.FileInfo -MemberType
ScriptProperty -MemberName Age -Value { [math]::Round(((Get-Date) -
$this.LastWriteTime).TotalDays) }
```

9. Query the contents of the current location and, optionally, format the output so that it looks like a table:

```
PS> Get-ChildItem . | Select-Object Name, Length, ComputerName,
Age, Modified | Format-Table -AutoSize
```

```
                                      Terminal                                          ×
PS /home/ram/random> Get-ChildItem . | Select-Object Name, Length, ComputerName, Age, Modi
fied | Format-Table -AutoSize

Name                  Length ComputerName Age Modified
----                  ------ ------------ --- --------
cities
bangalore.jpg         0      galago        20  20/06/2018 13:15:14
coffee.jpg            211787 galago        20  20/06/2018 13:24:47
crunched-numbers.csv  464    galago        9   01/07/2018 19:59:04
demo.doc              0      galago        20  20/06/2018 13:15:14
file-list.csv         1917   galago        8   02/07/2018 12:14:26
file-list.xml         73088  galago        8   02/07/2018 13:40:16
himalayas.jpg         0      galago        20  20/06/2018 13:15:14
matrix-like-wm.mp4    5001938 galago       20  20/06/2018 13:26:10
my-plugin.rb          0      galago        20  20/06/2018 13:15:14
piratos-wowa.me.mp3   3747493 galago       20  20/06/2018 13:28:42
random-text-1.txt     4680   galago        9   01/07/2018 18:13:27
random-text-2.txt     4500   galago        9   01/07/2018 18:14:28
screenshot-001.png    0      galago        20  20/06/2018 13:15:14
screenshot-002.png    0      galago        20  20/06/2018 13:15:14
screenshot-003.png    0      galago        20  20/06/2018 13:15:14
volcano-copy.jpg      78954  galago        10  30/06/2018 11:34:15
volcano.jpg           63538  galago        20  20/06/2018 13:23:23
```

10. Do the same for any directory in the filesystem, with the only condition being that the directory should contain at least one file, and not just more directories:

```
PS> Get-ChildItem ./cities/ | Select-Object Name, Length,
ComputerName, Age, Modified | Format-Table –AutoSize
```

How it works...

In the first section, we added members to the objects within a certain variable. This was a command-line-prompt-style extension to the *Creating a custom object from a returned object* recipe, which was, by all means, a little more efficient in the context. However, the changes we made to the object remained only while the $FilesWithAge variable was valid. The object returned by Get-ChildItem was not modified at all.

There is an important point to note here: $this. We have come across the automatic variable, $_ (or $PSItem, after PowerShell V3) when dealing with objects passed through the pipeline; this variable holds the current instance of the object in the pipeline. However, when we have to perform an object extension, we use the automatic variable, $this. Why? Because the property being referred to is being referred within the parent object (the object returned by Get-ChildItem). External methods would be able to use $_. In a way, $_ does not even exist yet when performing member addition. Also, $this, in fact, refers to the object itself, which is returned by Get-ChildItem, and not just an instance of it.

When we would like to get a member as part of the object itself throughout the session, irrespective of the validity of a certain variable or the object instance, we extend the type data itself. Therefore, no matter what context you run the cmdlet in, you would get the additional members you added. Of course, the formatting rules in PowerShell may still not let those members appear in the output by default. You can always call the specific members, though, such as using Select-Object for properties, or simply using the member access operator on the properties: (Get-ChildItem .).Age.

For this, we use the Update-TypeData cmdlet. Update-TypeData, in this context, requires the TypeName, which, as we have already seen, can be determined using Get-Member on the returned object.

We mentioned four things in the Update-TypeData statements:

- The type name
- The member type
- The member name
- The member value

The member type accepts several values, of which we use three:

1. AliasProperty, which is simply a reference to another member within the object. The new property is just another name of an existing property. Therefore, the Value parameter can just take the name of the existing member.
2. NoteProperty, which is a static value. In our case, we can use the hostname as the static value.
3. ScriptProperty, which is essentially a calculation. We calculate the time span between the date when it was last modified and the current date. This calculation is the Value for the member, and accepts a script block.

This modification to the object will be valid as long as the session is valid; the change is not persistent across sessions. That brings us to the next recipe, where we will be making object modifications stick across sessions.

See also

- The *Selecting columns from the output* recipe in `Chapter 4`, *Passing Data through the Pipeline*

Retaining object modifications across sessions

In the previous recipe, *Understanding the extension of type data*, we used the `Update-TypeData` cmdlet to add members. However, we said that the update was valid as long as the session was. Now, there are two ways by which we could make the type data stick across sessions:

- Using the PowerShell profile
- Using an XML file

The PowerShell profile is straightforward. However, usually, the type data extension and formatting rules are packaged as part of PowerShell modules, and adding code to the profile is not particularly helpful in that case. In this recipe, we will write a simple XML (`.ps1xml`) file that we will load so that we can extend the type data.

Getting ready

Restart your PowerShell session so that the custom data type extension is discarded.

How to do it...

We need an XML file. You can either use the `New-Item` cmdlet to create one, or simply use your favorite text editor. We will use Visual Studio Code for this recipe. Follow these steps to get started:

1. Open your text editor and create a new empty file, and save it as `CustomTypes.ps1xml`.

2. Add the following content to the XML file. Ensure that you don't change the case:

```xml
<?xml version="1.0" encoding="utf-8" ?>
<Types>
 <Type>
   <Name>System.IO.FileInfo</Name>
   <Members>
     <AliasProperty>
       <Name>Modified</Name>
       <ReferencedMemberName>LastWriteTime</ReferencedMemberName>
     </AliasProperty>
     <ScriptProperty>
       <Name>Age</Name>
       <GetScriptBlock>[math]::Round(((Get-Date) -
$this.LastWriteTime).TotalDays)</GetScriptBlock>
     </ScriptProperty>
     <NoteProperty>
       <Name>ItemType</Name>
       <Value>File</Value>
     </NoteProperty>
   </Members>
 </Type>
</Types>
```

3. Save the file at a convenient location.

4. Back at the terminal (or the **PowerShell Integrated Console**), enter the following command to update the type data using the XML. Note the `PrependPath` parameter:

```
PS> Update-TypeData -PrependPath
~/Documents/code/github/powershell/ch05/CustomTypes.ps1xml
```

5. Now, list out all the files within any directory of your choice:

```
PS> Get-ChildItem . -File | Select-Object Name, Length, Age,
Modified
```

You should see the new properties that you created:

```
                                        Terminal                                    ⊗
PS /home/ram/random> Get-ChildItem . -File | Select-Object Name, Length, Age, Modified

Name                  Length Age Modified
----                  ------ --- --------
bangalore.jpg              0  21 20/06/2018 13:15:14
coffee.jpg            211787  21 20/06/2018 13:24:47
crunched-numbers.csv     464  10 01/07/2018 19:59:04
demo.doc                   0  21 20/06/2018 13:15:14
file-list.csv           1917   9 02/07/2018 12:14:26
file-list.xml          73088   9 02/07/2018 13:40:16
himalayas.jpg              0  21 20/06/2018 13:15:14
matrix-like-wm.mp4   5001938  21 20/06/2018 13:26:10
my-plugin.rb               0  21 20/06/2018 13:15:14
```

 It is advised that you never modify the PS1XML files in the $PSHome directory. They are digitally signed by Microsoft and could be replaced with new versions during upgrades or patches.

How it works...

Custom types and formats are mostly used while creating custom modules. Rarely do administrators need to modify the types or formats for stock PowerShell modules. When you do need to modify custom types or formats, create a new PS1XML; do not modify the stock files, since they are digitally signed, and modifying them would break your setup.

Think of this PS1XML file as a regular XML file. Here is a simpler way of showing the structure. Remember that each type and each of the members within must have a name:

```
Types
-- Type
---- Members
------ [The custom properties and methods you define]
```

In essence, using the XML for type extension is not very different from how we performed type extension in the previous recipe, except this uses an XML file, which makes the setup more portable. When we work on creating our custom modules, we will look at packaging the types along with the modules, and, at that time, we will look in at how to work the paths in detail. For now, we load the XML by manually specifying the exact path to the file. If you would like to load these custom types for every session of yours, you can easily call the PS1XML file from your profile. The portability aspect here is that the XML can easily be shared or deployed; only the loading would be manual, or would be done through the profile—much simpler than adding cmdlets to profiles.

When updating the type data using cmdlets, we used the `Name` and `Value` parameters, along with the `MemberType` parameter. PowerShell understood the context and set up the types accordingly. In the case of XML, though, you must remember to use the correct tags for each of the member types. For instance, for `AliasProperty`, the tags within should be `Name` and `ReferencedMemberName` (as in the following code); for `ScriptProperty`, they should be `Name` and `GetScriptBlock`; for `NoteProperty`, the tags should be `Name` and `Value`:

```
<AliasProperty>
    <Name>Modified</Name>
    <ReferencedMemberName>LastWriteTime</ReferencedMemberName>
</AliasProperty>
```

Also, remember not to enclose the entire script block in braces when placing the statement within the `GetScriptBlock` tag:

```
<GetScriptBlock>
  [math]::Round(((Get-Date) - $this.LastWriteTime).TotalDays)
</GetScriptBlock>
```

Do not do this:

```
<GetScriptBlock>
  { [math]::Round(((Get-Date) - $this.LastWriteTime).TotalDays) }
</GetScriptBlock>
```

When loading the XML, we use the `PrependPath` parameter to load our XML before the built-in types are loaded. To load them after the built-in types, there is no need to use the `AppendPath` parameter, unless the situation really needs it, since `AppendPath` is the default. Why do the parameters matter? They determine the precedence of loading the types.

The XML file shown may look like having a large number of items. Use the indent guide in Visual Studio Code to guide you through reading the XML. The file, in reality, is very simple to read. Reading it will help you understand how the properties are defined.

See also

- The Update-TypeData cmdlet (https://docs.microsoft.com/en-us/powershell/module/microsoft.powershell.utility/update-typedata?view=powershell-6)
- The Types.ps1xml file (https://docs.microsoft.com/en-us/powershell/module/microsoft.powershell.core/about/about_types.ps1xml?view=powershell-6)

Removing custom type data

Now that we know how to create and update type data, the next step for us is to learn how to remove the type data. Removing the type data requires us to get the type data first. In this recipe, we will learn about the process of removing type data, whether it was updated using cmdlets or an XML file.

How to do it...

The first step is to understand that a cmdlet can output one or more types of objects. For instance, in our case, Get-ChildItem will output System.IO.DirectoryInfo, as well as System.IO.FileInfo. Let's learn how to work with these:

1. Get the type of the object returned by the cmdlet:

   ```
   PS> Get-ChildItem | Get-Member | Select-Object TypeName -Unique
   ```

2. Two types are returned. We created the custom members in the second type. Assign this to a variable:

   ```
   PS> $TypeData = Get-ChildItem | Get-Member | Select-Object -ExpandProperty TypeName -Unique -Last 1
   ```

3. Get the type data information. Expand its members to see if the custom members are shown:

```
PS> Get-TypeData -TypeName $TypeData | Select-Object -
ExpandProperty Members
```

The output shows Age as one of the members:

```
                                  Terminal                                  ⊗
PS /home/ram/random> Get-TypeData -TypeName $TypeData | Select-Object -ExpandProperty Memb
ers

Key          Value
---          -----
Mode         System.Management.Automation.Runspaces.CodePropertyData
VersionInfo  System.Management.Automation.Runspaces.ScriptPropertyData
BaseName     System.Management.Automation.Runspaces.ScriptPropertyData
Target       System.Management.Automation.Runspaces.CodePropertyData
LinkType     System.Management.Automation.Runspaces.CodePropertyData
Modified     System.Management.Automation.Runspaces.AliasPropertyData
Age          System.Management.Automation.Runspaces.ScriptPropertyData
```

4. Now, remove the type data:

```
PS> Remove-TypeData -TypeName $TypeData
```

How it works...

The process is straightforward. If you query the help information for the TypeName parameter of Remove-TypeData, you will notice that it accepts the type name input via the pipeline by property value as well as the property name. Recall the *Understanding pipeline-enabled parameters* recipe from Chapter 4, *Passing Data through the Pipeline*, and look at the object returned by Get-TypeData for more insight.

The Remove-TypeData cmdlet removes the type data from the current session. This removal is as ephemeral as type addition is. Therefore, the default types and formats are not permanently removed by the cmdlet; this is the reason why you can run this within PowerShell, without administrator privileges. Also, remember that the underlying XML files are not deleted either: they are custom or stock.

See also

- The *Understanding pipeline-enabled parameters* recipe from `Chapter 4`, *Passing Data through the Pipeline*

Understanding variables

That concludes this chapter. It is time to take a break so that you can assimilate what you have learned. Later, experiment with different data types, create variables, see what type of objects they contain, and what members each object contains. We did not explicitly talk much about variables in this chapter, other than environment variables, but we used variables in almost every recipe. Ponder over (or, better yet, practically try out) these questions:

1. What can be assigned to a variable?
2. What does the variable contain—the entire object?
3. Can I refer to one single property of the object that a variable contains, if it contains the entire object?
4. Can I assign a certain member and not the entire object to a variable?
5. What if the member is a whole object in itself? (Hint: use `Get-Member` on the variable to find out.)
6. What happens when I use `Select-Object` with `-ExpandProperty` and assign the value to a variable? What type is the variable then?

Finding out the answers to these questions will help you understand more about the variables, now that you have used them so much.

6
Working with Strings

In this chapter, we will cover the following recipes:

- Creating a literal string
- Creating an expanding string
- Understanding Here-Strings
- Using basic string methods
- Performing string matching operations
- Replacing substrings with strings
- Splitting and combining strings
- Using the formatting operator

Introduction

Over the last few chapters, we attempted to build a foundational understanding of how PowerShell works. In this chapter, we turn from the taxiway to the runway. Starting with this chapter, we will work with the recipes much faster, given that we have set the foundation in understanding and using PowerShell already.

Before we go any further, the one thing that is left before we push the throttle levers is knowing about the operators we are going to be using. So, here is an overview of them before we jump into the recipes. Over the next few recipes (and possibly a couple of chapters), we will try to use each of these operators in our operations.

Operators are something we have all already studied at some point or another. Operators in PowerShell can be classified into the following nine categories:

1. Arithmetic operators
2. Assignment operators
3. Comparison operators

4. Logical operators
5. Redirection operators
6. Split and Join operators
7. Type operators
8. Unary operators
9. Special operators

Instead of going into too much theory, run the following code to see how the operators work. This should be enough to introduce us to the functionality of operators. We will put them to real use in the upcoming recipes. Here is a general explanation for each of the operators.

Arithmetic operators perform arithmetic operators such as addition and division. In PowerShell, we use them in the same way that they are used in mathematics. These operators work on two or more operands. Therefore, to add two numbers in PowerShell, you would do the following:

```
PS> 5 + 71
```

Assignment operators assign values from their right to the operand to their left, either directly (=) or after a modification (+=):

```
PS> $Number = 5
PS> $Number += 71
```

Comparison operators compare two operands and return a Boolean output. In most languages, we use > for greater than and == for equals. In PowerShell, they have been abbreviated, and are used along with a hyphen, as follows:

- > is denoted as -gt
- >= is denoted as -ge
- != is denoted as -ne

To check if 5 is greater than 2 in PowerShell, run the following code:

```
PS> 5 -gt 2
```

 In PowerShell, we use the automatic variables $true and $false to indicate TRUE and FALSE, respectively. This is the recommended approach as opposed to using 1 and 0 to mean TRUE and FALSE.

There are other comparison operators in PowerShell, apart from the regular logical comparison operators we are used to in other languages. Two examples are -match and -like. (Their inverses are -notmatch and -notlike.) They have case-sensitive variants as well, such as -cmatch and -cnotlike. By default, matching operations in PowerShell are case-insensitive. However, if you would still like to explicitly make an operation case-insensitive, you could use the -imatch or -inotlike operators. Here are a few examples:

```
PS> 'Hello world!' -like '*world*'

PS> 'Hello world!' -cmatch 'world' # Notice the absence of wildcards.
```

Bitwise operators (such as -bor and -band) fall under this category as well.

Another important subclass is regarding Containment operators. They look for elements within an array, like so:

```
PS> 'Hello', 'world', 'is', 'a', 'great', 'phrase' -contains 'world'
```

PowerShell supports logical operators as well. A few examples are -and, -or, -nand, and -xor.

Redirection operators redirect output to other streams or files. The operators are very similar to what we are used to in Bash. A couple of examples are > (which sends the output to the file and overwrites the content if the file had any) and >> (which appends the output to the specified file).

Split and Join operators (surprise!) split strings and join substrings. PowerShell rocks -split '' would give you two elements, PowerShell and Rocks; the space would be used up in the split.

There are two type operators in PowerShell:

- -is verifies if a certain object is of the specified type
- -as tries to change the object to the specified type

A cast operator performs an action similar to -as:

```
PS> ('13 July 2018' -as [datetime])
PS> ([datetime]'13 July 2018')
```

These convert the object type and also let us use the member properties and methods of the resultant object type. Pipe these to Get-Member to see if the object type has been modified.

Unary operators are operators such as ++ and --, which work on a single operand.

An array subexpression operator—denoted by @()—initializes an array. Let's take an example of a pangram:

```
PS> # Create an array of strings and add them to a variable.
PS> 'a', 'quick', 'brown', 'fox', 'jumps', 'over', 'the', 'lazy', 'dog' |
ForEach-Object { $Pangram += $PSItem }
PS> $Pangram # Call the variable
```

As you can see, the entire chunk of text came out as a single element, aquickbrownfoxjumpsoverthelazydog. To initialize $Pangram as an array instead, we can use the Array Subexpression Operator like so:

```
PS> $Pangram = @() # Initialize $Pangram as an array
PS> 'a', 'quick', 'brown', 'fox', 'jumps', 'over', 'the', 'lazy', 'dog' |
ForEach-Object { $Pangram += $PSItem }
PS> $Pangram # Call the variable
```

Alternatively, we can leverage the comma operator:

```
PS> Remove-Variable Pangram # Delete the variable
PS> 'a', 'quick', 'brown', 'fox', 'jumps', 'over', 'the', 'lazy', 'dog' |
ForEach-Object { $Pangram += , $PSItem }
PS> $Pangram # Call the variable
```

To call a specific element from an array, use the index operator. To fetch the third word from the $Pangram array, use the following command:

```
PS> $Pangram[2]
```

A subexpression operator—denoted by $()—makes PowerShell execute the subexpression (the expression within the parentheses following the $) first, and then the rest of the expression. For instance, to see what time it would be six hours from now, and display the same within a string, we would use the following expression:

```
PS> "Six hours from now, it would be $((Get-Date).AddHours(6))."
```

Here, (Get-Date).AddHours(6) was executed first, and then it was shown as part of the string we specified.

The range operator—denoted by ..—creates an array with the elements specified, within the range specified. To create an array of numbers from 43 to 67, use the following code:

```
PS> 43..67
```

Also, try `[char]97..[char]106` to get all of the ASCII characters within the range.

Special operators are operators such as the dot-sourcing operator, the member access operator, the call operator, the formatting operator, the pipeline operator, and so on. We have already used the dot-sourcing operator and the member access operator (both: `.`), the call operator (`&`), and the pipeline operator (`|`). We will cover the formatting operator (`-f`) in our recipes in this chapter.

Run `Get-Help about_Operators` with or without `-Online` to find out more.

Creating a literal string

Text is something we instantly relate to. Having a textual representation of the world around us is arguably the most important invention of man. It is the same with modern computers as well—we started with textual programming and a text-based interface. Most programming today happens using text.

Closely related are strings. Bash is all string. Linux administration, so far, has been all string. Now, there is PowerShell. Is everything changing? No; PowerShell lets us work with strings just like the other shells do. There are some constraints with PowerShell, but those can be easily addressed using .NET accelerators related to strings. These are advanced concepts and rare scenarios, and, therefore, nothing to worry about.

How to do it...

In this recipe, we will create a simple literal string. Is there a non-literal string? Yes, but we'll look at that one in the next recipe. Follow these steps to complete this recipe:

1. Open a Terminal window and launch PowerShell on it.
2. Enter the following code to get the object type:

```
PS> 'I am a string.' | Get-Member | Select-Object TypeName -Unique
```

3. What if you wanted to use a contraction for I am?

```
PS> 'I'm a string.'
```

4. PowerShell waits for a prompt. Enter another single quote and press the *Enter* key.

You should receive an error that there was an unexpected token.

5. Enter two quotes for the contraction instead of one, like so:

```
PS> 'I''m a string.'
```

6. Now, try to show the value of your home directory within the string:

```
PS> 'I''m a string, and the home directory I''ve been asked to show
is $HOME.'
```

7. This did not show you the path to your home directory. Is it possible to force a line break?

```
PS> 'I''m a string.`nI love showing up on the screen.'
```

How it works...

We saw three things in this recipe. We simply put some text between two single quotes and the text echoed. There was no need for a cmdlet. Second, to show a quote within a literal string, you add two quotes. This instructs PowerShell that the quotation mark is part of the string. Third, variables and escape characters appear as they are when included within a literal string.

The `n is a line break. In Bash (and possibly many other programming languages as well), we are used to using \n for a line break. PowerShell uses ` as the escape character, just like .NET. PowerShell was created with system administrators in mind. While Unix-like operating systems use / as the separator in paths, Windows uses \. .NET and PowerShell use ` (the backtick) to avoid confusion.

Creating an expanding string

In the previous recipe, we created a really simple literal (or non-expanding) string. A literal string shows everything specified, as it is. An expanding string, on the other hand, is a little different.

In this recipe, we will create expanding strings. In the process, we will probably take this exercise up a notch.

Getting ready

Query the list of directories under your lab directory. If you have not already, clone the Git repository that accompanies this book and use the quick-and-dirty `Initialize-PacktPs6CoreLinuxLab.ps1` script under the `ch04` directory. Run the script to get the necessary files. If not, specify the path to any directory that has files, like so:

```
PS> $Random = Get-ChildItem -Path $HOME\random
```

How to do it...

Let's try to achieve the same thing as in the previous recipe, but use double quotes this time in place of single quotes. Follow these steps to complete this recipe:

1. Enter the following code to get the object type:

   ```
   PS> "I am a string." | Get-Member | Select-Object TypeName -Unique
   ```

2. What if you wanted to use a contraction for I am?

   ```
   PS> "I'm a string."
   ```

3. That worked without a problem, but what if you wanted to add double quotes within double quotes?

   ```
   PS> "I'm a string, and I'm currently being "double-quote"
   challenged"
   ```

   Here is what this looks like:

4. Correct, even the colors did not look right. Try the same syntax that you did in the previous recipe:

   ```
   PS> "I'm a string, and I'm currently being ""double-quote""
   challenged"
   ```

5. The colors changed, and it all works well. But wait a minute, we discussed something about the escape character. Would it work here?

```
PS> "I'm a string, and I'm currently being `"double-quote`"
challenged"
```

6. Now, try to show the value of your home directory within the string:

```
PS> "I'm a string, and the home directory I've been asked to show
is $HOME."
```

Note how $HOME was replaced by the actual path:

7. What about a line break?

```
PS> "I'm a string.`nI love showing up on the screen."
```

Here is what you get:

8. What if we wanted to show the paths within directories, from within a string?

```
PS> "The files and directories under random are:`n$Random"
```

9. Try to get the full path of each of those files:

```
PS> "The files and directories under random are:`n$Random.FullName"
```

The .`FullName` was simply added to the output text:

```
                               Terminal                                 ⊗
PS /home/ram> "The files and directories under random are:`n$Random.FullName"
The files and directories under random are:
cities bangalore.jpg coffee.jpg crunched-numbers.csv demo.doc file-list.csv file-list.xml
himalayas.jpg matrix-like-wm.mp4 my-plugin.rb new-dir-paths.txt piratos-wowa.me.mp3 random
-text-1.txt random-text-2.txt random-text.txt screenshot-001.png screenshot-002.png screen
shot-003.png volcano-copy.jpg volcano.jpg.FullName
PS /home/ram> []
```

10. Let's try the subexpression operator; enclose $Random.FullName within $():

    ```
    PS> "The files and directories under random
    are:`n$($Random.FullName)"
    ```

11. Let's try to add two strings:

    ```
    PS> "I'm a string. " + "I love showing up on the screen."
    ```

There we have it; our recipe.

How it works...

Here are our observations:

- The object type did not change when using double quotes.
- Two double quotes made PowerShell show double quotes within the string.
- The variable was expanded, and the path to the home directory was shown. This is important.
- Escape sequences worked.
- The names of the files in the random directory were shown. Only the filenames were shown, and the names were separated by spaces.
- The full path was not shown.

The strings we defined in this recipe were all expanding strings. Expanding strings expand the variables and respect escape sequences. One thing to remember is that one kind of string is not better than the other; it is about the context.

The output string did not show the mode, last write time, or other details from $Random, because of the formatting set on System.IO.DirectoryInfo and System.IO.FileInfo.

Also, when we called the full path without the subexpression operator, PowerShell interpreted $Random as a variable, but thought .FullName was part of the string; it simply added .FullName to the string. The subexpression operator made PowerShell compute $Random.FullName first, and then placed the computed output in place of the subexpression.

We also saw another way to concatenate strings: using the + operator:

```
'The quick brown fox jumps over the lazy dog' -split ' ' | ForEach-Object {
$Pangram += $PSItem }
```

Understanding Here-Strings

We now know how to write a literal string and an expanding string. The next string to cover is the Here-String, which is a little special. Most strings are declared in a single line at the Terminal. We use escape sequences to separate the lines.

Imagine that you are in a situation wherein you are asked to write an input file that's going to be used to create 20 directories in a specific structure. You do not have a text editor handy. All you have is the Terminal, and PowerShell loaded on it. Here are the paths that need to be created:

```
./dir-01/dir-07/dir-09/dir-13/
./dir-02/dir-05/dir-06/
./dir-03/dir-08/dir-10/
./dir-04/dir-11/dir-12/dir-14/
./dir-04/dir-11/dir-12/dir-15/
./dir-04/dir-11/dir-12/dir-16/
./dir-04/dir-11/dir-12/dir-17/
./dir-04/dir-11/dir-12/dir-18/dir-19/
./dir-04/dir-11/dir-12/dir-18/dir-20/
```

Don't worry about actually creating a directory. All you have to do is create the input file.

How to do it...

What we want to achieve is a block of text—a single string, without too many complicated notations such as escape characters or concatenation. Follow these steps to complete this recipe:

1. At the prompt, type in the following:

```
PS> @'
./dir-01/dir-07/dir-09/dir-13/
./dir-02/dir-05/dir-06/
./dir-03/dir-08/dir-10/
./dir-04/dir-11/dir-12/dir-14/
./dir-04/dir-11/dir-12/dir-15/
./dir-04/dir-11/dir-12/dir-16/
./dir-04/dir-11/dir-12/dir-17/
./dir-04/dir-11/dir-12/dir-18/dir-19/
./dir-04/dir-11/dir-12/dir-18/dir-20/
'@
```

2. Press the *Enter* key to see what the output is.
3. Now, send this output to a text file. Name it whatever you want:

```
PS> @'
./dir-01/dir-07/dir-09/dir-13/
./dir-02/dir-05/dir-06/
./dir-03/dir-08/dir-10/
./dir-04/dir-11/dir-12/dir-14/
./dir-04/dir-11/dir-12/dir-15/
./dir-04/dir-11/dir-12/dir-16/
./dir-04/dir-11/dir-12/dir-17/
./dir-04/dir-11/dir-12/dir-18/dir-19/
./dir-04/dir-11/dir-12/dir-18/dir-20/
'@ | Out-File ./input-file.txt
```

Is this a string or an array?

4. Either assign the whole text block to a variable and call the Count property, or do it this way:

```
PS> (@'
./dir-01/dir-07/dir-09/dir-13/
./dir-02/dir-05/dir-06/
./dir-03/dir-08/dir-10/
./dir-04/dir-11/dir-12/dir-14/
./dir-04/dir-11/dir-12/dir-15/
./dir-04/dir-11/dir-12/dir-16/
```

```
./dir-04/dir-11/dir-12/dir-17/
./dir-04/dir-11/dir-12/dir-18/dir-19/
./dir-04/dir-11/dir-12/dir-18/dir-20/
'@) .Count
```

This way will create relative paths, based on the present working directory. What if you wanted these directories to be created within the home directory of the user who runs it?

5. Run the following code to create an expanding here-string (double quotes), and if the output is satisfactory, send it to `input-file-expanding.txt`:

```
PS> @"
$HOME/dir-01/dir-07/dir-09/dir-13/
$HOME/dir-02/dir-05/dir-06/
$HOME/dir-03/dir-08/dir-10/
$HOME/dir-04/dir-11/dir-12/dir-14/
$HOME/dir-04/dir-11/dir-12/dir-15/
$HOME/dir-04/dir-11/dir-12/dir-16/
$HOME/dir-04/dir-11/dir-12/dir-17/
$HOME/dir-04/dir-11/dir-12/dir-18/dir-19/
$HOME/dir-04/dir-11/dir-12/dir-18/dir-20/
"@
```

How it works...

Here-Strings help you write text blocks, including line breaks. You do not need to use line break escape sequences to do this. Here, strings begin with @' or @", and end with '@ or "@. There are a few conditions to writing here-strings, though:

-   The string beginner (@' or @") should not be followed by anything—even a trailing white space
-   The string terminator ('@ or "@) should be at the very beginning of the prompt or the line—no leading characters

This means that the content should not fall on either of these lines.

Here-strings preserve everything that you mention within the text block. Therefore, if your text block contains four spaces before the first character in every line, those would be preserved too. Here-strings also come in expanding and non-expanding variants, and, as shown by the Count property, the entire content is a single string, not an array.

Then how do you create multiple files? Let's worry about that in the *Splitting and combining strings* recipe.

Using basic string methods

We saw a few operators in the introduction to this chapter, of which quite a few were string-related. Some of these capabilities are given within the `System.String` object as methods to offer a quicker way to perform some operations—such as splitting strings, joining strings, replacing strings, changing cases, creating substrings, removing substrings, and so on.

In this recipe, we will look at a few scenarios based on the input file we created in the *Understanding Here-Strings* recipe. A loop will not be required for these actions since they are simple, single operations. We will learn about looping through these files in the *Flow Control using Branches and Loops* chapter so that we can work with more complex scenarios.

Here are the operations that need to be performed on the input file:

1. Remove the leading . in the paths. (Use the file you created from the non-expanding here-string.)
2. Trim the path of the leading and trailing /.
3. List out the directories that would be created from each element.
4. Get only the number in the name of the fifth directory in the list.
5. The directories need to be all uppercase because that's what the boss wants.
6. Replace the hyphens with spaces.

Getting ready

This recipe assumes that you have sent the output of each of the literal here-strings to the file. If not, follow the *Understanding Here-Strings* recipe and send the output of the non-expanding here-string to the file.

Run the following to import the contents of the file into a variable:

```
PS> $LiteralString = Get-Content ./ch06/03-input-file.txt
```

How to do it...

Before we dive into the recipe, it is important to remember that these method-based operations work in simple situations. Complex operations may require the operators that we discussed. An example for a non-simple situation is when we have to use regular expressions. Follow these steps to complete this recipe:

1. At the Terminal, enter the following code to remove the leading .. Use an assignment operator to modify the contents of the variable:

```
PS> $LiteralString = $LiteralString.TrimStart('.')
```

2. Type in the following code to remove the leading as well as trailing slashes:

```
PS> $LiteralString.TrimStart('/').TrimEnd('/')
```

3. Can we reduce keystrokes (apart from tab-completion, that is)? Keep assigning the results back to the same variable:

```
PS> $LiteralString.Trim('/')
PS> $LiteralString = $LiteralString.Trim('/')
```

4. To list out the directories that would be created, use the split() method. This will create some repeating elements. Select only the unique values:

```
PS> $LiteralString = $LiteralString.Split('/') | Select-Object -
Unique
```

5. Now, to get the number from the name, use the following code (do not assign the value back to the variable):

```
PS> $LiteralString[4] # Get the fifth element from the array

PS> $LiteralString[4].IndexOf('-') # Get the index of the hyphen

PS> $LiteralString[4].Substring($LiteralString[4].IndexOf('-')) #
Get the substring based on the index

PS> $LiteralString[4].Substring($LiteralString[4].IndexOf('-') + 1)
# Skip the hyphen
```

6. To make all of the directory names uppercase, use the following command:

```
PS> $LiteralString = $LiteralString.ToUpper()
```

7. To replace all of the hyphens with spaces, use the following command:

```
PS> $LiteralString = $LiteralString.Replace('-', ' ')
```

How it works...

The `TrimStart()` method removes the specified character from the beginning of the string. The `TrimEnd()` method removes the specified character at the end of the string. If we have to remove the same character at both ends of the string, we use the `Trim()` method with the specified character. If you do not specify any character as the argument to any of the methods, white space will be removed from the string.

The `split()` method splits the strings at the specified character, and creates an array of the split strings.

We use the index operator to pick the fifth value from the array. Then, we find the index of the hyphen within the resultant string. Next, we create a substring using the `Substring()` method and instruct it to start at the index of the hyphen. The `Substring()` method accepts two arguments (the beginning and the end indices of the substring). If you specify only one index, PowerShell will pick up the single-parameter variant of the method and create a substring starting at the specified index, ending at the end of the string.

 For those that are interested, this is an example of overloading in object-oriented programming.

Next, we added 1 to the index to omit the hyphen. Remember to perform the addition outside of the `IndexOf()` method.

The `ToUpper()` method converts the entire string into uppercase. There is also `ToLower()`, which does the opposite case conversion.

The `Replace()` method replaces the first argument with the second. These methods work on the entire string. Therefore, you may use the `Replace()` method to replace the entire string with another string. For example:

```
PS> $LiteralString.Replace('DIR', 'FOLDER')
```

However, do note that wildcard or regular expression matching will not work with the `Replace()` method.

See also

- The *Replacing substrings within strings* recipe

Performing string matching operations

Matching operations are mostly performed using the `-like`, `-notlike`, `-match`, and `-notmatch` operators. These also come in case-sensitive (`-clike`, `-cnotmatch`) and forced case-insensitive (`-inotlike`, `-imatch`) variants.

We have a situation for this recipe.

One of your friends works for a travel agency and gets an automated CSV file of sites that contain great articles of categories including travel, and lifestyle. (The aggregator service that creates this CSV file has its own algorithms to decide what is great, and does not care about disagreements.) This list is delivered to the agency every day at 7 AM. The list, however, only contains the names of the sites and their home page links. BBC may or may not feature in the list for the day. If the list contains BBC, he wants a query that will fetch the links to all Travel stories from the home page. Here is a sample:

Name	HomeURL
BBC	http://www.bbc.com/
Reuters	https://in.reuters.com/
Associated Press	https://www.ap.org/en-gb/
Philippine News	http://www.pna.gov.ph/
Al Jazeera	http://www.aljazeera.net/portal
Bloomberg	https://www.bloomberg.com/
The Hindu	https://www.thehindu.com/

How to do it...

This task involves PowerShell visiting a web page and picking up the links. You can use the `Invoke-WebRequest` cmdlet for this. To add perspective, `Invoke-WebRequest` shares many similarities with `curl` and `wget`. This recipe also involves the use of a simple `if` statement. The syntax and working of the statement will be covered in the *Flow Control using Branches and Loops* chapter.

You ask your friend to save the CSV with the same name at the home location. You will take care of deleting the file after processing. You send him the steps, which are as follows:

1. Import the CSV file into the session and save it in a variable:

```
$CsvImport = Import-Csv ./ch06/05-sitelist.csv
```

2. Next, you find out if BBC features in the list by using an `if` block:

```
if ($CsvImport.Name -contains 'BBC') { "Process the file." }
```

3. Use `Invoke-WebRequest` within the script block to retrieve the links:

```
$Uri = ($CsvImport | Where-Object Name -EQ 'BBC').HomeURL
(Invoke-WebRequest -Uri $Uri).Links | Select-Object href
```

   Now that you have the links, you filter the links that contain /travel/ in them. You notice that there are links such as /travel/, as well as http://www.bbc.com/travel/, which takes you to the Travel page.

4. Filter out only the articles: they may be stories, photos, or other forms of content:

```
(Invoke-WebRequest -Uri $Uri).Links | Where-Object {$PSItem.href -
Like '*/travel/*' -and $PSItem.href -NotLike '*/travel/'} | Select-
Object href -Unique
```

   However, you would like a simpler way to filter the links:

```
(Invoke-WebRequest -Uri $Uri).Links | Where-Object href -match
'/travel/.+' | Select-Object -ExpandProperty href -Unique
```

5. Build the complete script. Place the links in a text file:

```
$CsvImport = Import-Csv ./ch06/05-sitelist.csv
if ($CsvImport.Name -contains 'BBC') {
    $Uri = ($CsvImport | Where-Object Name -EQ 'BBC').HomeURL
    (Invoke-WebRequest -Uri $Uri).Links |
    Where-Object href -match '/travel/.+' |
    Select-Object -ExpandProperty href -Unique
}
Remove-Item ./ch06/05-sitelist.csv
```

6. Send your friend the instructions on how to run the script.

How it works...

The `-Like` operator matches wildcard characters and sees if the given substring is present in the string. On the other hand, the `-Match` operator matches regular expression patterns to validate strings. The `-contains` operator sees if the specified element exists in the given array.

The `Invoke-WebRequest` cmdlet gives out an object that contains several properties. `Links` contains more properties within itself (`Links : {@{outerHTML...`). Expand this property and get its members:

```
PS> Invoke-WebRequest -Uri 'http://www.bbc.com' | Select-Object -
ExpandProperty Links | Get-Member
```

However, for ease of use, we will pick the entire `Links` property:

```
PS> (Invoke-WebRequest -Uri 'http://www.bbc.com').Links
```

At the first step after importing the file, we check whether the `$CsvImport.Name` array contains BBC. Then, we use the `-Like` operator to find `/travel/`. We include everything that contains `/travel/`, and then exclude the strings that end with `/travel/`. However, in this particular situation, this seems like a query that's a little longer than what is required:

```
# ...
Where-Object {$PSItem.href -Like '*/travel/*' -and $PSItem.href -NotLike
'*/travel/'}
# ...
```

Therefore, we will use regular expression matching to get only those links that have `/travel/`, followed by any character other than null:

```
# ...
Where-Object href -match '/travel/.+'
# ...
```

You then select only the links (and not the column header) and send the output to a file, and delete the input file to clean up.

There's more...

There is an automatic variable, `$Matches`, which contains all of the matches that are found during an operation:

```
PS> "Hey, there! I'm using PowerShell." -match "([a-z]+)'([a-z]+)"
```

Calling `$Matches` now would list out the following:

- The complete match (`I'm`, in this case)
- The groups (pattern within the parentheses: `I` and `m`, in our case)

The would be listed out as a hashtable. (You will learn more about hashtables in `Chapter 9`, *Using Arrays and Hashtables*; for now, think of them as a simple tabular representation of a list.)

Replacing substrings within strings

Now that we know how to match strings, we should also be able to replace substrings in a string.

The situation for this recipe is that one of your friends has subscribed to this aggregator that sends him blog posts in plain text. (I know—how great would that be for you, and so horrible for the maintainers of commercial websites!) The issue, though, is that the aggregator sends her only one file with all the content loaded into it. You can see the file and understand that it is, in fact, Markdown with YAML, and agree to help her make the file pure Markdown so that it can be rendered into clean HTML.

The file for use in this recipe is available in this book's GitHub repository.

How to do it...

The contents of the file are something like this:

```
...
The post is quite long for a read. Let's give ourselves a break here, and
resume in the next post.

---
title: Enter PowerShell
date: '2017-04-04 12:00'
tags:
- windows
- powershell
---

In the last post, we spoke about how it was a challenge to get data using
the CLI, for programmatic use.
```

To start with the operation of stripping the YAML out, you first need to load the content into PowerShell. Follow these steps to complete this recipe:

1. Get the content into the session:

```
PS> $String = Get-Content ./ch06/06-rawcontent.txt -Raw
```

2. In case you got the file with CRLF (carriage return and line feed, which is mostly the case with Windows) instead of LF (most *nix systems), replace CRLF with LF:

```
PS> $String = $String -replace '\r\n', '\n'
```

3. All we have to do now is replace `title:` with #, and remove the leading and trailing YAML boundaries:

```
PS> $String = $String -replace '---\ntitle:', '#'
PS> $String = $String -replace '((^#|\n#)\s.+\n)(.+\n)+-{3}\n',
'$1'
PS> $String | Out-File ./ch06/06-puregfm.md
```

4. Perform a `diff` to see the difference between the files:

```
PS> diff ./ch06/06-rawcontent.txt ./ch06/06-puregfm.md
```

You can use the Git commands from within PowerShell. As established earlier, PowerShell does not interfere with the shell commands, and so all Bash commands work as Bash commands themselves; syntax and everything.

I simply replaced the contents in the input file with the output so that I can use `git diff`. Here is the first heading that's replaced by PowerShell:

```
                                        Terminal                          _  ×
diff --git a/ch06/06-rawcontent.txt b/ch06/06-rawcontent.txt
index 101c83d..99d8bbe 100644
--- a/ch06/06-rawcontent.txt
+++ b/ch06/06-rawcontent.txt
@@ -1,10 +1,4 @@
----
-title: Command line, anybody?
-date: '2017-04-01 21:17'
-tags:
-- windows
-category: tyro
----
+# Command line, anybody?

 We're Windows people. We love the GUI. We don't use the boring plain window with grey tex
t. All that is so yesterday, aye? We are more used to moving the mouse, clicking at places
, and then touch the keyboard only when we have something to type. We love that experience
, be it Aero&trade; effect, or some other sassy visuals. Command line, again, is so yester
day.

@@ -26,13 +20,7 @@ It's now time to download Windows PowerShell.

 It will ask you for a restart, so be prepared. Once it's done, you're all set to follow t
:
```

And here is another screenshot to show that the replacement happened within the rest of the text as well:

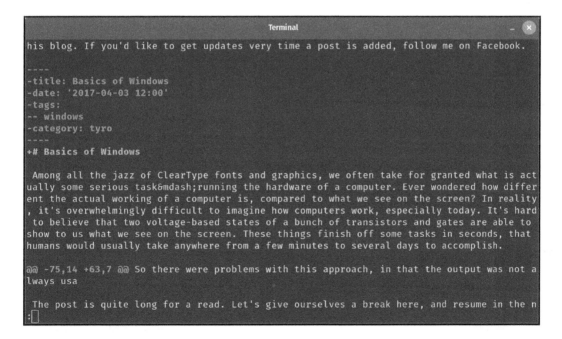

How it works...

To understand the entirety of how this worked, you will need to know about regular expressions.

First, there are important considerations when using the `Get-Content` cmdlet. The output of the cmdlet is *not* a single string, but an array of strings. PowerShell terminates a string at a line break when using `Get-Content`. Therefore, PowerShell will be unable to match newline characters. Using the `-Raw` switch imports the content as a single string; we need the entire text as a single block. However, now, the ^ anchor works only for the beginning of the entire text. To compensate for this, we use `^#|\n#` in the regex to match the first-level heading notation.

The `-replace` operator is similar to the `Replace()` method that's available in strings, except that the operator supports regular expressions, while the method does not. The operator takes the matching string as the first argument and the replacement string as the second, and replaces all occurrences of the matching string with the replacement string. The replacement string can be a simple string, as in the case of #, or one or more of the matched patterns. In the latter case, we use the $ notation to replace the group.

Note that $1 should be a literal string to denote a match in the regular expression; ensure that you don't use the expanding string or a variable notation. Use single quotes only.

 A brief note on the regex used in this recipe: the first matching-and-replacement was simple: three hyphens, followed by a newline, followed by `title:`.

For the second operation, we create logical groups:

- (Beginning with # *or* newline followed by #), followed by a white space, followed by any number of any character (other than a newline), and a newline. These are post titles, and we want them retained.
- Any number of zero or more characters (other than newline) followed by a newline, followed by three hyphens followed by a newline.

There's more...

Try out the same recipe with `Get-Content ./path/to/file.txt | Out-String -Stream` to learn more about the `-Stream` switch.

Splitting and combining strings

Now that we have learned how to match and replace substrings, the next step for us in the journey of strings in PowerShell is to learn to split and combine them. This will leave us with understanding formatting operators so that we can learn to use strings effectively in PowerShell.

In this scenario, we have to create a log cleanup script that takes input in the form of a CSV file. This CSV file contains multiple rows of input, each being a location that needs regular cleanup, the number of days, worth of files to retain, the extension of the files to be cleaned up, and the paths to be excluded. The paths to be excluded must have multiple paths, separated by a semicolon. Here is a sample:

Path	Retention	Extension	Exclusion
/home/coolapp/logs	7	.log	/home/coolapp/logs/devicelogs;/home/coolapp/logs/install

Your task is to only split the exclusion paths so that they can be processed, and join them in a human-understandable way to echo on the Terminal.

How to do it...

Our task is simple. We are only going to write the code block that will take the input and separate the various fields into variables. The exclusion list should be a single array variable. When displaying the output, we will display each exclusion path on separate lines. Follow these steps to complete this recipe:

1. At the Terminal, type in the following:

```
PS> $PathInfo = Import-Csv './ch06/07-input.csv'

PS> # Looping construct here
PS> $ExclusionPaths = $PathInfo.Exclusion -split ';'

PS> # Some code block to handle deletion and other things

PS> Write-Host "These $($ExclusionPaths.Count) paths will be
excluded from deletion: $($ExclusionPaths -join ', ')"
PS> # End loop
```

2. Since the script has run in the current session, you can fetch the values of the variables. Run the following commands to see what values you get:

```
PS> $PathInfo
PS> $ExclusionPaths
PS> $ExclusionPaths -join ', '
```

3. Note how the values differ.

How it works...

How this works is simple. Based on how comfortable we are with scripting and how readable we would like to make the scripts, we assign values to variables. In our case, for the sake of ease of use, we split `$PathInfo.Exclusion -split ';'` into `$ExclusionPaths`.

`$PathInfo.Exclusion` is a single string. However, `$ExclusionPaths` is a string array (which is why the `.Count` property returned 2).

When we had to display the array in a single human-readable sentence, we used the `-join` operator to join the two elements with a comma and a space. This works for any number of elements in the array.

Using the formatting operator

Learning about strings is incomplete without formatting. The formatting operator in PowerShell helps with formatting strings the way we want them. There are several options available with the operator, some of which we will see in the *How it works...* section of this recipe. This helps us with several situations, such as generating an HTML report from the output of a cmdlet. You can create complex output files without having to worry about missing out tags or introducing errors when constructing these structured files.

In this recipe, we will look into a simple usage of the formatting operator. The following is the situation.

You have been hired by a bank to provide them with a series of automation solutions. The Recovery Division of the credit card department has a follow-up team that calls up defaulting customers. Given the financial situation, there are many who are behind on their bills. Consequently, the volume of calls each of these team members makes has increased. They are now too busy to type out emails, looking at the email address of the customer, typing the title, the due amount, and so on. The system is able to generate a simple text file with the details necessary for an email. Your job is to generate a `mailto:` link, with all the necessary details, which will then be embedded into the customer profile so that the associates simply have to click the link to send emails to the defaulters. A sample input file is as follows:

 It must be noted that this script assumes that all of the input is uniform (as given in the following code), with one file generated per customer, each file containing the title in the first line, the full name on the second, and so on. When building a real-life automation solution, ensure that standardization of the input is factored in.

```
Mr
Bilbo Baggins
9149-4554-2127-8685
Bag End, The Shire, Hobbiton, Middle Earth
bilbo.baggins@middlearthmail.me
0069928789312
8472
```

The output should be something like this:

```
<a href="mailto:bilbo.baggins@middlearthmail.me?subject=Payment due for
9149-4554-2127-8685&body=Dear Mr Bilbo Baggins,

Hope you are doing well.

This is to notify you that the payment of $8,472.00 for card number
9149-4554-2127-8685 has not been received as yet. We tried to call you at
006-992-878-9312, but could not reach you. We have mailed the statement to
the address: Bag End, The Shire, Hobbiton, Middle Earth.

Please write to us in case you need any assistance, or have queries.

Regards,
Central Bank of Imaginary Realms">Send email</a>
```

How to do it...

The solution is pretty simple, and you are going to involve the formatting operator. Follow these steps to create the function to take care of this task:

1. Open a Terminal window and import the contents of the file:

```
PS> $Details = Get-Content ./ch06/08-details.txt
```

2. Now, build the `mailto:` block:

```
PS> $Link = @'
<a href="mailto:{4}?subject=Payment due for {2}&body=Dear {0} {1},

Hope you are doing well.

This is to notify you that the payment of {6:c} for card number {2}
has not been received as yet. We tried to call you at {5:00#-###-
###-####}, but could not reach you. We have mailed the statement to
the address: {3}.

Please write to us in case you need any assistance, have queries,
or would like any of the details corrected.

Regards,
Central Bank of Imaginary Fields">Send email</a>
'@
```

3. Finally, generate the link with the details filled in. Note that the sequence of the details plays a vital role:

```
PS> $Link -f $Details[0], $Details[1], $Details[2], $Details[3],
$Details[4], [int64]$Details[5], [int]$Details[6]
```

How it works...

String formatting with the formatting operator is simple. To make this easier to understand, let's understand that there are two components to this: the component before the formatting operator, and the component after the formatting operator. Therefore, the sequence that you specify to the command is as follows:

1. The string to be output
2. The formatting operator
3. The content to be inserted into the string

Therefore, the third component is the actual data.

The string to be output contains the formatting instructions. These instructions can be further divided into three:

1. The index (mandatory)
2. The alignment specifier (optional)
3. The format string

Together, they are specified within braces as `{index, alignment: formatString}`. In our recipe, we used only the index and the formatting string.

The `$Details` variable was an array. Therefore, we could refer to the elements with the index operator (`$Details[0]`). This way, we form the sequence of items to be passed into the string. We passed the email address as the fifth element, and we instructed the formatting operator to place the fifth element, (`...-f $Details[0], $Details[1], $Details[2], $Details[3], $Details[4]...`), in the sequence, right after `mailto:` in the resultant string (`mailto:{4}`). Therefore, if we said `{4}`, it would mean the fifth element after `-f`.

Next comes the alignment. If you would like a series of spaces to be added to the left or the right of the content being formatted, you could use the alignment specifier. The index and the alignment specifier are separated by a comma. Therefore, if you say `"{0,8}"` `-f` `'Joe'`, you would get   Joe; if you said `"{0,-8}"` `-f` `'Joe'`, you would get Joe .

The format string is important. It shows the output in the format specified. In our recipe, we use `:c` to show the number as $8,472.00. We use `00#-###-###-####` to show the 13 digit number as a phone number; here, the two initial zeros tell PowerShell to pad the number with zeros, while the hashes are simple placeholders. This way, the number does not get displayed as `69928....`.

When we want to tell PowerShell that the phone number and the amount due are not strings, we use the cast operator to cast the strings as `int64` and `int`.

The format string helps you show the content as decimal digits, in scientific notation, percentages, hexadecimal numbers, and various date strings, among other formats. For instance, you could display 3.141592653589 accurately to up to four decimal places by using "{0:n4}" -f 3.141592653589. Here, n says that the content needs to be treated as a number, and 4 instructs PowerShell to make the output accurate to four digits after the decimal point.

There's more...

Here are some exercises to try out:

1. Show the Avogadro number, 6,02,21,40,76,00,00,00,00,00,00,000, in scientific notation. The number of digits after the decimal point before the *e* should be three.
2. Show 65,535 as a hexadecimal number.
3. Show 58.25354 as a percentage.
4. Format the current date as yyyy-MM-dd without using the -Format parameter of Get-Date.

Done? Here are the solutions:

1. "{0:e3}" -f 602214076000000000000000
2. "0x{0:x}" -f 65535
3. "{0:p}" -f 58.25354
4. "{0:yyyy-MM-dd}" -f (Get-Date)

7
Flow Control Using Branches and Loops

In this chapter, we will cover the following recipes:

- Using `If-ElseIf-Else` conditions to control script flow
- Using `Switch-Case` conditions to control script flow
- Learning to use delays
- Writing a basic looping construct
- Writing a more complex loop on a predefined array
- Using the `For` loop construct
- Using the `While` loop construct
- Cleaning empty directories using the `Do-While` construct
- Cleaning empty directories using the `Do-Until` construct

Introduction

Just like working with strings, flow control is also a favorite part of PowerShell to me.

Most Linux administrators and Bash scripters will already be familiar with concepts such as loops and branches, which we will use to complete these recipes. The only difference we will see is that we are dealing with objects, and a more readable, streamlined process of scripting.

Using If–ElseIf–Else conditions to control script flow

We have seen how operators work. Try out more of these operators until it becomes second nature to you. Most of the flow control, as well as filtration in scripts, happens using these operators.

In this recipe, we are going to look at conditional script flow, also known as branching. In essence, branching works on two conditions (correct: $true and $false). This is generally achieved using two constructs:

- The If–ElseIf–Else construct
- The Switch–Case construct

In this recipe, we will give ourselves a simple problem to solve: finding out if today is one of the days of the weekend.

Getting ready

These recipes require that you to try them out so that you understand how they work. These work better on an integrated scripting environment (preferably Visual Studio Code) than at the prompt. To run the scripts in Visual Studio Code, use the *F5* key. These recipes should work identically on Windows PowerShell 3.0+ as well: the syntax for these constructs is exactly the same in PowerShell and Windows PowerShell.

How to do it...

Open a new PowerShell file in Visual Studio Code:

1. Enter the following in the code pane to simply find out if it is a weekend day:

```
$Date = Get-Date

if ($Date.DayOfWeek -in 'Saturday', 'Sunday') {
    Write-Host 'We party on weekends!' -BackgroundColor Yellow -
ForegroundColor Black
}
```

2. If you would like to get an output on weekdays as well, use the following code:

```
$Date = Get-Date
if ($Date.DayOfWeek -in 'Saturday', 'Sunday') {
    Write-Host 'It is a weekend!'
}
else {
    Write-Host 'It is a weekday.'
}
```

3. If you would like to jazz it up a little, and use the whole of if-elseif-else, use the following code:

```
$Date = Get-Date

if ($Date.DayOfWeek -in 'Saturday', 'Sunday') {
    Write-Host 'We party on weekends!' -BackgroundColor Yellow -
ForegroundColor Black
}
elseif ($Date.DayOfWeek -eq 'Wednesday') {
    Write-Host 'Half the week is over, and I want to do so much
more!'
}
else {
    Write-Host 'Work is worship. Ahem!'
}
```

In general, Write-Output is a better cmdlet to use than Write-Host. Write-Host writes the output only to the host; this output cannot be sent to anything else without manipulation. Use Write-Host only on occasions that need it.

How it works...

Simple branching could work with just the If statement. The statement checks for truth, and executes the code block based on the outcome of the condition. In the case of either-or, where there are only two conditions, use If-Else. When there are more than two possible outcomes, use If-ElseIf-Else. The else block is the catch-all.

Using Switch–Case conditions to control script flow

If–ElseIf–Else works when you have outcomes coming in categories (weekdays being five days, weekends being two). When the outcomes are specific and/or too many in number, it could be a little tedious to use the If–ElseIf–Else construct. To understand this better, let's give ourselves a scenario.

The dress code at your workplace is decided by a child, who likes everyone wearing the colors of the rainbow. Since she does not like anyone working weekends, she's not a big fan of orange, and absolutely hates yellow. She has come up with the following scheme (she doesn't know of Monday Blues yet): red on Mondays, violet on Tuesdays, indigo on Wednesdays, blue on Thursdays, green on Fridays, and orange during the weekends.

How to do it...

This situation will require a whole round of If–ElseIf–Else statements. A more efficient way of handling this situation is to use the Switch–Case construct:

1. Open a new PowerShell file and add the following content to it:

```
$Date = Get-Date

switch ($Date.DayOfWeek) {
    'Monday' { Write-Output 'Red' }
    'Tuesday' { Write-Output 'Violet' }
    'Wednesday' { Write-Output 'Indigo' }
    'Thursday' { Write-Output 'Blue' }
    'Friday' { Write-Output 'Green' }
    Default { Write-Output 'Orange' }
}
```

2. If you would rather omit Default and use a wildcard matching for the weekends, use the following code:

```
$Date = Get-Date

switch -Wildcard ($Date.DayOfWeek) {
    'Monday' { Write-Output 'Red' }
    'Tuesday' { Write-Output 'Violet' }
    'Wednesday' { Write-Output 'Indigo' }
    'Thursday' { Write-Output 'Blue' }
    'Friday' { Write-Output 'Green' }
```

```
        'S*' { Write-Output 'Orange' }
    }
```

How it works...

As we can see, it is more efficient to write, execute, as well as troubleshoot a `Switch-Case` construct in such situations, rather than writing a series of `If-ElseIf-ElseIf-ElseIf-...-Else` statements. To define a catch-all action in `Switch-Case`, use `Default`.

The `Switch-Case` construct also supports wildcard (`-Wildcard`) and regex (`-Regex`). In general, it is not a good practice to omit `Default` unless all the possible outcomes have been covered.

The working of `Switch-Case` is simple: it checks the condition against all the values among the definitions, and whenever it finds a condition to be true, it executes the corresponding script block. Therefore, if three conditions among five are met, the three script blocks will be executed. This is a little unlike `If-ElseIf-Else`, which exits out of the branching construct the moment the first `$true` is met and the script block is executed. Therefore, if you want only one outcome from the construct, consider adding the `break` keyword in every script block to break out of the construct the moment a `$true` is encountered. For example, check out the following code:

```
    ...
        'Monday' {
            Write-Output 'Red'
            break
        }
    ...
```

Of course, in this particular situation, it is not necessary, since the outcome would be exclusive.

Learning to use delays

PowerShell usually runs one statement after another; the current statement must return the buffer (so to speak) for the next step to begin execution. However, in some cases, you still require a wait; situations where the buffer could be returned before the desired outcome is achieved.

While setting up something like this may require some manipulation, to keep it simple, let's just assume that we need five seconds to register what day it is (sure, disbelief works), before being instructed what to wear.

How to do it...

Let's combine the two scripts from the previous recipe, *Using Switch-Case conditions to control script flow*.

Open a new file and type in the following:

```
$Date = Get-Date

if ($Date.DayOfWeek -in 'Saturday', 'Sunday') {
    Write-Host 'We party on weekends!' -BackgroundColor Yellow -
ForegroundColor Black
}
elseif ($Date.DayOfWeek -eq 'Wednesday') {
    Write-Host 'Half the week is over, and I want to do so much more!'
}
else {
    Write-Host 'Work is worship. Ahem!'
}

Start-Sleep -Seconds 5

$Date = Get-Date

switch ($Date.DayOfWeek) {
    'Monday' { Write-Output 'Wear red.'; break }
    'Tuesday' { Write-Output 'Wear violet.'; break }
    'Wednesday' { Write-Output 'Wear indigo.'; break }
    'Thursday' { Write-Output 'Wear blue.'; break }
    'Friday' { Write-Output 'Wear green.'; break }
    Default { Write-Output 'Poor you, working today. Wear orange.';
break }
}
```

Here is a sample output:

```
                                    Terminal                                 _  ⊗
PS /home/ram/Documents/code/github/powershell> & ./ch07/03-Wait-BeforeDressCode.ps1
We party on weekends!
Poor you, working today. Wear orange.
PS /home/ram/Documents/code/github/powershell> []
```

How it works...

The reason this is a separate recipe is that it is part of flow control, and is useful in some specific situations. The `Start-Sleep` cmdlet accepts `Seconds` or `Milliseconds` as input, and waits for that amount of time to pass before processing the next instruction.

Writing a basic looping construct

Automation is perhaps only half-complete without loops. After all, the point of automation in most situations is making the computer do what is repetitive. There are six looping constructs in PowerShell in all:

- Looping using `Foreach-Object`
- The `Foreach` loop
- The `For` loop
- The `While` loop
- The `Do-While` loop
- The `Do-Until` loop

The `Foreach-Object` looping construct is perhaps the simplest of them all.

Let's imagine that we have a list of five guests to a certain event, and you would like to greet them each individually.

How to do it...

Let's assume that the guests are Mr Jain, Mr Jacobs, Ms Sanders, Mr Shah, and Mr Hugo:

1. Open a new file in Visual Studio Code and, in the script pane, type the following:

```
$GuestsRaw = Read-Host "Enter the guest names, separated by commas"
$Guests = $GuestsRaw -split ",$([regex]'[\s]*')"

$Guests | ForEach-Object { Write-Output "Welcome, $PSItem!" }
```

2. Run the script and at the prompt, type in the names of the guests:

```
PS> Mr Jain, Mr Jacobs, Ms Sanders, Mr Shah, Mr Hugo
```

How it works...

First, you take in the input through a prompt from the host. The raw guest list is taken in. PowerShell then splits the input string based on the commas and a regular expression match (this is necessary so that it works regardless of whether the input contains a space after the comma or not: not all users are alike). We use the -split and cast operators for the operation.

The loop part comes in at Foreach-Object. You pass the array object into the pipeline. The Foreach-Object cmdlet picks up the array, and processes one element at a time. When referring to the element within the loop, you use the $PSItem (that is, $_) automatic variable, since the object has been passed through the pipeline.

Writing a more complex loop on a predefined array

In the *Writing a basic loop construct* recipe, we passed content through the pipeline into an in-place Foreach-Object loop. Now, let's consider that we have these same guests, but specific seats have been allotted to them. We would like to show the seats to the guests. You have the following table in CSV format:

Name	Seat
Mr Jain	A-12
Mr Jacobs	C-28
Ms Sanders	B-17
Mr Shah	M-22
Mr Hugo	E-08

How to do it...

The assumption here is that each row has 40 seats, and that the aisle goes through the center of the hall. Follow these steps to get started:

1. If you have not cloned the repository, you could create your own CSV file. Either copy the comma-separated content in the following code block, or create a CSV file using PowerShell:

```
PS> @'
Name,Seat
Mr Jain,A-12
Mr Jacobs,C-28
Ms Sanders,B-17
Mr Shah,M-22
Mr Hugo,E-08
'@ | Out-File -Path './ch07/05-Write-GuestSeatDetails.csv'
```

2. Open a new PowerShell file in Visual Studio Code and type in the following script:

```
$Guests = Import-Csv './ch07/05-Write-GuestSeatDetails.csv'

foreach ($Guest in $Guests) {
    $RowIdentifier = [byte][char](($Guest.Seat -split '-
')[0].ToUpper())
    $RowNumber = ($RowIdentifier - 64).ToString()

    switch -Regex ($RowNumber) {
        '1(1|2|3)$' { $RowNumber += 'th'; break }
        '.?1$'      { $RowNumber += 'st'; break }
        '.?2$'      { $RowNumber += 'nd'; break }
        '.?3$'      { $RowNumber += 'rd'; break }
        Default     { $RowNumber += 'th'; break }
    }

    $SeatNumber = ($Guest.Seat -split "-")[1]

    if ($SeatNumber -gt 20) {
        $Side = 'right'
    }
    else {
        $Side = 'left'
    }

    Start-Sleep -Seconds 1
    Write-Host "Welcome, $($Guest.Name)! " -NoNewline
```

```
        Start-Sleep -Seconds 1
        Write-Host "Your seat is in the $RowNumber row, to the $Side
the aisle."
    }
```

3. Run the script.

    The output shows personalized greetings and the seat locations:

```
                                    Terminal                              _  ⊗
PS /home/ram/Documents/code/github/powershell> & ./ch07/05-Write-GuestSeatDetails.ps1
Welcome, Mr Jain! Your seat is in the 1st row, to the left the aisle.
Welcome, Mr Jacobs! Your seat is in the 3rd row, to the right the aisle.
Welcome, Ms Sanders! Your seat is in the 2nd row, to the left the aisle.
Welcome, Mr Shah! Your seat is in the 13th row, to the right the aisle.
Welcome, Mr Hugo! Your seat is in the 5th row, to the left the aisle.
PS /home/ram/Documents/code/github/powershell> []
```

How it works...

The main idea here is the use of the `foreach` statement. When using the `Foreach` loop construct, you refer to each element with a variable; variables are not identified with an index, in this case. For every iteration, in our case, `$Guest` picks one value from `$Guests`, in sequence, so that the current element can be referred to using `$Guest`. Also, `$Guest in $Guests` has been used to make it more English-like. To PowerShell, it would not matter if you said `$Item in $Guests` or `$Person in $Guests`.

The seat numbers have a pattern: an alpha row identifier, followed by a hyphen, followed by the numeric seat identifier.

The seat number is a string. We split it at –, pick the first element in the resultant array, convert it to uppercase (in case it isn't already), convert this letter to a character, and then use the `[byte]` cast operator to find its ASCII identifier. And, yes, we subtract 64 from it (so A becomes 1).

To be able to use the number with `Switch-Case` without errors, we convert the number back into a string. We make the number friendly for use in a sentence. We take the second (numeric) part of the array to see which side of the aisle the seat is located on. We combine all of these to get the resultant greeting-and-guidance strings, which are displayed after a delay of one second each.

There are two kinds of foreach statement in PowerShell: one that follows the pipeline (which is in fact an alias for the Foreach-Object cmdlet), and the foreach looping statement itself that this recipe talks about. To identify which is which, see if foreach follows a pipeline: if it does, it is the alias; if the line itself begins with foreach, it is the foreach looping statement.

Using the For loop construct

The Foreach loop and the For loop are different in that the latter uses an index to perform operations. We need a variable to control the flow, whose values form a range. Let's re-implement the same solution that we used in the *Writing a more complex loop on a predefined array* recipe, but with a For loop construct instead.

How to do it...

The assumptions that are made are the same as those in the *Writing a more complex loop on a predefined array* recipe. Follow these steps to get started:

1. Open a new file and paste the following content into it:

```
$Guests = Import-Csv './ch07/05-Write-GuestSeatDetails.csv'

for ($CurrentGuest = 0; $CurrentGuest -lt $Guests.Length;
$CurrentGuest++) {
    $Guest = $Guests[$CurrentGuest]

    $RowIdentifier = [byte][char](($Guest.Seat -split '-
')[0].ToUpper())
    $RowNumber = ($RowIdentifier - 64).ToString()
    switch -Regex ($RowNumber) {
        '1(1|2|3)$' { $RowNumber += 'th'; break }
        '.?1$'      { $RowNumber += 'st'; break }
        '.?2$'      { $RowNumber += 'nd'; break }
        '.?3$'      { $RowNumber += 'rd'; break }
        Default     { $RowNumber += 'th'; break }
    }

    $SeatNumber = ($Guest.Seat -split "-")[1]
    if ($SeatNumber -gt 20) {
        $Side = 'right'
    }
```

```
        else {
            $Side = 'left'
        }

        Start-Sleep -Seconds 1
        Write-Host "Welcome, $($Guest.Name)! " -NoNewline #
Subexpression `$Guest.Name` to be computed first.
        Start-Sleep -Seconds 1
        Write-Host "Your seat is in the $RowNumber row, to the $Side
the aisle."
        }
```

2. Run the script.

How it works...

Some of you might be pointing out that the foreach construct was simpler than the for construct in this case, and you would be right. In my stint as an administrator, I may have used the for construct fewer than 10 times over the last three years, compared to the hundreds of times I used foreach. The For construct has its own uses; use with a predefined array is one of the less-efficient ones.

Regardless, for works as long as the object is an array. $CurrentGuest is the index we use, which ranges from 0 through the total elements in $Guests—1. The loop starts with the index being initialized at 0 in this case, and after every iteration of the script block, the index is incremented ($CurrentGuest++).

One operation where for would be more efficient than foreach is if every alternate guest had to be greeted (rude, I know). In that case, the third part of the definition of for would have been $CurrentGuest += 2.

 $CurrentGuest + 2 instead of $CurrentGuest += 2 would make this loop infinite, since the value of $CurrentGuest would not be changed at all.

Using the While loop construct

We will create two scripts in this recipe: the first one to establish the similarities between For and While, and the other to lay the foundation to understanding the Do-While and Do-Until constructs. This way, the learning will be incremental, and the understanding will be easier.

For the first script, the scenario is the same as described in the previous recipe, *Using the For loop construct*. For the second, the task is to take the year number as input and find the date for Mother's Day in that year.

How to do it...

First, continue with the assumptions that you had for the previous recipe:

1. Open a new file and paste the following content into it:

```
$Guests = Import-Csv './ch07/05-Write-GuestSeatDetails.csv'
$CurrentGuest = 0

while ($CurrentGuest -lt $Guests.Length) {
    $Guest = $Guests[$CurrentGuest]

    $RowIdentifier = [byte][char](($Guest.Seat -split '-
')[0].ToUpper())
    $RowNumber = ($RowIdentifier - 64).ToString()

    switch -Regex ($RowNumber) {
        '1(1|2|3)$' { $RowNumber += 'th'; break }
        '.?1$'      { $RowNumber += 'st'; break }
        '.?2$'      { $RowNumber += 'nd'; break }
        '.?3$'      { $RowNumber += 'rd'; break }
        Default     { $RowNumber += 'th'; break }
    }

    $SeatNumber = ($Guest.Seat -split "-")[1]

    if ($SeatNumber -gt 20) { $Side = 'right' }
    else { $Side = 'left' }

    Start-Sleep -Seconds 1
    Write-Host "Welcome, $($Guest.Name)! " -NoNewline
    Start-Sleep -Seconds 1
    Write-Host "Your seat is in the $RowNumber row, to the $Side
the aisle."
```

```
        $CurrentGuest++
    }
```

2. Run the script; the output should be the same as that of the previous recipe.
3. Now, create a new PowerShell file and add the following code:

```
$Year = Read-Host "Enter the year (YYYY) you would like to find
Mothers' Day for"

$CurrentDay = Get-Date "01 May $Year"

while ($CurrentDay.DayOfWeek -ne 'Sunday') {
    $CurrentDay = $CurrentDay.AddDays(1)
}
$MothersDay = $CurrentDay.AddDays(7)

Write-Output "Mothers' Day falls on
$($MothersDay.ToLongDateString())."
```

4. Run the script. Enter any year and you should get the date for Mother's Day for that year.

How it works...

Every finite looping construct requires three things:

- The starting point
- The stopping point
- The way to proceed toward the stopping point

In the case of the `Foreach` construct, the entire logic is pre-coded. It takes an entire array, finds the starting and stopping points, and moves toward the stopping point one step at a time. The `For` construct has these parameters declared in the loop declaration statements itself, and each parameter is separated by a semicolon.

The `While` loop is not very different. Its starting point is defined outside of the loop, the stopping point is the only condition passed, and the operation on the index is specified within the loop. These three parameters have been highlighted in the scripts. The initialization should happen outside the loop so that it is not modified during the course of the loop. The operation on the index should happen for every iteration so that the loop moves in some direction. Therefore, this operation falls within the loop.

Be a little careful with the `While` loop; you are more prone to getting an infinite loop, because it is easy to forget to add the starting point or the operation to move toward the stopping point.

Now, on to Mother's Day. We first get the date object for May 1 for that year, so we can manipulate it using its members. This date is the starting point. We then specify the condition, keep the loop going if the day is not a Sunday. Then, we add one day at every iteration. After every iteration, the variable is checked against the condition. Finally, when the first Sunday is encountered, the variable comes out of the loop. We then add a week to it to find the second Sunday, and output the long date version of the value of `$MothersDay`.

Cleaning empty directories using the Do–While construct

In the previous recipe, we found the second Sunday of May using the year as input. We used a `While` loop for that. The `While` loop checks the condition before even starting the iteration. If the condition returns `$false` at the very beginning, the loop would not even begin, for instance, if you input the year as `2016`.

`Do–While` is a little different; the loop is executed once, regardless of whether the condition is true or not. The condition is checked only after the first iteration.

The scenario for this recipe is that we want to delete all empty directories within a certain directory.

Getting ready

To work with this recipe, let's create a few empty directories within `$HOME/random`. Use the input file that is part of the Git repository of this book to create the directories:

```
PS> Get-Content ./ch07/08-input-file.txt | ForEach-Object { New-Item
$($PSItem -replace '\.', "$HOME/random") -ItemType Directory }
```

How to do it...

If you run the following recipe within the `random` lab directory, all of its empty subdirectories will be deleted. Follow these steps to get started:

1. Open a new file and paste the following content into it:

```
do {
    $AllDirectories = (Get-ChildItem -Path $HOME/random -Recurse -
Directory).FullName
    $EmptyDirectories = $AllDirectories | Where-Object {(Get-
ChildItem $PSItem).Count -eq 0}
    $EmptyDirectories | Remove-Item
} while ($EmptyDirectories.Count -gt 0)
```

2. Let's add some logging to it so that we know what's happening:

```
$Iteration = 0
do {
    $AllDirectories = (Get-ChildItem -Path $HOME/random -Recurse -
Directory).FullName
    $EmptyDirectories = $AllDirectories | Where-Object {(Get-
ChildItem $PSItem).Count -eq 0}
    $EmptyDirectories | Remove-Item

    Write-Output "Iteration $Iteration. Removed the following
$($EmptyDirectories.Count) directories."
    $EmptyDirectories
    $Iteration++
} while ($EmptyDirectories.Count -gt 0)
```

Note how there was an empty iteration, 5. This shows the nature of a `Do-While` loop:

How it works...

The execution is similar to the While construct, however, as shown by Iteration 0, the Do–While construct executes the script block once without checking the condition. In our case, we queried the empty directories within the loop. If we had placed this query outside of the loop, we would have had to place it within as well, for loop control. This is inefficient programming.

PowerShell found nine empty directories during the execution of the script block. When the condition check happened after the execution, 9 was evaluated to be greater than 0. The loop ran again. This time, the value of $EmptyDirectories.Count was evaluated to be 4. The loop ran again, and this time again, the value was 4, which is greater than 0; the condition was still $true. During the next run, $EmptyDirectories.Count was evaluated to be 2, then 1, and then, during the last run, 0. This time, the outcome of the condition became $false, and the loop exited. Essentially, the loop statement was: Go on while the count is more than zero.

See also

- The *Taking actions on the returned objects* recipe in Chapter 4, *Passing Data through the Pipeline*

Cleaning empty directories using the Do–Until construct

It is easy to confuse Do–While and Do–Until, since they share a lot of similarities. However, the difference between them is in fact pretty clear. The Do–While loop executes as long as the outcome of the condition check is $true, and exits the moment it becomes $false. Do–Until is the opposite: the loop continues as long as the condition check returns $false, and stops the moment the condition check returns $true.

Let's use the same scenario of cleaning up empty folders, this time using the Do–Until loop.

Getting ready

To work with this recipe, let's create a few empty directories within $HOME/random. Use the input file that is part of the Git repository of this book to create the directories:

```
PS> Get-Content ./ch07/08-input-file.txt | ForEach-Object { New-Item
$($PSItem -replace '\.', "$HOME/random") -ItemType Directory }
```

How to do it...

You will need to rerun the command to create the empty directories. Follow these steps to get started:

1. Open a new file and paste the following content into it:

```
$Iteration = 0
do {
    $AllDirectories = (Get-ChildItem -Path $HOME/random -Recurse -
Directory).FullName
    $EmptyDirectories = $AllDirectories | Where-Object { (Get-
ChildItem $PSItem).Count -eq 0}
    $EmptyDirectories | Remove-Item
    $Count = $EmptyDirectories.Count

    Write-Output "Iteration $Iteration`nRemoved the following
$Count directories. '$Count = 0' is $($Count -eq 0)"
    $EmptyDirectories
    $Iteration++
} until ($Count -eq 0)
```

2. Note the change in behavior this time and compare it with the run of `Do-While`.

Note how there was an empty iteration 5, just like with the `Do-While` loop:

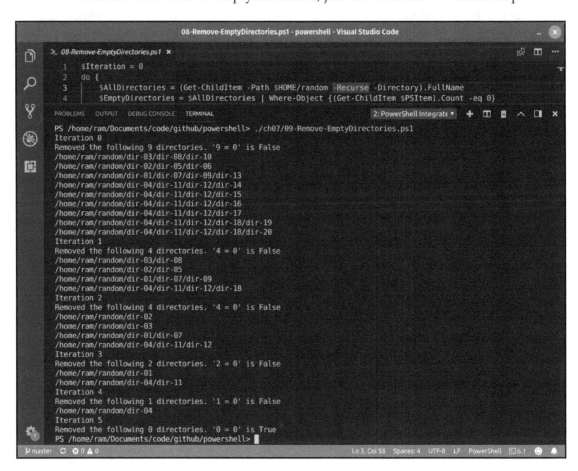

How it works...

This time, it was made evident in the interactive output how it works. The first run happened without checking for the condition. At the end of the run, the condition was checked for. 9 is greater than 0, and not equal. The outcome was `$false`, so the loop continued. It went on this way until the count came down to 0 (making the outcome of the condition `$true`), at which point, the loop exited. Essentially, the loop statement was: Go on until the count becomes zero.

8
Performing Calculations

In this chapter, we will discuss the following topics:

- Performing arithmetic operations
- Performing calculations on the output
- Working with administrative constants
- Working with calculated properties
- Working with binary numbers
- Performing base conversions

Introduction

Performing calculations is an integral part of automation. Of course, PowerShell allows for it. PowerShell also takes things up a level by providing administrators with what is called administrative constants, which help ease calculations (which will be addressed in the following recipes). We will first look at common arithmetic operations, and then move toward using the concepts on outputs using calculated properties, as we saw in `Chapter 4`, *Passing Data through the Pipeline*.

We will also look at cases where we could ease automation using binary numbers to identify flags, perform base conversion, and, finally, use some of the .NET accelerators or cast operators to simplify scripting.

Performing arithmetic operations

As administrators, we do not often use arithmetic operations, such as the `sin`, `cos`, `log`, and `exp` operations. However, it is possible to do all of them on PowerShell, since PowerShell can leverage .NET. In general, we may use these operations as administrators: `Abs` (as in absolute), `Ceiling`, `Floor`, `Round`, and `Truncate`. In this recipe, we will use three of these methods, based on the scenario we have. Use of the other methods is very similar.

Here is the scenario. You have an application that creates logs throughout the day. These logs consume a lot of space. You would like to clean up logs that are between 30 and 31 days old. You are not allowed to use a dual condition for comparison.

Create a function that looks for files that are 30 days old. Your script should also say how much of the log space was cleared, rounded off to the nearest megabyte.

Getting ready

Run the `Initialize-PacktPs6CoreLinuxLab.ps1` script from within the `ch04` directory of the book's GitHub repository. This is just so we have some files to work on. Next, run the `01-Set-LastWriteTime.ps1` script from within the `ch08` directory of the repository.

If you would like to specify a path other than `~/random` for the content, add `-Path '//your/custom/path'` to the last line of `01-Set-LastWriteTime.ps1` as well as `Initialize-PacktPs6CoreLinuxLab.ps1`:

```
PS> # Last line of file: Initialize-PacktPs6CoreLinuxLab.ps1
PS> Initialize-PacktPs6CoreLinuxLab -Path ./path/of/your/choice/

PS> # Last line of file: 01-Set-LastWriteTime.ps1
PS> Set-LastWriteTime -Path ./path/of/your/choice/
```

How to do it...

Navigate to the directory that contains your lab files, using the `Set-Location` cmdlet; here is where all the action happens. If you did not specify a custom `-Path` when running the scripts, it should be `~/random`:

1. Open the terminal and, using a code editor (`vi`, `nano`, or VS Code), create a new file called `01-Clear-LogFiles.ps1`. Remember, CamelCase is just a convention.

2. Enter the following content. I suggest typing it by yourself rather than copying and pasting it:

```
# Change this to match ./path/of/your/choice/ from the
aforementioned scripts
$LabPath = "$HOME/random"

$Today = Get-Date
$TotalFileSize = 0

$FilesToDelete = Get-ChildItem $LabPath -Recurse -File | Where-
Object {[math]::Floor(($Today - $_.LastWriteTime).TotalDays) -eq
30}


Write-Host "The following files will be deleted:"
Write-Host $FilesToDelete.FullName

foreach ($File in $FilesToDelete) {
    $TotalFileSize += $File.Length
    Remove-Item -Path $File -WhatIf
}

Write-Host "Total space cleared:
$([math]::Round($TotalFileSize/[math]::Pow(1024, 2))) MB"
```

There is no need to actually delete the files. If you would like to anyway, remove the `–WhatIf` switch from line 12.

It is recommended to use Visual Studio Code to write this script since its IntelliSense autocompletion is very helpful. You could write this script at the terminal itself, in which case, use shorter versions of parameters and tab-completions as necessary.

How it works...

The `[math]::` accelerator allows us to use the methods of the `System.Math` class. The `Round()` method accepts one or two arguments; in the case of a single argument, the rounding happens to the nearest integer. The optional second parameter specifies the number of digits after the decimal point.

The `Pow()` method is almost self-explanatory: 1024^2, in our case. The `Floor()` method brought down numbers from 30.00 to less than 31.00, down to 30.

This is what we did:

1. We listed out the files to delete: we subtracted the `LastWriteTime` from today, and performed a `Floor()` operation on it since we were not allowed to use the – and operator
2. We displayed the files
3. We performed a remove operation on each of the files, while also adding the size of each of the files to `$TotalFileSize`
4. Finally, we divided `$TotalFileSize` by 1024^2 and rounded it off to the nearest MB

See also

1. `System.Math` Methods (Microsoft documentation: `https://docs.microsoft.com/en-us/dotnet/api/system.math?redirectedfrom=MSDNview=netframework-4.7.2#methods`)

Performing calculations on the output

In the previous recipe, we performed some nifty calculations on the objects themselves, and listed out files that were 30 days old. In the process, we also output the total amount of space to be cleared. In this recipe, we will output this information as a PowerShell object, and also perform a small calculation during output.

Here is the scenario. Modify the script you created in the *Performing arithmetic operations* recipe to output a structured `PSCustomObject`. The output should have the total number of files in the directory, files that are 30 days old, and the total amount of space cleared (without any calculations). Also, separately, show the amount of space cleared by the cleanup, in MB.

Getting ready

Run the `Initialize-PacktPs6CoreLinuxLab.ps1` script from within the ch04 directory of the book's GitHub repository. This is just so we have some files to work on. Next, run the script, `01-Set-LastWriteTime.ps1`, from within the ch08 directory of the repository.

If you would like to specify a path other than ~/random for the content, add –Path
'//your/custom/path' to the last line of 01-Set-LastWriteTime.ps1 as well
as Initialize-PacktPs6CoreLinuxLab.ps1:

```
PS> # Last line of file: Initialize-PacktPs6CoreLinuxLab.ps1
PS> Initialize-PacktPs6CoreLinuxLab -Path ./path/of/your/choice/

PS> # Last line of file: 01-Set-LastWriteTime.ps1
PS> Set-LastWriteTime -Path ./path/of/your/choice/
```

How to do it

We will simply build on the previous recipe to save ourselves some time and effort. The
changes from the script in the previous recipe have been emboldened:

1. Open your favorite code editor, enter the following in the file, and save the file as
   a ps1 file:

```
# Change this to match ./path/of/your/choice/ from the
aforementioned scripts
$LabPath = "$HOME/random"

$Today = Get-Date
$TotalFileSize = 0

$AllFiles = Get-ChildItem $LabPath -Recurse -File
$FilesToDelete = $AllFiles | Where-Object {[math]::Floor(($Today -
$_.LastWriteTime).TotalDays) -eq 30}


Write-Host "The following files will be deleted:"
Write-Host $FilesToDelete.FullName

foreach ($File in $FilesToDelete) {
    $TotalFileSize += $File.Length
    Remove-Item -Path $File -WhatIf
}

New-Object -TypeName psobject -Property @{
    TotalFiles = $AllFiles.Count
    FilesToDelete = $FilesToDelete.Count
    SpaceCleared = $TotalFileSize
}
```

2. Call the PowerShell script:

```
PS> & ./ch08/02-Clear-LogFiles.ps1
```

This produces the following output:

3. Now, pick just the `SpaceCleared` parameter:

```
PS> (& $HOME/Documents/code/github/powershell/ch08/02-Clear-
LogFiles.ps1).SpaceCleared
```

Note the reference to the `SpaceCleared` property, and the output just before the prompt:

4. Divide the output by $1,024^2$ to get the value in MB:

```
PS> (& $HOME/Documents/code/github/powershell/ch08/02-Clear-
LogFiles.ps1).SpaceCleared/[math]::Pow(1024, 2)
```

Similar to the preceding output, the total space cleared in MB is shown in the following screenshot:

```
Terminal                                                          –  ⊗
PS /home/ram/Documents/code/github/powershell> (& ./ch08/02-Clear-LogFiles.ps1).SpaceCleared
/[math]::Pow(1024, 2)
The following files will be deleted:
/home/ram/random/my-plugin.rb /home/ram/random/piratos-wowa.me.mp3 /home/ram/random/random-t
ext.txt /home/ram/random/screenshot-001.png /home/ram/random/screenshot-002.png /home/ram/ra
ndom/screenshot-003.png /home/ram/random/volcano.jpg /home/ram/random/cities/cairo.html /hom
e/ram/random/cities/dubai.html /home/ram/random/cities/mumbai.html /home/ram/random/cities/n
yc.html /home/ram/random/cities/paris.html
8.71955299377441
PS /home/ram/Documents/code/github/powershell>
```

How it works...

Not only cmdlets and functions, but scripts also output objects. In the previous recipe, this was a string object; in this, it was a PSCustomObject. This way, even though the information gathered from both the recipes was the same, we were able to process the output further by running calculations on the fly.

There's more...

1. Perform a Round() operation on SpaceCleared to get the output in MB, with two digits after the decimal point.
2. Show the number of files that were omitted from deletion.

Assign the output object of the script to a variable, $FileCleanupInfo = (& //path/to/02-Clear-LogFiles.ps1), in order to make things easier.

Working with administrative constants

The one thing that may have irked a few of us was how difficult it was to convert the Length property to MB. We had to apply [math]::Pow(1024, 2). Simplify the output of the previous recipe.

Also, imagine that you have these files loaded on a 250 GB drive, and you would like to see what percent of space was cleared.

Getting ready

Run the script, `Initialize-PacktPs6CoreLinuxLab.ps1` from within
the `ch04` directory of the book's GitHub repository. This is just so we have some files to
work on. Next, run the script, `01-Set-LastWriteTime.ps1` from within
the `ch08` directory of the repository.

If you would like to specify a path other than `~/random` for the content, add `-Path`
`'//your/custom/path'` to the last line of `01-Set-LastWriteTime.ps1` as well
as `Initialize-PacktPs6CoreLinuxLab.ps1`:

```
PS> # Last line of file: Initialize-PacktPs6CoreLinuxLab.ps1
PS> Initialize-PacktPs6CoreLinuxLab -Path ./path/of/your/choice/

PS> # Last line of file: 01-Set-LastWriteTime.ps1
PS> Set-LastWriteTime -Path ./path/of/your/choice/
```

How to do it...

We will use the same script as the previous recipe:

1. Assign the object returned by the previous recipe to a variable:

   ```
   PS> $FileCleanupInfo = (& /ch08/02-Clear-LogFiles.ps1)
   ```

2. Call the `SpaceCleared` property and divide it by administrative constants:

   ```
   PS> $FileCleanupInfo.SpaceCleared/1KB
   ```

   ```
   PS> $FileCleanupInfo.SpaceCleared/1MB
   ```

   ```
   PS> $FileCleanupInfo.SpaceCleared/1GB
   ```

   Note how the results are not just the numbers divided by powers of 1,000:

```
Terminal                                                              _  ✕
PS /home/ram/Documents/code/github/powershell> $FileCleanupInfo.SpaceCleared/1kb
8928.822265625
PS /home/ram/Documents/code/github/powershell> $FileCleanupInfo.SpaceCleared/1mb
8.71955299377441
PS /home/ram/Documents/code/github/powershell> $FileCleanupInfo.SpaceCleared/1gb
0.00851518847048283
PS /home/ram/Documents/code/github/powershell> █
```

3. To calculate what percentage of space got cleared from a 250 GB hard disk, do the following:

```
PS> ($FileCleanupInfo.SpaceCleared)/(250*1e9)*100
```

An almost negligible number in our case, but here it is:

```
Terminal                                                              _  ⊗
PS /home/ram/Documents/code/github/powershell> $FileCleanupInfo.SpaceCleared/(250*1e9)*100
0.0036572456
PS /home/ram/Documents/code/github/powershell> 
```

How it works...

PowerShell has been created with administrators in mind. Given that we rely on a myriad of file operations on a regular basis, PowerShell contains administrative constants. These constants represent powers of 1,024 ($1,024^1$, $1,024^2$, $1,024^3$, and so on).

Hard drive and flash drive manufacturers usually use powers of 1,000 to represent drive sizes. In our recipe, we use the scientific notation to convert the size of the drive into bytes.

Working with calculated properties

If you read through the *Selecting columns from the output* recipe, in Chapter 4, *Passing Data through the Pipeline*, you may skip this recipe. This recipe has been created in the interest of context, as well as for those who have skipped that chapter/recipe.

Calculated properties is another form of performing calculations on the fly. Here is the scenario. You need a report of all the files present in a certain directory, with the names of the files, the last modified date, the full paths, and the sizes in MB.

Getting ready

If you do not have the lab files or you deleted the files in the previous recipe, run the script, Initialize-PacktPs6CoreLinuxLab.ps1, from within the ch04 directory of the book's GitHub repository. Next, run the script, Set-LastWriteTime.ps1, from within the ch08 directory of the repository.

How to do it...

This is going to be a one-liner.

At the terminal, type the following and press the *Enter* key:

```
PS> Get-ChildItem -file -rec | Select-Object name, lastwritetime, @{n =
'Size'; e = {[math]::Round($_.Length/1MB, 3)}}

PS> # Verbose version: Get-ChildItem -File -Recurse | Select-Object Name,
LastWriteTime, @{Name = "Size"; Expression = {
[math]::Round($PSItem.Length/1MB, 3) }}
```

How it works...

A calculated property takes in two things: the name of the property and the expression that would produce the desired result. Technically, this is a hashtable with n (or Name) and e (or Expression) being the two name-value pairs. The Expression in itself is a script block. When broken down into lines, the query looks like this:

```
Get-ChildItem -File -Recurse | Select-Object Name, LastWriteTime, @{
    Name = "Size"
    Expression = {
        [math]::Round($PSItem.Length/1MB, 3)
    }
}
```

Since we separated the Name and the Expression by a line, we do not need the semicolon anymore.

Calculated properties come in handy in situation where you do not really want to create a new script, but instead want some information at the terminal itself, as though running a query. The value of Name is the name of the property, and the values in the column are determined by the expression.

Working with binary numbers

In the interest of specificity, we are going to use the hexadecimal notification for this recipe. If you have worked with colors on your computer, chances are that you are aware of RGB. The levels of these primary colors are commonly represented as numbers ranging from 0 to 255 (24-bit colors). You may have also come across the hexadecimal representation of these colors, especially if you have worked with HTML/CSS.

The scenario here is to write a simple script that converts any given hexadecimal code into decimal RGB.

How to do it...

We will assume that the input is going to be with or without the # (as in `55bc9a` or `#55bc9a`):

1. Open a new PowerShell file and type the following:

```
$Rgb = Read-Host "Enter the hexadecimal RGB value"
$TrimmedRgb = $Rgb.Substring($Rgb.Length - 6)

$R = $TrimmedRgb.Substring(0, 2)
$G = $TrimmedRgb.Substring(2, 2)
$B = $TrimmedRgb.Substring(4, 2)

"Here are the R, G and B levels for the supplied hex value:"
$R, $G, $B | ForEach-Object { [int]("0x" + $PSItem) }
```

2. Run the script.
3. Enter any valid hexadecimal RGB value, with or without the preceding #. Press the *Enter* key.

   Here is an example:

```
Terminal
PS /home/ram/Documents/code/github/powershell> ./ch08/05-ConvertTo-Rgb.ps1
Enter the hexadecimal RGB value: #23feab
Here are the R, G and B levels for the supplied hex value:
35
254
171
PS /home/ram/Documents/code/github/powershell>
```

How it works...

First, we will look at how the script works to separate the R, G, and B values. We first trim the hexadecimal string to exclude the # in case there is one. We need the last six characters of the string. Therefore, we use PowerShell to begin the substring at 1 in case there is a # and 0 in case the string is six characters long. We then pick two characters at a time, starting at 0 (of the trimmed string), 2, and 4.

The conversion happens at the last line. First, we instruct PowerShell that we would like an integer output using the cast operator. Then, we tell PowerShell that the string is a hexadecimal string by adding `0x` to its beginning.

This is a simple way of converting a hexadecimal into an integer. Next, we will look at a few other conversions.

Performing base conversions

The previous recipe was a simple conversion using a cast operator and string addition. Next, we will look at converting an integer into multiple bases, such as octal, hexadecimal, and binary strings.

How to do it...

The input will be taken as a string. The output would also be string, but with octal, hexadecimal, and binary representations. We will use a .NET accelerator for this:

1. Open a new PowerShell file and type the following:

```
$InputString = Read-Host "Enter an integer"

Write-Host "Octal representation: " -NoNewline
Write-Host "$([Convert]::ToString($InputString, 8))"

Write-Host "Hexadecimal representation: " -NoNewline
Write-Host "$([Convert]::ToString($InputString, 16))"

Write-Host "Binary representation: " -NoNewline
Write-Host "$([Convert]::ToString($InputString, 2))"
```

2. Run the script and enter an integer to get the octal, hexadecimal, and binary representations of it.

Do not forget to try negative numbers as well:

```
                                    Terminal                              _  ⊗
PS /home/ram/Documents/code/github/powershell> & ./ch08/06-ConvertTo-OtherBases.ps1
Enter an integer: 89
Octal representation: 131
Hexadecimal representation: 59
Binary representation: 1011001
PS /home/ram/Documents/code/github/powershell> []
```

How it works...

This recipe leverages the [System.Convert] .NET accelerator. The input and the output of the script are strings.

The ToString() method accepts input in the form of int64. When only one argument is passed, the integer is output as it is, except the object type is no longer int, but string. The optional second argument passed to the method is the base: 2 stands for decimal, 8 stands for octal, and 16 stands for hexadecimal.

There's more...

When I was learning PowerShell, I came across a recipe, *Work with Numbers as Binary*, in the book *Windows PowerShell Cookbook* by Lee Holmes, where he showed how file attribute flags worked in PowerShell. To see what attributes are available in PowerShell for files and directories, and see their decimal and binary representations, enter the following at the PowerShell prompt:

```
PS> [Enum]::GetValues([System.IO.FileAttributes]) | Select-Object `
@{ n = 'Property'; e = { $_ } }, `
@{ n = 'Integer'; e = { [int]$_ } }, `
@{ n = 'Hexadecimal'; e = { [Convert]::ToString([int]$_, 16) } }, `
@{ n = 'Binary'; e = { [Convert]::ToString([int]$_, 2) } }
```

This is what the command gives you:

```
                                    Terminal                              _  ⊗
PS /home/ram/Documents/code/github/powershell> [Enum]::GetValues([System.IO.FileAttributes
]) | Select-Object `
>> @{ n = 'Property'; e = { $_ } },
>> @{ n = 'Integer'; e = { [int]$_ } },
>> @{ n = 'Hexadecimal'; e = { [Convert]::ToString([int]$_, 16) } },
>> @{ n = 'Binary'; e = { [Convert]::ToString([int]$_, 2) } }

        Property Integer Hexadecimal Binary
        -------- ------- ----------- ------
        ReadOnly       1 1           1
          Hidden       2 2           10
          System       4 4           100
       Directory      16 10          10000
         Archive      32 20          100000
          Device      64 40          1000000
          Normal     128 80          10000000
       Temporary     256 100         100000000
      SparseFile     512 200         1000000000
     ReparsePoint   1024 400         10000000000
      Compressed    2048 800         100000000000
         Offline    4096 1000        1000000000000
NotContentIndexed   8192 2000        10000000000000
       Encrypted   16384 4000        100000000000000
 IntegrityStream   32768 8000        1000000000000000
     NoScrubData  131072 20000       100000000000000000

PS /home/ram/Documents/code/github/powershell> []
```

That brings us to the end of this chapter. Basic arithmetic calculations have been omitted since they are no different from any of the most common languages.

Using Arrays and Hashtables

9

In this chapter, we will cover the following recipes:

- Creating and working with a simple array
- Accessing and manipulating array items
- Sorting an array
- Searching for an item in an array
- Combining arrays
- Item matching in an array
- Removing elements from an array
- Comparing arrays
- Creating a simple hashtable
- Performing simple tasks on a hashtable

Introduction

System automation without arrays is almost unthinkable. Everywhere there is a list of entities to be worked on, chances are, the implementation uses arrays. PowerShell is no exception. PowerShell works with single-dimensional as well as multidimensional arrays. Multidimensional arrays are of two types: jagged and non-jagged. We will look into what they are shortly.

Another very important concept in PowerShell is that of hashtables. Think of hashtables as named arrays (or, more appropriately, associative arrays). Hashtables provide us with a very systematic way to handle arrays, which we will see in the last couple of recipes of this chapter.

Replace `pwsh` with `pwsh-preview` in all of the following instances of `pwsh` if you are using PowerShell (Preview).

Creating and working with a simple array

In this recipe, we will see how to initialize a simple array and work with it. And here is the scenario. You have, let's say, a unique requirement. You want to know the process that is consuming the least of the processor time. To this, you add the top five processes consuming the most processor time. Information on how much of what is being used is not necessary; just the name would suffice.

How to do it...

We will first get the process consuming the least CPU and assign it to a variable:

1. Now, run the following to get the process consuming the least processor time and assign it to a variable:

```
PS> $Process = get-process | sort-object cpu | select-object -fi 1
-expand processname
PS> # Verbose version: $Process = Get-Process | Sort-Object CPU |
Select-Object -First 1 -ExpandProperty ProcessName
```

2. Next, select the top five processes using the most CPU and add them to this list. Also, call the variable to see the contents, and get the count:

```
PS> $Process += get-process | sort-object cpu | select-object -last
5 -expand processname
PS> # Verbose version: $Process += Get-Process | Sort-Object CPU |
Select-Object -Last 5 -ExpandProperty ProcessName

PS> "These are the $($Process.Count) processes you asked for:";
$Process
```

3. That was a single string, and not helpful at all. Let's now create a script at the terminal and run it:

```
$Process = @()
$Process += Get-Process | Sort-Object CPU | Select-Object -
ExpandProperty ProcessName -First 1
$Process += Get-Process | Sort-Object CPU | Select-Object -
ExpandProperty ProcessName -Last 5
"These are the $($Process.Count) processes you asked for:";
$Process
```

Alternatively, use the following:

```
$Process = , (Get-Process | Sort-Object CPU | Select-Object -
ExpandProperty ProcessName -First 1) $Process += Get-Process |
Sort-Object CPU | Select-Object -ExpandProperty ProcessName -Last 5
"These are the $($Process.Count) processes you asked for:";
$Process
```

In both the cases, you should get six processes, as expected.

How it works...

This recipe was aimed at initializing and adding content to an array. We used two cases here. In the first case, we added the name of one process to a variable, and tried to add five more to it. However, the value assigned to the variable at the end of it turned out to be a string, not an array as we may have expected. This happened because the + operator, when used with strings, concatenates strings. $Process was a string; we never told PowerShell that we wanted an array.

In the third step, we initialized an array using @(). And then, we used the += assignment operator to add content to the now-empty array. Remember that you must use the += assignment operator when adding content to the empty array; using the = operator will again assign a string to the variable, because the = assignment operator replaces content within the variable.

In the alternate method, we used a shorter way of telling PowerShell that $Process is an array; we used a comma, followed by the expression we would like to evaluate. Then, we used the += assignment operator to add the top five CPU hogs to the variable.

At the output line, we used a subexpression operator ($()) to show the process count.

There's more...

This is a little note on using multidimensional arrays in PowerShell. We did not include a recipe for it because, while multidimensional arrays are supported in PowerShell, there are very limited practical applications to them; a hashtable or a PowerShell custom object is preferred (and more efficient).

Multidimensional arrays in PowerShell are of two types:

- Jagged multidimensional array
- Non-jagged multidimensional array

A jagged array is one whose members contain a non-uniform number of members, such as the following:

```
 1,  2,  3,  4,  5
 6,  7,  8
 9, 10, 11, 12, 13, 14
15, 16, 17, 18
19, 20
```

It can be created using the following syntax:

```
$JaggedArray = @(
    (1, 2, 3, 4, 5),
    (6, 7, 8),
    (9, 10, 11, 12, 13, 14),
    (15, 16, 17, 18),
    (19, 20)
)
```

We also have non-jagged arrays in PowerShell:

```
 1,  2,  3,  4,  5
 6,  7,  8,  9, 10
11, 12, 13, 14, 15
16, 17, 18, 19, 20
```

They need to be initialized as a new object:

```
$MultiDimensionalArray = New-Object -TypeName "int[,]" 4, 5
$Count = 1

for ([int]$i = 0; $i -lt 4; $i++) {
    for ([int]$j = 0; $j -lt 5; $j++) {
        $MultiDimensionalArray[$i,$j] = $Count
        $Count++
    }
}

# Access a random member from within the array:
$MultiDimensionalArray[2,3]
```

Accessing and manipulating array items

In this recipe, we will look at using the array in administration.

The scenario is that one of the administrative assistants has sent you a list of names in the FirstName LastName format. You need to change the format to LastName, FirstName so that you can process it further in a system that requires that format. The list contains over 100 names, and manual manipulation is ruled out.

How to do it...

We need a simple script to accomplish this. The assumption made for this recipe is that all names consist of two words, separated by a space. Each line in the input file contains only one name.

Here is the logical flow:

1. Import the content. Get-Content would import the names as an array of strings. However, we will not manipulate this array.
2. Use a foreach loop to go through the names one by one.
3. Split the first name and the last name. (Each FirstName LastName pair will be an array consisting of two strings.)
4. Place the last name, place a comma, and then place the first name.
5. Optionally, output the content to a file.

The following script will accomplish this:

```
$Names = Get-Content ./ch09/02-names.txt
$NewNames = @()

foreach ($Name in $Names) {
    $Name = $Name -split ' '
    $NewName = $Name[1], $Name[0] -join ', '

    $NewNames += $NewName
}
$NewNames
```

How it works...

This script block is a simple implementation of array manipulation. The first line of the script imports the names from the input file into the $Names variable.

We initialize a new array, $NewNames, to store the names in the LastName, FirstName format. Get-Content imports the text in the input file in the form of an array, the newline character being the separator of elements. Since $Names is an array, using the foreach loop to perform operations on the elements is possible.

Within the loop, we split the single string into two strings using the split operator. This, of course, converts $Name from a string into an array; the first name is the first element of the array, and the last name is the second. Next we perform a concatenation using the join operator.

We then add the values of $NewName to the $NewNames array to get all the names together.

There's more...

Try the same operation using the Foreach-Object cmdlet instead of the foreach loop.

See also

- *Writing a basic looping construct* from Chapter 7, *Flow Control Using Branches and Loops*
- *Writing a more complex loop on a predefined array* from Chapter 7, *Flow Control Using Branches and Loops*
- *Splitting and combining strings* from Chapter 6, *Working with Strings*

Sorting an array

Sorting an array is no different from sorting anything else in PowerShell. PowerShell treats arrays as objects, too. This recipe will be simple.

The scenario is that you need to sort the names given in the previous recipe based on the first name. Then, you need to convert the names to the LastName, FirstName format.

How to do it...

This recipe is simple. We simply add another cmdlet to the first line of the script. Here is the flow:

1. Import the content using `Get-Content`. Pipe this output to `Sort-Object`.
2. Use a `foreach` loop to go through the names one by one.
3. Split the first name and the last name, swap them, and separate them with a comma and a space.

The following script will accomplish this:

```
$Names = Get-Content ./ch09/02-names.txt | Sort-Object
$NewNames = @()

foreach ($Name in $Names) {
    $Name = $Name -split ' '
    $NewName = $Name[1], $Name[0] -join ', '

    $NewNames += $NewName
}
$NewNames
```

How it works...

The sorting happens at the first line. `Get-Content` imports the name as an array of strings. At this point, the input object is an array. `Sort-Object` then sorts the elements in this object. From here on, the process is the same as the *Accessing and manipulating array items* recipe.

Of course, there are other ways to do this, one being to replace the last line of the script with the following:

```
$NewNames = $NewNames | Sort-Object
```

There's more...

Create a CSV with first names and last names as two different columns. Add the age of each of these members to the CSV. Now, sort based on the age, then on the last name.

See also

- *Sorting the output* from Chapter 4, *Passing Data through the Pipeline*

Searching for an item in an array

It is exceedingly simple in PowerShell to look for an element in an array.

The scenario for you is that you need to know if the list of names that was output from the *Accessing and manipulating array items* recipe contains the name, Torres, Leon.

How to do it

We will build on the *Accessing and manipulating array items* recipe. Here is the flow:

1. Import the names from the text file
2. Flip the first and the last names so the format is LastName, FirstName
3. Look for the element Torres, Leon within the newly constructed array

The following script would accomplish this:.

```
$Names = Get-Content ./ch09/02-names.txt
$NewNames = @()

foreach ($Name in $Names) {
    $Name = $Name -split ' '
    $NewName = $Name[1], $Name[0] -join ', '

    $NewNames += $NewName
}
if ($NewNames -contains 'Torres, Leon') {
    Write-Host "Found Leon Torres in the list!"
}
```

How it works...

The emboldened line in the script is the one that performs the search. The `contains` comparison operator, as we discussed in `Chapter 6`, *Working with Strings*, looks for an element in an array. One important point to note is that the `contains` operator always looks for an exact match. Therefore, `$NewNames -contains 'Torres, L*'` will not work.

See also

- Containment operators in *Introduction* of `Chapter 6`, *Working with Strings*

Combining arrays

You have already combined arrays when adding elements to an array. The point is, combining two arrays is no different than adding elements to an array. Here is the scenario. You have two lists, each 10 names long. You have to combine them into a single list of 20 names.

How to do it...

The process is simple. This is the flow we are going to follow:

1. Import the contents of the first file into a variable
2. Import the contents of the second file into another variable
3. Combine the arrays

And this is the script that will help you with this:

```
$ListOne = Get-Content ./ch09/05-list-one.txt
$ListTwo = Get-Content ./ch09/05-list-two.txt

"List one contains $($ListOne.Count) items."
"List two contains $($ListTwo.Count) items."

$CombinedList = $ListOne + $ListTwo

$CombinedList
```

How it works...

In this recipe, we did not initialize an array, because we already had two arrays as the input. When we created $CombinedList, PowerShell understood, from the assignment operation, that the resultant object type should be an array. When ListOne and ListTwo were added, PowerShell, instead of combining all the names into a single string, simply combined the two arrays and added each array as arrays themselves.

One important point to note here is that when an array is created, it is of a fixed length. In other words, suppose you said $ListOne += $ListTwo; the $ListOne array does not directly get altered, since the length of $ListOne is fixed at 10. PowerShell, in the background, measures the lengths of the two arrays in question, creates a temporary array of length 20, adds the elements of both the source arrays into this array, and then re-initializes $ListOne as an array of length 20 and assigns all the elements from the temporary array into $ListOne.

Item matching in an array

In the *Searching for an item in an array* recipe, we searched for a specific name using the contains comparison operator. This way, we looked for a complete element, without wildcards or regex.

In this recipe, we will use wildcard and regex matching to find elements that match a pattern.

Build on the *Accessing and manipulating array items* recipe and look for individuals whose last names end with son. Perform this search using the like and the match comparison operators.

How to do it...

The flow is simple. All we have to do is replace the contains operator with like or match:

1. Import the names from the text file.
2. Look for the elements that end with son within the newly constructed array.
3. Flip the first and last names so the format is LastName, FirstName:

```
$Names = Get-Content ./ch09/02-names.txt
$Names = $Names -match 'son$'
```

```
# or $Names = $Names -like '*son'

$NewNames = @()

foreach ($Name in $Names) {
    $Name = $Name -split ' '
    $NewName = $Name[1], $Name[0] -join ', '

    $NewNames += $NewName
}
$NewNames
```

Alternatively, you could swap the second and the third steps and use a slightly different approach:

```
$Names = Get-Content ./ch09/02-names.txt
$NewNames = @()

foreach ($Name in $Names) {
    $Name = $Name -split ' '
    $NewName = $Name[1], $Name[0] -join ', '

    $NewNames += $NewName
}
"Using the match operator:"
$NewNames -match 'son,'

"Using the like operator:"
$NewNames -like '*son,*'
```

Depending on the number of elements in the array, the processing time in the second approach may be higher given that PowerShell would have to swap positions of the first and last names a greater number of times.

How it works...

The `match` and `like` comparison operators can take input as single elements or as arrays. When the operators are used on arrays, the comparison operation runs on each of the elements of the array. Think of this as being equivalent to the `Where-Object`-based filtration. In other words, `$NewNames -match 'son'` is very similar to using `$NewNames | Where-Object { $PsItem -match 'son' }`.

That brings us to performing some more complex filtration; when such a need arises, use the `Where-Object` cmdlet instead of a plain `match` or `like` on the array. Performing Boolean AND or OR operations with plain matching and multiple conditions will only produce a Boolean output. For instance, if you are using the name list supplied with the chapter, the output to the following would only be `True`:

```
$NewNames -match 'son,' -and $NewName -notmatch 'Erick'
```

There's more...

Find the individuals in the list whose last names end with `son`, and whose first names do not contain `Erick`.

Removing elements from an array

Removing elements from an array is not as straightforward as adding elements to an array. Adding two arrays is as simple as using the + arithmetic operator or the += assignment operator. Removing objects, on the other hand, can be done in either of the following two ways:

- Filter out objects that you do not want and assign the rest of the array to a new array
- Use the `System.Collections.ArrayList` class

Create a list of all the files and directories within `~/random`. Remove the paths within `dir-04`.

How to do it...

We will perform this task in two ways. Here is the first way:

1. List out all the paths within the `$HOME/random` directory. (Replace all instances of `$HOME/random` with the path to your lab directory if you changed the defaults in the script.).
2. Filter out paths that do not match `dir-04`.
3. Show the list.

Here is the script that performs these actions:

```
$Paths = (Get-ChildItem $HOME/random -Recurse).FullName
$Paths = $Paths | Where-Object {$PSItem -notmatch "^$HOME/random/dir-04"}
Write-Output "Here is the list of paths within the lab directory, without
those within dir-04:`n`n"
$Paths
```

The second method would be using the `System.Collections.ArrayList` class:

1. List out all the paths within the $HOME/random directory
2. List out all the paths that have $HOME/random/dir-04 in them
3. Remove these paths from the list of directories, using the `Remove()` method of the `System.Collections.ArrayList` class

Here is the script that performs these actions:

```
$AllPaths = New-Object -TypeName System.Collections.ArrayList
foreach ($Path in (Get-ChildItem $HOME/random -Recurse)) {
[void]$AllPaths.Add($Path.FullName)
}

$PathsToExclude = $AllPaths -match "^$HOME/random/dir-04"

foreach ($Dir4Path in $PathsToExclude) {
$AllPaths.Remove($Dir4Path)
}

Write-Output "Here is the list of paths within the lab directory, without
those within dir-04:`n`n"
$AllPaths
```

How it works...

This is relatively simple to understand. We use a simple comparison operation to exclude those elements that we don't want, and then assign the resultant array back to the original array. This is the first way of doing it.

The other, not-so-simple, way of performing deletions is using the .NET class, `System.Collections.Arraylist`. This class has methods specific to array operations. Therefore, in some situations, the `Remove()` method may seem like a better option to use rather than performing filtration on the array. It is noteworthy that these methods may show undesirable console output. This is because the methods were created with programming in mind; these are neither native to PowerShell, nor entirely meant for administration. To avoid the console output, use `[void]` before the variable name (do not use `| Out-Null`).

Comparing arrays

Array comparison, although fun, can seem to be a little bit of a technical overkill to implement using programming or scripting, the reason being the necessity to loop through the entire arrays and perform comparisons. In PowerShell, though, this task is as simple as passing two arguments to a cmdlet. In Linux, we have the `diff` tool to help us compare the contents of two files.

Imagine that you had an input file with 30 server names. One of the administrators in the team picked up the list and performed modifications to it by adding and removing a few server names. This list was not source-controlled. Luckily, the administrator did not replace the file, but created a new copy. You would like to review the file before approving the changes made. You want to see which servers were added and which were removed.

How to do it...

PowerShell has a cmdlet for this task. Here is the script that can handle it:

```
$MyServers  = Get-Content ./ch09/08-server-names-01.txt
$ModServers = Get-Content ./ch09/08-server-names-02.txt

Compare-Object $MyServers $ModServers
# Verbose version: Compare-Object -ReferenceObject $MyServers -
DifferenceObject $ModServers
```

Here is the output of that command:

```
Terminal                                                            _  ⊗
PS /home/ram/Documents/code/github/powershell> & ./ch09/08-Compare-ServerName.ps1

InputObject SideIndicator
----------- -------------
heinap      =>
aptoor      =>
shaeco      =>
modusp      =>
hulont      =>
jublam      =>
urilip      =>
exeini      =>
eullib      =>
kemers      <=
bysher      <=
arsure      <=
uphawa      <=
chlelo      <=
zioldy      <=
dirlec      <=
aoradu      <=
honclu      <=

PS /home/ram/Documents/code/github/powershell> []
```

How it works...

The `Compare-Object` cmdlet is designed to take in a reference object (your list of servers in this case) and a difference object (the list that your fellow administrator sent you). It compares the contents and shows on the screen which of the objects contains it; the reference object indicated by the left arrow and the difference object by the right arrow. The cmdlet has other parameters as well, such as a switch to include the objects that are equal, and/or exclude the differences.

Creating a simple hashtable

To be honest, if you followed the course of this book without skipping recipes, you have already seen a few hashtable demonstrations. However, it has not been shown in this light so far. So, off we go.

You would like to create a list of processes and the amount of working set each of them uses. You would like to access each of the processes by name. You do not require any detail from the process table other than the working set. As an example, show the amount of working set used by pwsh.

How to do it...

The script is a simple three-liner:

1. Initialize a hashtable
2. List out all the processes
3. Add the process name as well as the working set to the new array you created

The following script can accomplish this task:

```
$Processes = @{}
Get-Process | ForEach-Object { $Processes[$PSItem.Name] = $PSItem.WS/1MB }
$Processes['pwsh']
```

Optionally, you can also go for a foreach looping construct instead of the Foreach-Object cmdlet.

How it works...

What we just created was an associative array, also known as a hashtable. These are arrays with named elements. Instead of accessing the values using an index, we use a name.

In this recipe, we associate the process name to the working set of each of the processes running in the system.

The first step is to initialize a hashtable. An array is initialized using @(), whereas a hashtable is initialized using @{}. The next step is to add data as we would to an array. However, when adding content to an array, we simply add the values. In the case of hashtables, though, each value must be accompanied by a name. Therefore, we use the $Variable['Name'] = Value format.

In this recipe, we add content to the hashtable using a Foreach-Object loop. And when it comes to calling an element, we call it as $Variable['Name'].

Content can also be modified. For instance, if you would like to manually modify the working set value for `pwsh` or `code`, you could use the following:

```
Terminal                                                          _  ✕
PS /home/ram/Documents/code/github/powershell> . ./ch09/09-New-MemoryList.ps1
227.16015625
PS /home/ram/Documents/code/github/powershell> $Processes.'pwsh' = 150
PS /home/ram/Documents/code/github/powershell> $Processes['pwsh']
150
PS /home/ram/Documents/code/github/powershell> $Processes['code']
119.3125
PS /home/ram/Documents/code/github/powershell> $Processes.'code' = 21
PS /home/ram/Documents/code/github/powershell> $Processes['code']
21
PS /home/ram/Documents/code/github/powershell> # If you do not have `code` running, call a
 different process.
```

The syntax dictates using quotes around the name within the square brackets, and, when assigning values to element names, using quotes when the name contains non-alphanumeric characters (as demonstrated in the cases of `pwsh` and `code`).

You can also manually create a hashtable. Here is how to do this:

```
$Hashtable = @{
    pwsh     = 12
    inkscape = 23
    atom     = 15
}
```

Performing simple tasks on a hashtable

Now that we know how to create a hashtable, we can start working with it. The scenario for us here is this. You need to create a verbose report of all the processes currently running on your computer. The report should have the following information:

- The number of processes running on the computer
- Whether PowerShell is running on the computer
- Processes sorted by name
- Average working set used

In addition, you also need to count the number of processes after removing `pwsh` from it, and then clear the hashtable.

How to do it...

Perform the following steps:

1. Create a report template
2. Fill in the values from queries using the methods that are part of the hashtable object

Here is the script that will help you accomplish the tasks. Create a new PS1 file and add the following content to it.

The script is available as `10-New-ProcessReport.ps1` within the `ch09` directory of the code repository that accompanies the book:

```
$Processes = @{}
Get-Process | ForEach-Object { $Processes[$PSItem.Name] = $PSItem.WS/1MB }

$Report = "The computer is currently running $($Processes.Count)
processes."

if ($Processes.Contains('pwsh')) {
    $Report += "`n`nPowerShell is also running at the moment."
    $Processes.Remove('pwsh')
}
else {
    $Report += "`n`nPowerShell is not running at the moment."
}

$Report += "`n`nFollowing is the list of processes currently running,
sorted by name:"

$Report += "`n`n$(($Processes.GetEnumerator() | Sort-Object Name).Name -
join "`n")"

$Report += "`n`nThe average working set used is $(($Processes.Values |
Measure-Object -Average).Average) MB. There are $($Processes.Count)
processes running, apart from PowerShell."

$Processes.Clear()

$Report += "`n`n$($Processes.Count) processes left after clearing the
list."

$Report
```

How it works...

The first two lines in the script have already been seen: they initialize a hashtable and add the processes to the hashtable. The rest of the script simply uses the members of the hashtable to give us the necessary information. For instance, `Count` is a property within the object. The `Contains()` method looks for the key, `pwsh`, and reports `True` or `False` based on whether it finds the key. The `Remove()` method removes the element identified by the key.

If you simply call `$Processes`, the list will be unsorted. In order to sort the keys or values, we use the `GetEnumerator()` method, so that PowerShell treats the hashtable as an object with two properties (`Name` and `Value`). Only then will you be able to sort the hashtable by name or value.

> If you create a hashtable manually and call the hashtable to see its keys and values, you will see that they are not sorted in any particular way. When manually creating a hashtable, if you would like to control the sequence of the key-value pairs, use the (ordered) cast operator when initializing the hashtable (`[ordered]@{}` instead of the plain `@{}`).

We can also call only the names or the values. When applicable, you can also perform arithmetic operations on the values using the `Measure-Object` cmdlet.

Clearing the hashtable is as simple as calling the `Clear()` method from within the hashtable object.

Call `$Processes | Get-Member` to list out all the properties and methods of the object:

```
                                   Terminal                              _  ⊗

PS /home/ram/Documents/code/github/powershell> $Processes | Get-Member


   TypeName: System.Collections.Hashtable

Name               MemberType            Definition
----               ----------            ----------
Add                Method                void Add(System.Object key, System.Object valu...
Clear              Method                void Clear(), void IDictionary.Clear()
Clone              Method                System.Object Clone(), System.Object ICloneabl...
Contains           Method                bool Contains(System.Object key), bool IDictio...
ContainsKey        Method                bool ContainsKey(System.Object key)
ContainsValue      Method                bool ContainsValue(System.Object value)
CopyTo             Method                void CopyTo(array array, int arrayIndex), void...
Equals             Method                bool Equals(System.Object obj)
GetEnumerator      Method                System.Collections.IDictionaryEnumerator GetEn...
GetHashCode        Method                int GetHashCode()
GetObjectData      Method                void GetObjectData(System.Runtime.Serializatio...
GetType            Method                type GetType()
OnDeserialization  Method                void OnDeserialization(System.Object sender), ...
Remove             Method                void Remove(System.Object key), void IDictiona...
ToString           Method                string ToString()
Item               ParameterizedProperty System.Object Item(System.Object key) {get;set;}
Count              Property              int Count {get;}
```

That brings us to the end of this chapter, and a little closer to being comfortable with PowerShell scripting. As noted before, where PowerShell really excels is in handling structured data. Everything is an object.

Handling Files and Directories

10

In this chapter, we are going to discuss the following topics:

- Reading content from a file
- Sending output to a file
- Adding and setting content to a file
- Searching for content
- Working with locations
- Working with files and directories
- Listing files and directories
- Working with structured and unstructured files

Introduction

The initial design of PowerShell is considered a replacement for DOS commands. The new design features allowed a certain degree of modernization and adaptation to the changing need of the growing market. In fact, the initial design is a clone from Unix/Linux Bash concepts, such as the pipe, aliases, and so on.

Working with files is arguably the most important part of being an IT pro, especially in the Linux environment, where everything is a file. This type of management helps with modularity, not to mention easy readability. Configuration files, so far, have been plain text and using them for administration has been about strings. PowerShell is a little ahead in this case: apart from handling simple files (which we call unstructured files), PowerShell can also handle structured files, and much better, because of its object-oriented nature. Structured files, such as JSON, are where PowerShell shines the most, because using them as objects is simple, straightforward, and efficient in PowerShell.

This chapter is all about working with files and directories. You will learn to read content from files, send output to files, and work with structured and unstructured files.

Reading content from a file

One of the most basic operations of the file is reading content from a file. So far, we have been reading content from file as a block of text. The PowerShell cmdlet for this operation is Get-Content. And it works a little different than expected. This recipe is aimed at explaining how different it is.

The task for this recipe is simple. You must display details of the file on the screen, as follows:

1. Show the details of a file
2. Read the first seven lines from the file
3. Read the last five lines of the file
4. Read content from the 11th to the 13th line of the file
5. Display the number of characters, words, and lines in the file
6. Import the contents of the file into a variable

How to do it...

Perform the following steps:

1. Create a dummy file at ~/random. This script uses the code repository of the book as the location.

2. If you would like, create the file yourself using the following script block:

```
PS> for ($j = 0; $j -lt 100; $j++) { $($i = 0; while ($i -lt 8) {
(-join ((65..90) + (97..122) | Get-Random -Count 8 | ForEach-Object
{ [char]$_ })).ToString(); $i++ }) -join ' ' | Out-File ./ch10/01-
random-text.txt -Append }
```

3. Next, use the following script to get the necessary details:

```
Write-Host "File details:"

Get-Item ./ch10/01-random-text.txt

"Here are the first seven lines from the file."

Get-Content ./ch10/01-random-text.txt -ReadCount 7 | Select-Object
-First 1

"Here are the last five lines from the file."
```

```
Get-Content ./ch10/01-random-text.txt -Tail 5

"Here are the eleventh to the thirteenth lines."

Get-Content ./ch10/01-random-text.txt | Select-Object -First 3 -
Skip 10

"And here are some details about the content in the file."

Get-Content ./ch10/01-random-text.txt | Measure-Object -Character -
Word -Line

"Finally, the content will be imported into a variable. Let us see
if the content is a single block of text or not."

$Content = Get-Content ./ch10/01-random-text.txt

"There are $($Content.Count) elements in the variable."
"When read as raw content, the number of elements is $((Get-Content
./ch10/01-random-text.txt -Raw).Count)"
```

Take the time to read the output.

 Get-Content with the -Tail parameter finds its primary use in reading log files. If you would like to follow along as the file is updated, use the -Wait switch parameter as well. This will update the output as content is added to the file in question. Like so: Get-Content ./ch10/01-random-text.txt -Tail 5 -Wait.

How it works...

The first task is relatively simple. It shows you the details about the file. Think of this as peeking into the file properties. If you would like more details, pipe the first line of the command to Select-Object *.

The second line is very important. The ReadCount parameter instructs Get-Content to read *n* lines in a shot, and pass it along the pipeline. In our case, note how we have used -ReadCount 7 | Select-Object -First 1 to read the first seven lines. In this case, Get-Content read the first seven lines of the file as a single block.

To read the last five lines of the file, we use the Tail parameter. However, in this case, the number of elements (lines) is retained; the imported content is an array of five strings, not a single block containing five lines. More on this in just a moment.

To get the 11th to the 13th lines, we skip the first 10 lines, and pick only three lines. Simple enough.

Since the output object is a string, the `Measure-Object` cmdlet supports characters, words (groups of characters separated by spaces), and lines. The output says that we have 100 lines in the script, so many characters, and so many words.

The 100 lines is consistent with the number of elements present in `$Content`. This means that `Get-Content` imported the text as an array of 100 elements, the elements separated by a newline character in the file. This is an important point to note, because we are used to file content being read as a single block, with the newline characters preserved. PowerShell handles reading text from a file as an array of strings.

Using the `Raw` switch, however, changes this behavior. In this case, PowerShell imports the text as you would expect, in a single block, with the newline characters retained.

Getting content as an array of strings is primarily useful when we use a simple text file as an input file. Imagine you want to get some details about a certain 100 servers. You could simply place all the names in a file and make PowerShell import the names as separate names, thereby allowing you to use looping constructs such as `foreach`.

See also

- The *Replacing substrings within strings* recipe in `Chapter 6`, *Working with Strings*

Sending output to a file

Reading content from files is one part of using files for administration; sending output to files is another. This recipe is intended to show you the options available to send output to files. In PowerShell, the process works through redirection. We will mainly look at the following:

- The `Out-File` cmdlet
- The `Tee-Object` cmdlet
- Redirection operators

The scenario for this recipe is as follows:

1. Send the list of the contents of ~/random/dir-04 to a file called ~/random/file-list.txt.

2. Try to list the contents of ~/random/dir-05. This would throw an error (because there is no such directory as ~/random/dir-05). This error must be sent to ~/random/error.txt.

3. Use Write-Host to write a note that the list of contents of the directory, ~/random/dir-03, is being appended to ~/random/file-list.txt; this console message should go to ~/random/message.txt.

4. Append the list of the contents of ~/random/dir-03 to ~/random/file-list.txt, while also displaying the list on the console.

Getting ready...

In order to go through this lab recipe, you need the lab set up. If you have not already done so, run the quick-and-dirty Initialize-PacktPs6CoreLinuxLab.ps1 script, under the ch04 directory, within the https://github.com/PacktPublishing/PowerShell-6.0-Linux-Administration-Cookbook repository. Run the script to get the necessary files.

Next, use the input file that we created in the *Understanding Here-Strings* recipe in Chapter 6, *Working with Strings*, to create files within the lab directory. Change the value of $LabPath to point to your lab directory:

```
PS> $LabPath = "$HOME/random"
PS> Get-Content ./ch06/03-input-file.txt | ForEach-Object { New-Item -Path
(Join-Path $LabPath -ChildPath $PSItem) -ItemType Directory -Force }
```

Go through the *Understanding Here-Strings* recipe from Chapter 6, *Working with Strings*, to create the directories needed for this recipe.

How to do it...

Here are the cmdlets we will use to accomplish these tasks:

1. The Get-ChildItem cmdlet to list out the contents, and Out-File across the pipeline (or the familiar redirection operator, >; they both work in PowerShell) to send the list of contents to a file.

2. The `Get-ChildItem` cmdlet to list the contents, and the `Out-File` cmdlet across the pipeline to send the error to the file. Everything that is displayed on the console should go to the file this way, shouldn't it?

3. The `Write-Host` cmdlet to display content on the screen, and, as usual, the `Out-File` cmdlet or the redirection operator to send the message to the file.

4. Again, the `Get-ChildItem` cmdlet to list the contents, and the `Tee-Object` cmdlet with the `Append` switch parameter (or the familiar redirect-and-append operator, >>) to append the file with the new list along with showing the content on the screen.

Proceed to write the script. This script has been saved as `ch10/02-Write-ContentOne.ps1` within the code repository that accompanies this book:

```
Get-ChildItem $HOME/random/dir-04 > $HOME/random/file-list.txt

Get-ChildItem $HOME/random/dir-05 > $HOME/random/error.txt

Write-Host "Listing the contents of ~/random/dir-03 and appending the list
to file-list.txt." > $HOME/random/message.txt

Get-ChildItem $HOME/random/dir-03 | Tee-Object $HOME/random/file-list.txt -
Append
```

The files, `message.txt` and `error.txt`, are empty, and the message and the error have appeared on the console:

```
                                   Terminal                                  ✕
PS /home/ram> & /home/ram/Documents/code/github/powershell/ch11/02-Test-Redirection.ps1
Get-ChildItem : Cannot find path '/home/ram/random/dir-05' because it does not exist.
At /home/ram/Documents/code/github/powershell/ch11/02-Test-Redirection.ps1:3 char:1
+ Get-ChildItem $HOME/random/dir-05 > $HOME/random/error.txt
+ ~~~~~~~~~~~~~~~~~~~~~~~~~~~~~~~~~~~~~~~~~~~~~~~~~~~~~~~~~~~~~
+ CategoryInfo          : ObjectNotFound: (/home/ram/random/dir-05:String) [Get-ChildItem]
, ItemNotFoundException
+ FullyQualifiedErrorId : PathNotFound,Microsoft.PowerShell.Commands.GetChildItemCommand

Listing the contents of ~/random/dir-03 and appending the list to file-list.txt.


    Directory: /home/ram/random/dir-03


Mode                LastWriteTime         Length Name
----                -------------         ------ ----
d-----         7/16/18     4:18 AM               dir-08


PS /home/ram>
```

Modify the script a little now. This script has been saved as `ch10/02-Write-ContentTwo.ps1` within the code repository that accompanies this book:

```
Get-ChildItem $HOME/random/dir-04 > $HOME/random/file-list.txt

Get-ChildItem $HOME/random/dir-05 2>&1 | Out-File $HOME/random/error.txt

Write-Host "Listing the contents of ~/random/dir-03 and appending the list
to file-list.txt." 6>&1 | Out-File $HOME/random/message.txt

Get-ChildItem $HOME/random/dir-03 | Tee-Object $HOME/random/file-list.txt -
Append
```

If we read the files, `error.txt` and `message.txt`, after running the modified script, you see the error and the message in the files:

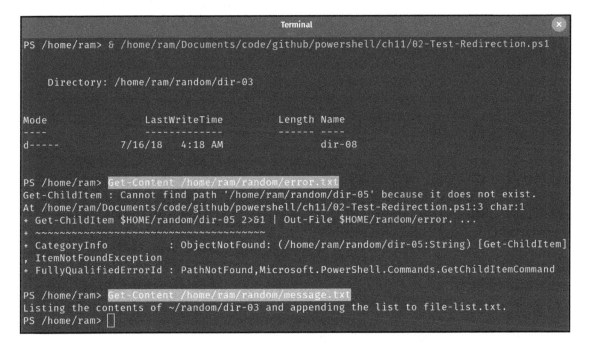

> In order to avoid confusion, the last > operator in `2>&1 >`
> `$HOME/random/error.txt` has been replaced by the pipeline and the
> `Out-File` cmdlet.

How it works...

First, a (rather long) note on streams. And this is very important.

There are six streams in PowerShell (Core, and Windows PowerShell 5.0+):

1. Success stream
2. Error stream
3. Warning stream
4. Verbose stream
5. Debug stream
6. Information stream

Think of them as separate parallel lines that never meet each other by themselves. PowerShell uses all of these six streams to send output. By default, the output destination of all of these streams is the host program, which, in our case, is the terminal emulator.

The success stream is where the actual output is sent to. Therefore, output from all the cmdlets and all success stories, is sent to the success stream. The pipeline, the redirection operator, and the redirect-and-append operator also work only on the Success stream. Streams 2 through 5 are self-explanatory: the errors go to the error stream, warnings go to the warning stream, and so on.

`Write-Host` is used when a message is to be shown on the host. Until PowerShell 5.0, `Write-Host` did not write anything to any of the streams; it simply bypassed all streams and went straight to the host program. Therefore, `Write-Host` was a little too evasive and dirty. During PowerShell 5.0, the team decided to bring in something that would retain the capabilities of `Write-Host` for backward compatibility, but make `Write-Host` content go to a stream. Obviously, to prevent what those who understand PowerShell streams call polluting the stream, `Write-Host` content had to be kept separate from the five aforementioned streams. So, a new stream called the information stream was introduced, along with the `Write-Information` cmdlet and a few information-related functionalities. `Write-Host` was programmed to write content to the information stream. While it is still argued that the verbose stream should be used to communicate with the user during script execution, it is still nice to have the plain old kind of interaction with the user using `Write-Host`. Now let's look at how the recipe works.

Initially, we pick the simple redirection operator or the `Out-File` cmdlet; both of them perform the same task: pass the content of the success stream to a file. The difference between the two, apart from the fact that the former is an operator and the latter is a cmdlet, is that, in the case of the operator, you can simply add the operator to the end of the command, add a space, and type in the path to the file. Therefore, if you use the operator, the syntax would be `command > //path/to/file`, whereas, for `Out-File`, it would be `command | Out-File //path/to/file`.

The error and the host message were not part of the Success stream. Therefore, they did not get sent to the respective files initially, but instead got sent straight to the default output of all the streams: the host program.

The order of the stream names is as mentioned at the beginning of this section. The third redirection operator (after > and >>) redirects data between streams, and the syntax is `SourceStreamNumber>&DestinationStreamNumber`. Therefore, to redirect the contents of the error stream to the success stream (so we can use the file redirection operator or the pipeline), we use `2>&1`. To redirect the contents of the Information stream to the Success stream, we use `6>&1`. When we use this redirection, you would notice that the error and the console message are not shown on the screen anymore, but instead go further in the path we specified (in our case, down the pipeline to `Out-File`).

Another point to note is that `Out-File`, by default, rewrites the specified file with the new content. In order to change that behavior and make the cmdlet append content to the existing content in the file, we use the `Append` switch parameter.

If you would like the contents of the Success stream passed on further through the pipeline along with being sent to a file or a variable, use the `Tee-Object` cmdlet; think of the letter T, if you are not already familiar with the `tee` command in Linux. If we do not add a pipeline after the `Tee-Object` cmdlet, the contents of the Success stream would be sent to the host, which is the default outlet, along with being sent to the specified file or variable. This is what happens at the last line of our script. The positional parameter at position 0 (the first, unnamed parameter) is `FilePath`, whose value is the output file. Like `Out-File`, the `Tee-Object` cmdlet also rewrites the contents of the file by default, unless overridden by `Append`.

See also

- Read more about redirection using the following command: `Get-Help about_Redirection`.

Adding and setting content to a file

Redirecting output or sending output to a file is a simple process. PowerShell also allows us to add, remove, or replace content in the files using the other three `Content` cmdlets (`Get-Command *content` or `Get-Command -Noun Content`). So, here is the scenario for the recipe.

You sent some text to the `message.txt` file, in the last recipe. Change the text to `Successfully sent the contents of ~/random/dir-03 and appending the list to file-list.txt`. Then, add the date to the `message.txt` and `file-list.txt` files. Finally, empty the `error.txt` file.

Getting ready

The files this recipe uses were created in the previous recipe. If you do not have the files, either create three files with those names and add content to them manually, or follow the *How to do it...* section of the previous recipe, *Sending output to a file*, to generate the files.

How to do it...

This is another simple recipe. The concept, though, is a very important one when dealing with files. Let's look at solving the situation we are presented with.

Here is the script that would address the problem in question:

```
#region Copy files to a backup directory before proceeding:
New-Item $HOME/random/backup/ -it Directory -f
# Verbose version New-Item -Path $HOME/random/backup -ItemType Directory -
Force # -Force to avoid errors in case when the directory already exists
Copy-Item $HOME/random/message.txt, $HOME/random/file-list.txt,
$HOME/random/error.txt $HOME/random/backup/
# Verbose version: Copy-Item -Path $HOME/random/message.txt,
$HOME/random/file-list.txt, $HOME/random/error.txt -Destination
$HOME/random/backup/
```

```
#endregion

#region Commence operations

Set-Content $HOME/random/message.txt "Successfully sent the contents of
~/random/dir-03 and appending the list to file-list.txt"
# Verbose version: Set-Content -Path $HOME/random/message.txt -Value
"Successfully sent the contents of ~/random/dir-03 and appending the list
to file-list.txt"

Add-Content $HOME/random/message.txt, $HOME/random/file-list.txt (Get-Date)
# Verbose version: Add-Content -Path $HOME/random/message.txt,
$HOME/random/file-list.txt -Value (Get-Date)

Clear-Content $HOME/random/error.txt
# Verbose version: Clear-Content -Path $HOME/random/error.txt

#endregion

"Here are the contents before and after the modifications:"

"Message (before):"
Get-Content $HOME/random/backup/message.txt

"Message (now):"
Get-Content $HOME/random/message.txt

Read-Host "Press ENTER to continue"
# Verbose version Read-Host -Prompt "Press ENTER to continue"

"File list (before):"
Get-Content $HOME/random/backup/file-list.txt

"File list (now):"
Get-Content $HOME/random/file-list.txt

Read-Host "Press ENTER to continue"

"Error (before):"
Get-Content $HOME/random/backup/error.txt

"Error (now):"
Get-Content $HOME/random/error.txt
```

If you like, open the files in your favorite code editor or use `cat` to see how the files have been modified. You can even use the `diff` command in Linux or use the `Compare-Object` PowerShell cmdlet to compare the contents of the backed-up and the current files.

Here is a snapshot of the outputs at different stages. The following screenshot shows the details about the contents of `message.txt`:

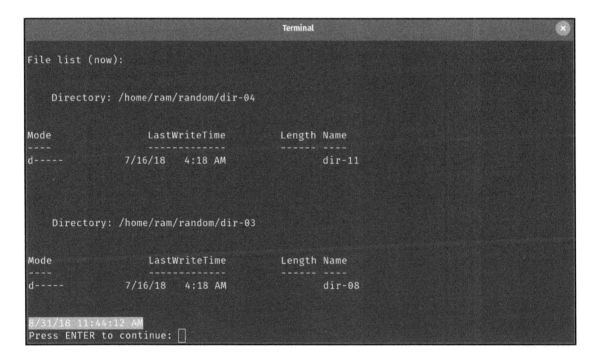

```
Terminal                                                                    ⊗
PS /home/ram/Documents/code/github/powershell/ch11> & ./03-Modify-FileContent.ps1


    Directory: /home/ram/random


Mode                LastWriteTime         Length Name
----                -------------         ------ ----
d-----         8/31/18   11:44 AM                backup
Here are the contents before and after the modifications:
Message (before):
Listing the contents of ~/random/dir-03 and appending the list to file-list.txt.
Message (now):
Successfully sent the contents of ~/random/dir-03 and appending the list to file-list.txt
8/31/18 11:44:12 AM
Press ENTER to continue: []
```

The contents of `file-list.txt` are shown in the following screenshot. Note the date on the last line of both the files:

```
Terminal                                                                    ⊗

File list (now):


    Directory: /home/ram/random/dir-04


Mode                LastWriteTime         Length Name
----                -------------         ------ ----
d-----         7/16/18    4:18 AM                dir-11




    Directory: /home/ram/random/dir-03


Mode                LastWriteTime         Length Name
----                -------------         ------ ----
d-----         7/16/18    4:18 AM                dir-08


8/31/18 11:44:12 AM
Press ENTER to continue: []
```

How it works...

You would have seen the use of `#region` and `#endregion` here for the first time in this book. This construct is used to enable code folding in code editors, as well as to be simple logical boundaries to visually help readers understand the script. They are by no means necessary.

The first region in the script merely backs up the three files in order to restore them if need be, given that using variables for this seems a little too volatile.

The three cmdlets we use in this recipe are `Set-Content`, `Add-Content`, and `Clear-Content`. The `Set-Content` cmdlet replaces the contents in a file (or files, with the paths separated by commas; the `Path` parameter in all the three cmdlets accepts a string array as input).

The `Add-Content` cmdlet adds the specified `Value` to the end of the existing file(s), acting similar to `Out-File` with `Append` or the `>>` operator. The `Clear-Content` cmdlet empties the file(s).

Searching for content

It is uncommon for a Linux administrator to be unfamiliar with `grep`, `sed`, and `awk`. PowerShell has similar functionalities built in, although these cmdlets and operators deal with text as objects, rather than as plain strings. There are little nuances that we would need to remember when working with PowerShell. In this recipe, we will look at searching for content in files from within PowerShell. The `Select-String` cmdlet, our string-related operators, such as `like` and `match`, and the object-based pipeline collectively help us with this.

Imagine you have a collection of markdown files. These files contain PowerShell code blocks. You have to perform the following steps:

1. Find the PowerShell code blocks present in the files within the directory. Show the filename, the line number, and the match, each on a separate line.
2. Contextually show what each of those code blocks is for. This time, use the properties from within the returned object, and show the output as a table.
3. List out all the files that contain the word `command` in them. Show how many times the word appears in each of the files. Exclude the first cheatsheet for the first chapter.

4. List out all the files that contain the word `PowerShell` (case-sensitive) in them.
5. Place all of this content in a single text file, so that it can be sent as a report.

Getting ready

You need some text files for this recipe. The easiest way to do it is to clone the repository for the book, and use the cheatsheets. Another way is to download a few text files to work with. In the latter case, you would need to modify the script to suit your search strings, filenames, and extensions. This recipe assumes that you have the repository cloned.

How to do it...

The task here is primarily to look for text patterns. We use the following script to accomplish these tasks (it is recommended that you view this script in a code editor—the file is available as `04-Search-FileForPattern.ps1` within the `ch10` directory):

 Modify the values for `$ReportPath` and `$CheatsheetPath` to suit your setup and preferences.

```
$ReportPath = "$HOME/random/FileSearchReport.txt"
$CheatsheetPath = "$HOME/Documents/code/github/powershell/cheatsheets"

if (!(Test-Path $ReportPath)) {
    New-Item $ReportPath -ItemType File -Force
}

"Here are the PowerShell code blocks present within the cheatsheets." |
Out-File $ReportPath
Select-String '```powershell' $CheatsheetPath/*.md |
    ForEach-Object {
        $PSItem = $PSItem -split ':'
        Write-Output "File Name: $($PSItem[0])"
        Write-Output "Line number: $($PSItem[1])"
        Write-Output "Pattern: $($PSItem[2])`n"
    } | Out-File $ReportPath -Append

<# Verbose version:
Select-String -Pattern '```powershell' -Path $CheatsheetPath/*.md
#>

"Here is a contextual report of all the PowerShell code blocks:" | Out-File
```

```
$ReportPath -Append
Select-String '```powershell' $CheatsheetPath/*.md -Context 2, 2 |
    Select-Object Path, LineNumber, `
    @{ Name = "Before"; Expression = { $PsItem.Context.PreContext -join
"`n" } }, `
    @{ Name = "After"; Expression = { $PsItem.Context.PostContext -join
"`n" } } |
        Format-List | Out-File $ReportPath -Append

"Here are the files that contain the word, 'command' in them, except the
cheatsheet for the first chapter:" | Out-File $ReportPath -Append
Select-String 'command' $CheatsheetPath/*.md -Exclude '*chapter-01.md' |
    Group-Object Path |
        Select-Object Name, Count |
            Format-Table -AutoSize | Out-File $ReportPath -Append

"Here are the files that contain the word, 'PowerShell' in them." | Out-
File $ReportPath -Append
Select-String -CaseSensitive 'PowerShell' $CheatsheetPath/*.md -Exclude
'*chapter-01.md' |
    Select-Object Path -Unique |
        Format-Table -AutoSize | Out-File $ReportPath -Append
```

How it works...

The script may seem fairly long, and complicated. However, if you look at it piece by piece, there are four pieces to it. And here is how each of them works.

The first piece introduces you to searching for patterns in files. We already saw `Select-String` in Chapter 1, *Introducing PowerShell Core*, where we looked for a certain string within the Help documentation. That was when a certain string content was passed through the pipeline to `Select-String`. In this recipe, however, we leverage the file-handling capabilities of the cmdlet by passing the file path(s) as well as the pattern that we are looking for. `Select-String` returns the matches as an array, each element being the complete line that contains the pattern. In our case, the line and the match are the same, since the pattern in question itself appears as a line in the files.

 A little note on markdown and code blocks: ```powershell tells the GitHub-Flavored Markdown renderer that the content that follows is a code block, and that it is PowerShell code. ``` itself stands for the code fence. When the name of the language follows, it aids in syntax highlighting.

Since this result is in the form of an array, we are able to use `Foreach-Object` on it. Within the script block, we split the results at `:`, and display the contents in a meaningful manner, all using string manipulation.

The majority of the second piece is simply the definition of the calculated properties. (So much for formatting!) What is important is that the results that are shown on the screen are simply formatted textual representation of the actual result object; a concise way of showing the `Path`, the `LineNumber`, and the `Line` that contains the pattern. The piece demonstrates leveraging the object model to get the path, the line number, and two lines before and after the matched line. Two lines is defined in `Select-String`, using the `Context` parameter. The first number that appears after `-Context` is the number of lines before the one that contains the pattern in question, and the second is the number of lines after. The `PreContext` and `PostContext` properties are arrays themselves (because PowerShell treats each line as a separate string). Therefore, we `join` the elements with a newline character. Finally, we format the content as a list, since that would make the most sense in this situation. If you would rather export this as a CSV file, use a different character for `-join`, and replace `Format-List` with `Export-Csv`.

The third piece leverages `Group-Object` so that it shows us the number of matches with `Count` in its output. We also use the `Exclude` parameter in `Select-String` and specify the file we would like to exclude. This matches the complete path of the file; therefore, you either give the complete path, or use a wildcard, depending on the context.

The fourth piece is similar to the third, except that we are not concerned about the count. Therefore, we simply pick the `Path` property from the output of `Select-String`, and use the `Unique` parameter of `Select-Object` to show a file only once, not once per match. Also, we use the `CaseSensitive` parameter in `Select-String`, for case-sensitive pattern matching.

Working with locations

Without a doubt, working with locations is an important aspect of scripting when working with files and directories. This recipe deals with file and directory objects, their properties, and a few cmdlets that help with paths.

The scenario for this recipe is that you need to find the location where the script is running from. You need to find the complete path of the script. Also, similar to the lab setup script, create a new path (do not create the files yet) within the home directory, and create dummy file paths within the new directory (again, no actual files yet). The important point to remember is that this script should be platform-agnostic; it should run without errors on Windows, Linux, and macOS environments. Also, you have a group of users using your computer. Find out which among those users has a directory called `random` within their home directory. (Launch PowerShell with `sudo` for this task.)

How to do it...

The last point is important here, because the `home` directory is located in entirely different locations on Linux and Windows (macOS behaves similarly to Linux in this regard). Also important is the fact that a space in Unix-like systems is specified with a backslash, which is an escape character here. On Windows, the backslash is the path separator.

> In many (or perhaps most) situations, it does not matter whether you use the / or the \ character as the path separator in PowerShell on Windows or on Windows PowerShell. However, as with any situations, using a forward slash on Windows as the path separator could cause errors in scripts.

This is the flow we will use for this recipe:

1. In the first part of the script, call for the present working directory.
2. In the second part, call for the complete path of the script.
3. Next, use `New-Item` to create files within a directory, using `Join-Path` to create complete paths

   Type in and run the following script:

```
"The script is located within:"
$PSScriptRoot

Read-Host "Press Enter to continue"

"Here is the complete path to the script that was run:"
$PSCommandPath

Read-Host "Press Enter to continue"

"Here are the file paths asked for, as per the scenario:"
'random-text.txt', 'himalayas.jpg', 'crunched-numbers.csv',
```

```
'screenshot-001.png', 'screenshot-002.png', 'screenshot-003.png',
'demo.doc', 'my-plugin.rb' | ForEach-Object { Join-Path -Path $HOME
-ChildPath $PSItem }
```

4. Finally, list out the paths to `random` from within `/home`; in other words, the list of directories within `/home` that contain `random`:

```
PS> exit
$ sudo pwsh
PS> Resolve-Path /home/*/random/ | Split-Path -Parent | Split-Path
-Leaf
```

Now, to how it all worked.

How it works...

The current location, or the present working directory, can be gotten in different ways:

- By calling the `$pwd` automatic variable
- By calling the `Get-Location` cmdlet at the terminal (this will not work within a script)
- Using the `$PSScriptRoot` automatic variable, when calling for a location within a script

Also, there is an automatic variable called `$PSCommandPath`, which stores the location of a script being executed. Again, if you call this variable at the terminal, it will not give you any value.

When creating paths, in order to eliminate possibilities of errors in resolution, it is best to use the `Join-Path` cmdlet, with the necessary arguments. Based on the system the script is being run on, `Join-Path` will use the right path separator and create the complete path. `Join-Path` works with other PowerShell providers as well; therefore, it will work with, for example, the `Variable` provider or even the Windows Registry. Use the `Resolve` switch parameter to check whether the path that was created after joining the path and the child path exists or not. `Join-Path` is particularly useful when creating a certain directory at multiple parent paths; for instance, when you want to complete a child path, `TestDir`, under `/home`, `/etc`, `/var`, and `/boot`:

```
Join-Path /home, /etc, /var, /boot -ChildPath TestDir
```

When creating multiple files under the new demo directory, we used a single parent path, and multiple child paths. The `ChildPath` parameter accepts only a single string, and therefore we send an array of the string into the pipeline, and then use `Foreach-Object` for the `ChildPath`:

```
# Create a single path at multiple parent paths:
Join-Path /home, /etc, /var, /boot -ChildPath TestDir

# Create multiple child paths at a parent directory:
'file1.txt', 'file2.txt', 'file3.txt' | ForEach-Object { Join-Path -Path
$HOME/dir/ -ChildPath $PSItem }
```

At the fourth step, we use the `Resolve-Path` cmdlet along with a wildcard for the directory name. This returns output, such as `/home/ram/random`. We need `ram` in this example. For this, we use the `Split-Path` cmdlet; we pick the `Parent` at the first step, thereby picking `/home/ram`, and then we pick the `Leaf` (or the child directory), which is now `ram` in this example.

See also

- The *Listing the various providers in PowerShell* recipe from `Chapter 1`, *Introducing PowerShell Core*

Working with files and directories

In the previous recipe, *Working with locations*, we created paths. In this recipe, we will create actual files and directories. The scenario is this:

1. You have the `random` directory within `$HOME`. This directory contains `dir-01`, `dir-02`, `dir-03`, and `dir-04`. Create a file, called `demo.txt` within all of these four directories.
2. Create new empty files, `random-text.txt`, `himalayas.jpg`, `crunched-numbers.csv`, `screenshot-001.png`, `screenshot-002.png`, `screenshot-003.png`, `demo.doc`, and `my-plugin.rb`, within `$HOME/random/dir-01`.
3. Rename `screenshot-001.png` as `myscreenshot.png`.
4. Copy `myscreenshot.png` into `dir-02`.
5. Finally, remove the `dir-04` directory, and everything within it.

Ensure that the script is platform-agnostic.

How to do it...

Again, this is quite a set of tasks to do. Let's get cracking and spawn a little script to do this for us:

```
Set-Location (Join-Path $HOME random)

Join-Path dir-01, dir-02, dir-03, dir-04 -ChildPath demo.txt | ForEach-
Object { New-Item $PSItem -ItemType File } 'random-text.txt',
'himalayas.jpg', 'crunched-numbers.csv', 'screenshot-001.png',
'screenshot-002.png', 'screenshot-003.png', 'demo.doc', 'my-plugin.rb' |
ForEach-Object { New-Item (Join-Path dir-01 -ChildPath $PSItem) -ItemType
File } Rename-Item screenshot-001.png myscreenshot.png # Verbose version:
Rename-Item -Path screenshot-001.png -NewName myscreenshot.png
Copy-Item myscreenshot.png dir-02
# Verbose version: Copy-Item -Path myscreenshot.png -Destination ./dir-02

Remove-Item dir-04 -Recurse
# Verbose version: Remove-Item -Path dir-04 -Recurse
```

How it works...

The first task that this recipe does is create files and directories. By providing multiple parent paths to the `Join-Path` cmdlet, we create `demo.txt` at four locations. We use the `Foreach-Object` cmdlet to perform this iterative task. Next, we twist the process a little; we pass several strings into the pipeline, and then use a `Join-Path` subexpression within `New-Item`, thereby creating multiple child paths at the parent location.

`New-Item` can create items based on what you define as the `ItemType`.

Next, we rename a file using the `Rename-Item` cmdlet, copy a file using the `Copy-Item` cmdlet, and recursively delete a directory using the `Remove-Item` cmdlet with the `Recurse` switch.

Many (but not all) parameters in PowerShell accept wildcard input. This is indicated by `Accept wildcard characters?` shown upon running `Get-Help` with the `Full` switch parameter or the `Parameter` parameter. For example, the `ChildPath` parameter in `Join-Path` cannot work with wildcard characters in paths.

Any providers that support the concept of items automatically support these cmdlets as well.

There's more...

Try to rename all screenshots as captures. For instance, `screenshot-001.png` should be renamed as `capture-001.png`.

Listing files and directories

This chapter would be incomplete without a recipe on working with file lists. We have already seen some of the concepts in our previous recipes. However, for the sake of completeness, we will write a script that lists out files of type `.mp4` within our random directory that are more than seven days old and larger than 100 KB. Also, list out the five largest files in the lot.

How to do it...

Let's pick the location as `$HOME/random`. We don't know under what directory these `.mp4` files would be. Therefore, do the following:

1. Perform a recursive listing of files
2. Add a parameter, `Name`, that lists out only the `.mp4` files
3. Use the `CreationTime` property of the file to determine the age
4. Perform a filter based on the size (`Length`) of the file
5. Use the `Sort-Object` and the `Select-Object` cmdlets to pick the five largest files

Here is the script that would help us with this task:

```
$ThresholdDate = (Get-Date).AddDays(-7)

Get-ChildItem $HOME/random -rec -na *.mp4  | Where-Object { $_.CreationTime
-lt $ThresholdDate -and $_.Length -gt 100KB }
# Verbose version: Get-ChildItem $HOME/random -Recurse -Name *.mp4  |
Where-Object -FilterScript { $PSItem.CreationTime -lt $ThresholdDate -and
$PSItem.Length -gt 100KB }

Get-ChildItem $HOME/random -Recurse | Sort-Object Length -Descending |
Select-Object -First 5
# Verbose version: Get-ChildItem -Path $HOME/random -Recurse | Sort-Object
-Property Length -Descending | Select-Object -First 5
```

The path parameter in `Get-ChildItem` accepts an array as input.
Therefore, you could write `Get-ChildItem $HOME/random,`
`$HOME/random/dir-01` to get the contents of the two paths.

How it works...

This recipe primarily concentrates on `Get-ChildItem` and its parameters. The `Recurse`
switch parameter recursively lists out all paths within the specified path. The `Name`
parameter makes PowerShell list out those sub-paths that match the pattern specified.

The rest in this script is about passing the output object from `Get-ChildItem` into different
other cmdlets for further processing. We use the `Where-Object` cmdlet and a filter script
that compares the date of creation of the file and the current date, and then compares the
size of the file. We also use the administrative constant (`100KB`).

When picking the five largest files, we first sort the files by size in descending order, and
select the first five from the list.

Again, `Get-ChildItem` and `Get-Item` do not only work with files and folders; they also
work with other objects within the `Env:`, `Alias:`, `Cert:`, `Variable:`, and other providers.

There's more...

Find out the difference between `Get-Item` and `Get-ChildItem`.

Working with structured and unstructured files

In this modern world, we tend to deal with a lot of information. In some cases, the data is stored in a structured way (for example, CSV, XML, JSON, and so on). And in some other cases, the data is stored in an unstructured away, such as log files, `.txt`, and so on.

We have already been dealing with unstructured files so far in this book. PowerShell works well with either type of file. Where PowerShell really stands out is how it handles structured data, and, by extension, structured files. In many cases, in fact, a simple one-liner is sufficient for PowerShell to parse data into an object.

We had an interesting situation once at work. One of our clients uses a certain MDM application. At one point, the email application that is part of the MDM suite started crashing on the users. The users found that reinstalling the app fixed the crash. And one of the IT managers at the client's wanted a list of users who reinstalled the application. Upon checking the logs, we found something interesting: the log files were `.log` files, and the files had single lines of entries, which had some characters in the beginning, after which the log pretty much looked like valid JSON. The `08-mdm-reinstall-log.log` file, within the `ch10` directory of the code repository of the book contains a sample log that looks similar to what we got on the server. The report that needs to be extracted from this data should have the timestamp, the username, and the email address of the user. Here is a line from the log file:

```
2018-09-06T00:09:45.351-0500 - CORE Exchange[Body: DeviceActionEvent
{"eventTypeId":"979dba5297b4c8c8a9fb59d25f33fd2a","timestamp":1536210585273
,"tenantId":1,"tenantGuid":"5b73c758-57af-47b2-a6d4-
d7b6c52cb5e5","externalTenantId":"S650643799","correlationId":"7876c65b-2ba
4-7648-9a94-1ef6fb492c3b","hostName":"svrbbp.mydomain.com","version":"5.63.
87-
SNAPSHOT","severity":"CLEARED","tags":["device_action","user","userdevice"]
,"userDeviceInfo":{"enrollmentType":"MDM_CONTROLS","perimeterUuid":"afa5786
9b-3f76-7e74-98d8-ab725136a663","userInfo":{"userGuid":"af78905c-806f-49a8-
b491-3f3fc26564e5","userName":"NBFA091","emailAddress":"Joyce.Rose@mydomain
.com"},"deviceInfo":{"deviceOSFamily":"ios","id":1332,"udid":"4a77839994785
77b7746dc774657b992","guid":"6657bc4e-19d5-b4bc-
b05c-2e3c63190a11"},"perimeterState":"ENROLLED"},"deviceActionType":"INSTAL
L_APP"}]
```

How to do it...

This is, in fact, very simple. Here is the high-level flow of what we want to do:

1. Loop through each line of the log. We will use `Get-Content` and the `foreach` loop construct for this.
2. Perform a simple string manipulation to get the timestamp.
3. Parse the JSON to get the username as well as the email address.

Here is the script that will perform this operation.

```
$AllLogLines = Get-Content ./ch10/08-mdm-reinstall-log.log
$UserTable = @()

foreach ($Line in $AllLogLines) {
    $Timestamp = ($Line.Split(' '))[0]

    $Line = $Line -replace ".+(DeviceActionEvent)\ \{", '{'
    $Line = $Line -replace '\]$'

    # Alternatively: $Line = $Line | Select-String -Pattern '(\{.*})' |
ForEach-Object { $PSItem.Matches | ForEach-Object { $PSItem.Value } }

    $JsonData = ConvertFrom-Json $Line
    $UserInfo = $JsonData.userDeviceInfo.userInfo

    $Record = [ordered]@{
        Timestamp       = Get-Date $Timestamp -Format d
        Username        = $UserInfo.userName
        EmailAddress    = $UserInfo.emailAddress
    }

    $UserTable += New-Object -TypeName psobject -Property $Record
}
$UserTable = $UserTable | Sort-Object Username -Unique | Sort-Object
Timestamp
$UserTable
```

Run the script and you should see a table with the required information. Optionally, you can export this into a CSV file. You know how.

 If you run the script as it is, it is important that you run it at the terminal. If you plan to run this script from Visual Studio Code, change the first line of the script to $AllLogLines = Get-Content ./08-mdm-reinstall-log.log by removing ch10/ to avoid errors.

How it works...

The first step in the script is to read the contents of the log file. Get-Content reads the content, each line in the file being a separate element in a string array. Next, we initialize the variable that will contain our object. We use the foreach loop construct to perform operations on each of the log lines.

Now to a single log entry. The first thing we do here is split the log at whitespace, and pick the first element in it, because the structure of the log line tells us that the timestamp is in the beginning. We use the split method within the string object and pick the timestamp.

Next, we perform a couple of simple string replacement operations (or the single alternative operation) using the replace operator (or Select-String in the case of the alternative method). This is to remove the non-JSON part of the log line. (You can always perform a syntax check online on any of the JSON entries. There are several services, such as https://jsonlint.com/ and https://codebeautify.org/jsonvalidator, available to help you. If not, simply follow what your code editor tells you.)

The magic really happens at the `ConvertFrom-Json` line, where PowerShell quite effortlessly parses the JSON data and converts it into an object with the keys and values being the properties and property values, respectively. Now, `$JsonData` has the complete JSON content within it. We now have two ways: either inspect the `$JsonData` variable using the Visual Studio Code debugger, or simply format the JSON using an online service and then go down property by property. I took the former approach, by adding a breakpoint and using the Visual Studio Code debugger. Note the left-hand bar. We will learn more about this process at a later point:

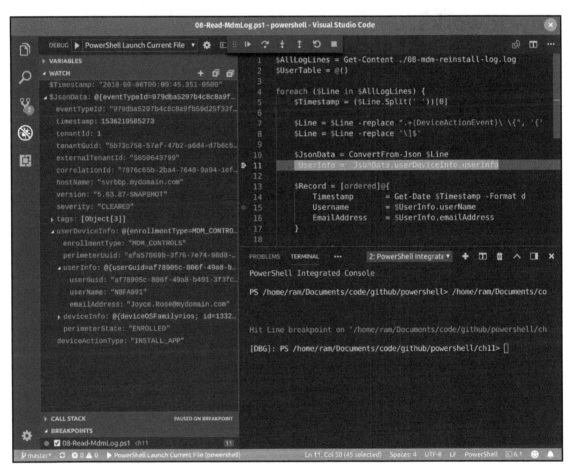

We then create an ordered hashtable, with the keys being the property names and the values being the values of the keys. We transpose the hashtables in every iteration into a custom PowerShell object, which we finally call at the end of the script to show the table.

There's more...

This is just the tip of the iceberg. Read through the *Adding custom properties to an object recipe* in Chapter 5, *Using Variables and Objects*, to learn how to work with PowerShell objects and make your scripts much more efficient than you are used to.

Building Scripts and Functions

11

In this chapter, we will cover the following recipes:

- Writing a simple script
- Reading input from the host
- Displaying an interactive menu
- Showing progress of execution
- Defining arguments for a script
- Writing a simple function
- Working with a script block
- Measuring running duration

Introduction

Scripts are arguably the primary mode of automation using PowerShell. And, just like with Bash or sh, a PowerShell script is nothing but a series of instructions, along with some much-needed branching and looping. The pipeline makes handling data very simple from the moment you understand the concept of objects—this is the difference from the scripting framework available in Linux.

In this chapter, we will proceed with creating scripts that accept input at the terminal. Then, we will learn how to create functions so that we can leverage modularity as well as transfer objects between your functions and other functions, or even cmdlets.

Writing a simple script

In a way, this book began with a script: the lab setup script. This recipe is here to show you that a simple script is nothing more than a series of commands put together. Now, we have been writing scripts throughout this book. However, some of the information may have been scattered across different chapters and recipes. In this recipe, we will bring it all together and write a simple script. Also, given the cookbook structure of this book, it is important that we cover this topic for those who skipped straight to this point.

The scenario here is that you have to write a script that will give out the current date and time, and show the hostname of the computer the script is running on. It also welcomes the user by his/her username. The catch here is that you need to have a space in the name of the script, and you need to ensure that the script should be called in a platform-agnostic manner.

How to do it...

The requirements are simple. Four things are required of us:

- The script must have a name that contains a space
- We must write out the current date and time
- We must show the host name
- We must greet the user by their username

Create a file called simple `script.ps1`. Add the following content to it:

```
Get-Date

hostname

Write-Output "Hello, $env:username!"
```

Then, call the script:

```
PS> & './simple script.ps1'
```

How it works...

Now to the part where this is rocket science. First, identify the payload. Calculate the orbital velocity and the rotational velocity of the Earth. Next... you get the point. However, here are a couple of things to remember when you want to run a script.

A script, when called simply, will load, execute, and exit. It will not store anything in the memory—neither the functions, nor the variables and other data. If you want the variables, functions, and other information retained in the session, the script has to be called in a specific way, like so:

```
PS> # To retain variable and function information in the session:
PS> . ./path/to/script.ps1

PS> # To simply have PowerShell run the script:
PS> & ./path/to/script.ps1
```

In Bash, we simply add a backslash before the space, that is, if there is a space in the path name. In PowerShell, especially when running a script on Windows, it will not work, because in Windows the backslash is the path separator. The other option would be to enclose the complete path in quotes. However, by default, PowerShell considers anything enclosed in quotes to be a string. Therefore, in order to tell PowerShell to read the path as the path, we use either of the call operators, & or ., based on the situation. We have demonstrated using both of these techniques in the preceding code.

Reading input from the host

Admittedly, reading input given by the user at the host is not among the best things for automation. However, in some situations, it is necessary. Let's not leave such stones unturned, at least. In this recipe, we will ask the user for their name, and then display the greeting along with the date. Optionally, you can have a space in the name of the script.

How to do it...

This is straightforward. If you are comfortable using command discovery, you can simply use get-command *host to get the information. Modify the script we created for the *Writing a simple script* recipe to get the desired script:

```
Get-Date

hostname
```

```
Write-Output "Hello, $(Read-Host "Enter your name")!"
# Verbose version: Write-Output "Hello, $(Read-Host -Prompt "Enter your
name")!"
```

That is all it is; run the script:

```
PS> & './simple prompt script.ps1'
```

How it works...

`Read-Host` takes input from the host, and then passes on the received object to the calling function. In our case, we have the `Read-Host` placed within a subexpression, and the caller is the `Write-Output` cmdlet. Therefore, it takes in the name as the input and then passes it on to the `Write-Output` cmdlet.

Optionally, if you are not comfortable using a subexpression, you can assign the value to a variable, and call the variable with `Write-Output`:

```
$Name = Read-Host "Enter your name"
Write-Output "Hello, $Name!"
```

Displaying an interactive menu

Many of our clients outsource their Service Desks to offshore service providers. Many of these Service Desk agents are not comfortable running commands or scripts, and some of our clients are uncomfortable providing Service Desk agents with a no-UI script. One such L1 Support team came to us with a requirement for a script to partially automate account termination backup. Most importantly, we were asked to provide the agents with a textual menu that they would interact with to start the right kind of backup (mailbox, membership, home drive, and so on).

In this recipe, we will replicate that menu, but not actually call the backup functions.

How to do it...

The requirements are simple. We will create a script that displays the following menu:

1. Mailbox backup
2. Home drive backup
3. Mailbox and home drive backup
4. Mailbox, home drive, and group membership backup

Here is the script that will show this menu:

```
$Menu = @'
Hello! Welcome to the Terminated Account Backup Utility (TABU)!

1. Mailbox backup
2. Home drive backup
3. Mailbox and home drive backup
4. Mailbox, home drive, and group membership backup

Choose your backup type and enter the corresponding number
'@

$Choice = Read-Host $Menu

switch ($Choice) {
    1 {
        "You chose the mailbox backup. Initiating..."
        # Call the corresponding function here.
    }
    2 {
        "You chose the home drive backup. Initiating..."
        # Call the corresponding function here.
    }
    3 {
        "You chose to back up the mailbox as well as the home drive.
Initiating..."
        # Call the corresponding function here.
    }
    4 {
        "You chose a complete backup. This person must be imporant!
Initiating..."
        # Call the corresponding function here.
    }
    Default {
        "Invalid selection. Please try again."
    }
}
```

How it works...

This is another of the hard-to-tackle rocket science problems. To oversimplify this, the choice is assigned to the variable, and a `Switch-Case` block is made to proceed with the task based on the branch chosen.

See also

- The *Using Switch–Case conditions to control script flow* recipe from `Chapter 7`, *Flow Control using Branches and Loops*

Showing progress of execution

The whole point of automation is that it helps handle repetitive, tedious, and long-running tasks. For instance, the mailbox backup script that I spoke about in the previous recipe, *Displaying an interactive menu,* took a long time to back up large mailboxes. Sometimes, staring at a terminal that seems to do nothing is unnerving—not to mention not knowing whether the script is actually doing something or not.

This is where writing progress comes into the picture. Here is the task: count 25 seconds and write progress for the percentage of time elapsed.

How to do it...

This is a percentage-based progress writing. Therefore, we need to know the total time beforehand. We will calculate the percentage based on the elapsed time, and we will pass it to the `Write-Progress` cmdlet, which we will use to write the progress of our task. Follow these steps to get started:

1. Create a new `.ps1` file using Visual Studio Code.
2. Enter the following content into the file:

```
$TotalTime = 25
$CurrentTime = 0

do {
    Write-Progress -Activity 'Counting to 25' -Status "Elapsed
time: $CurrentTime seconds" -PercentComplete ($CurrentTime /
$TotalTime * 100)
```

```
        Start-Sleep 1
        $CurrentTime++
    } until ($CurrentTime -eq $TotalTime)
```

3. Switch to a terminal emulator (the **Integrated Terminal** does not show progress) and launch PowerShell.
4. Call the script and watch its progress.

Here is a screenshot of what the progress looks like:

How it works...

This cmdlet is designed to show the progress of tasks on the console. In our case, there are three parts to the progress:

- The activity (mandatory)
- The current status
- The progress bar

The progress bar is enabled using the `PercentComplete` parameter. The current `Status` is also dynamic, just like `PercentComplete`. The activity is mandatory (without which there would be no point in writing the progress anyway), and does not change until the end of the activity.

In a production scenario, we either use a status cmdlet (such as `Get-MailboxExportRequestStatistics`, in the case of mailbox export) or the count to calculate the total completion percentage, and supply the values to the parameters of `Write-Progress`. `Write-Progress` is usually used with a suitable looping construct, since the progress has to be rewritten based on the progress of the task. Therefore, in the case of cmdlets that are accompanied by a statistics cmdlet, we begin the task outside of the loop and then get its statistics within the loop, the values of which are assigned to the progress parameters.

In the case of count and other such quantifiable tasks, we perform the tasks within the loop. For instance, when copying items from one location to another, we would list out all the paths (recursively), calculate the total size of the content being transferred (and assign it to say, $TotalSize), use a foreach loop to copy the files from the source to the destination, and, within the foreach loop, right after the Copy-Item cmdlet, we would, say, add to $TransferredSize the Length of the file we just transferred. PercentComplete would be calculated as $TransferredSize / $TotalSize * 100:

```
foreach ($Item in $AllPaths) {
    Copy-Item $Item.Path $DestinationPath
    $TransferredSize += $Item.Length
    Write-Progress -Activity 'Copying files' -Status "Copied $($Item.Name)
to $DestinationPath" -PercentComplete ($TransferredSize / $TotalSize * 100)
}
```

See also

- The *Writing a more complex loop on a predefined array* recipe in Chapter 7, *Flow Control Using Branches and Loops*

Defining arguments for a script

Scripts help with a good amount of automation. Most administrators that I have come across like to create self-contained scripts. However, this means that you have to hardcode a lot of information that you may not want someone to read, such as passwords or keys. This is a limitation with scripts that contain everything in them. Of course, another way to handle such a situation is to use secure files such as a CLI XML with the password or key stored as a secure string, which will work only on that computer, only with your sign-in. But then, what if someone else wanted to use your script with their credentials?

You get the point. Hardcoding certain things is not a very flexible way to do this—it kills modularity. The other option available to us is to prompt the user for such information. But what if you were writing a script to be used unattended? What if you had your credentials in a secure location stored as a secure CLI XML, but had to use a script stored in a location that is accessible to everyone, and you had to call your script in an unattended mode? What if you could pass arguments to scripts just like you could with cmdlets?

At the time of writing this book, conversion to and from secure strings does not work on PowerShell on Linux. However, this is expected to be fixed in an upcoming release.

Modify the countdown script to accept `TotalTime` as an argument, with the default value being 25. Call this script for a countdown from 40.

How to do it...

The difference between the previous script and the one you need to write now is only one line:

1. Create a copy of the script that you created for the *Showing progress of execution* recipe.
2. Replace the first line, `$TotalTime = 25`, with `param ($TotalTime = 25)`.
3. Switch to the terminal, place an `&` and a space, and type in the relative path to the script. Add a space, type a hyphen, and hit the *Tab* key. The `TotalTime` parameter should auto-resolve.

Now, you can start a seconds-based count to any positive integer you pass to this parameter, like so:

```
Terminal                                                                    ✕
PS /home/ram> & ./Documents/code/github/powershell/ch12/05-Start-Count.ps1 -TotalTime 10

 Counting to 10
    Elapsed time: 5 seconds
    [ooooooooooooooooooooooooooooooooooooooo                                  ]
```

How it works...

What we did in this recipe was create a parameter for the script. We simply converted a plain vanilla variable into a parameter. A parameter is, in fact, very similar to a variable, except that it can be accessed from outside of the script or function. To convert a variable into a parameter, we place the variable within the `param ()` definition.

If a value is assigned to this variable within the `param ()` block, this value becomes its default value, which will be used if no value is specified when calling the script. Quite a few parameter options are available when defining a parameter. However, for this recipe, we will stick with the bare basics.

The working of the rest of the script is similar to the one in the *Showing progress of execution* recipe.

Writing a simple function

Scripts are a great way to automate tasks. However, a fundamental limitation with a script is that only one kind of task can be handled by a simple script. For instance, if you wanted to achieve two goals, that is, count down from 21 and copy two files from one location to another, you would need to write two different scripts to perform the tasks. Wouldn't it be great if you could write a single script for the two tasks and run either of them by choice? This way, you have a smaller number of scripts to manage.

Secondly, writing a script to perform a very complex task would involve several sub-tasks. If a single script is written for all the sub-tasks, the script would become monolithic. This has its own drawbacks, the first one being the challenges in reusing the code.

Functions help with this. With functions, you can separate the sub-tasks, and make each function do only one thing, which is what any software design person would tell you to do. This makes the script more flexible, and code reuse easy. Not to mention that if you wanted to perform a certain task multiple times in a single session, you would just have to call the script once, and only the function every subsequent time, rather than specifying the path and calling the script every time.

Convert the script that you wrote for the *Defining arguments for a script* recipe into a function.

How to do it...

This is, again, a very simple task. Follow these steps to perform the conversion, and understand how to call the function in the final step:

1. Create a copy of the script you created for the *Showing progress of execution* recipe.
2. At the first line, define the function with the following code:

```
function Start-Count {
```

Go to the end of the script, and close the braces to complete the function. The complete script should look like this:

```
function Start-Count {
    param ($TotalTime = 25)

    $CurrentTime = 0

    while ($CurrentTime -le $TotalTime) {
        Write-Progress -Activity "Counting to $TotalTime" -Status
"Elapsed time: $CurrentTime seconds" -PercentComplete ($CurrentTime
/ $TotalTime * 100)
        Start-Sleep 1
        $CurrentTime++
    }
}
```

3. Load the script using the dot calling operator at the terminal:

   PS> . ./ch11/06-Start-Count.ps1

   If you are using VS Code IDE, simply run the script with *F5*.

4. Call the function. Optionally, supply a value to the `TotalTime` parameter:

   PS> Start-Count -TotalTime 5

Here is a screenshot of the function running. Note how similar it looks to a cmdlet:

```
                                    Terminal                                    ⊗
PS /home/ram/Documents/code/github/powershell> . ./ch12/06-Start-Count.ps1
PS /home/ram/Documents/code/github/powershell> Start-Count -TotalTime 10

 Counting to 10
    Elapsed time: 4 seconds
    [ooooooooooooooooooooooooooooooooo                                        ]
```

How it works...

When you convert a script into a function, the function retains all of the capabilities of a script. However, simply calling the script is not sufficient when you want to get tasks done. Now, you first load the script—and all of the functions and other parts of it—into the session, and then call the function of your choice. Functions may or may not contain parameters. When present, parameters can be called along with the function, just like how you would a cmdlet. However, it would not be as follows:

```
PS> Start-Count.TotalTime(5)
```

Instead, it would be like this:

```
PS> Start-Count -TotalTime 5
```

 We will look at how to make it Start-Count 5 in Chapter 12, *Advanced Concepts of Functions*.

Remember to call the scripts that contain functions with the dot calling operator and not the ampersand. If you call a script with the ampersand calling operator, the script will simply run; the functions within will not be loaded into the session, and so you won't be able to call the functions.

See also

- The *Dot-sourcing a PowerShell script* recipe in Chapter 2, *Preparing for Administration using PowerShell*

Working with a script block

Again, script blocks are nothing new to us. We have, in fact, used script blocks at several places in this book, such as the Foreach-Object cmdlet. Think of script blocks as somewhere in between a script and a function.

Implement the same functionality as the Start-Count function, but using a script block.

How to do it...

The process is simple:

1. Create a copy of the `06-Start-Count.ps1` file.
2. Replace the first line with `$MyScriptBlock = {`. The file should now look like the following:

```
$MyScriptBlock = {
    param ($TotalTime = 25)

    $CurrentTime = 0

    while ($CurrentTime -le $TotalTime) {
        Write-Progress -Activity "Counting to $TotalTime" -Status
"Elapsed time: $CurrentTime seconds" -PercentComplete ($CurrentTime
/ $TotalTime * 100)
        Start-Sleep 1
        $CurrentTime++
    }
}
```

3. Now, call the script with the dot calling operator so that the variable is loaded into the session.
4. Call the variable with the `&` calling operator to run the script. Optionally, pass a value to the `TotalTime` parameter:

```
PS> . ./ch11/07-Start-Count.ps1
PS> & $MyScriptBlock 10
PS> # Verbose version: & $MyScriptBlock -TotalTime 10
```

Here is what the run will look like:

```
                              Terminal                              ⓧ
PS /home/ram/Documents/code/github/powershell> . ./ch12/07-Start-Count.ps1
PS /home/ram/Documents/code/github/powershell> & $MyScriptBlock -TotalTime 10
▯
Counting to 10
    Elapsed time: 5 seconds
    [ooooooooooooooooooooooooooooooooooooooooo                              ]
```

How it works...

A script block is essentially a series of PowerShell instructions, packaged within curly braces. These allow for a different level of flexibility by having the capability to be assigned to a variable. In this recipe, we assigned a script block to a variable. We do not change anything otherwise, including the parameter we defined in the function. This is to show that a script block is not very different from a function or a script file.

If, at the terminal, after calling the script file with a dot calling operator, you simply run $MyScriptBlock, the output will show the entire script block without the outermost opening and closing braces. This may give you the impression that this is nothing but a string. However, when you run $MyScriptBlock | Get-Member, you would be shown the type name as System.Management.Automation.ScriptBlock.

A script block, just like a function, can accept parameter input as well, and the syntax is no different from that of a param block within a function or a script file.

When calling the script block, you call it with the ampersand calling operator. This way, you instruct PowerShell that the variable has to be executed, and not just displayed on the host.

Alternatively, you can use the following code:

```
PS> Invoke-Command $MyScriptBlock -args 10
PS> # Verbose version: Invoke-Command -ScriptBlock $MyScriptBlock -
ArgumentList 10
```

The ArgumentList or the args parameter may seem confusing at first. In our case, the script block has only one argument, TotalTime. It was, therefore, simple to use ArgumentList. In cases where there are multiple parameters specified in the script block, you would specify only the values to the script block parameters, in the order of the appearance of the arguments.

Note that if you use the ampersand calling operator, you will be able to call the parameters by name; this will not work with Invoke-Command, as noted in the information block. Therefore, using a calling operator is preferred over Invoke-Command in most cases.

Script blocks are useful when you write functions that accept input in the form of a script block, which will be executed when necessary. Two examples of these would be the Invoke-Command and Start-Job cmdlets.

Measuring running duration

Optimization is the key to efficient automation. While shorter duration does not always stand for optimization, it is an important part of optimization. Here is the scenario:

You have a friend who has just learned how to use PowerShell, and they are excited about `Select-Object` *, which they just found out shows information that is not usually visible with the vanilla `Get-ChildItem`. You ask them why they want to use `Select-Object` *, and they say it's because they would like to get the `CreationTime` of the files as well. Of course, you are trying to tell them that they are not efficiently querying the metadata. They ask for proof.

How to do it...

Open a terminal window to show your friend the difference between the commands:

1. At the prompt, enter the following (point `Get-ChildItem` to any valid directory with a noticeable number of files):

   ```
   PS> $AllAttributes = measure-command { gci $HOME/random/ -rec |
   select * }
   PS> # Verbose version: Measure-Command -Expression { Get-ChildItem
   $HOME/random -Recurse | Select-Object * }
   ```

2. And then, to compare, type in the following:

   ```
   PS> $SelectAttributes = measure-command { gci $HOME/random/ -rec |
   select name, fullname, creationtime }
   PS> # Verbose version: Measure-Command -Expression { Get-ChildItem
   $HOME/random/ -Recurse | Select-Object Name, FullName, CreationTime
   }
   PS> ($allattributes - $selectattributes).totalmilliseconds
   ```

Smile when your friend says you took longer than 200 ms to type out the three property names.

How it works...

The cmdlet that helps find the total runtime of any command or a script block is `Measure-Command`. While this cmdlet can take `PSObject` as input, the convention here is to use the `Expression` parameter. This parameter accepts a script block as input, which is what we pass to it, in our case. The cmdlet evaluates for how long the script block ran, and shows us the output as a `System.TimeSpan` object.

Now, on to the point that your friend mentioned you taking longer than 200 ms to merely write the properties. I was once tasked with creating a script that performed some filtration on Active Directory objects based on a couple of properties. We observed that the script took about 25 minutes to run in that environment. After some minor changes to the script, we were able to reduce the runtime to about 23 minutes.

When we checked each statement in the script for its runtime, we found that a single query within a `foreach` loop was taking about 200 milliseconds to run. Multiplied by well over 65,000 entities, the total time went over 20 minutes. We changed the logic at this step, and achieved a reduction of about 60%. 60% of 200 milliseconds may be a mere 120 milliseconds, but when the number of objects where the operation is performed increases, the total time taken shoots up. Little things add up.

See also

- *Software disenchantment* (http://tonsky.me/blog/disenchantment/) by Nikita Prokopov, the author of the beautiful font Fira Sans

Important points to remember

While writing scripts and functions is straightforward in most situations, there are cases where you are required to write complex scripts whose lengths run in hundreds of lines. In such situations, it is important that you remember the following points.

Using Host cmdlets

There are five `Host` cmdlets that help you `Clear` the host, `Get` information about the host, send `Out` the output to the host, `Read` information from the host, and `Write` information to the host.

PowerShell is a shell—an engine—as Don Jones points out in his `powershell.org` article (`https://powershell.org/2013/10/the-shell-vs-the-host/`). The Host is what hosts this engine, or interacts with the engine on your behalf. This is to reiterate that `Host` cmdlets send output to the sixth stream, called the information stream. The only stream that interacts with the pipeline, though, is the first, or the success stream. Behind the scenes, when PowerShell does not find an entity at the end of the pipeline to accept the output of the success stream, the output is redirected to the host (think `| Out-Host`).

Imagine the setup to be like this: there is a room, which has a heap of wet clothes. There is a camera pointing to the clothes, right near the window. The camera is hooked up to a large display, which is placed at the window, instead of plain glass. You can look into the room only through the display. At the moment, you can see the wet clothes on the screen. You cannot touch them, smell them, or weigh them; only see them.

The wet clothes are passed through a pipe into an electric dryer. The dried clothes are sent out of the machine. What you see now is dry clothes, and you know they are dry because someone just picked them up and unfurled them, and the clothes unfurled rather smoothly.

Now, imagine you placed the dryer right next to you, between you and the screen. The sequence now is, wet clothes | camera | screen | dryer | you. Can you take the image and dry it? Or do the wet clothes physically disappear if you turn off the screen? In this analogy, the camera acts as the formatting rules—the interface between the camera—the display is the information stream, and the screen is the host.

Returning objects from functions

We are probably tired of reading that PowerShell works on objects. We also know that text is a form of object. Now, it is important to know how to return objects from functions and scripts.

In most programming languages, we use the `return` keyword to return content from functions. PowerShell has no such requirements; there is no need to use the `return` keyword to return objects from within functions or scripts. In PowerShell, we simply call the variable or use a statement that outputs content, and this is the `return` statement in itself. The convention is that as well: no `return` statements in functions and scripts. If you would like to use it anyway because you are used to it because of languages such as C++, feel free to use it. PowerShell will output content based on the cmdlet or statement used, regardless of the keyword.

One important point to note is that exports may be affected by how content is returned from the functions. For instance, check out the following code:

```
function Test-Return {
    try {
        Test-Path $HOME/random/ -ErrorAction Stop
        $Files = Get-ChildItem $HOME/random/ -Recurse -File
        $Files
    }
    catch {
        Write-Error "Could not find the path specified."
    }
}

Test-Return | Export-Csv $HOME/random/FileListExport.csv
```

This won't record anything in the CSV file. The reason is that the `Test-Path` statement in line #3 would return a `System.Boolean` object, while `$Files` would return a `System.IO.FileInfo` object. The `Export-Csv` cmdlet would not be able to parse the Boolean object into CSV. To see that two kinds of members are returned by the function, you can pipe the function to the `Get-Member` cmdlet. Also, note that using the return keyword for `$Files` and omitting it from line #3 will not affect the objects returned by the function.

Naming functions

As we saw in the previous recipes, functions can be used like we use cmdlets. When we define parameters, they can be used along with the function, just like how we use parameters with cmdlets. Therefore, it is a convention to name the functions in the Verb-Noun format as well. This way, it is almost intuitive to use them, since we are used to cmdlets now. Also, when these functions are packed into a module and shared, they can, again, be used just like cmdlets.

It is natural for us to create functions in the conventional form—how we do it in other programming languages—however, naming the PowerShell functions the PowerShell way would make things easier for everyone who uses your functions. Also, after loading the modules, `Get-Command` would show the functions you packaged into your module. In that case, which would be easier to use in PowerShell in the context of `Get-Command`: the conventional `burgerDetails` or `Get-Burger`?

12
Advanced Concepts of Functions

In this chapter, we will cover the following recipes:

- Defining parameters
- Working with parameter aliases
- Working with parameter sets
- Adding default values to the parameter
- Adding validation to parameter input
- Handling dependencies and prerequisites
- Adding safety switches to functions
- Adding help to functions
- Adding support for pipeline input
- Using the Main function
- Writing a script module
- Handling module cleanup

Introduction

Personally, this part of PowerShell is among my favorites. The reason for this is the amount of control these concepts give you when you try to extend your work beyond simply running scripts to get things done. Functions that are packaged into a module give you a great productivity boost. It also means a smaller inventory of scripts, and close to no management overhead.

Without too much introduction, let us get down to business.

Defining parameters

In Chapter 11, *Building Scripts and Functions*, we defined parameters in scripts as well as functions. That was a simple parameter, where we simply defined the parameter name. With parameters in PowerShell, you can get as vague or as specific as you want. The idea is to keep things as standard or as flexible as you want. The flexible model may work in a single environment, however, the more standardized approach is advisable when creating shareable scripts (which is generally encouraged).

Here is the scenario for this recipe: modify the Start-Count function, which you created in the previous chapter, to remove the default value for TotalTime and make the parameter mandatory. Also, allow the user to define the CurrentTime parameter as well. Define the positions in such a way that the user can use Start-Count 5 10 if they want the script to count from 5 to 10.

Getting ready

Read the *How to do it...* part of the *Writing a simple function* recipe in Chapter 11, *Building Scripts and Functions*. We will use the same function here to extend it a little.

How to do it...

The modifications will be simple, but they will make a significant difference to how the script behaves:

1. Create a new PowerShell script file and paste the contents from the *How to do it...* section of the *Writing a simple function* recipe into the text window.
2. Make the modifications as follows. Do not copy and paste. Writing them by yourself will help you understand what you are doing:

```
function Start-Count {
    param (
        # The current time, or the starting point
        [Parameter(Mandatory=$true, Position=0)]
        [int]
        $CurrentTime,

        # The total number of seconds to count
        [Parameter(Mandatory=$true, Position=1)]
        [int]
        $TotalTime
```

```
        )

    while ($CurrentTime -le $TotalTime) {
        Write-Progress -Activity "Counting to $TotalTime" -Status
"Counting: $CurrentTime seconds" -PercentComplete ($CurrentTime /
$TotalTime * 100)
        Start-Sleep 1
        $CurrentTime++
    }
}
```

3. Run the script and call the function like so:

```
PS> . ./ch12/01-Start-Count.ps1
PS> Start-Count 5 10
PS> # Verbose version: Start-Count -CurrentTime 5 -TotalTime 10
```

How it works...

Note how we wrote a multiline `param()` block this time. This makes the script more readable. PowerShell understands this, and reads the entire `param()` block as follows:

```
param([Parameter(Mandatory=$true, Position=0)][int]$CurrentTime,
[Parameter(Mandatory=$true, Position=1)][int]$TotalTime)
```

The simple definition (without all the specifications) would simply be `param($CurrentTime, $TotalTime)`. The primary point of this recipe, though, is the specifications.

Use the snippets available in Visual Studio Code if you do not want to type the whole content, or do not remember the exact syntax. The snippets and IntelliSense suggestions improve the speed of creating functions, along with avoiding potential errors. To invoke snippets or suggestions, use the *Ctrl + Space* key combination.

It is customary to add a comment to each parameter in the definition. This helps improve readability. The `[Parameter()]` block contains specifications (`AttributeValues`) such as whether the parameter is mandatory, input what position should be assigned to the parameter, what parameter set the parameter belongs to, whether it can accept input through the pipeline, and so on.

We generally do not make a parameter mandatory, along with assigning a default value to it. That would be redundant.

The next line in the definition is the data type of the parameter. PowerShell understands the data type based on the context most of the time, however, explicitly defining it reduces room for error. This is also where you would specify whether the parameter is an array. Therefore, if you were to take an array of numbers as input for TotalTime, you would define it in the following way:

```
[Parameter(Mandatory=$true, Position=1)]
[int[]]
$TotalTime
```

When a parameter is made mandatory, PowerShell will automatically prompt the user for input for the parameter, that is, if the user does not specify values to them while calling the function:

```
Terminal                                                          ⊗
PS /home/ram/Documents/code/github/powershell/ch13> . ./01-Start-Count.ps1
PS /home/ram/Documents/code/github/powershell/ch13> Start-Count

cmdlet Start-Count at command pipeline position 1
Supply values for the following parameters:
CurrentTime: []
```

If the parameter accepts array input, PowerShell will prompt the user in the following way:

```
PS> TotalTime[0]: 3
TotalTime[1]:
```

If you are finished with the array, just send a blank element and PowerShell will take that as the end of the array.

Also note that position numbers start with 0. Therefore, the first parameter input will be associated with the parameter whose position is 0.

There's more...

Now that you know about the positional parameter, the mandatory parameter, and the default value of a parameter, attempt to modify the function to make it accept two kinds of input:

1. Count from 0 in case only one argument is specified. Here, take `TotalTime` as the only input:

   PS> Start-Count 10

2. In case a user specifies both the start time and the end time, start at the `CurrentTime` and stop counting at `TotalTime`:

   PS> Start-Count 3 9

   Do not make the user call the parameters by name.

Compare your script with the `01-Start-CountFlexible.ps1` script, which is a solution to this requirement.

See also

- Advanced Function Parameter Attributes (TechNet – Social): `https://social.technet.microsoft.com/wiki/contents/articles/15994.powershell-advanced-function-parameter-attributes.aspx`

Working with parameter aliases

We've already seen in the previous recipes that parameters can be called without having to specify the entire name, but enough characters to uniquely identify them. For instance, if `ComputerName` were a parameter, and the cmdlet had no other parameter that starts with c, we could simply say `-c MyPc` instead of `-ComputerName MyPc`. However, if the cmdlet also had a `ComputerType` parameter, then you would have to call `ComputerName -computern MyPc`, at the very least.

In such situations, especially when running commands on the terminal, we could use a shorter version of these parameter names. This is one of the situations where parameter aliases help. You will notice that, in many cmdlets, you could specify the `ComputerName` as `cn`.

Modify the function we created in the previous recipe to accept ct and from as the aliases for the CurrentTime, and tt and to for the TotalTime.

How to do it...

Parameter aliases are set when defining the parameters. Modify the script as follows to define the parameter aliases:

```
function Start-Count {
    param (
        # The current time, or the starting point
        [Parameter(Mandatory=$false)]
        [Alias("CT","From")]
        [int]
        $CurrentTime=0,

        # The total number of seconds to count
        [Parameter(Mandatory=$true, Position=1)]
        [Alias("TT","To")]
        [int]
        $TotalTime
    )

    while ($CurrentTime -le $TotalTime) {
        Write-Progress -Activity "Counting to $TotalTime" -Status
"Counting: $CurrentTime seconds" -PercentComplete ($CurrentTime /
$TotalTime * 100)
        Start-Sleep 1
        $CurrentTime++
    }
}
```

Call the script:

```
PS> . ./ch12/02-Start-Count.ps1
PS> Start-Count -tt 7
```

How it works...

The process of defining the alias is rather self-explanatory once we know the syntax. However, parameter aliases serve a purpose that's a little more on the functional side than serving as keystroke reducers: backward compatibility. PowerShell has evolved over time. Standardization may not have come into PowerShell overnight. From time to time, the creators of PowerShell modules have had to rename parameters in order to either make them adhere to standards, or to enhance functionality.

However, doing this could potentially break several scripts out there, many of which may have been shared publicly and used by hundreds of teams worldwide. Therefore, the old names of these parameters would be converted into aliases for the new, more standard names.

Working with parameter sets

In the *Updating and using Help* recipe in `Chapter 1`, *Introducing PowerShell Core*, we saw the term `Parameter Set`. We also read that parameters that are present in one parameter set, but absent in another, cannot be combined with a parameter from the latter set. Parameter sets are useful when we have either conflicting functionalities or functionalities that do not get along.

In this recipe, we will create a function that will be used to relay messages. If a text message is sent, the function calls another function called `Send-TextMessage`, which sends an SMS to the recipient, or `New-VoiceCall`, which is designed to make a voice call through the phone system in your company. `Send-TextMessage` and `New-VoiceCall` are already present in the system. Our task is to write a function that accepts a phone number as one of the inputs, and either the path to the WAV file or the SMS message.

How to do it...

This recipe is not dependent on any of the recipes we have already seen. We will create the function from scratch. What we are going to create is a wrapper function. The assumption here is that we already have the two functions, `Send-TextMessage` and `New-VoiceCall`. Follow these steps to get started:

1. Open a new PowerShell script file and enter the following into the text field:

```
function New-PersonalMessage {
    [CmdletBinding(DefaultParameterSetName='Audio')]
```

```
            param (
                # The phone number
                [Parameter(Mandatory=$true, Position=0,
        ParameterSetName='Audio')]
                [Parameter(Mandatory=$true, Position=0,
        ParameterSetName='Text')]
                [string]
                $PhoneNumber,

                # The path to the WAV file
                [Parameter(Mandatory=$true, Position=1,
        ParameterSetName='Audio')]
                [string]
                $WavPath,

                # The message to be sent
                [Parameter(Mandatory=$true, Position=1,
        ParameterSetName='Text')]
                [string]
                $Message
            )
            if ($WavPath) {
                New-VoiceCall -PhoneNumber $PhoneNumber -FilePath $WavPath
            }
            else {
                Send-TextMessage -PhoneNumber $PhoneNumber -Message
        $Message
            }
        }
```

2. Run the script using the *F5* key.
3. Run the following command to show the help information:

   PS> Get-Help New-PersonalMessage

   Note the parameter sets:

```
Terminal                                                         ⊗
PS /home/ram/Documents/code/github/powershell> Get-Help New-PersonalMessage

NAME
    New-PersonalMessage

SYNTAX
    New-PersonalMessage [-PhoneNumber] <string> [-WavPath] <string> [<CommonParameters>]

    New-PersonalMessage [-PhoneNumber] <string> [-Message] <string> [<CommonParameters>]
```

How it works...

Parameter sets have been created so that two incompatible actions are not called for by a cmdlet. However, some parameters can or must be part of multiple parameter sets (for example, the phone number).

To define these parameters, we must begin with CmdletBinding, right after defining the function. On this line, we mention the default parameter set name. This helps when using positional and/or mandatory parameters. Next, when defining the parameters, we specify the parameter set that each of the parameters belongs to. If a parameter belongs to more than one parameter set, we specify all of the parameter sets on separate lines (in our case, the PhoneNumber parameter).

When you run the Get-Help cmdlet for the new wrapper function we created, you will be able to see the parameter sets. Now, when you have to send a message, you could either call the New-PersonalMessage cmdlet with a phone number and the path to the WAV file, or with a phone number and the message body.

Adding default values to the parameter

Sometimes, it is possible to give a parameter in a function a default value. In this case, we do not specify the parameter as a mandatory one (if we do, the function will disregard the default value and prompt for a value anyway).

In this recipe, we will revisit the count function and focus on the default value.

How to do it...

We will use the same script that we did in the *Defining parameters* recipe, with two small changes in it. Create a PowerShell script file with the following content:

```
function Start-Count {
    param (
        # The current time, or the starting point
        [Parameter(Mandatory=$false)]
        [Alias("CT", "From")]
        [int]
        $CurrentTime=0,

        # The total number of seconds to count
        [Parameter(Mandatory=$false, Position=1)]
```

```
        [Alias("TT", "To")]
        [int]
        $TotalTime=10
    )

    while ($CurrentTime -le $TotalTime) {
        Write-Progress -Activity "Counting to $TotalTime" -Status
    "Counting: $CurrentTime seconds" -PercentComplete ($CurrentTime /
    $TotalTime * 100)
        Start-Sleep 1
        $CurrentTime++
    }
}
```

At the terminal, dot-source and run the script. Call the function without passing any parameters.

How it works...

Sometimes, it is possible to assign a default value to a parameter so that the administrators do not have to necessarily specify any value to it when calling the cmdlet. One of the examples for this is the ResultSize parameter in the Get-Mailbox cmdlet in Microsoft Exchange. By default, calling Get-Mailbox without any parameter would return 1,000 mailboxes.

The default value, of course, can be overridden by explicitly specifying a value for the parameter when calling the function. Let's say we're running the following code:

```
PS> Start-Count
```

This would count to 10. To override this behavior—to, say, make the function count to 4—you would call the following:

```
PS> Start-Count -to 4
```

Do not make the parameter mandatory if it has a default value. Not only does it defeat the purpose of having a default value by prompting for input anyway, but it is also illogical to do so.

Adding validation to parameter input

You may be in a situation where a null value is not acceptable for a parameter, or there may be situations that require you to restrict the input you receive. While such situations can be handled with branch-based validation, that would mean dedicating some amount of code to such validation. Parameter validation can help here, without you having to worry too much about what construct to use for the validation.

Moreover, parameter validation can also assist with tab completion!

The scenario for this recipe is to limit the value of `TotalTime` to one of 5, 10, 15 and 20 seconds.

How to do it...

Modify the script we used in the previous recipe, *Adding default values to a parameter*, to the following:

```
function Start-Count {
    param (
        # The current time, or the starting point
        [Parameter(Mandatory=$false)]
        [Alias("CT", "From")]
        [int]
        $CurrentTime=0,

        # The total number of seconds to count
        [Parameter(Mandatory=$false, Position=1)]
        [Alias("TT", "To")]
        [ValidateSet(5, 10, 15, 20)]
        [int]
        $TotalTime=10
    )

    while ($CurrentTime -le $TotalTime) {
        Write-Progress -Activity "Counting to $TotalTime" -Status
"Counting: $CurrentTime seconds" -PercentComplete ($CurrentTime /
$TotalTime * 100)
        Start-Sleep 1
        $CurrentTime++
    }
}
```

Run the following command and read the error:

```
PS> Start-Count -TotalTime 6
```

How it works...

PowerShell provides a range of options for parameter validation. These are simply pre-recorded functions that reduce the amount of time you spend validating the input, and at the same time give errors that are readable. PowerShell also allows us to create our own parameter validation logic. However, that is out of the scope of this book.

In our recipe, we use the ValidateSet attribute, which accepts a series of inputs as a set and ensures that the input sent to TotalTime is one of 5, 10, 15, or 20 seconds. There are more validation options available, such as ValidateNotNullOrEmpty, ValidateRange, ValidateCount, ValidatePattern, or even—when you have your own script block —ValidateScript.

Handling dependencies and prerequisites

A function, in fact, is made of three blocks, apart from the param() block. These are begin, process, and end.

By default, whatever you specify after the param() block will be treated as belonging to process, unless you specify otherwise.

Create a wrapper function to create three files, test1.txt, test2.txt, and test3.txt. However, before creating the files, output the date. You must be able to call the function like so:

```
PS> New-File 'test1.txt', 'test2.txt', 'test3.txt'
```

How to do it...

The logic is simple. We will use a begin block to show the date, and have the file creation part in the process block. The process block will have a looping construct to create the files.

Open a new PowerShell script file and enter the following:

```
function New-File {
    param (
        # The path to the file (or the name)
        [Parameter(Mandatory=$true, Position=0)]
        [string[]]
        $Path
    )
    begin {
        Write-Host "$(Get-Date)"
    }
    process {
        foreach ($Item in $Path) {
            New-Item -Path $Item -ItemType File
        }
    }
    end {}
}
```

Now, call the function as specified in the requirement:

```
PS> New-File 'test1.txt', 'test2.txt', 'test3.txt'
```

How it works...

The begin block contains a block of code that runs once per function call. Going by this method, the begin block will execute once, and then the entire process block will run for each of the objects passed into the function (either as a parameter, or via the pipeline).

Whatever is in the process block is the actual code for the function. This executes once for each object in the pipeline. We did not use the end block for this recipe, but it can be used if you would like your function to perform a post-processing step.

Typically, in production environments, we use the begin block to handle prerequisites, such as loading a certain module that is required in the process block. We add these steps in a try-catch block, with the break keyword in the catch block, to prevent the execution of the process block altogether if the prerequisite fails:

```
function myFunction {
    param ([string]$myParameter)

    begin {
        try {
            # Load the myAwesomeModule -ErrorAction Stop
```

```
        }
        catch {
            "Uh oh, That module did not load."
            break
        }
    }
    process { <# Do some amazing stuff here. #> }
}
```

When PowerShell encounters the `break` keyword within the `begin` block, it prevents the `process` block from executing. This means that there's no unnecessary processing, no barrage of errors, and no mess.

In the `end` block, we usually place commands for any cleanup that we would want to perform after the function is executed.

Adding safety switches to functions

It is common to hear the phrase – PowerShell looks out for you, when anyone talks about how PowerShell is friendly. What they really mean is that PowerShell has several functionalities that help you not mess up. This is achieved by using methods such as the `ShouldProcess` method, or, in other words, the `WhatIf` parameter. Also, in cases where what you are going to do with the function is drastic, you could also add a `Confirm` parameter to it.

Supporting both of these functionalities can be tricky sometimes. In this recipe, you will add a `WhatIf` switch to the file creation process so that the user knows what would happen if they ran the cmdlet, and add a `Confirm` switch to ask the user whether they would really like to create the files.

How to do it...

There are two requirements here. We will add the functionalities to the same function, `New-File`.

Open a new file window, copy the contents of the `06-New-File.ps1` file, and make some changes so that the script looks like this:

```
function New-File {
    [CmdletBinding(
        ConfirmImpact='High',
```

```
            SupportsShouldProcess=$true
    )]
    param (
        # The path to the file (or the name)
        [Parameter(Mandatory=$true, Position=0)]
        [string[]]
        $Path
    )
    begin {
        Write-Host "$(Get-Date)"
    }
    process {
        foreach ($Item in $Path) {
            if ($PSCmdlet.ShouldProcess("$PsScriptRoot", "Create $Path")) {
                New-Item -Path $Item -ItemType File
            }
        }
    }
    end {}
}
```

Run the script and call the function with three file-names as parameters. Dot-source the script; don't just call it. Alternatively, you could run the script using the *F5* key when in Visual Studio Code:

```
PS> . ./ch12/07-New-File.ps1
PS> New-File file1.txt, file2.txt -WhatIf
PS> New-File file1.txt, file2.txt
```

Here is a screenshot of the output for the cmdlet being run with and without -WhatIf:

```
                              Terminal                              _  ⊗
PS /home/ram/Documents/code/github/powershell> New-File file1.txt, file2.txt -WhatIf
11/15/2018 23:04:36
What if: Performing the operation "Create file1.txt file2.txt" on target "/home/ram/Docume
nts/code/github/powershell/ch12".
What if: Performing the operation "Create file1.txt file2.txt" on target "/home/ram/Docume
nts/code/github/powershell/ch12".
PS /home/ram/Documents/code/github/powershell> New-File file1.txt, file2.txt
11/15/2018 23:06:09

Confirm
Are you sure you want to perform this action?
Performing the operation "Create file1.txt file2.txt" on target
"/home/ram/Documents/code/github/powershell/ch12".
[Y] Yes  [A] Yes to All  [N] No  [L] No to All  [S] Suspend  [?] Help (default is "Y"): █
```

Optionally, remove the files you just created if you answered Y to the confirmation prompt.

How it works...

PowerShell is capable of making changes to your system in such a drastic way that sometimes it is simply scary—this is no different than any other shell, such as Bash. Therefore, there are two very important functionalities built into PowerShell that help ensure that you do not accidentally do what you did not intend to.

The first among these capabilities is the `ShouldContinue` capability, or the `Confirm` parameter. As the name suggests, it asks you whether the operation should continue. In order to ask this, though, it needs some information that is useful to you. We will get to that in a moment.

The first change compared to `06-New-File.ps1`, as you may have noticed, is the `[CmdletBinding()]` line, right before the parameter declaration. This attribute technically converts your regular function into an advanced function. The first attribute we declare is the `ConfirmImpact` attribute, and this governs whether there is a confirmation prompt.

Every session of PowerShell contains an automatic variable called `$ConfirmPreference`, which is, by default, set at `High`. This means that there would be a confirm prompt if there is a confirmation impact of high or above. The confirmation impact is governed by the `ConfirmImpact` attribute, which is, by default, `Medium`. Now, if the value of the `ConfirmImpact` attribute is greater than or equal to that of the `$ConfirmPreference` variable, there would be a confirmation prompt. Since the impact is medium by default, and the preference is set at high, PowerShell does not ask us to confirm every action we perform.

In our function, we set the value of `ConfirmImpact` to the same as that of `$ConfirmPreference`, and therefore enable the confirmation prompt.

The next attribute we set is `SupportsShouldProcess`. This enables the `WhatIf` parameter. However, merely setting `SupportsShouldProcess` to `$true` does not exactly tell the script what to tell the user when they use `WhatIf`. Therefore, we use the `$PsCmdlet.ShouldProcess()` method within the script.

> You could simply use `SupportsShouldProcess` instead of `SupportsShouldProcess=$true` and avoid redundancy. However, if you want your script to support PowerShell 2.0 or older, assigning `$true` to it is necessary.

The `ShouldProcess()` method within `$PsCmdlet` (yes, `CmdletBinding` enables us to use this variable as well), by default, takes in one input, which is the target. When just the target is passed, the output—when `-WhatIf` is called—says the following:

```
What if: Performing the operation "<Cmdlet Name>" on target "<Specified
target>".
```

If you would like to manually specify what operation the function performs instead of letting PowerShell pick the cmdlet name, specify that action as the second argument:

```
if ($PsCmdlet.ShouldProcess("$PsScriptRoot", "Create $Path") {
```

These two arguments also help with the confirmation prompt. The prompt uses the same data to ask you whether you would like to perform said operation on said target.

We use the `if` construct here because we want to make the `What if` output available only when `WhatIf` is called (or with the confirmation prompt when the `ConfirmImpact` is higher than or the same as the `ConfirmPreference`).

Adding help to functions

PowerShell is strong on help documentation. This is reflected in the extensive documentation given in all of the first-party cmdlets as well as most third-party and community cmdlets. As seen in `Chapter 1`, *Introducing PowerShell Core*, the `Get-Help` cmdlet itself runs in different modes, such as `Example` and `Full`.

Let's add some help documentation to the `Start-Count` cmdlet.

How to do it...

Help in PowerShell is comment-based. Therefore, add the following comment block right after the function declaration:

```
function Start-Count {
    <#
    .SYNOPSIS
    This cmdlet counts seconds by accepting a from and a to value. The from
value is optional.
    .DESCRIPTION
    This cmdlet is a counting function. It accepts two parameters: the
TotalTime being the "to" and CurrentTime being the "from". CurrentTime
defaults to 0 if not specified.
```

```
.PARAMETER CurrentTime
The starting point, in seconds.
.PARAMETER TotalTime
The stopping point, in seconds.
.EXAMPLE
Start-Count 10 15
.NOTES
Created as a demo for PowerShell 6.0 Linux Administration Cookbook
#>
param (
    # The current time, or the starting point
    [Parameter(Mandatory=$false)]
    [Alias("CT", "From")]
    [int]
    $CurrentTime=0,

    # The total number of seconds to count
    [Parameter(Mandatory=$false, Position=1)]
    [Alias("TT", "To")]
    [ValidateSet(5, 10, 15, 20)]
    [int]
    $TotalTime=10
)

while ($CurrentTime -le $TotalTime) {
    Write-Progress -Activity "Counting to $TotalTime" -Status
"Counting: $CurrentTime seconds" -PercentComplete ($CurrentTime /
$TotalTime * 100)
    Start-Sleep 1
    $CurrentTime++
    }
}
```

Run the script within Visual Studio Code, and then, at the **Integrated Terminal**, run `Get-Help` on this cmdlet.

It is not necessary to generate this documentation manually by typing the name of each of the parameters. Add a line before the function declaration when in Visual Studio Code and type `##`, after you are done writing the entire function. The PowerShell extension will automatically generate the help documentation based on the parameters you have declared. Use tabs to move through sections in the document.

How it works...

The formatting of the PowerShell help documentation is very specific. PowerShell, even without what you just added, would make `Get-Help` possible on the cmdlet, although the help information would only show the parameters, which parameter is mandatory, and so on. If you would like to provide the user with more information on each of the parameters (which is recommended, by the way), add this help documentation.

PowerShell typically looks for this large, formatted comment block before the function declaration or right after it. While it is possible that PowerShell recognizes these in more places, it is recommended that the help document be added right before the function declaration or right after.

PowerShell also recognizes (all the instances of) the `.EXAMPLE` heading and shows its contents when the `Examples` switch parameter is called along with `Get-Help`.

Adding support for pipeline input

Administrators who are used to shell scripting cannot live without the pipeline. Without one cmdlet interacting with another, the extent of automation is drastically reduced. Adding support for pipeline input is also one of the configuration options you set in the `param()` block of a function.

Let's add support for pipeline input to the `New-File` cmdlet so that you can send an array of strings through the pipeline for the filename.

How to do it...

This capability will require a single change to the existing script. Follow these steps to get started:

1. Copy the content from `07-New-File.ps1` and paste it into a new file.
2. Change the `[Parameter()]` declaration for the `Path` parameter:

```
function New-File {
    [CmdletBinding(
        ConfirmImpact='High',
        SupportsShouldProcess=$true
    )]
    param (
        # The path to the file (or the name)
```

```
        [Parameter(Mandatory=$true, Position=0, ValueFromPipeline)]
        [string[]]
        $Path
    )
    begin {
        Write-Host "$(Get-Date)"
    }
    process {
        foreach ($Item in $Path) {
            if ($PSCmdlet.ShouldProcess("$PsScriptRoot", "Create
$Path")) {
                New-Item -Path $Item -ItemType File
            }
        }
    }
    end {}
}
```

How it works...

There are really two ways to make a cmdlet accept input through the pipeline. Each of these two ways has two sub-ways to accept input, so to speak:

- Accept input by type:
  - With coercion
  - Without coercion
- Accept input by parameter name:
  - With coercion
  - Without coercion

In this recipe, we will make the cmdlet accept input without coercion. In this case, the data type of the Path parameter is the same as the content being passed through the pipeline: a string array. In the case of accepting input with coercion, PowerShell will try to convert the content passed through the pipeline to the type that is accepted by the parameter, such as a valid date-like string to a datetime object.

In the case of accepting input by parameter name, the input will be chosen based on whether the property name matches the name of the parameter. If we had to implement this in our case, we could have sent a PsCustomObject through the pipeline, with Path as one of the property names in the object. This would have been matched with the parameter name in the New-File cmdlet, and the new files would have been created.

There's more...

- Make the `New-File` cmdlet accept input based on the property name
- Read the Help text for both the types (parameter by type and by name) and observe the differences

Using the Main function

It is a good practice to make a function do only one thing. This means that, when writing a script that must do a series of tasks, you will need multiple functions. In such a case, one function will call another to perform the task. The structure of the script, then, would be to have the called function written before the calling function. When working with several functions within a script, the entire structure could look upside-down.

Now, reading and understanding the script may feel a little challenging.

For instance, I wrote a script for one of my clients that helped them heal a Citrix Virtual Desktop Agent server if it unregistered itself from the Controller for any of several reasons. This script was over 300 lines long, and had a dozen functions that would do the following:

- Find if a server was unregistered
- Send out `server unregistered` and other notifications to the Service Desk and/or the concerned teams
- Place the server in maintenance mode in order to prevent user connections
- Attempt a restart of the Citrix Desktop Service and purge Prelogon connections
- Wait and watch the resource consumption and perform a few diagnostics and troubleshooting steps
- Send a notification to the connected users that the server will be taken down for maintenance
- Attempt a server restart if nothing works by issuing a simple Restart-Computer account
- If the restart doesn't work, connect using VMware PowerCLI and perform a forceful restart
- Perform post-restart steps and, finally, check if the server was registered with the Controller

At a glance, however, an administrator would not be able to understand what the script is doing, and which is the actual function that governs all of these tasks.

Write two functions: one to generate filenames and another to create those files. Use the former function in conjunction with the latter to create 10 files. Ensure that the script is readable.

How to do it...

We will only write the first function; we already have a function to create the files. Follow these steps to get started:

1. Write the function to generate the filenames. Make this function really simple and bare-bones:

```
function New-FileName {
    param (
        # The name of the file
        [Parameter(Mandatory=$false)]
        [string]
        $Prefix='File',

        # The number of files to be generated
        [Parameter(Mandatory=$false, Position=1)]
        [int]
        $Count=1
    )

    begin {
        $InitCount = 1
    }

    process {
        while ($InitCount -le $Count) {
            Write-Output $Prefix$InitCount
            $InitCount++
        }
    }
}
```

2. Copy and paste the `New-File` function from `09-New-File.ps1`. You may want to remove the `ConfirmPreference` line from the function if you do not want the function to prompt you to confirm the file's creation.

3. Add the following to the beginning of the script:

```
function Main {
    New-FileName -Count 10 | New-File
}
```

4. Call the `Main` function at the end:

```
Main
```

How it works...

This process of creating a main function and calling it in the end is just so that the reader knows the ultimate intent right at the beginning of the script, and that it is not an absolute necessity.

PowerShell works on the scripts in the same manner as it does on the terminal. This is done to give a unified experience, as well as to provide script writers with the ability to test out their snippets on the terminal if they want to, or even actually run the snippets on the terminal.

You can only run those functions that have already been declared; a function that is not yet written (or read by PowerShell) cannot be run. In the case of long-running scripts with several functions, it is possible for a user to feel lost, regarding what the script is actually supposed to achieve.

To be clear about the ultimate intent and call the functions sequentially, we use the `Main`, `Function1 – FunctionN` construct and then, finally, call the `Main` function in the end. To maintain readability, the first thing we do is create the `Main` function. If there weren't the `Main` function, we would have had the following line at the end of the script:

```
New-FileName -Count 10 | New-File
```

We simply declare the `Main` function, write our functions that do the tasks, and then call the already declared `Main` function at the end. This way, we execute the functions in the right sequence and, at the same time, show the user what the actual intent is.

It is not necessary that the `Main` function be called `Main`. It is just a convention to call it so, especially because we are used to it in many languages, such as C++.

Writing a script module

A module in PowerShell is a package that may contain functions/cmdlets, variables, aliases, providers, and so on. Modules extend the capabilities of PowerShell, and can be as simple as containing just one wrapper function or as complex as allowing the user to completely manage their entire cloud infrastructure. At its core, PowerShell is only an engine; the shafts, the wheels, the body, and so on are all due to the modules.

Modules can be of different kinds, based on how they are constructed. Some examples include Binary Module, Script Module, and Manifest Module.

The focus of this recipe (and, really this book) is the Script Module.

Convert the `10-New-File.ps1` script into a module so that the users get the ability to generate filenames, as well as create files. Make changes to the script in such a way that the users see only the `New-File` cmdlet. Finally, use the `Generate` switch parameter to generate the filenames.

How to do it...

We will create a script module with two functions. We will call one function from another. The latter function will be exposed for use. Follow these steps to get started:

1. Start a new PowerShell session.
2. Create a copy of the `10-New-File.ps1` file and call it `11-New-File.psm1`.
3. Replace the contents of the file with the following:

```
function New-FileName {
    param (
        # The name of the file
        [Parameter(Mandatory=$false)]
        [string]
        $Prefix='File',

        # The number of files to be generated
        [Parameter(Mandatory=$false, Position=1)]
        [int]
        $Count=1
    )

    begin {
        $InitCount = 1
    }
```

```
    process {
        while ($InitCount -le $Count) {
            Write-Output $Prefix$InitCount
            $InitCount++
        }
    }
}

function New-File {
    [CmdletBinding(
        SupportsShouldProcess=$true,
        DefaultParameterSetName='File'
    )]
    param (
        # The path to the file (or the name)
        [Parameter(Mandatory=$true, Position=0, ValueFromPipeline,
ParameterSetName='File')]
        [string[]]
        $Path,

        # Whether files need to be generated
        [Parameter(Mandatory=$true, ParameterSetName='Generate')]
        [switch]
        $Generate,

        # Number of files to be generated
        [Parameter(Mandatory=$false, ParameterSetName='Generate')]
        [int]
        $Count=1
    )
    begin {
        Write-Host "$(Get-Date)"
    }
    process {
        if ($Generate) {
            $Path = New-FileName -Count $Count
        }
        foreach ($Item in $Path) {
            if ($PSCmdlet.ShouldProcess("$PsScriptRoot", "Create
$Path")) {
                New-Item -Path $Item -ItemType File
            }
        }
    }
    end {}
}
```

3. Next, add the following to the end of the file:

```
Export-ModuleMember New-File
```

4. Load the module:

```
PS> Import-Module ./ch12/11-New-File.psm1
```

5. Try to call the New-FileName function (it will not autocomplete).
6. Call the New-File cmdlet with the Generate switch:

```
PS> New-File -Generate -Count 4
```

Optionally, remove the if block for ShouldProcess if you do not want to be prompted each time a file is created. Of course, let the New-Item line remain.

How it works...

Script Modules are almost like scripts. When loading a PowerShell script, you would call the script with the . calling operator, and then use the functions within. In the case of a module, though, you use the Import-Module cmdlet. A module could be a collection of functions that have been saved as a psm1 file. As already mentioned, a module can be a simple one like the module we discussed in this recipe, or one that is much more complex and has many, many components.

In this recipe, the module exports only one member, which is the New-File cmdlet; the New-FileName function is not exposed for use. This is done using the Export-ModuleMember cmdlet. Had the cmdlet not been used, both functions would have been exported. The New-FileName function calls the New-FileName cmdlet from within it.

When loading the module, we provide the complete path to the module file. If you would like to load the module without giving the complete path, save the module file in one of the paths in $env:PsModulePath. PowerShell looks for module files within these paths and loads them simply by name.

The other benefit of saving the module file in one of the $env:PsModulePath paths is that Get-Module -ListAvailable (the modules available to be loaded) will show your custom module as well.

See also

- The *Installing modules from the repository* recipe from `Chapter 1`, *Introducing PowerShell Core*

Handling module cleanup

In the case of a simple script module, you may not necessarily need to handle module cleanup. However, when you write more complex modules, it is necessary that the module members be cleaned up when the module is removed.

Set up the cleanup of the custom module you created in the previous recipe, *Writing a script module*; simply write a host output stating that the module has been cleaned up. The cleanup should take place upon invoking `Remove-Module`. You also need to ensure that the the module cleanup happens, even if the PowerShell session is terminated without invoking `Remove-Module`.

How to do it...

Add the following block to the end of your module file and save the file:

```
$MyInvocation.MyCommand.ScriptBlock.Module.OnRemove = {
    Write-Output "Module cleaned up."
}

Register-EngineEvent PowerShell.Exiting {
    Remove-Module '12-New-File'
}
```

Remove the module from the session to see what this does.

How it works...

Members of a module share private state. In the case of simple script modules like the one in this recipe, it is not quite necessary to perform explicit cleanup. However, it is good to know how it can be done.

There are two aspects to consider:

- The module is unloaded using the `Remove-Module` cmdlet
- The PowerShell session is terminated without the user running `Remove-Module`

To perform a task (or tasks) upon running the `Remove-Module` cmdlet on the module in question, you must create a script block with the cmdlets that should be run during the module removal. This script block is then assigned to the `$MyInvocation.MyCommand.ScriptBlock.Module.OnRemove` object. In our case, we do not perform a real cleanup; we simply display a line that says that the module has been cleaned up. This `Write-Host` line can be replaced with actual cleanup commands, as and when required.

The second situation is if the module was never removed, but the PowerShell session was terminated. Termination of the session is an engine event, and tasks to be invoked in such situations should be sent to the engine. Therefore, we use the `Register-EngineEvent` cmdlet with the `PowerShell.Exiting` identifier. Here, we simply add the `Remove-Module` cmdlet, which in turn invokes the `$MyInvocation.MyCommand.ScriptBlock.Module.OnRemove` script block, thereby gracefully handling the cleanup.

Debugging and Error Handling

13

In this chapter, we will cover the following recipes:

- Writing debug output
- Running a script in Debug mode
- Using breakpoints
- Using conditional breakpoints
- Using exit codes
- Working with the Error variable
- Controlling flow based on errors
- Sending verbose output to a file

Introduction

As much as it's fun writing scripts, encountering errors and hidden bugs is a serious pain point. During the days of PowerShell ISE (which is still a thing in Windows PowerShell), debugging was not very intuitive. Today, we have Visual Studio Code, which proves to be a much better PowerShell scripting environment and has the necessary tools in its user interface.

It is important to mention at this point that if you are not using a Desktop Environment on your Linux system, you will need to stick with the debugging cmdlets. This chapter will point out those cmdlets as necessary so that you can use a code editor such as Vim and still be able to use the debugging tools without a graphical user interface.

The Debug tab of Visual Studio Code

Today, Microsoft suggests using Visual Studio Code as the PowerShell scripting environment. Installing the PowerShell extension with Visual Studio Code enables all of the capabilities of the PowerShell Integrated Scripting Environment and more.

The Debug tab in Visual Studio Code helps you get under the hood and debug scripts. Get yourself a copy of Visual Studio Code and install the PowerShell extension to it by following the *Installing Visual Studio Code* recipe in `Chapter 2`, *Preparing for Administration Using PowerShell*.

The Debug panel can be accessed either by clicking on the Debug button on the sidebar or using the key combination *Ctrl + Shift + D*.

The first thing you will notice in the Debug panel is the Run button, which is right next to a dropdown where you can select the launch configuration. We will use the default, **PowerShell Launch Current File**. These configurations can be seen and modified by clicking on the gear icon, which opens the `launch.json` file. Any configuration you add here will be shown as an option in the dropdown.

Next in the panel is the **Variables** pane. This pane shows all of the variables that have been created and used in the script so far, including the relevant automatic variables. These variables are shown as objects themselves, which means that any of their member properties are also shown in this view upon expanding the relevant variables. If you would like to keep an eye on specific variables, these can be added to the **Watch List**. This would be helpful when debugging scripts so that you don't have to navigate a sea of variables. The values will change as required as we step through the code.

The next pane is the **Call stack** pane. This pane shows the call stack within the current script. Finally, there is the **Breakpoints** pane, which list out all the breakpoints set in the script. Very straightforward.

Writing debug output

Traditionally, while writing scripts, we have used regular console output, also known as print-style debugging. This often leads to a lot of text in the output. Of course, this can be cleaned up once the scripting is complete, but that is still additional work, not to mention the need to add all of the debug output again during further development, changes, or extension. Also, as the complexity of the script increases, so does the complexity of debugging using console text.

Enter: the extensive built-in debugging capabilities of PowerShell.

Write a debug output for the `New-File` function that you created in the previous chapter.

Getting ready

Here are the requirements that need to be met before we get into the recipes:

1. Install Visual Studio Code and configure it to run PowerShell by referring to the *Installing Visual Studio Code* recipe from `Chapter 2`, *Preparing for Administration Using PowerShell.*

2. Optionally, clone the repository that accompanies this book so that you have the necessary scripts to work with:

```
$ git clone
https://github.com/PacktPublishing/PowerShell-Core-Linux-Administra
tors-Cookbook book-code
```

How to do it...

We will pick the simplest file to ensure focus:

1. Create a copy of the `ch12/06-New-File.ps1` file. This file can be found in the code repository that accompanies this book.

2. Add a few `Write-Debug` lines to it.

3. Now, either change the `DebugPreference` to `Continue` from `SilentlyContinue`, or add `[CmdletBinding()]` to the function. If you chose the latter approach of adding `[CmdletBinding()]` to the script, this is what the final script should look like:

```
function New-File {
    [CmdletBinding()]
    param (
        # The path to the file (or the name)
        [Parameter(Mandatory=$true, Position=0)]
        [string[]]
        $Path
    )
    Write-Debug "Entered the process block."
    foreach ($Item in $Path) {
        Write-Debug "Iterating for item, $Item."
        New-Item -Path $Path -ItemType File
```

```
        }
    }
```

Next, load the script and call the function with the `Debug` switch. Confirm your actions through each step and read the debug output:

```
PS> New-File -Path ./MyFile.txt -Debug
```

How it works...

The actual debug output is written using the `Write-Debug` cmdlet within the script. Whether the debug output is written or not is governed by two things:

1. Using the `DebugPreference` automatic variable. This variable resets itself to `SilentlyContinue` for each session. `SilentlyContinue` will make the script go on without the debug output being displayed. Setting the `DebugPreference` to `Continue` would change this behavior and display the debug output.
2. Converting a function into an advanced function by simply declaring `CmdletBinding()`. This way, you would be able to easily control the debug display using the `Debug` switch. Whenever you need the debug display, simply call the function with the `Debug` switch; during the other times, the debug output would be silent, unless overridden by the `DebugPreference` variable.

One point to remember is that when turning on debug output using the `DebugPreference` variable, the functions will not confirm each of your actions like it does when you use the `Debug` switch.

Running a script in Debug mode

We saw that adding `CmdletBinding()` and using the debug switch when calling the script shows us debug output. However, what if your function is not designed to support debugging or you are not using a function at all? What if you would like to step through each of the steps in the script?

Run the following script in Debug mode:

```
function New-File {
    param (
        # The path to the file (or the name)
        [Parameter(Mandatory=$true, Position=0)]
        [string[]]
```

```
        $Path
    )
    begin {
        Write-Debug "Entered the begin block."
        Write-Host "$(Get-Date)"
    }
    process {
        Write-Debug "Entered the process block."
        foreach ($Item in $Path) {
            Write-Debug "Iterating for item, $Item."
            New-Item -Path $Path -ItemType File
        }
    }
    end {
        Write-Debug "Entered the end block."
    }
}
```

How to do it...

We used a cmdlet to run scripts and functions in Debug mode. Follow these steps to get started:

1. Run `Set-PsDebug -Step` to go into `Debug` mode
2. Run the script by either dot-sourcing the script or using the Debug tab of Visual Studio Code
3. Call the `New-File` function with an appropriate parameter
4. Exit Debug mode when the script run is complete by using the same cmdlet with the `Off` switch:

```
PS> Set-PsDebug -Off
```

How it works...

To enter Debug mode in PowerShell, use the `Set-PsDebug` cmdlet with the `Step` switch to step through the entire process, whatever the script is designed to do. At each step, we can peek into the objects to see what value they hold and perform diagnostics.

Running the `Set-PsDebug` cmdlet when in Debug mode with the `Off` parameter exits Debug mode. You can change the behavior of Debug mode from within the Debug mode itself by using other parameters such as `Trace` or `Strict`.

Tracing errors

Sometimes, errors or unexpected outputs are evasive. This situation can get complicated when the script is long.

Identify and trace the issue in the following script:

```
function Set-Name {
    $Name = @()
    $Name = Read-Host "Enter first name"
    $Name += Read-Host "Enter middle name (press Enter for blank)"
    $Name += Read-Host "Enter surname"

    $Count = $Name.Count
    $Converter = (Get-Culture).TextInfo

    switch ($Count) {
        2 {
            "$($Converter.ToTitleCase($Name[1])),
$($Converter.ToTitleCase($Name[0]))"
        }
        3 {
            "$($Converter.ToTitleCase($Name[2])),
$($Converter.ToTitleCase($Name[0])) $($Converter.ToTitleCase($Name[1]))"
        }
        Default {
            Write-Host "Invalid input."
        }
    }
}
Set-Name
```

How to do it...

First of all, we will check whether there was an issue in this script in the first place.

The intention of this function is to get the first name, the middle name, and the surname. Next, it looks at how many strings have been input. If there are two, the name is displayed as Surname, FirstName; if there are three, the name is displayed as Surname, FirstName, MiddleName. However, in the case of this script, no matter how many inputs you give, the output is Invalid input. Follow these steps to get started:

1. Enter Debug mode with trace by using the Trace parameter. Enter 1 or 2 as the value for Trace.

2. Run the script and call the function.
3. Enter the first name and the surname.
4. Observe the output. Note how the execution enters the `Default` block.
5. Exit Debug mode and set a breakpoint at line 10:

```
PS> Set-PSBreakpoint -Script ./ch13/03-Set-Name.ps1 -Line 10
```

6. Run the script and call the function.
7. Enter the values as before.
8. At the `DBG` prompt, call `$Count` to see what its value is.
9. Check the assignments and fix the issue (see line 3 of the script).

How it works...

The `Trace` parameter helps trace the error. By default, the trace level is 0. Therefore, no trace output is shown. When the trace level is set to 1, it only shows each of the lines that were run; when set to 2, the debug information is more verbose: PowerShell tells you what it is doing at each step.

At step 4, we can see that the issue seems to be with what was within `$Name`. Therefore, we set a breakpoint at line 10. (In fact, setting the breakpoint at 8 also would have worked.) The execution pauses at the breakpoint, and, at this point, you can look at the value of `$Count` by simply calling it. Tracing back to what could have caused this wrong count, we arrive at line 3, where we can see that the type of `$Name` was changed from an array to a string because of a wrong assignment operator.

The `Set-PsDebug` cmdlet, along with the `Trace` parameter, lets you go line by line and shows you the flow of the script. Combined with the breakpoint feature, this helps you find issues with scripts more quickly.

Using breakpoints

Breakpoints are crucial to debugging. They help us halt the execution of the script at a desired point and then step through the process slowly. Breakpoints can be created in PowerShell in two ways: using the breakpoint controls in a visual editor (such as Visual Studio Code) or using cmdlets.

Set a breakpoint at line 17 in the script that you used in the previous recipe, *Writing debug output.*

Perform this action on Visual Studio Code as well as the Vim-and-PowerShell-terminal combo.

How to do it...

This process is very simple in Visual Studio Code. All you have to do is open the file in question, hover your mouse around the left of the line number until a red dot appears, and click it to turn the red dot on:

```
02-New-File.ps1 - powershell - Visual Studio Code

DEBUG ▶ PowerShell L: ▼  ⚙ ⊡        ≥ 02-New-File.ps1 ×

▲ VARIABLES                        1    function New-File {
                                   2        [CmdletBinding()]
                                   3        param (
                                   4            # The path to the file (or the name)
                                   5            [Parameter(Mandatory=$true, Position=0)]
                                   6            [string[]]
                                   7            $Path
                                   8        )
▲ WATCH                            9    begin {
                                  10        Write-Debug "Entered the begin block."
                                  11        Write-Host "$(Get-Date)"
                                  12    }
                                  13    process {
                                  14        Write-Debug "Entered the process block."
                                  15        foreach ($Item in $Path) {
                                  16            Write-Debug "Iterating for item, $Item."
                              ●   17            New-Item -Path $Path -ItemType File
▲ CALL STACK                      18        }
                                  19    }
                                  20    end {
                                  21        Write-Debug "Entered the end block."
                                  22    }
                                  23 }



▲ BREAKPOINTS
  ● ☑ 02-New-File.ps1  ch14      17
⚡ master  ↻ ⊗0 ⚠0                             Ln 20, Col 10   Spaces: 4   UTF-8   LF   PowerShell  6.1  ☺ ▲
```

To make the script halt at the breakpoint, call the function from within the script. Here is what the script should look like:

```
function New-File {
    [CmdletBinding()]
    param (
        # The path to the file (or the name)
        [Parameter(Mandatory=$true, Position=0)]
        [string[]]
        $Path
    )
    begin {
        Write-Debug "Entered the begin block."
        Write-Host "$(Get-Date)"
    }
    process {
        Write-Debug "Entered the process block."
        foreach ($Item in $Path) {
            Write-Debug "Iterating for item, $Item."
            New-Item -Path $Path -ItemType File
        }
    }
    end {
        Write-Debug "Entered the end block."
    }
}

New-File One.txt
```

If you are, however, not using a desktop environment, use the text editor of your choice to write the script. I use Vim:

1. Turn on line numbers. On Vim, press the *Escape* key and enter `set number`.

Here is what it should look like now:

```
                                      Terminal                                  ⊗
 1 function New-File {
 2     [CmdletBinding()]
 3     param (
 4         # The path to the file (or the name)
 5         [Parameter(Mandatory=$true, Position=0)]
 6         [string[]]
 7         $Path
 8     )
 9     begin {
10         Write-Debug "Entered the begin block."
11         Write-Host "$(Get-Date)"
12     }
13     process {
14         Write-Debug "Entered the process block."
15         foreach ($Item in $Path) {
16             Write-Debug "Iterating for item, $Item."
17 □           New-Item -Path $Path -ItemType File
18         }
19     }
20     end {
21         Write-Debug "Entered the end block."
22     }
23 }
:set number                                                        17,1            All
```

2. Note down the line number where you would like to place the breakpoint.
3. Exit Vim and call the following cmdlet to set the breakpoint:

```
PS> Set-PSBreakpoint -Script ./ch13/04-New-File.ps1 -Line 17
```

To find out how the breakpoint works, simply run the script. You do this by entering debugging mode—this applies to both Visual Studio Code as well as the PowerShell Terminal:

```
                          Terminal                                    ⊗
PS /home/ram/Documents/code/github/powershell> Set-PSBreakpoint -Script ./ch14/02-New-File
.ps1 -Line 17

  ID Script                Line Command              Variable           Action
  -- ------                ---- -------              --------           ------
   1 02-New-File.ps1         17

PS /home/ram/Documents/code/github/powershell> . ./ch14/02-New-File.ps1
10/08/2018 01:49:10
Entering debug mode. Use h or ? for help.

Hit Line breakpoint on '/home/ram/Documents/code/github/powershell/ch14/02-New-File.ps1:17
'

At /home/ram/Documents/code/github/powershell/ch14/02-New-File.ps1:17 char:13
+             New-Item -Path $Path -ItemType File
+             ~~~~~~~~~~~~~~~~~~~~~~~~~~~~~~~~~~~~
[DBG]: PS /home/ram/Documents/code/github/powershell>> █
```

Follow the on-screen instructions when on the terminal, and the on-screen control keys on top of the script pane when in Visual Studio Code, to step through the script.

To remove a breakpoint, click on the red dot when using the GUI, or list out the breakpoints using `Get-PsBreakpoint` and then remove the breakpoint using `Remove-PsBreakpoint`, along with the relevant identifier.

How it works...

When you create a breakpoint and call the script, the execution halts at the breakpoint. From this point on, you could decide on how to step through the script. In the meanwhile, as you may have noticed, you will see updates happening to the variables, which can be seen in real time on the left-hand side of the screen, as discussed in the *The Debug tab of Visual Studio Code* recipe.

 Remember that, when adding a breakpoint in a function, you must call the function from within the script (hence the last line of the script). If you just create a function and add a breakpoint to it, and call the function from the terminal (instead of from within the script), you would not enter debug mode. This applies to both cmdlet-based breakpoints as well as breakpoints on an IDE.

When in the debug mode on the terminal, you could call each of the variables and objects available in the script, just like how you would on a normal prompt. You will notice the prompt change to `[DBG]: PS>>` instead of `PS>`.

Using conditional breakpoints

As we write more and more scripts, the need to debug our scripts reduces. When we get there, we tend to learn which parts of the scripts may require debugging, and debug only those parts based on specific situations. This is something that conditional breakpoints can help with.

Create a conditional breakpoint for when the number of elements in the `$Name` array is less than two, given the following script:

```
function Set-Name {
    $Name = @()
    $Name = Read-Host "Enter first name"
    $Name += Read-Host "Enter middle name (press Enter for blank)"
    $Name += Read-Host "Enter surname"

    $Count = $Name.Count
    $Converter = (Get-Culture).TextInfo

    switch ($Count) {
        2 {
            "$($Converter.ToTitleCase($Name[1])),
$($Converter.ToTitleCase($Name[0]))"
        }
        3 {
            "$($Converter.ToTitleCase($Name[2])),
$($Converter.ToTitleCase($Name[0])) $($Converter.ToTitleCase($Name[1]))"
        }
        Default {
            Write-Host "Invalid input."
        }
    }
}
Set-Name
```

How to do it...

First, we will create a script block that contains the conditional statement. We will then use this script block with the `Set-PsBreakpoint` cmdlet.

Here is the script block:

```
PS> $Condition = { if ($Count -lt 2) { break } }
```

Next, place a breakpoint when the specified condition is satisfied. First, remove any existing breakpoints:

```
PS> Get-PSBreakpoint | Remove-PsBreakpoint
PS> Set-PSBreakpoint ./ch13/05-Set-Name.ps1 9 -Action $Condition
PS> # Verbose version: Set-PSBreakpoint -Script ./ch13/05-Set-Name.ps1 -
Line 9 -Action $Condition
PS> ./ch13/05-Set-Name.ps1
```

When you hit the condition (which you will, in this case), you will enter debug mode, wherein you can start your debugging process.

How it works...

First things first: we assign a script block to the `$Condition` variable. You tell PowerShell that the value of the variable is of the script block type by enclosing the entire condition in curly braces.

Next, we proceed with setting the breakpoint in the same way as in the previous recipe, *Using breakpoints*, except we add the `Action` parameter. This action parameter contains the condition. The breakpoint is activated only if the condition is met. To verify this, change the assignment operator on line 3 to += from =, remove the breakpoint, and use the same conditional breakpoint. This time, your script will simply execute without hitting the `break`.

Using exit codes

Error codes are ubiquitous. PowerShell is no exception.

Find out whether the following command generated an error, and if it did, show the error code:

```
PS> ping ghostname
```

Would the same technique work with the following command?

```
PS> Get-Item $HOME/random/randompackage.zip -ErrorAction SilentlyContinue
```

How to do it...

We will place the given cmdlet within a script and try to find whether the line generated an error, and if it did, find its error code.

Create a script with the following and run it. Dot-sourcing the script is optional:

```
ping ghostname

if (!$?) {
    Write-Host "PowerShell seems to have encountered an error while running
the last command."
}

Write-Host "The exit code for the last operation is $LASTEXITCODE."

Remove-Variable LASTEXITCODE

Get-Item $HOME/random/randompackage.zip -ErrorAction SilentlyContinue

if (!$?) {
    Write-Host "PowerShell seems to have encountered an error while running
the last command."
}

Write-Host "The exit code for the last operation is $LASTEXITCODE."
```

Observe the output:

```
Terminal                                                           - ⊗
PS /home/ram/Documents/code/github/powershell/ch13> . ./05-Find-Item.ps1
ping: ghostname: Name or service not known
PowerShell seems to have encountered an error while running the last command.
The exit code for the last operation is 2.
PowerShell seems to have encountered an error while running the last command.
The exit code for the last operation is .
PS /home/ram/Documents/code/github/powershell/ch13> 
```

How it works...

Note that the first command given to us is a native Linux command; the second is a PowerShell command.

We use two automatic variables here to find out whether there was an error in execution. The first is `$?`, which checks if the last command executed without an error. The value the variable holds is Boolean, that is, `TRUE`, standing for successful execution. In our script, we negate this in order to use it with the `if` block.

The other variable is `$LASTEXITCODE`, which contains the exit code of the last command. In our case, the exit code was 2. The `ping: ghostname: Name or service not known` error is also displayed.

In the second command, we use `-ErrorAction SilentlyContinue` to hide errors at the terminal. However, these errors are still recorded by PowerShell – they are simply not sent to the host. In this case, you will notice that `$LASTEXITCODE` is empty. This is because this variable is assigned the value of error codes from native applications. Errors from PowerShell cmdlets and scripts are handled in a different way, as shown in the next recipe, *Working with the Error variable*.

Working with the Error variable

Error codes have traditionally helped identify how errors are caused; the numbers have meanings tagged to them. Today, when we see codes such as 404 or 503, we instantly know what they mean. PowerShell operates a little differently.

Find out whether the following command will result in an error. If it does, show details about the error:

```
PS> Get-Item $HOME/random/randompackage.zip -ErrorAction SilentlyContinue
```

How to do it...

Let us make the series of steps we would like to take into a script.

Create a new PowerShell script file and add the following to it:

```
Get-Item $HOME/random/randompackage.zip -ErrorAction SilentlyContinue

if (!$?) {
```

```
      Write-Host "PowerShell seems to have encountered an error while running
   the last command."
   }

   $Error[0] | Select-Object -Property *
```

Execute this script to get error details.

How it works...

Traditionally, a non-zero exit code means that the command or the script did not complete as intended. Querying the exit code told us whether there was an error in execution, and what the error was related to.

In PowerShell, we use the automatic variable $? to find out whether there was an error in the last command, or whether the last script exited in error; this addresses the first part.

The automatic variable $Error keeps track of all of the errors that occurred in the current PowerShell session. The last error gets stored as the first element in the $Error array. Errors in PowerShell have several properties, such as Exception (the name of the exception, as well as the description), TargetObject (the object on which the action was intended), FullyQualifiedErrorId (to facilitate searching the documentation as well as the forums for troubleshooting information, irrespective of what language PowerShell is used in, thereby not restricting searches to English), and so on.

The $Error variable records errors, irrespective of what the error action preferences are, and enables us to take actions based on the error, such as when using a try–catch block.

If you would like to clear the error messages instead of starting a new PowerShell session just so that the errors are cleared, use the clear method that's available in $Error: call $Error.Clear().

Controlling flow based on errors

There are situations where errors can be handled by scripts. For instance, let's say that you are trying to create a file at a certain location during an operation. Say you want to save this file within the Logs directory within your home directory. Your home directory does not contain a Logs directory just yet. You want to make your script handle the creation of the directory if it encounters ItemNotFoundException.

You have the lab directory that you created for use with this book. You need to create a log file within a directory called `LogDir`, situated within the lab directory. If `LogDir` does not exist, the script should create it upon encountering the appropriate exception.

How to do it...

The first step for creating actions depending on the situation is identifying the situation itself. In this case, it is specifically identifying the exception. Follow these steps to get started:

1. Run the following command to find the name of the exception:

   ```
   PS> New-Item random/log.log
   PS> $Error | select *
   ```

2. Look for the following line: Exception : System.IO.DirectoryNotFoundException: Could not find a part of the path. The exception that occurred here is System.IO.DirectoryNotFoundException.

3. Now, create a new script file and add the following content to it:

```
function New-LogFile {
    param (
        # The path to the log file
        [Parameter(Mandatory=$false)]
        [string]
        $Path = "$HOME/random/LogDir",

        # The name of the log file
        [Parameter(Mandatory=$false)]
        [string]
        $Name = 'MyLog.log'
    )

    try {
        New-Item "$Path/$Name" -ItemType File -ErrorAction Stop
    }
    catch [System.IO.DirectoryNotFoundException] {
        New-Item $Path -ItemType Directory -Force
        New-LogFile
    }
    catch {
        "Some error other than DirectoryNotFound"
    }
}
```

The script should now execute without errors.

How it works...

Errors can be broadly classified into two kinds: terminating and non-terminating errors. In this recipe, we used the try–catch construct to handle errors and actions related to them. The catch statement executes in case of errors in the try block, but only if the error in the try block is terminating. In our situation, though, the error returned upon not finding that the directory is a non-terminating error. For the catch block to be executed, we need to make the error a terminating one.

There are two ways to handle this. Either set the $ErrorActionPreference variable to Stop, or explicitly make errors generated by the New-Item statement terminate. The latter approach is recommended (and used in this recipe,) since that gives us better control over error handling – we should choose which errors should be terminating errors. To make errors from a specific statement terminate, we must apply the common parameter ErrorAction and set Stop as its value. We place the statement, along with the ErrorAction parameter, in the try block.

We write two catch blocks: one specifically for the error caused by the directory that doesn't exist, and another that's a catch-all catch block. In the first catch block, we specify the name of the exception. Within this block, we specify the action to be taken upon this exception being thrown.

Now, when the script is executed and the function is called, PowerShell promptly goes to the first catch block and creates the directory, and calls the function again.

If you would like to see the flow of the script, enter debug mode with the Step parameter. Refer to the *Running a script in debug mode* recipe for more information.

See also

- The *Running a script in debug mode* recipe

Sending verbose output to a file

We looked at streams in the *Sending output to a file* recipe in `Chapter 10`, *Handling Files and Directories*, wherein we redirected errors and informational output to files. However, this was done in steps: we redirected the non-Success output (error, information, and so on) to the Success stream first, and then piped the same to `Out-File`. To redirect output between streams, we used the redirection operator, `>&`.

In this recipe, you will write verbose output and directly send the verbose output to a file called `verbose.log`, and redirect errors to `error.log`. Here is the script that you will work with:

```
function New-LogFile {
    param (
        # The path to the log file
        [Parameter(Mandatory=$false)]
        [string]
        $Path = "$HOME/random/LogDir",

        # The name of the log file
        [Parameter(Mandatory=$false)]
        [string]
        $Name = 'MyLog.log'
    )

    try {
        New-Item "$Path/$Name" -ItemType File -ErrorAction Stop
    }
    catch [System.IO.DirectoryNotFoundException] {
        New-Item $Path -ItemType Directory -Force
        New-LogFile
    }
    catch {
        Write-Error $_
    }
}
New-LogFile
```

How to do it...

The main idea here seems to be the verbose logging of actions. Modify the script to look like the following:

```
function New-LogFile {
    param (
        # The path to the log file
        [Parameter(Mandatory=$false)]
        [string]
        $Path = "$HOME/random/LogDir",

        # The name of the log file
        [Parameter(Mandatory=$false)]
        [string]
        $Name = 'MyLog.log'
    )

    try {
        Write-Verbose "Creating the file, $Name at $Path."
        New-Item "$Path/$Name" -ItemType File -ErrorAction Stop
    }
    catch [System.IO.DirectoryNotFoundException] {
        Write-Verbose "System.IO.DirectoryNotFoundException encountered."
        Write-Verbose "Creating the directory, $Path."
        New-Item $Path -ItemType Directory -Force
        Write-Verbose "Calling the function."
        New-LogFile
    }
    catch {
        Write-Verbose "Catch-all. There was an error."
        Write-Error $_
    }
}
New-LogFile -Verbose 4>> verbose.log 2>> error.log
```

Run the script and read the files that just got created.

How it works...

This script is simple. We create a function and define its parameters. Next, we clear the contents of the $Error variable, say, for a clean slate. (This is not always recommended. Clear the error variable only if you know for sure that you do not want the previous errors from the current session.) We then proceed to write some verbose content for every step the function takes by using the Write-Verbose cmdlet. This content is suppressed by default ($VerbosePreference is set to SilentlyContinue by default). We use the -Verbose common parameter to make the function generate the verbose output.

As we saw in the *Sending output to a file* recipe, the PowerShell has six streams:

- Success
- Error
- Warning
- Verbose
- Debug
- Information

In this recipe unlike the *Sending output to a file* recipe in Chapter 10, *Handling Files and Directories*—we directly send the verbose output to a file by redirecting the output of the fourth stream to a file by using a redirection (with append) operator rather than first sending the non-Success output to the Success stream. (The latter is popularly known as **polluting the Success stream**.) At the same line, we also instruct PowerShell to send the output of the second stream—the error stream—to another file.

 By default, >> stands for 1>>, or "append Success stream to file". Change the 1 to any of the streams you would like to redirect to a file so that you can redirect the output of that stream.

You will notice that the error.log file is empty. This is because we handled the error (System.IO.DirectoryNotFoundException) that occurred. Run the script a second time to get a different error – System.IO.IOException – which is handled by actually writing the error to the Error stream (using Write-Error). This content will be sent through the Error stream, and will appear in error.log.

14
Enterprise Administration Using PowerShell

In this chapter, we will cover the following recipes:

- Installing OpenSSH on Windows
- Configuring OpenSSH using `sshd_config` on Windows
- Installing and configuring OpenSSH on Linux
- Testing PowerShell remoting with OpenSSH
- Testing PowerShell remoting with OpenSSH using keys between Linux machines
- Testing PowerShell remoting with OpenSSH using keys between Linux and Windows machines
- Managing the administration of remote machines with PowerShell Jobs
- Generating HTML reports
- Sending email messages

Introduction to OpenSSH

SSH (**Secure Shell**) is a protocol that's used for connecting one computer to another. It's commonly and widely used for system administration such as software updates, configuration management, and deployment on Linux and macOS machines. SSH is a vital—and the most valuable—tool in a Linux system administrator's toolbox.

There's lots of SSH client software available on the market. This software is used to set up a connection to an SSH server, and it is available for all of the major computer operating systems. Linux distros have the SSH application built in, and is accessible through Terminal. Windows now has options available for testing the connection using a protocol named OpenSSH. PowerShell is using SSH to build a connection and as a transport layer for remoting. This is standard SSH behavior.

Keep in mind that you can change settings while using SSH that can prevent you from being able to log back in. If you shut down a network interface, commit incorrect network settings, block the service with a firewall, or shut down the SSH service, you risk cutting off your own access.

And, of course, local and remote network conditions can cause access problems. If a computer allows remote access, there needs to be a way to control who can log in and work on the system. With SSH, access is controlled either through the use of a username and password being set up by an administrator on the remote server, or a cryptographic key pair that's been generated by the user and shared with the server. Key-based access is the more secure option, and as such it's increasingly common.

It's also the preferred way of accessing Linux servers on many popular cloud services, such as Amazon Web Services and Microsoft Azure. SSH encrypts the connection between a client and the server so that information that's been sent back and forth is more secure than with other types of remote access protocols, such as FTP or Telnet.

Installing OpenSSH on Windows

As we mentioned earlier, Windows doesn't bundle with an SSH software component, so you'll need to download the SSH software piece. One of the most popular among many SSH software providers is PuTTY, and it stands as first choice for many administrators. It's easy to download, and you can find a download link at `http://www.putty.org`. The installation is a simple copy of the executable from the `Downloads` folder. Paste it under the `C:\Program Files (x86)` folder. Now, SSH is available for both Linux and Windows platforms. It is that easy to set up SSH on Windows. In these recipes, we'll look at how to configure SSH on a Windows host.

Getting ready

The SSH software component needs to be installed on all target machines. Let's install the SSH client (`ssh.exe`) and SSH server (`sshd.exe`) software pieces so that you can experiment with PowerShell remoting to and from the targeted machines.

The `New-PSSession`, `Enter-PSSession`, and `Invoke-Command` cmdlets now have the new parameter sets `HostName` and `UserName` to facilitate PowerShell remoting.

The following prerequisite needs to be met before you proceed with the OpenSSH installation and configuration on Windows:

- You must have PowerShell 6.1 installed on a Windows machine

How to do it...

For Windows, follow these steps to configure SSH for PowerShell remoting:

1. Based on the OS type, download the latest OpenSSH build (`https://github.com/PowerShell/Win32-OpenSSH/releases`).
2. In this case, it is 64-bit, so the `OpenSSH-Win64.zip` file is downloaded.
3. Extract the files to `C:\Program Files\`.
4. Now, the files are saved under `C:\Program Files\OpenSSH-Win64`. Rename the folder to OpenSSH.
5. Open the PowerShell console with an elevated permission and then run the following:

   ```
   PS> powershell.exe -ExecutionPolicy Bypass -File "C:\Program
   Files\OpenSSH\install-sshd.ps1"
   ```

6. Next, add the OpenSSH path to the environment variable:

   ```
   PS> $ENV:Path+=";C:\Program Files\OpenSSH;"
   ```

7. To make the changes permanent, edit the registry entry, like so:

   ```
   PS> Set-ItemProperty -Path
   'Registry::HKEY_LOCAL_MACHINE\System\CurrentControlSet\Control\Sess
   ion Manager\Environment' -Name PATH -Value $env:Path
   ```

8. Next, start the OpenSSH services:

   ```
   PS> Get-Service ssh*
   PS> Start-Service ssh*
   ```

9. Open the firewall to allow inbound SSH connections. If you're on Windows 10, or Windows 2008 R2 or below, run the following command:

   ```
   c:\> netsh advfirewall firewall add rule name=sshd dir=in
   action=allow protocol=TCP localport=22
   ```

To open SSH for Windows 2012 servers and above, run the following command:

```
PS> New-NetFirewallRule -Name sshd -DisplayName 'OpenSSH Server (sshd)' -
Enabled True -Direction Inbound -Protocol TCP -Action Allow -LocalPort 22
```

10. Restart the `sshd` service:

```
PS> Restart-Service ssh*
```

11. Repeat the preceding steps for all Windows machines.

How it works...

The SSH protocol is not native to the Windows operating system. It doesn't bundle with Windows components. RDP-, WinRM-, or PowerShell-native components are used to connect to remote Windows servers. and that's always been the case. But if you really need an SSH server running on a Windows machine, then PowerShell Open SSH is the option for you.

PowerShell OpenSSH remoting lets you do basic PowerShell session remoting from Windows to Windows, Windows to Linux, Linux to Windows, and Linux to Linux. This is done by creating a PowerShell hosting process on the target machine as an SSH subsystem.

As you will notice, the process differs significantly from enabling remoting for WinRM. One big difference is that you no longer need the `Enable-PSremoting` cmdlet.

If you configure a default shell, ensure that the OpenSSH installation path is in the system `PATH`. If not already present, amend the system `PATH` and restart the `sshd` service. SCP and SFTP have been tested to work with PowerShell.

There's more...

To uninstall OpenSSH, start PowerShell as an administrator and follow these steps:

1. Browse to the OpenSSH directory:

```
PS> cd 'C:\Program Files\OpenSSH'
```

2. Run the uninstall script:

```
PS> powershell.exe -ExecutionPolicy Bypass -File uninstall-sshd.ps1
```

See also

- Refer to Comparison of SSH Servers article (https://en.wikipedia.org/wiki/Comparison_of_SSH_servers) for more information
- Refer to the installation and procedure document to install PowerShell Core on Windows (https://docs.microsoft.com/en-us/powershell/scripting/setup/installing-powershell-core-on-windows?view=powershell-6).

Configuring OpenSSH using sshd_config on Windows

In this recipe, we will discuss the OpenSSH system-wide configuration file sshd_config for Windows. It allows us to set options at the server so that configuration parameters control the operation of the client programs. Let's list the required OpenSSH parameters so that you can configure your OpenSSH.

On Windows, the sshd_config file is at the location where you installed OpenSSH. On Linux, it's at /etc/ssh/sshd_config.

Getting ready

To edit the ssh_config file, go to the /ssh/sshd_config. log. Locate the file with elevated permission so that you can edit the file.

On Windows, locate the cmd.exe executable, right-click it, and select **Run as Administrator** to edit the ssh_config file.

How to do it...

Let's look at how we can change the required parameters in the `ssh_config` file by following these steps:

1. First, navigate to the location where you installed OpenSSH: `%PROGRAMDATA%\ssh`.
2. Open the `sshd_config` file in Notepad or TextPad or any other available editors.
3. Enable `PasswordAuthentication`:

       PasswordAuthentication yes

4. Enable the optional `PubKeyAuthentication`:

       PubKeyAuthentication yes

5. Add the following PowerShell Subsystem entry:

       Subsystem powershell c:/program files/powershell/6.1.0-
       preview.1/pwsh.exe -sshs -NoLogo -NoProfile

    For interoperability reasons, in the actual path, `C:\Program Files\powershell\6.1.0-preview.1\` is changed to `C:/Program Files/powershell/6.1.0-preview.1/`. The backslash `\` is changed to a forward slash `/`.

6. Restart the sshd service:

       PS> Restart-Service ssh*

How it works...

Let's take a look at a few of the configuration parameters in the SSH server configuration file. Of course, it's not possible to cover them all here, but I'll highlight a few common ones that are used and tested to configure OpenSSH. The SSH Server configuration is `/etc/ssh/sshd_config`. Let's open `vi /etc/ssh/sshd_config`, SSH daemon the configuration file, and scroll down a little bit. The first thing you'll see is Port 22. It's commented out, so if you uncomment this by removing the pound sign, you can change the port that the server listens on.

You notice that all of the lines that start with a hash are comments and defaults. A configuration item is a combination of key-value pairs. The commented lines with key-value pairs are usually the defaults. For instance, look at the Port 22—this line is commented because the default port it listens to is 22. If you want to change the SSH Server Port, uncomment it by removing the # and edit value. Also, note that you should leave the message as part of a good practice. Let's leave the default value now. Moving on to the authentication section, you can change the grace time for the login, and if you change `PermitRootLogin` to be uncommented and change the value to `no`, the root won't be able to log in. This is a good security practice to observe. Continue scrolling down; there's an option that says `PasswordAuthentication`. Uncomment this line and change the value to `Yes`. If it's set to `No`, the user won't be able to log in with a password—they'll need to use a key. Let's discuss this in the upcoming recipe.

I'll continue scrolling past some of the more advanced options. Down toward the bottom is an option called `Banner`. If you uncomment that and change the value of none to a path or a text file, you can display some text when a user logs in.

Next, add the `pwsh.exe` file to the `Subsystems` section. The subsystems are the layers of abstraction or a set of predefined instructions in the configuration file that are used for the successful invocation of remote commands from the client machines. A subsystem entry allows you to invoke the PowerShell console as a daemon process.

If you make any changes to this file, you will need to restart the SSH server in order for those changes to take effect. You can do this by writing `service sshd restart`.

There's more...

To get a complete listing of `sshd_config`, type `man sshd_config` and hit the *Enter* key.

Installing and configuring OpenSSH on Linux

In this recipe, we'll look at how to install OpenSSH and how to configure parameters in the `sshd_configure` file. Most Linux distributions come with an SSH server already baked in. You don't need to do this if you've already installed an SSH server.

Getting ready

To get started, install the latest PowerShell 6 build from GitHub (https://docs.microsoft.com/en-us/powershell/scripting/setup/installing-powershell-core-on-linux?view=powershell-6). Next, install the OpenSSH server package on Linux.

How to do it...

Let's dive deep into the installation steps and procedures to configure SSH Server on Linux:

1. To install Ubuntu SSH, run the following command:

   ```
   $ sudo apt install openssh-client openssh-server
   ```

2. Next, edit the sshd configuration file using the vi editor or any other available editors:

   ```
   # vi /etc/ssh/sshd_config
   ```

    To edit the /etc/ssh/sshd_config file on Linux, log in to the terminal with root credentials and navigate to the sshd_config file located under the configuration directory.

3. Enable PasswordAuthentication:

   ```
   PasswordAuthentication yes
   ```

4. Enable the optional PubKeyAuthentication:

   ```
   PubKeyAuthentication yes
   ```

5. Add the following PowerShell Subsystem entry:

   ```
   Subsystem powershell /usr/bin/pwsh -sshs -NoLogo -NoProfile
   ```

6. Restart the sshd service:

   ```
   $ sudo service sshd restart
   ```

How it works...

The installation is pretty simple and straightforward. If you're in the Debian world (Ubuntu or Mint), use `apt`. If you're in the Red Hat world, which includes CentOS and Fedora, use `yum`. In this case, the host is Ubuntu, so run the `sudo apt install OpenSSH-Server` command to install the OpenSSH Server package and use `sudo apt install OpenSSH -Client` to install the OpenSSH client.

The next step is to edit the `sshd_config` file. I would recommend reading the previous recipe to get a strong hold of configuring OpenSSH on various Linux distros. Type in `vi /etc/ssh/sshd_config`, which will open up the SSH daemon configuration file. If you're not using the root user, you'll need to use sudo for this.

There's more...

The one recommended place to start SSH troubleshooting steps is the Ubuntu community for SSH, which you can find at `help.ubuntu.com/community/SSH`.

See also

For detailed information about the configuration of `sshd_config`, refer to the previous recipe, *Configuring OpenSSH using sshd_config on Windows*.

Testing PowerShell remoting using OpenSSH

In this recipe, we'll look at how we can test PowerShell remoting using OpenSSH with the PowerShell 6 console. It is important to understand that you have to install OpenSSH on the local and remote machine.

You're going to see the PowerShell remoting connections between the following:

1. Windows to Windows
2. Windows to Linux
3. Linux to Windows
4. Linux to Linux

Getting ready

It is important to understand that you have to install OpenSSH on the local and remote machine. It is required that you follow the previous recipe's setup instructions and configurations for each of the host machines. Complete this step to get ready for this recipe:

1. To open the PowerShell console, type in `pwsh`.

How to do it...

The `New-PSSession`, `Enter-PSSession`, and `Invoke-Command` cmdlets are the three cmdlets that help with the PowerShell remoting feature. Let's dig further to dissect the internals of PowerShell remoting:

1. To create a session to a remote Windows machine, run the following command:

```
PS> $Session= New-PSSession -HostName wintel01 -UserName ram
ram@wintel01's password:
```

2. To display the session details, call the `$Session` variable on the PowerShell console:

```
PS> $session
```

3. To enter the remoting session, use the session parameter, along with the `Enter-PSSession` cmdlet:

```
PS> Enter-PSSession -Session $session
[wintel01]: PS>
```

4. To invoke the script on a remote machine, run the `Invoke-Command` cmdlet:

```
PS> Invoke-Command $session -ScriptBlock {Get-Process| Sort-Object
CPU -Descending|Select-Object
name,HandleCount,WorkingSet,PrivateMemorySize,VirtualMemorySize -
Firs
t 5|Format-Table -AutoSize}
```

5. Run the simple cmdlet to prove that the session is open and able to execute the PowerShell cmdlets:

```
PS> Get-Process |Sort-Object CPU |Select-Object -First 10
```

A sample output from the preceding command is shown in the following screenshot:

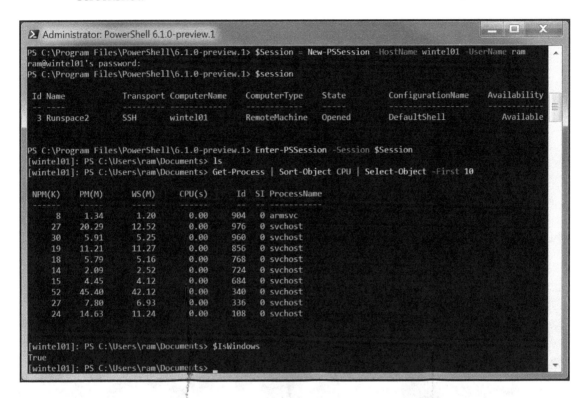

Let's create a session to a remote Linux machine (Ubuntu - 10.2.6.68) from a Windows host machine (Wintel01). The commands are no different for Windows, Linux, and macOS:

1. To create a session to a remote Linux machine, run the following command:

```
PS> New-PSSession -HostName 10.2.6.68 -UserName prashant
prashant@10.2.6.68's password:
```

2. To assign session details to a variable, run the following command:

```
PS> $session=New-PSSession -HostName 10.2.6.68 -UserName prashant
prashant@10.2.6.68's password:

PS> $Session
```

3. To enter the remote machine, use `Enter-PSSession`, along with the `Session` parameter:

```
PS> Enter-PSSession -Session $session
[10.2.6.68]: PS> cat /etc/lsb-release
[10.2.6.68]: PS> $IsLinux
```

4. To run the script on a remote Linux machine, call the `Invoke-Command` cmdlet:

```
[10.2.6.68]: PS> Invoke-Command $session -ScriptBlock {Get-Process|
Sort-Object CPU -Descending|Select-Object
name,HandleCount,WorkingSet,PrivateMemorySize,VirtualMemorySize -
Firs
t 5|Format-Table -AutoSize}

[10.2.6.68]: PS> Get-Process |Sort-Object CPU |Select-Object -First
10
```

This results in the following output:

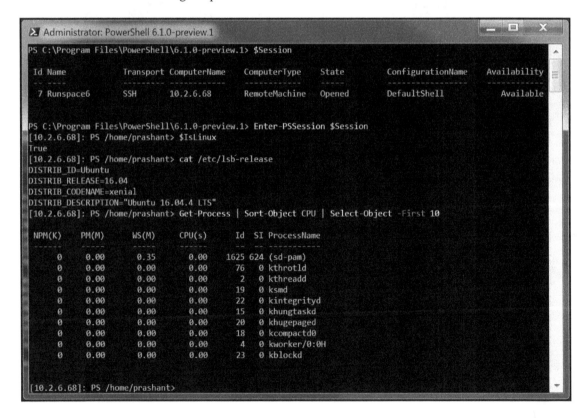

Let's create a session to a remote Windows machine (wintel01) from a Linux host (Ubuntu –
10.2.6.68) to prove that the commands and theories are applicable in the same way and
that it is platform-independent:

1. To create a session to a remote Windows machine, run the following command:

```
PS> Enter-PSSession -HostName wintel01 -UserName ram
ram@wintel01's password:
[wintel01]: PS> hostname
wintel01
```

2. To assign session details to a variable, run the following command:

```
PS> $session=New-PSSession -HostName wintel01 -UserName ram
ram@wintel01's password:
PS> $session
```

3. To enter a remote session, use `Enter-PSSession`, along with the `Session`
parameter:

```
PS> Enter-PSSession -Session $session
[wintel01]: PS> hostname
wintel01
```

4. To run the script on a remote Windows machine, call the `Invoke-
Command` cmdlet:

```
[wintel01]: PS> Invoke-Command $session -ScriptBlock {Get-Process|
Sort-Object CPU -Descending|Select-Object
name,HandleCount,WorkingSet,PrivateMemorySize,VirtualMemorySize -
First 5|Format-Table -AutoSize}

[wintel01]: PS> hostname
wintel01
[wintel01]: PS> $IsWindows
True
[wintel01]: PS> Get-Process|Sort-Object CPU -Descending |Select-
Object -First 5
```

This gives the following result:

```
● ● ●   Terminal
PS /home/prashant> $Session | Select-Object Id, Transport, ComputerName, State

Id Transport ComputerName State
-- --------- ------------ -----
 3 SSH       wintel01     Opened


PS /home/prashant> Enter-PSSession $Session
[wintel01]: PS C:\Users\ram\Documents> $IsWindows
True
[wintel01]: PS C:\Users\ram\Documents> Get-Process | Sort-Object CPU -Descending
 | Select-Object -First 5

NPM(K)    PM(M)     WS(M)    CPU(s)      Id  SI ProcessName
------    -----     -----    ------      --  -- -----------
    63    50.43     80.07      2.03    7040   0 pwsh
    62    38.13     65.94      1.70   10068   0 pwsh
     9    13.98     15.42      0.06    9176   0 audiodg
    10     2.52      7.18      0.03    1792   0 sshd
    10     2.45      7.08      0.03    4280   0 sshd

[wintel01]: PS C:\Users\ram\Documents> █
```

How it works...

SSH always sets up an encrypted connection between the remote and client machine. With the established connection, a shell is created. It works the same way as it does when you're locally logged on to the remote server.

The first time you connect to the remote server, SSH prompts you with a window, asking you to accept the server's host key. If it's your first time connecting to the server, this is normal. But if you've been connecting to an SSH server for a while and you suddenly see the message **The authenticity of host 'wintel01 (10.7.2.204)' can't be established. ECDSA key fingerprint is SHA256:2GnYAODZGB+UEuJjuSXrpgOP3gP4xI+rGCtCWfcvHbc. Are you sure you want to continue connecting (yes/no)?**, you might want to investigate a little bit before accepting the key. After configuring SSH, you can run a command using the `Invoke-command` cmdlet or any other supported cmdlets, as shown in the preceding screenshot.

Testing PowerShell remoting with OpenSSH using keys between Linux machines

In this recipe, you'll look at how you can configure SSH to allow logins to a remote system using cryptographic key files between two Linux machines.

Getting ready

On the remote system, you need to ensure that the SSH server package is installed. I'll do that here with `apt install OpenSSH-server`. And just like that, our system is able to host SSH connections. However, there are a few things we need to look at before we use SSH.

How to do it...

Let's dive deep into the steps to connect to a remote Linux (Ubuntu) machine from another Linux machine (CentOS):

1. On the CentOS Linux machine, check whether the SSH service is running or not. To do that, use the `systemctl` command:

   ```
   # systemctl status sshd
   ```

2. Next, check the firewall setting. By default, port 22 is open to allow inbound traffic:

   ```
   # ufw status
   ```

3. To generate a key-pair, run the `ssh-keygen` command and save the keys to the default location:

    The passphrase is left blank, but this is not a recommended practice. Use the Linux SSH native command `ssh-keygen` to generate keys.

   ```
   PS> ssh-keygen
   Generating public/private rsa key pair.
   Enter file in which to save the key (/home/packpub/.ssh/id_rsa):
   Enter passphrase (empty for no passphrase):
   ```

```
Enter same passphrase again:
Your identification has been saved in /home/packpub/.ssh/id_rsa.
Your public key has been saved in /home/packpub/.ssh/id_rsa.pub.
The key fingerprint is:
4a:a9:ca:63:85:b1:b2:f9:39:61:05:ef:1a:b8:e2:fd
packpub@localhost.localdomain
The key's randomart image is:
+--[ RSA 2048]----+
| |
| . |

| o |
| . o . |
| . * o S |
|o * oo . |
| * =. . |
|=.*o |
|o+=+.E |
+-----------------+
```

4. To copy the public key to the remote machine (Ubuntu -10.2.6.68), run the following command:

```
PS> ssh-copy-id prashant@10.2.6.68
/usr/bin/ssh-copy-id: INFO: attempting to log in with the new
key(s), to filter out any that are already installed
/usr/bin/ssh-copy-id: INFO: 1 key(s) remain to be installed -- if
you are prompted now it is to install the new keys
prashant@10.2.6.68's password:

Number of key(s) added: 1

Now try logging into the machine, with: "ssh 'prashant@10.2.6.68'"
and check to make sure that only the key(s) you wanted were added.

PS> Enter-PSSession -HostName 10.2.6.68 -UserName prashant
[10.2.6.68]: PS>
```

 Note: `ssh-copy-id` and `ssh-keygen` are Linux SSH native commands that are used in conjunction with PowerShell OpenSSH remoting.

5. To take a look at the local `know_hosts` file, run the following command:

```
$ cat ~/.ssh/known_hosts
```

6. Test the connection using a public key and run a few simple cmdlets on the remote machine:

```
PS> Enter-PSSession –HostName 10.2.6.68 –UserName prashant
[10.2.6.68]: PS> $IsLinux
True
[10.2.6.68]: PS> cat /etc/lsb-release
[10.2.6.68]: PS> Get-Process|Sort-Object CPU –Descending| Select-
Obejct –First 5
```

This results in the following output:

```
PS /home/packpub> Enter-PSSession –HostName 10.2.6.68 –UserName prashant
[10.2.6.68]: PS /home/prashant> $IsLinux
True
[10.2.6.68]: PS /home/prashant> cat /etc/lsb-release
DISTRIB_ID=Ubuntu
DISTRIB_RELEASE=16.04
DISTRIB_CODENAME=xenial
DISTRIB_DESCRIPTION="Ubuntu 16.04.4 LTS"
[10.2.6.68]: PS /home/prashant> Get-Process | Sort-Object CPU –Descending | S
elect-Object –First 5

  NPM(K)     PM(M)      WS(M)     CPU(s)       Id  SI ProcessName
  ------     -----      -----     ------       --  -- -----------
       0      0.00     141.70     108.37     2035 035 compiz
       0      0.00      64.84      21.01      824 824 Xorg
       0      0.00      71.04       5.21     3131 878 update-manager
       0      0.00      32.51       4.23     2229 736 gnome-terminal-
       0      0.00      84.56       3.72     2456 260 pwsh

[10.2.6.68]: PS /home/prashant>
```

How it works...

A key-pair is made up of two files: a private key file that a user keeps and a public key that is stored on the remote server. On using the SSH protocol, the user tries to establish the connection between server and client with the exchange key information to determine if the user is allowed to log on.

Let's take a look at the way we can generate a key-pair using a tool called SSH-keygen. It offers a lot of different options for changing the encryption algorithm, but in this case, the default values are used to generate a key-pair.

First, I'm asked where I want to save the key. The tool suggests the hidden `.ssh` folder in my `home` folder, under the name `id_RSA`. This is the default, but you can set any name you like. The SSH tool knows to look for a key here, so keeping it named like this can save a little bit of time.

On running the `ssh-copy-id` command, two things happen. First, the local public key is copied across the network to the remote machine and stored in the user's `authorized_keys` file. Second, the fingerprint of the remote machine is stored in the local user's `known_hosts` file.

After verifying every piece of the configuration, you will see that the test connections are successful.

There's more...

To enable port 22 on an Ubuntu machine, type in the following code:

```
# ufw allow 22/tcp
# systemctl restart ufw
# ufw enable
```

In Ubuntu, you can check the firewall settings by using `ufw status` to check whether it's active or not. If it's inactive, add a rule to allow port 22 access, that is, `sudo ufw allow 22/tcp`, and restart the firewall with `systemctl restart ufw`. Now, enable the firewall with `sudo ufw enable` and check its status.

Testing PowerShell remoting with OpenSSH using keys between Linux and Windows machines

In this recipe, you'll find out how to configure SSH to allow logins to a remote system by using cryptographic key files between two Linux and Windows machines.

Getting ready

On the remote Windows machine (**wintel01**), you need to ensure that the OpenSSH server package is installed and configured. You also need to copy the public key using any of the available tools. In this case, WinSCP has been installed so that it copies the `id_rsa.pub` file to the remote Windows machine.

How to do it...

Let's get started and set up the authorized key from the Linux host (CentOS) and send it to the remote Windows machine:

1. On the Linux host, to generate a key-pair, run the `ssh-keygen` command:

```
PS> ssh-keygen -t rsa
Generating public/private rsa key pair.
Enter file in which to save the key (/home/packpub/.ssh/id_rsa):
Enter passphrase (empty for no passphrase):
Enter same passphrase again:
Your identification has been saved in /home/packpub/.ssh/id_rsa.
Your public key has been saved in /home/packpub/.ssh/id_rsa.pub.
The key fingerprint is:
4a:a9:ca:63:85:b1:b2:f9:39:61:05:ef:1a:b8:e2:fd
packpub@localhost.localdomain
The key's randomart image is:
+--[ RSA 2048]----+
|  |
| . |
| o |
| . o . |
| . * o S |
|o * oo . |
| * =. . |
|=.*o |
|o+=+.E |
+-----------------+
```

2. Copy the `id_rsa.pub` public key to the `/tmp` directory:

```
PS> cp ~/.ssh/id_rsa.pub /tmp
```

3. To verify file permissions, run the `ls` command:

```
PS> ls /tmp/id_rsa.pub -lrt
-rw-------. 1 packpub packpub 411 Jul 26 11:45 /tmp/id_rsa.pub
```

4. On a Windows machine, create a `.ssh` folder under the `home` directory of the user. In this case, it's a `ram` account:

```
PS> mkdir .ssh

    Directory: C:\Users\ram
Mode LastWriteTime Length Name
---- ------------- ------ ----
d----- 7/26/2018 10:51 AM .ssh
```

5. Copy the `id_rsa.pub` file to a `.ssh` folder from Linux to Windows by using the WinSCP tool.

6. To view the content, run `cat    <filename>`:

```
PS> cat .\id_rsa.pub
ssh-rsa
AAAAB3NzaC1yc2EAAAADAQABAAAABAQC//zAtkDZclx26rU0+fvsYAD4MooiDzcGO56Y
ZOOCAtJrlF7L05vtoIXS8+UWj/FLGnn5hTLUnjMJPjfqfyT2rxjXqgb7QdpPEfTnOWB
MVaodHN38QRzYwziITXkE9I5BSePRSNpiX4yA3vsPVGM1DdYpZVqEMULDlW/Gfl4h6T
FWw9dHJZEi2NMeEIz2AEG27uvfCuOFsyQjho5gosKw99dDu0G6B7Zy26iZRz+xaQELn
+yIcHm4IG1Xe2DKW2gwn3KHaHnqUY0RvZcLMyjx5hejTx3Op73OOBtfk8cFHo3/86Mv
fQN4Ny2H0yGk7fIdX5Q3oJECgDCSPJ6mSWJCt packpub@localhost.localdomain
```

7. To append the content of the `id_rsa.pub` file to the `authorized_keys` file, use the following command:

```
PS> cat .\id_rsa.pub >>authorized_keys
```

8. To test the connection from the Linux machine to the Windows machine, run the following command:

```
PS> Enter-PSSession -HostName wintel01 -UserName ram
[wintel01]: PS>
```

How it works...

This works no differently to what we explained in the previous recipe. Let's verify the `.ssh` hidden directory and make sure that the public key file has got `rw` permission. By default, the permission is set while generating the public key. Type in `ls -l ~/.ssh` and hit the *Enter* key to verify the permission. We can see that a file called `id_rsa` (`private key` and a file called `id_rsa.pub` (`public key`) are listed. Let's view the public key's content with the `cat` command. Type in `cat ~/.ssh /id_rsa.pub` and hit the *Enter* key.

Now, create a .ssh folder at the user's home directory of the Windows machine and copy the public key to the .ssh folder using the WinSCP tool. After doing this, run the cat command to append it to the authorized_key file. Next, you will see that the Windows machine is ready to establish the connection with a key, that is, is without asking for a password.

See also

- Refer to the previous recipe's *How it works...* section to get more details of the SSH internals.

Running cmdlets on remote computers

In this recipe, you'll find out how to run the Get-Process cmdlet on remote machines. It is very important that you know how to learn and explore in PowerShell.

Getting ready

Let's take a look at the following example. Let's pretend that you are working with a Get-Process cmdlet for the first time.

How to do it...

Let's discuss how we can create a custom object. To start with, the script requires an input CSV file, and the file contains **Server** and **User** columns. Let's get started and create the content of the input CSV file:

1. To create an Input file, type in nano, followed by a filename:

   ```
   PS> nano input.csv
   ```

2. To view the contents of the input.csv file, type in cat, followed by a filename:

   ```
   PS> cat ./input.csv
   Server,user
   hfd01,ssh-test
   10.2.6.68,prashant
   ```

3. Use SSH to establish a session with the remote machine and run the `Invoke-command` cmdlet to execute a script block on the remote session:

```
PS> import-csv ./input.csv|%{
  Invoke-Command -HostName $_.Server -UserName $_.user -ScriptBlock
{ Get-Process |`
  select-object Handles,CPU, `
  @{name="NPM";Expression={[int]($_.NPM/1024)}}, `
  @{name="PM";Expression={[int]($_.PM/1024)}}, `
  @{name="WS";Expression={[int]($_.WS/1024)}}, `
  @{name="VM";Expression={[int]($_.VM/1MB)}}, `
  Id, ProcessName
}
}
```

How it works...

The input CSV file consists of the Windows and Linux machine's server details. The target machine name and intended user details are fetched from the CSV file using the `Import-CSV` cmdlet. The `Invoke-Command` cmdlet allows you to run commands or script on multiple remote computers. The most interesting fact about PowerShell is the PowerShell remoting management of remote machines. You can see that the script block doesn't feature the computer name parameter, but we are able to run the command on multiple remote machines using the hostname feature.

Managing the administration of remote machines with PowerShell Jobs

In this recipe, you'll find out how to manage multiple servers using PowerShell remoting, and using PowerShell jobs. PowerShell provides an interface that takes a command or the script and runs them in the background. PowerShell can run several different tasks simultaneously and is able to retrieve results.

Getting ready

Since you will be working with multiple servers and you are going to be sending multiple commands to the same remote machine, it is better to create a remote session and assign it to a variable. It is a much more efficient way to manage remote connections.

How to do it...

When you start a PowerShell background or remote job, the job starts in two modes: background and remote. However, the results do not appear immediately. Instead, the command returns an object that represents the background or remote job.

Let's look at a few simple examples to understand how PowerShell Jobs work:

1. To create a background job, run the `Start-job` cmdlet, followed by a `scriptblock` parameter:

   ```
   PS> start-job -ScriptBlock { Get-Process}
   ```

2. To create a remote job, run `Invoke-Command` with the `-asjob` parameter:

   ```
   PS> $session=New-PSSession -HostName hdf01 -UserName ssh-test
   $job=Invoke-Command -Session $session -ScriptBlock {Get-Process |
   Select-Object -First 5} -AsJob
   ```

3. To list the jobs, run the `Get-Job` command:

   ```
   PS> Get-Job

   Id Name PSJobTypeName State HasMoreData Location Command
   -- ---- ------------- ----- ----------- -------- -------
   22 Job22 RemoteJob Completed False hdf01 Get-Process | Select-O...
   24 Job24 BackgroundJob Completed True localhost dir
   ```

4. To create a local job on the remote machine, run the following command:

   ```
   PS> $j=Invoke-Command -Session $session -ScriptBlock {Start-Job -
   ScriptBlock {Get-Process}}
   PS>  Enter-PSSession -Session $session
   [hdf01]: PS> Get-Job

   Id Name PSJobTypeName State HasMoreData Location Command
   -- ---- ------------- ----- ----------- -------- -------
   1 Job1 BackgroundJob Completed True localhost Get-Process | Select-
   O...
   ```

5. To get the results of the remote job, run the `Receive-Job` command:

   ```
   PS>  Get-Job

   Id Name PSJobTypeName State HasMoreData Location Command
   -- ---- ------------- ----- ----------- -------- -------
   42 Job42 RemoteJob Completed True hdf01 Get-Process | Select-O...
   ```

```
#Passing job name 'Job42' as a parameter to Recieve-Job cmdlet
```

PS> Receive-Job -Name job42

```
NPM(K)  PM(M)  WS(M)  CPU(s)  Id SI ProcessName PSComputerName
------  -----  -----  ------  -- -- ----------- --------------
     8  1.41   1.29   0.00  1992  0 armsvc      hdf01
    47 34.38  40.13   0.00  3048  0 CcmExec     hdf01
     9  1.55   1.85   0.00  2020  0 CdfSvc      hdf01
    16  5.38   1.93   0.00  1816  0 CmRcService hdf01
    21 18.34   1.12   0.00  2540  1 Code        hdf01
```

```
# You can also pass job id
```

PS> Receive-Job -id 42

```
NPM(K)  PM(M)  WS(M)  CPU(s)  Id SI ProcessName PSComputerName
------  -----  -----  ------  -- -- ----------- --------------
     8  1.41   1.29   0.00  1992  0 armsvc      hdf01
    47 34.38  40.13   0.00  3048  0 CcmExec     hdf01
     9  1.55   1.85   0.00  2020  0 CdfSvc      hdf01
    16  5.38   1.93   0.00  1816  0 CmRcService hdf01
    21 18.34   1.12   0.00  2540  1 Code        hdf01
```

How it works...

The Start-Job cmdlet starts a normal background job. The remote connection is handled within the job script block. The script block runs as a separate PowerShell process. The remote connection is managed by Get-Process, so it is destroyed when the data is returned. Note that the location says localhost, which means that the job is running locally.

In the second job, you're using Invoke-Command to run the command and control the connection to the remote machine. Invoke-Command uses standard PowerShell remoting for connectivity to remote machines. The -AsJob parameter brings the PowerShell job engine into play. Note that, this time, the PSJobTypeName is RemoteJob and that the location is hdf01 (the remote machine).

The big difference is where the job runs. By using Start-Job, it runs locally and the code in the script block handles the connectivity. By using Invoke-Command, the job runs on the remote machine, but the results come back to the local machine.

There's more...

To remove all of the jobs, run the following command:

```
PS> Get-Job | Remove-Job
```

Generating HTML reports

HTML is one of the most simple and useful formats of all types when it comes to reporting – and PowerShell is perfectly capable of working with it. For example, let's say I need to pull process information from multiple remote machines and put it onto an intranet web server. You can do this with very little effort.

Getting ready

Let's pull the script from the GitHub repository for this book and pipe it to convert to HTML. We also need the `input.csv` file for remote machine traversing.

How to do it...

Let's see what this looks like by following these steps:

1. Save the following content in the `PSHTMLReport.ps1` file:

```
$Top = @()
$process =Import-Csv ./input.csv|% { Invoke-Command -HostName
$_.Server -UserName $_.User -ScriptBlock { Param($Server)
    Get-Process | Sort-Object CPU-Descending |`
 Select-Object Handles, CPU, `
 @{name = "NPM"; Expression = {[int]($_.NPM / 1024)}}, `
 @{name = "PM"; Expression = {[int]($_.PM / 1024)}}, `
 @{name = "WS"; Expression = {[int]($_.WS / 1024)}}, `
 @{name = "VM"; Expression = {[int]($_.VM / 1MB)}},`
 @{name = "ServerName"; Expression = {($server)}},`
  Id, ProcessName -First 5 }-Args $_.Server
}
foreach ($proc in $process)
{
    $row = New-Object -Type PSObject -Property @{
        ServerName = $proc.Servername
        ID = $proc.ID
```

```
            ProcessName = $proc.ProcessName
            NPM_KB = $proc.NPM
            PM_KB = $proc.PM
            WS_KB = $proc.WS
            VM_MB = $proc.VM
            CPU_S = $proc.CPU }
    $Top += $row
    }
    $Top | ConvertTo-Html |Out-File /tmp/out.html
```

2. To run the PowerShell script PSHTMLReport.ps1, run the following command:

    PS> ./PSHTMLReport.ps1

3. Navigate to the /tmp/out.html path to view the HTML content or use Invoke-Expression:

    PS> Invoke-Expression /tmp/out.html

How it works...

Building HTML tags in PowerShell is relatively simple. To do this, use the ConvertTo-Html cmdlet. PowerShell provides this. It takes an input object and converts it into an HTML tag. As you can see, the output is a concatenated array object and is piped into ConvertTo-Html. The console output will return a string of HTML tags. The string isn't that useful, so pipe it to out-file and mention the path. After doing this, check out the out.html file that this generated.

See also

- To find out more about ConvertTo-HTML, refer to the following link: https://docs.microsoft.com/en-us/powershell/module/microsoft.powershell.utility/convertto-html?view=powershell-6.

Sending email messages

In this recipe, you'll find out how to use the Send-MailMessage cmdlet to send an email to an intended recipient from within PowerShell.

Getting ready

This script is going to be an enhancement of the previous recipe.

How to do it...

Here's the script that will send the email message:

1. Save the following content in the `PSHTMLReport.ps1` file:

```
# inputfile - filelocation of the CSV file
$inputfile='/tmp/input.CSV'

# Output file
$outfile='/tmp/out.html'
#Email variable declaration
$from = 'donotreply@packtpublinux.com'
$to = 'pjayaram@gmail.com'
$cc = 'pjayaram@gmail.com'
$sub = 'Process Info-PowerShell Remoting'
$body = 'PowerShell script automation email to pull process related
information from Windows and Linux machines'
$attachment = $outfile
$smtpserver = 'packpublinux@smtp.com'

#declare the array to hold multiple values
$Top = @()
#the output of import-csv is assigned to a variable
$process =Import-Csv $inputfile|% { Invoke-Command -HostName
$_.Server -UserName $_.User -ScriptBlock { Param($Server)
 Get-Process | Sort-Object CPU-Descending |`
 Select-Object Handles, CPU, `
 @{name = "NPM"; Expression = {[int]($_.NPM / 1024)}}, `
 @{name = "PM"; Expression = {[int]($_.PM / 1024)}}, `
 @{name = "WS"; Expression = {[int]($_.WS / 1024)}}, `
 @{name = "VM"; Expression = {[int]($_.VM / 1MB)}},`
 @{name = "ServerName"; Expression = {($server)}},`
 Id, ProcessName -First 5 }-Args $_.Server
}
foreach ($proc in $process)
{
  $row = New-Object -Type PSObject -Property @{
  ServerName = $proc.Servername
  ID = $proc.ID
  ProcessName = $proc.ProcessName
 NPM_KB = $proc.NPM
```

```
 PM_KB = $proc.PM
WS_KB = $proc.WS
 VM_MB = $proc.VM
CPU_S = $proc.CPU
}
$Top += $row
}
$Top | ConvertTo-Html |Out-File $outfile

#Send Email output to intended recipients

$message = new-object System.Net.Mail.MailMessage
$message.From = $from
$message.To.Add($to)
$message.CC.Add($cc)
$message.IsBodyHtml = $True
$message.Subject = $sub
$attach = new-object Net.Mail.Attachment($attachment)
$message.Attachments.Add($attach)
$message.body = $body
$smtp = new-object Net.Mail.SmtpClient($smtpserver)
$smtp.Send($message)
```

2. In the script, modify the following variable as per the environment:

```
#Ouput file
$outfile='/tmp/out.html'
#Email variable declaration
$from = 'donotreply@packtpublinux.com'
$to = 'pjayaram@gmail.com'
$cc = 'pjayaram@gmail.com'
$sub = 'Process Info-PowerShell Remoting'
$body = 'PowerShell script automation email to pull process related
information from Windows and Linux machines'
$attachment = $outfile
$smtpserver = 'packpublinux@smtp.com'
```

 Nowadays, email notifications are vital for monitoring systems in real time. It's essential to know how to configure emails on servers. SMTP is a basic component that can be configured so that it can send email notifications. In this case, the configuration of SMTP is not discussed. It is assumed that you've preconfigured the SMTP server already.

3. Run the PowerShell script:

```
PS> ./PSHTMLReport.ps1
```

4. Go to your inbox and verify whether the email has been received or not.

How it works...

Turning the output of a PowerShell script into an automated email is a snap in PowerShell V2, thanks to a nifty new cmdlet called `Send-MailMessage`. `Send-MailMessage` sends out emails with the credentials of the current user (or an arbitrary user) and an SMTP server. `Send-MailMessage` can send HTML emails by using the `-BodyAsHtml` switch, and `ConvertTo-HTML` can take the output of a cmdlet and turn it into an HTML chunk.

15
PowerShell and Cloud Operations

In this chapter, we will discuss the following recipes:

- Installation of the `AzureRM.Netcore` (or ARM) PowerShell module on Linux machines
- Installation of the `AWSPowerShell.NetCore` module on Linux machines
- Discovering AzureRM cmdlets discovery functions
- Azure Cloud Shell in action
- Provisioning a Ubuntu 18.04-LTS VM using `AzureRM.Netcore` cmdlets on Azure Cloud
- Provisioning Linux VM using PowerShell script
- Provisioning Linux Docker containers using Docker Machine on Azure
- Performing management tasks using ARM PowerShell cmdlets
- PowerShell remoting to Azure VM using OpenSSH
- Managing AWS credentials
- Connecting an EC2 Linux instance using SSH from PowerShell

Introduction to PowerShell for Cloud operations on Azure and AWS

Microsoft's announcement about cross-platform product support raised many eyebrows with curiosity and sparked a lot of buzz. Now, Microsoft's latest announcements and developments toward open source projects is definitely a trend-setting factor in the IT market. This announcement prompted two big questions: why and how. There have been discussions on the porting of various components and software pieces using Drawbridge.

Interested? Well, first of all, PowerShell running on a Linux machine enables the user to run management tasks, such as provisioning resources, configuration, and auditing, on Linux. Now, let's say you write one script to perform the same tasks on Windows as well as Linux machines. On the same day that Microsoft made their announcement about cross-platform support, Amazon announced their AWS toolkit for PowerShell.

These developments led to a stage where cloud operations or cloud management tasks could be performed from any platform. Since Azure is so important and Azure Resource Manager is the way that Microsoft turned classical Azure into a cloud-oriented public cloud infrastructure, we will see how the AzureRM module works with PowerShell.

Why restrict ourselves to Azure? In this chapter, we will also discuss what AWS Tools for PowerShell Core have in store for us. Some of these tools include the following:

- **Compute and Networking**: Amazon **Elastic Compute Cloud** (**EC2**), Elastic Load Balancing, Route 53, and **Virtual Private Cloud** (**VPC**)
- **Database**: Amazon **Relational Database Service** (RDS), Redshift, and ElastiCache
- **Storage and Content Delivery**: Amazon **Simple Storage Service** (**S3**) and CloudFront
- **Deployment and Management**: AWS Elastic Beanstalk, CloudFormation, CloudWatch, and **Identity and Access Management** (**IAM**)
- **App Services**: Amazon **Simple Queue Service** (**SQS**), **Simple Notification Service** (**SNS**), and **Simple Email Service** (**SES**)

Installation of the AzureRM.Netcore PowerShell module on Linux machines

In this recipe, we will discuss the installation of the AzureRM.Netcore or (ARM) module on PowerShell. You're going to look at some of the features that are available with ARM PowerShell cmdlets and how you can use them.

Getting ready

In this section, you will learn how to get started with the AzureRm.Netcore module's installation:

1. Log on to the Terminal with your **superuser** (**SU**) account
2. Open the PowerShell console (pwsh)

How to do it...

You should have an SU session open now. Let's walk through the steps for installing the module:

1. To install the AzureRM.Netcore PowerShell module, run the Install-Module cmdlet, along with a module manifest, that is, AzureRM.Netcore:

```
PS> Install-Module -Name AzureRM.Netcore
```

2. You may get a warning based on the execution policy. Pick Yes to continue; this is a trusted module.
3. Now the module is ready and available for use. To import the cmdlets to the user session, run the Import-Module cmdlet:

```
PS> Import-Module -Name AzureRM.Netcore
```

4. Test the AzureRM cmdlets. To create a session, use `Login-AzureRmAccount`:

PS> Login-AzureRmAccount

```
                                       prashanth@packtpub:~                                       ● ● ●
[prashanth@packtpub ~]$ sudo pwsh
[sudo] password for prashanth:
PowerShell v6.1.0-preview.2
Copyright (c) Microsoft Corporation. All rights reserved.

https://aka.ms/pscore6-docs
Type 'help' to get help.

PS /home/prashanth> Install-Module -Name AzureRM.NetCore
PS /home/prashanth> Import-Module AzureRM.NetCore
PS /home/prashanth> Login-AzureRmAccount
WARNING: To sign in, use a web browser to open the page https://microsoft.com/devicelogin and enter the code G
52NDHXBV to authenticate.


Account         : PacktPubLinux@gmail.com
SubscriptionName : Free Trial
SubscriptionId   : 74d6872d-54f8-4240-91aa-4e19c7f0f18b
TenantId         : a06f3a07-c723-464e-99af-5fc73b85b372
Environment      : AzureCloud



PS /home/prashanth> █
```

5. Straight after that, you need to authenticate the device by going to `https://aka.ms./devicelogin` and entering an authentication code.

How it works...

The installation is no different from loading any other module. By now, you can say that that it is simple and straightforward. The `AzureRM.Netcore` module is built on .NET Core. However, the AzureRM module doesn't have all of the functionality to interact with Azure. The discussion around the development of `AzureRM.Netcore` is relatively prominent and active on GitHub, so it is expected that `AzureRM.Netcore` will match AzureRM very soon.

A few scripts might not run with the `AzureRM.Netcore` module. In order to run the scripts, fine-tuning is required and it will have to be adapted with a few modifications.

There's more...

It is recommended that you update the `AzureRM.Netcore` modules using the following command:

```
PS> Update-Module -Name AzureRM.Netcore
```

Installation of the AWSPowerShell.NetCore module on Linux machines

In this recipe, we will look at how to install the AWS PowerShell Core module on the Linux machine.

Amazon Web Services (AWS) offers a variety of tools, **Command-Line Interfaces (CLIs)**, and SDKs to manage and administrate AWS resources. In any of these cases, PowerShell stands at the top of the list because of the flexibility, language richness, and user-friendliness it provides. AWS Tools for PowerShell is cross-platform and is supported on Windows, Linux, and macOS platforms. Since PowerShell is built on .NET Core, it is very easy to refer .Net Core class libraries in the PowerShell scripts.

Getting ready

In this section, you will learn how to get started with the `AWSPowerShell.NetCore` module's installation:

1. Log on to the Terminal with your SU account
2. Open the PowerShell console
3. Type in `pwsh`

How to do it...

You should have an SU session open now. The AWS PowerShell Core module is accessible via the PSGallery. Let's follow these instructions to install the module:

1. To install the `AWSPowerShell.NetCore` PowerShell module, run the `Install-Module` cmdlet along with a module manifest name, that is, `AWSPowerShell.NetCore`:

    PS> Install-Module -Name AWSPowerShell.NetCore

    If you have trouble installing the module using the aforementioned command, try the following instead:

    PS> Install-Module -Scope CurrentUser -Name AWSPowerShell.NetCore

2. To import the cmdlets, run the `Import-Module` cmdlet:

    PS> Import-Module -Name AWSPowerShell.NetCore

3. Let's discover the AWS cmdlets by using the `Get-Module` cmdlet:

    PS> Get-Module -Name AWSPowerShell.NetCore

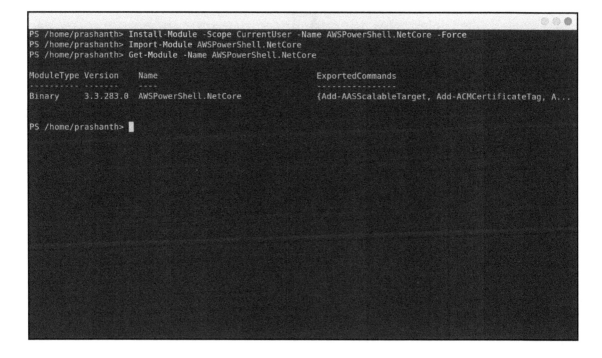

```
PS /home/prashanth> Install-Module -Scope CurrentUser -Name AWSPowerShell.NetCore -Force
PS /home/prashanth> Import-Module AWSPowerShell.NetCore
PS /home/prashanth> Get-Module -Name AWSPowerShell.NetCore

ModuleType Version    Name                    ExportedCommands
---------- -------    ----                    ----------------
Binary     3.3.283.0  AWSPowerShell.NetCore   {Add-AASScalableTarget, Add-ACMCertificateTag, A...

PS /home/prashanth>
```

4. You can further dissect the cmdlet discovery for a specific verb or noun part of the cmdlets:

```
PS> Get-Command Get*EC2* -Module AWSPowerShell.NetCore | ForEach-
Object {
[pscustomobject] @{
'Cmdlet' = $_.Name
'Description' = (Get-Help $_.Name).Description.Text }
} | Format-Table -Wrap
```

```
PS /home/prashanth> Get-Command Get*EC2* -Module AWSPowerShell.NetCore | ForEach-Object {
>> [pscustomobject] @{
>> 'Cmdlet' = $_.Name
>> 'Description' = (Get-Help $_.Name).Description.Text }
>> } | Format-Table -Wrap

Cmdlet                    Description
------                    -----------
Get-EC2AccountAttributes  Describes attributes of your AWS account. The following are the supported account
                          attributes:
                              - supported-platforms: Indicates whether your account can launch instances into
                          EC2-Classic and EC2-VPC, or only into EC2-VPC.
                              - default-vpc: The ID of the default VPC for your account, or none.
                              - max-instances: The maximum number of On-Demand Instances that you can run.
                              - vpc-max-security-groups-per-interface: The maximum number of security groups
                          that you can assign to a network interface.
                              - max-elastic-ips: The maximum number of Elastic IP addresses that you can
 allocate for use with EC2-Classic.
  - vpc-max-elastic-ips: The maximum number of Elastic IP addresses that you can
 allocate for use with EC2-VPC.
Get-EC2ExportTasks        Describes one or more of your export tasks.
Get-EC2FlowLogs           Describes one or more flow logs. To view the information in your flow logs (the log
                          streams for the network interfaces), you must use the CloudWatch Logs console or
                          the CloudWatch Logs API.This operation automatically pages all available results to
                          the pipeline - parameters related to iteration are only needed if you want to
                          manually control the paginated output.
Get-EC2Hosts              Describes one or more of your Dedicated Hosts.
                          The results describe only the Dedicated Hosts in the region you're currently using.
                          All listed instances consume capacity on your Dedicated Host. Dedicated Hosts that
                          have recently been released will be listed with the state released.
```

How it works...

The `AWSPowerShell.NetCore` module has been published to the PSGallery, and therefore is available for download and installation on PowerShell 6.0. Sometimes, the module does not install properly; launching `pwsh` as an administrator does not seem to help. However, when the scope is restricted to `CurrentUser`, the module installs without difficulties.

When listing out the cmdlets, we used the `pscustomobject` accelerator to create a custom PowerShell object with the name of the cmdlet and the description text of the cmdlet as its members. We used the `Wrap` parameter to wrap the contents in the table that was output so that we can read the description text without it being truncated.

There's more...

Use the `Update-Module` cmdlet to update the module:

```
PS> Update-Module -Name AWSPowerShell.NetCore
```

Discovering AzureRM cmdlets discovery functions

In this recipe, we will discuss the steps for managing Azure resources or services using **Azure Resource Manager** (**ARM**) PowerShell cmdlets. We will use the discovery cmdlets to list out the Azure cmdlets using keywords or patterns.

How to do it...

Getting the Azure cmdlets is a relatively simple task. For the benefit of those who came directly to this chapter, follow these steps:

1. Run the following command, which is a chain of `Get-Command`, `Group-Object`, `Sort-Object`, and `Format-Table` cmdlets, to group all of the available AzureRM cmdlets by verbs:

```
PS> Get-Command * -Type Cmdlet -Module AzureRM.Net* | Group-Object
-Property Verb | Sort-Object Count -Descending | Format-Table -
AutoSize
```

```
PS /home/prashanth> Get-Command * -Type Cmdlet -Module AzureRM.Net* | Group-Object -Property Verb | Sort-Objec
t Count -Descending | Format-Table -AutoSize

Count Name    Group
----- ----    -----
   82 Get     {Get-AzureRmApplicationGateway, Get-AzureRmApplicationGatewayAuthenticationCertificate, Get-A...
   59 New     {New-AzureRmApplicationGateway, New-AzureRmApplicationGatewayAuthenticationCertificate, New-A...
   51 Remove  {Remove-AzureRmApplicationGateway, Remove-AzureRmApplicationGatewayAuthenticationCertificate,...
   46 Set     {Set-AzureRmApplicationGateway, Set-AzureRmApplicationGatewayAuthenticationCertificate, Set-A...
   30 Add     {Add-AzureRmApplicationGatewayAuthenticationCertificate, Add-AzureRmApplicationGatewayBackend...
    4 Test    {Test-AzureRmDnsAvailability, Test-AzureRmNetworkWatcherConnectivity, Test-AzureRmNetworkWatc...
    3 Start   {Start-AzureRmApplicationGateway, Start-AzureRmNetworkWatcherConnectionMonitor, Start-AzureRm...
    3 Stop    {Stop-AzureRmApplicationGateway, Stop-AzureRmNetworkWatcherConnectionMonitor, Stop-AzureRmNet...
    2 Reset   {Reset-AzureRmVirtualNetworkGateway, Reset-AzureRmVirtualNetworkGatewayConnectionSharedKey}
    1 Move    {Move-AzureRmExpressRouteCircuit}
    1 Resize  {Resize-AzureRmVirtualNetworkGateway}


PS /home/prashanth> []
```

2. To get a detailed synopsis of the cmdlets, use the following PowerShell script. In the following example, the details of `Login-AzureRmAccount` are shown:

```
PS> Get-Command Login-Azure* -Module AzureRM* | ForEach-Object {
[pscustomobject] @{
'Name' = $_.Name
'Description' = (Get-Help $_.Name).Synopsis
}} | Format-Table -Wrap

Name Desc
---- ----
Login-AzureRmAccount
                        Connect-AzureRmAccount [-Environment <string>]
[-TenantId <string>] [-Subscription <string>] [-ContextName
<string>] [-Force] [-Scope <ContextModificationScope>] [-
DefaultProfile <IAzureContextContainer>] [-WhatIf]
                        [-Confirm] [<CommonParameters>]

                        Connect-AzureRmAccount -Credential
<pscredential> -ServicePrincipal -TenantId <string> [-Environment
<string>] [-Subscription <string>] [-ContextName <string>] [-Force]
[-Scope <ContextModificationScope>]
                        [-DefaultProfile <IAzureContextContainer>] [-
WhatIf] [-Confirm] [<CommonParameters>]
```

```
                      Connect-AzureRmAccount -CertificateThumbprint
<string> -ApplicationId <string> -ServicePrincipal -TenantId
<string> [-Environment <string>] [-Subscription <string>] [-
ContextName <string>] [-Force] [-Scope
 <ContextModificationScope>] [-DefaultProfile
<IAzureContextContainer>] [-WhatIf] [-Confirm] [<CommonParameters>]

 Connect-AzureRmAccount -AccessToken <string> -AccountId <string>
[-Environment <string>] [-TenantId <string>] [-GraphAccessToken
<string>] [-KeyVaultAccessToken <string>] [-Subscription <string>]
[-ContextName
 <string>] [-SkipValidation] [-Force] [-Scope
<ContextModificationScope>] [-DefaultProfile
<IAzureContextContainer>] [-WhatIf] [-Confirm] [<CommonParameters>]

 Connect-AzureRmAccount -Identity [-Environment <string>] [-
TenantId <string>] [-AccountId <string>] [-ManagedServicePort
<int>] [-ManagedServiceHostName <string>] [-ManagedServiceSecret
<securestring>]
 [-Subscription <string>] [-ContextName <string>] [-Force] [-Scope
<ContextModificationScope>] [-DefaultProfile
<IAzureContextContainer>] [-WhatIf] [-Confirm] [<CommonParameters>]
```

3. To view all cmdlets that contain VM in the `AzureRM.Compute` module, use the following code:

```
PS> Get-Command -Name '*VM*' -Module AzureRM.Compute.Netcore
```

How it works...

Cmdlet discovery is key when working with PowerShell, unless you are sure of what cmdlets you should use to meet your requirements. PowerShell is designed to provide the useful discovery of cmdlets so that it can display detailed information about them.

In this recipe, we will use cmdlet discovery, along with `Format-Table`, to format the name and the synopsis of the cmdlets in a way that makes reading them easier. We will also use a wildcard-based filtering of cmdlets to list the cmdlets that help manage virtual machines.

Azure Cloud Shell in action

At Build 2017, Microsoft announced the new Azure Cloud Shell, built into the Azure Portal, which made it easier than ever to use Azure PowerShell. With the Cloud Shell, you don't have to work around copying-and-pasting tokens to authenticate yourself. Also, it is always there. It even provides you with storage so that you can store your scripts.

The following features are some of its highlights:

- Browser-based integration on the Azure portal
- A choice between Bash and PowerShell consoles
- It's a lightweight tool that has multiple access points from various platforms, such as the following:
  - `portal.azure.com`
  - `shell.azure.com`
  - Azure CLI
  - Azure mobile app
  - VS Code Azure Extension
- Loads all Azure-related modules
- Storage support

Getting ready

To get started with PowerShell within the Azure Portal, go to `https://portal.azure.com` and register yourself for a free trial if you don't have one already. Next, click on the Cloud Shell icon on the top-right, next to the notifications (bell) icon.

Azure will ask you to create a storage account and a file share. Create one that will help you store PowerShell-related content. After you have created your storage account, your Cloud Shell will launch.

 You will be charged for the non-trial subscription as per how much you use it.

How to do it...

To navigate the Azure Cloud Shell, follow these steps:

1. Click the Cloud Shell icon in the top navigation bar of the Azure portal; select either **Bash** or **PowerShell**.
2. Click on the **Advanced** link to choose from the available subscriptions to create storage account and file share required for local mount.
3. Azure requires a storage account and a file share within that so that you can store content pertaining to the Cloud Shell. Therefore, choose a location that is closest to you and then enter the names of the storage account and the file share. If they don't exist, they will be created at this step.
4. If you chose **Bash**, type `pwsh` to open the PowerShell Core console:

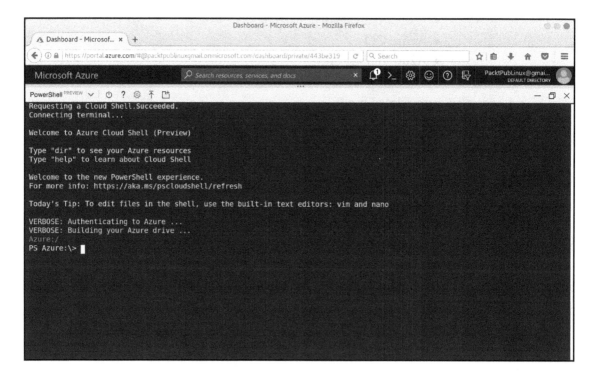

5. You can run PowerShell commands in the Cloud Shell, just as you would run them on the console:

    ```
    PS> Get-AzureRmVM
    ```

6. You can navigate the Azure resources as filesystem objects using `dir` or `ls` and `cd`.

How it works...

Azure Cloud Shell gives you the flexibility of choosing the shell experience that best suits the way you work. Linux users can opt for the **Bash** or the **PowerShell** consoles. You can run PowerShell cmdlets, navigate and manage resources, and run and save scripts on the Cloud Shell. The `Azure` PowerShell provider exposes data stores in a hierarchical manner (just like filesystem objects, as seen in the *Listing the various providers in PowerShell* recipe in `Chapter 1`, *Introducing PowerShell Core*). In other words, the data in your data store can be treated like files and directories so that you can navigate them using the `cd` or `dir` commands.

See also

- The *Listing various providers in PowerShell* recipe, from `Chapter 1`, *Introducing PowerShell Core*.
- Refer to the Cloud shell overview (`https://docs.microsoft.com/en-us/azure/cloud-shell/overview`) documentation for more information.

Provisioning a Ubuntu 18.04 LTS VM using AzureRM.Netcore cmdlets on the Azure Cloud

In this recipe, we'll discuss the steps required to build an Ubuntu 18.04 virtual machine on Azure, using the `AzureRm.Netcore` cmdlets.

This activity involves the following steps:

1. Setting up a Resource Group and a Resource
2. Creating a Storage Account
3. Setting up a virtual network
4. Configuring the network interface
5. Configuring the virtual machine

6. Setting up storage
7. Connecting to the VM

Getting ready

To get ready for setting up a VM using `AzureRm.Netcore` cmdlets, follow these steps:

1. Open a Terminal.
2. Launch PowerShell.
3. Load the `AzureRM.Netcore` module.

How to do it...

In this example, a virtual machine has been created with the name `myVM` and is running the latest version of Ubuntu:

1. Create a connection with Azure using the `Login-AzureRmAccount` cmdlet. Next, authenticate the device by following the instructions provided:

   ```
   PS> Login-AzureRmAccount
   ```

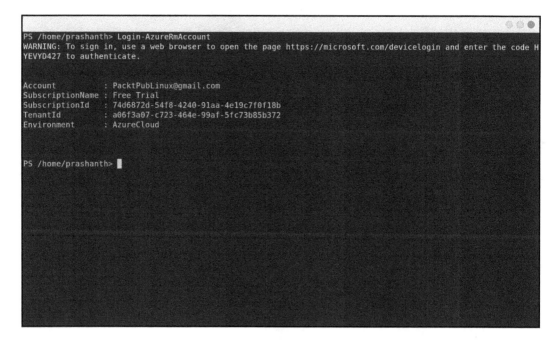

```
PS /home/prashanth> Login-AzureRmAccount
WARNING: To sign in, use a web browser to open the page https://microsoft.com/devicelogin and enter the code H
YEVYD427 to authenticate.


Account            : PacktPubLinux@gmail.com
SubscriptionName : Free Trial
SubscriptionId   : 74d6872d-54f8-4240-91aa-4e19c7f0f18b
TenantId          : a06f3a07-c723-464e-99af-5fc73b85b372
Environment        : AzureCloud



PS /home/prashanth>
```

2. Create a resource group with the `New-AzureRmResourceGroup` cmdlet:

```
PS> $ResourceGroup = 'packpub-demo'
PS> $Location = 'East US'
PS> New-AzureRmResourceGroup -Name $ResourceGroup -Location
$Location
```

3. Create a storage account with the `New-AzureRmStorageAccount` cmdlet:

```
PS> $StorageAcctName = 'packpubstorage'
PS> New-AzureRmStorageAccount -Name $StorageAcctName -
ResourceGroupName $ResourceGroup -Type Standard_LRS -Location
$Location
```

4. To set up and configure a virtual network, follow these commands:

```
PS> $VNet = 'packtpub-vnet'
PS> $Subnet = New-AzureRmVirtualNetworkSubnetConfig -Name
FrontendSubnet -AddressPrefix 10.0.1.0/24

PS> $VNet = New-AzureRmVirtualNetwork -Name $VNet -
ResourceGroupName $ResourceGroup -Location $Location -AddressPrefix
10.0.0.0/16 -Subnet $Subnet
```

5. Set up a network interface for the Ubuntu Linux machine using the subnet ID:

```
PS> $NicName = 'vm-nic'
PS> $Ip = New-AzureRmPublicIpAddress -Name $NicName -
ResourceGroupName $ResourceGroup -Location $Location -
AllocationMethod Dynamic
PS> $Nic = New-AzureRmNetworkInterface -Name $NicName -
ResourceGroupName $ResourceGroup -Location $Location -SubnetId
$VNet.Subnets[0].Id -PublicIpAddressId $Ip.Id
```

6. Configure the virtual machine:

```
PS> $VmName = 'ubuntu-packtpub'
PS> $Vm = New-AzureRmVMConfig -VMName $VmName -VMSize 'Basic_A1'
PS> $cred=Get-Credential

PowerShell credential request
Enter your credentials.
User: PacktPubLinux@gmail.com
Password for user PacktPubLinux@gmail.com: *******
PS> $Vm = Set-AzureRmVMOperatingSystem -VM $Vm -Linux -ComputerName
$VmName -Credential $Cred
```

```
NetworkRuleSet       : Microsoft.Azure.Commands.Management.Storage.Models.PSNetworkRuleSet
Context              : Microsoft.WindowsAzure.Commands.Common.Storage.LazyAzureStorageContext
ExtendedProperties   : {}


PS /home/prashanth> $VNet = 'packtpub-vnet'
PS /home/prashanth> $Subnet = New-AzureRmVirtualNetworkSubnetConfig  -Name FrontendSubnet -AddressPrefix 10.0.
1.0/24
PS /home/prashanth> $VNet = New-AzureRmVirtualNetwork -Name $VNet -ResourceGroupName $ResourceGroup -Location
$Location -AddressPrefix 10.0.0.0/16 -Subnet $Subnet
WARNING: The output object type of this cmdlet will be modified in a future release.
PS /home/prashanth> $NicName = 'vm-nic'
PS /home/prashanth> $Ip = New-AzureRmPublicIpAddress -Name $NicName -ResourceGroupName $ResourceGroup -Locatio
n $Location -AllocationMethod Dynamic
WARNING: The output object type of this cmdlet will be modified in a future release.
PS /home/prashanth> $Nic = New-AzureRmNetworkInterface -Name $NicName -ResourceGroupName $ResourceGroup -Locat
ion $Location -SubnetId $VNet.Subnets[0].Id -PublicIpAddressId $Ip.Id
WARNING: The output object type of this cmdlet will be modified in a future release.
PS /home/prashanth> $VmName = 'ubuntu-packtpub'
PS /home/prashanth> $Vm = New-AzureRmVMConfig -VMName $VmName -VMSize 'Basic_A1'
PS /home/prashanth> $Cred = Get-Credential

PowerShell credential request
Enter your credentials.
User: PacktPubLinux@gmail.com
Password for user PacktPubLinux@gmail.com: *************

PS /home/prashanth> $Vm = Set-AzureRmVMOperatingSystem -VM $Vm -Linux -ComputerName $VmName -Credential $Cred
PS /home/prashanth>
```

7. Get the VM images. The `Get-AzureRmVMImage*` cmdlets are used to search the marketplace for images. These cmdlets help find the publisher, offer, SKU, and optionally a version of the specific image:

```
PS> Get-AzureRmVMImagePublisher -Location $Location
PS> Get-AzureRmVMImageOffer -Location $Location -PublisherName
'Canonical'
PS> Get-AzureRmVMImageSku -Location $Location -PublisherName
'Canonical' -Offer 'UbuntuServer'
```

```
Ubuntu_Snappy_Core_Docker Canonical      eastus   /Subscriptions/74d6872d-54f8-4240-91aa-4e19c7f0f18b/Provi...

PS /home/prashanth> Get-AzureRmVMImageSku -Location $Location -PublisherName 'Canonical' -Offer 'UbuntuServer'

Skus                  Offer         PublisherName Location Id
----                  -----         ------------- -------- --
12.04.3-LTS           UbuntuServer Canonical      eastus   /Subscriptions/74d6872d-54f8-4240-91aa-4e19c7f0f18b/...
12.04.4-LTS           UbuntuServer Canonical      eastus   /Subscriptions/74d6872d-54f8-4240-91aa-4e19c7f0f18b/...
12.04.5-DAILY-LTS UbuntuServer Canonical      eastus   /Subscriptions/74d6872d-54f8-4240-91aa-4e19c7f0f18b/...
12.04.5-LTS           UbuntuServer Canonical      eastus   /Subscriptions/74d6872d-54f8-4240-91aa-4e19c7f0f18b/...
14.04.0-LTS           UbuntuServer Canonical      eastus   /Subscriptions/74d6872d-54f8-4240-91aa-4e19c7f0f18b/...
14.04.1-LTS           UbuntuServer Canonical      eastus   /Subscriptions/74d6872d-54f8-4240-91aa-4e19c7f0f18b/...
14.04.2-LTS           UbuntuServer Canonical      eastus   /Subscriptions/74d6872d-54f8-4240-91aa-4e19c7f0f18b/...
14.04.3-LTS           UbuntuServer Canonical      eastus   /Subscriptions/74d6872d-54f8-4240-91aa-4e19c7f0f18b/...
14.04.4-LTS           UbuntuServer Canonical      eastus   /Subscriptions/74d6872d-54f8-4240-91aa-4e19c7f0f18b/...
14.04.5-DAILY-LTS UbuntuServer Canonical      eastus   /Subscriptions/74d6872d-54f8-4240-91aa-4e19c7f0f18b/...
14.04.5-LTS           UbuntuServer Canonical      eastus   /Subscriptions/74d6872d-54f8-4240-91aa-4e19c7f0f18b/...
16.04-DAILY-LTS   UbuntuServer Canonical      eastus   /Subscriptions/74d6872d-54f8-4240-91aa-4e19c7f0f18b/...
16.04-LTS             UbuntuServer Canonical      eastus   /Subscriptions/74d6872d-54f8-4240-91aa-4e19c7f0f18b/...
16.04.0-LTS           UbuntuServer Canonical      eastus   /Subscriptions/74d6872d-54f8-4240-91aa-4e19c7f0f18b/...
17.10                 UbuntuServer Canonical      eastus   /Subscriptions/74d6872d-54f8-4240-91aa-4e19c7f0f18b/...
17.10-DAILY           UbuntuServer Canonical      eastus   /Subscriptions/74d6872d-54f8-4240-91aa-4e19c7f0f18b/...
18.04-DAILY-LTS   UbuntuServer Canonical      eastus   /Subscriptions/74d6872d-54f8-4240-91aa-4e19c7f0f18b/...
18.04-LTS             UbuntuServer Canonical      eastus   /Subscriptions/74d6872d-54f8-4240-91aa-4e19c7f0f18b/...
18.10-DAILY           UbuntuServer Canonical      eastus   /Subscriptions/74d6872d-54f8-4240-91aa-4e19c7f0f18b/...

PS /home/prashanth>
```

8. Set up the image source and add network configuration:

```
PS> $Vm = Set-AzureRmVMSourceImage -VM $Vm -PublisherName
'Canonical' -Offer 'UbuntuServer' -Skus '18.04-LTS' -Version
'latest'
PS> $Vm = Add-AzureRmVMNetworkInterface -VM $Vm -Id $Nic.Id
```

9. Configure the disk **URI (Uniform Resource Identifier):**

```
PS> $DiskName = 'ub-disk-packtpub'
PS> $StorageAccount = Get-AzureRmStorageAccount -ResourceGroupName
$ResourceGroup -Name $StorageAcctName
PS> $OsDiskUri =
$StorageAccount.PrimaryEndpoints.Blob.ToString()+'vhds/'+$DiskName+
'.vhd'
PS> $OsDiskUri
https://packtpubstorageacct.blob.core.windows.net/vhds/ub-disk-pack
tpub.vhd
PS> $Vm = Set-AzureRmVMOSDisk -VM $Vm -Name $Diskname -VhdUri
$OsDiskuri -CreateOption FromImage
```

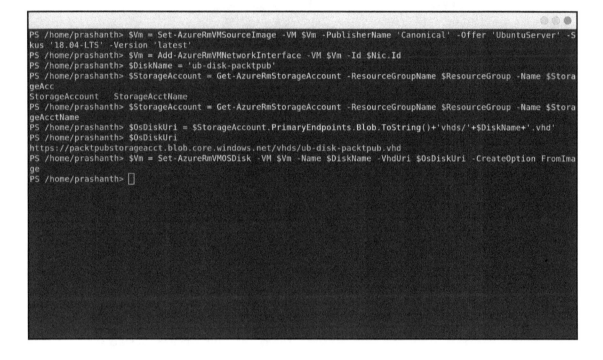

10. Deploy the VM with a specific image. The command may take a while to complete:

```
PS> New-AzureRmVM -ResourceGroupName $resourceGroup -Location
$location -VM $vm

RequestId IsSuccessStatusCode StatusCode ReasonPhrase
--------- ------------------- ---------- ------------
                        True OK OK
```

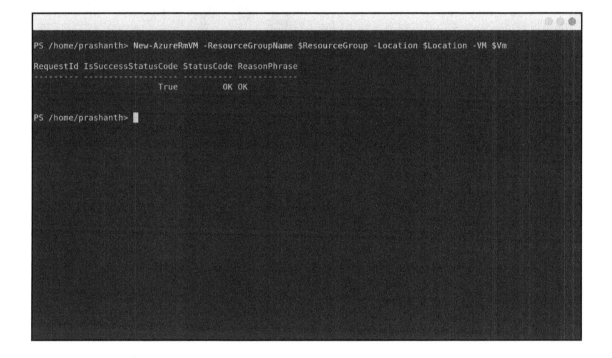

11. To get the assigned public IP address of VM, use the `Get-AzureRMPublicIPAddress` cmdlet:

```
PS> Get-AzureRmPublicIpAddress -ResourceGroupName $ResourceGroup
```

```
PS /home/prashanth> Get-AzureRmPublicIpAddress -ResourceGroupName $ResourceGroup

Name                    : vm-nic
ResourceGroupName       : packtpub-demo
Location                : eastus
Id                      : /subscriptions/74d6872d-54f8-4240-91aa-4e19c7f0f18b/resourceGroups/packtpub-demo/
                          providers/Microsoft.Network/publicIPAddresses/vm-nic
Etag                    : W/"0433bb40-1e6c-4d94-bce1-c273a1a58515"
ResourceGuid            : 14337550-ba7e-48df-8ba8-7dedff9f3d3b
ProvisioningState       : Succeeded
Tags                    :
PublicIpAllocationMethod : Dynamic
IpAddress               : 168.62.42.54
PublicIpAddressVersion  : IPv4
IdleTimeoutInMinutes    : 4
IpConfiguration         : {
                            "Id": "/subscriptions/74d6872d-54f8-4240-91aa-4e19c7f0f18b/resourceGroups/packt
                          pub-demo/providers/Microsoft.Network/networkInterfaces/vm-nic/ipConfigurations/ip
                          config1"
                          }
DnsSettings             : null
Zones                   : {}
Sku                     : {
                            "Name": "Basic"
                          }
IpTags                  : []
```

12. Note down the IP address.

13. Open a new Terminal and connect to the newly created VM using SSH. Use the password that you used for your Azure account:

```
$ ssh PacktPubLinux@gmail.com@168.62.42.54
PacktPubLinux@gmail.com@168.62.42.54's password:
Welcome to Ubuntu 18.04 LTS (GNU/Linux 4.15.0-1013-azure x86_64)
_

_

_

PacktPubLinux@gmail.com@ubuntu-packtpub:~$
```

How it works...

The primary point to note here is the Resource Group. A Resource Group in Azure is a logical container that contains assets, which could be anything that Azure offers: virtual disks, virtual machines, virtual networks, and so on. The usual practice is to group all of the resources that are related into a single Resource Group. For this demo, we created a resource group called `packtpub-demo`, in the `East US` region, using the `New-AzureRmResourceGroup` cmdlet. The location and the name are specified when creating the Resource Group.

The rest of the flow is straightforward. The next step is to create a Storage Account using `New-AzureRmStorageAccount`. While a Resource Group can contain several kinds of assets, a Storage Account contains storage-related assets, such as blobs (or binary large object), disks, or tables. Storage Accounts have types, the choices being Standard and Premium. We will choose Standard, and along with that, choose the replication as well: Locally Redundant Storage.

Next, we configure the virtual network with subnetting by using `New-AzureRmVirtualNetworkSubnetConfig` and `New-AzureRmVirtualNetwork`. Then, we create a dynamic IP configuration using `New-AzureRmPublicIpAddress`, create an NIC (`New-AzureRmNetworkInterface`), and assign the dynamic IP address to it, within the subnet.

Finally, we choose to build the virtual machine. We set the name and the size (`New-AzureRmVMConfig`), and then we set the credentials and operating system (`Set-AzureRmVMOperatingSystem`). We look for VM images (`Get-AzureRmVMImageSku`), set up the image source, and add the network configuration to the virtual machine (`Add-AzureRmVMNetworkInterface`). We configure the disk and create the string that will identify the disk in our resource group (this string must be a complete URI). We then tie in all of the disk-related configuration together using `Set-AzureRmVMOSDisk` and attach the image to it to build an OS disk. Finally, we tie all of the bits together and deploy the virtual machine using `New-AzureRmVM`.

We find the public IP address for the virtual machine using `Get-AzureRmPublicIpAddress` and make an SSH connection to it.

The one question that must be nagging some of us is why we use variables when we can simply pass the values when necessary. The reason for this is that variables facilitate not remembering arbitrary names and values. They offer the flexibility of simply using names. As you will discover in the *There's more...* section of this recipe, they simplify calling more commands.

There's more...

The `Remove-AzureRmResourceGroup` cmdlet removes the specified resource group and all of the resources contained within it. To clean up the deployment, run the following cmdlet:

```
PS> Remove-AzureRmResourceGroup -Name $ResourceGroup
```

Provisioning Linux Docker containers using Docker Machine on Azure

In this recipe, you will understand some of the concepts of the Docker Machine tool and the steps that are required to deploy an Azure Docker container VM using Docker Machine.

Docker Machine is a tool that lets you install Docker Engine on virtual hosts and manage the hosts with commands. Using `docker-machine` commands, you can start, inspect, stop, and restart a managed host, upgrade the Docker client and daemon, and configure a Docker client to talk to your host. Docker Machine uses drivers to enable deployment to different platforms. In this recipe, we will go over the steps to provision a VM running Docker on Microsoft Azure.

Getting ready

It is recommended that you meet the following listed prerequisites before proceeding with the recipe:

1. Open a session with your SU account.
2. To install `docker-machine`, run the following commands:

```
# base=https://github.com/docker/machine/releases/download/v0.14.0
&&
> curl -L $base/docker-machine-$(uname -s)-$(uname -m) >
/tmp/docker-machine &&
> sudo install /tmp/docker-machine /usr/local/bin/docker-machine
  % Total % Received % Xferd Average Speed Time Time Time Current
                            Dload Upload Total Spent Left
Speed
100 617 0 617 0 0 1458 0 --:--:-- --:--:-- --:--:-- 1458
100 26.7M 100 26.7M 0 0 5043k 0 0:00:05 0:00:05 --:--:-- 6265k
```

3. Open a PowerShell session by typing `pwsh`.
4. Import the `AzureRM.Netcore` module using `Import-Module`:

```
PS> Import-Module -Name AzureRM.Netcore
```

How to do it...

We know that the modules have been loaded and that the `docker-machine` tool is installed. Now, we can manage our Docker VMs. Follow these steps to complete this recipe:

1. Connect to an Azure session. Run the following cmdlet and follow the instructions that appear as a warning:

   ```
   PS> Connect-AzureRmAccount
   ```

2. Create a resource group by running the following command:

   ```
   PS> $ResourceGroup = 'packpub-demo'
   PS> $Location = 'East US'
   PS> New-AzureRmResourceGroup -Name $ResourceGroup -Location
   $Location
   ```

3. Create a new storage account:

   ```
   PS> $StorageAcctName = 'packpubstorageacct'
   PS> New-AzureRmStorageAccount -Name $StorageAcctName -
   ResourceGroupName $ResourceGroup -Type Standard_LRS -Location
   $Location
   ```

4. Retrieve the Azure subscription ID and assign it to a variable:

   ```
   PS> $SubscriptionId = (Get-AzureRmContext).Subscription.Id
   ```

5. To provision a VM, run the following `docker-machine` command:

```
PS> docker-machine create --driver azure `
--azure-subscription-id $SubscriptionId `
--azure-resource-group $ResourceGroup `
--azure-location $Location `
--azure-ssh-user $env:USERNAME `
--azure-open-port 22 `
--azure-image "Canonical:UbuntuServer:18.04-LTS:latest" `
--azure-size "Standard_D2_v2" `
packtpub-ubuntu
```

```
PS /home/prashanth> docker-machine create -d azure `
>> --azure-subscription-id $subscriptionId `
>> --azure-resource-group $resourceGroup `
>> --azure-location $location `
>> --azure-ssh-user prashanth `
>> --azure-open-port 22 `
>> --azure-image "Canonical:UbuntuServer:18.04-LTS:latest" `
>> --azure-size "Standard_D2_v2" `
>> packtpub-ubuntu
Running pre-create checks...
(packtpub-ubuntu) Microsoft Azure: To sign in, use a web browser to open the page https://microsoft.com/devic
elogin and enter the code HKC855GB6 to authenticate.
(packtpub-ubuntu) Completed machine pre-create checks.
Creating machine...
(packtpub-ubuntu) Querying existing resource group.  name="packtpub-demo"
(packtpub-ubuntu) Resource group "packtpub-demo" already exists.
(packtpub-ubuntu) Configuring availability set.  name="docker-machine"
(packtpub-ubuntu) Configuring network security group.  name="packtpub-ubuntu-firewall" location="East US"
(packtpub-ubuntu) Querying if virtual network already exists.  name="docker-machine-vnet" rg="packtpub-demo"
location="East US"
(packtpub-ubuntu) Creating virtual network.  name="docker-machine-vnet" rg="packtpub-demo" location="East US"
(packtpub-ubuntu) Configuring subnet.  vnet="docker-machine-vnet" cidr="192.168.0.0/16" name="docker-machine"
(packtpub-ubuntu) Creating public IP address.  name="packtpub-ubuntu-ip" static=false
(packtpub-ubuntu) Creating network interface.  name="packtpub-ubuntu-nic"
(packtpub-ubuntu) Creating storage account.  sku=Standard_LRS name="vhdsau8lr8vk4bfa69uqiuvj" location="East
US"
(packtpub-ubuntu) Creating virtual machine.  name="packtpub-ubuntu" location="East US" size="Standard_D2_v2"
username="prashanth" osImage="Canonical:UbuntuServer:18.04-LTS:latest"
Waiting for machine to be running, this may take a few minutes...
Detecting operating system of created instance...
```

6. Connect to the newly created `packtpub-ubuntu` VM:

PS> docker-machine ssh packtpub-ubuntu

prashanth@packtpub-ubuntu:~$

```
                          prashanth@packtpub-ubuntu: ~                      ● ● ●
Copying certs to the local machine directory...
Copying certs to the remote machine...
Setting Docker configuration on the remote daemon...
Checking connection to Docker...
Docker is up and running!
To see how to connect your Docker Client to the Docker Engine running on this virtual machine, run: /usr/loca
l/bin/docker-machine env packtpub-ubuntu
PS /home/prashanth> docker-machine ssh packtpub-ubuntu
Welcome to Ubuntu 18.04 LTS (GNU/Linux 4.15.0-1013-azure x86_64)

 * Documentation:  https://help.ubuntu.com
 * Management:     https://landscape.canonical.com
 * Support:        https://ubuntu.com/advantage

  System information as of Fri Jul  6 09:51:46 UTC 2018

  System load:  0.01            Processes:             127
  Usage of /:   4.8% of 28.90GB Users logged in:       0
  Memory usage: 6%              IP address for eth0:   192.168.0.4
  Swap usage:   0%              IP address for docker0: 172.17.0.1


  Get cloud support with Ubuntu Advantage Cloud Guest:
    http://www.ubuntu.com/business/services/cloud

22 packages can be updated.
6 updates are security updates.

prashanth@packtpub-ubuntu:~$ ▯
```

7. Test the configuration:

```
$ sudo -s
# ls
# yum

Command 'yum' not found, but can be installed with:

apt install yum

# apt install yum
```

How it works...

This recipe details how to use the Docker Machine tool to create hosts in Azure. The `docker-machine` command creates a Linux virtual machine in Azure and installs and configures the Docker engine. This lets you manage your Docker hosts in Azure using the same local tools and workflows. To use `docker-machine`, refer the installation document at `https://docs.docker.com/machine/install-machine/` and install it on the Linux machine.

Docker Machine is a tool that uses the Azure driver to enable the deployment of virtual machines on the Azure platform. In this recipe, we saw the steps to provision an Ubuntu VM by running the `docker-machine` command on Azure and deploying containers to the VM.

The provisioning of a new VM is no different than the process of VM creation.

To create a VM, the following default steps are carried out in a series:

1. Run and validate the pre-creation checks.
2. After completing the machine pre-creation checks, initiate the VM creation process.
3. Query to see whether the resource group `packtpub-dockerdemo` exists. The command reuses the same resource group since it is available.
4. Configure the availability set.
5. Configure the network security group for `packtpub-ubuntu-firewall` for the specified location.
6. Create a virtual network called `docker-machine-vnet` for the `packtpub-dockerdemo` resource group and, for the specified location, use East US.
7. Configure the `docker-machine` subnet for the `docker-machine-vnet` virtual network using CIDR `192.168.0.0/16`.
8. Create a dynamic public IP address named `packtpub-ubuntu-ip`.
9. Create a network interface called `packtpub-ubuntu-nic`.
10. Create a storage account called `vhdstk3mnxdlg5i9n65vcif0` under `Standard_LRS`.
11. Proceed to create the `packtpub-ubuntu` virtual machine with the specified VM size of `Standard_D2_v2`. We also specify the login username, followed by the OS image, `Canonical:UbuntuServer:18.04-LTS:latest`.

There's more...

To ensure that we don't coin new names and to save unwanted costs on the resources, clean up the resource group when your lab session ends. Run the following command to do so:

```
PS> Remove-AzureRmResourceGroup -Name $ResourceGroup
```

See also

- Docker Machine overview (`https://docs.docker.com/machine/`)
- To get the details of the different Azure regions, refer to `https://azure.microsoft.com/en-in/global-infrastructure/regions/`.

Provisioning Linux VM using PowerShell script

In this recipe, we will use a PowerShell script to create a virtual machine on Azure. In its essence, it is simply a series of instructions in PowerShell that are executed one after the other, as we have already seen in the previous chapters in this book.

Getting ready

If you followed the recipes in the previous chapters, you should already have Visual Studio Code installed on your system. If not, go ahead and install VS Code, following the instructions in the *Installing Visual Studio Code* recipe in `Chapter 2`, *Preparing for Administration Using PowerShell*.

Once you have Visual Studio Code installed, follow these steps to get started:

1. Launch Visual Studio Code
2. Open the integrated PowerShell Terminal
3. Load the `AzureRM.Netcore` module

How to do it...

We are now ready to write and execute the script:

1. In the script pane, paste the following content:

```
Param(
# Variables for common values
    [string]$ResourceGroup = "packtpub-rg",
    [string]$storageAcctName = "packtstorage",
    [string]$Location = "East US",
    [string]$VNetName = "packtpub-vnet",
    [string]$NicName = "packtpub-vm-nic",
    [string]$DiskName = "packtUbuntu",
    [string]$VmName = "packtpub-ubuntu"
)

# Check for open session
Connect-AzureRmAccount

# Create user object
$Cred = Get-Credential -Message "Enter username and password of
administrator credentials"

# Create a resource group
New-AzureRmResourceGroup -Name $ResourceGroup -Location $Location

# Create a storage account
New-AzureRmStorageAccount -Name $storageAcctName -ResourceGroupName
$ResourceGroup -Type Standard_LRS -Location $Location

# Create a subnet configuration
$SubNetCfg = New-AzureRmVirtualNetworkSubnetConfig -Name mySubnet -
AddressPrefix 10.0.1.0/24

# Create a virtual network
$VNet = New-AzureRmVirtualNetwork -Name $VNetName -
ResourceGroupName $ResourceGroup -Location $Location -AddressPrefix
10.0.0.0/16 -Subnet $SubNetCfg

# Create a public IP address and specify a DNS name
$Ip = New-AzureRmPublicIpAddress -Name $NicName -ResourceGroupName
$ResourceGroup -Location $Location -AlLocationMethod Dynamic

# Create a virtual network card and associate with public IP
address and NSG
$Nic = New-AzureRmNetworkInterface -Name $NicName -
ResourceGroupName $ResourceGroup -Location $Location -SubnetId
```

```
$VNet.Subnets[0].Id -PublicIpAddressId $Ip.Id

# Create a blob storage
$StorageAccount = Get-AzureRmStorageAccount -ResourceGroupName
$ResourceGroup -Name $storageAcctName
$OsDiskUri =
$StorageAccount.PrimaryEndpoints.Blob.ToString()+'vhds/'+$DiskName+
".vhd"

# Create a virtual machine configuration
$Vm = New-AzureRmVMConfig -VMName $VmName -VMSize "Basic_A1"
$Vm = Set-AzureRmVMOperatingSystem -VM $Vm -Linux -ComputerName
$VmName -Credential $Cred
$Vm = Set-AzureRmVMSourceImage -VM $Vm -PublisherName 'Canonical' -
Offer 'UbuntuServer' -Skus '18.04-LTS' -Version 'latest'
$Vm = Add-AzureRmVMNetworkInterface -VM $Vm -Id $Nic.Id
$Vm = Set-AzureRmVMOSDisk -VM $Vm -Name $DiskName -VhdUri
$OsDiskUri -CreateOption fromImage

# Create a virtual machine
New-AzureRmVM -ResourceGroupName $ResourceGroup -Location $Location
-VM $Vm
```

2. Run the script by pressing the *F5* key.
3. Watch out for errors. In most cases, there should be none. However, if you do get any, check whether the script has been pasted/typed verbatim.

How it works...

The script is an example of creating a Ubuntu 18.04-LTS virtual machine. At the beginning of the script, we define its parameters and their values.

This script is nothing but a collection of the commands you ran for the *Provisioning a Ubuntu 18.04 LTS virtual machine using AzureRM.NetCore cmdlets* recipe, with the difference being the initial declaration of the parameters. These parameters can be declared in the beginning, just like in this script, or be configured to take in input based on your requirements.

How it works is simple: the commands are run one line after another, while retaining the values of the variables. Once the script finishes running and the virtual machine is created, the buffer is returned for further commands.

There's more...

Do not clean up the resources this time if you plan to go through the next recipe, *Performing management tasks using ARM PowerShell cmdlets*, immediately. If not, it is a good idea to clean up the resource group and redo this recipe when you plan to go through *Performing management tasks using ARM PowerShell cmdlets*.

Performing management tasks using ARM PowerShell cmdlets

In this recipe, we will walk through the management tasks that will be carried out during the virtual machine's creation life cycle. We will look at tasks such as starting, stopping, and deleting a virtual machine using the Cloud Shell.

Getting ready

Read the *Azure Cloud Shell in action* recipe and set up the Cloud Shell if you haven't already. Then, follow these steps to get started:

1. Connect to the Azure Portal (`https://portal.azure.com`).
2. Click the PowerShell icon to launch the Cloud Shell.

How to do it...

Run the following commands, one after the other, to perform the required operations on the virtual machine:

1. To stop a virtual machine, type in the following commands:

```
PS Azure:> $ResourceGroup = 'packtpub-rg'
PS Azure:> $Vm = 'packtpub-ubuntu'
PS Azure:> Stop-AzureRmVM -ResourceGroupName $ResourceGroup -Name
$Vm -Force
```

2. You can also navigate the Azure resources using commands such as `cd` and `dir`, and run the command to stop one or more virtual machines by using `where` with conditional logic:

```
PS Azure:>  Get-AzureRmVM | Where-Object {$_.Name -match "ubun"}

ResourceGroupName Name Location VmSize OsType NIC ProvisioningState
Zone
----------------- ---- -------- ------ ------ --- -----------------
----
PACKTPUB-RG packtpub-ubuntu eastus Basic_A1 Linux packtpub-vm-nic
Succeeded


PS Azure:> Get-AzureRmVM | Where-Object {$_.Name -match "ubun"} |
Stop-AzureRmVM
```

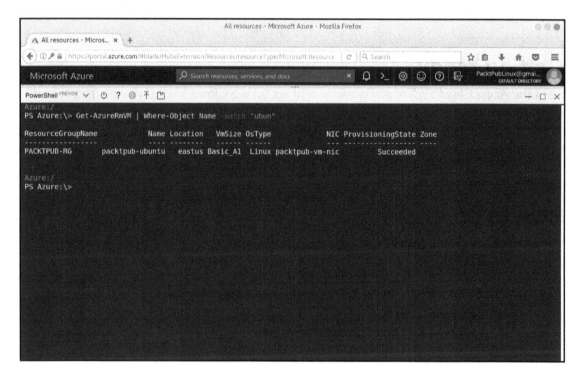

3. To start the virtual machine with the `Start-AzureRmVM` cmdlet, run the following command:

```
PS Azure:> Start-AzureRmVM -ResourceGroupName $ResourceGroup -Name
$Vm
```

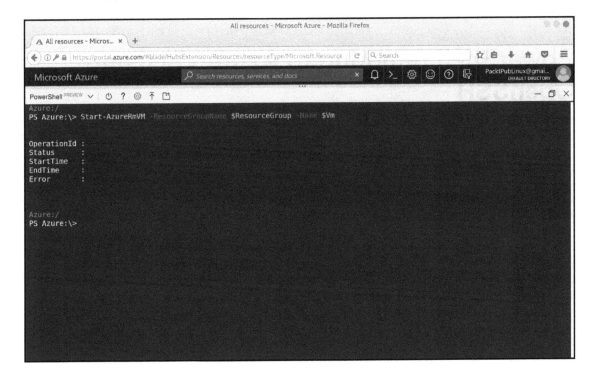

4. To delete a resource group with the `Remove-AzureRmResourceGroup` cmdlet, run the following command:

```
PS Azure:> $ResourceGroup = 'PACKTPUB-RG'
PS Azure:> Remove-AzureRmResourceGroup -Name $ResourceGroup -Force
```

How it works...

This recipe is an example of using pipeline and variables. Going by the PowerShell philosophy of using objects throughout, starting, stopping, and removing virtual machines (or any of the Azure resources, for that matter) seems simple using the console.

PowerShell remoting to Azure VM using OpenSSH

In this recipe, we will look at how to connect to a remote Linux VM using PowerShell remoting. OpenSSH, which originated as part of the OpenBSD project and is commonly used across the BSD, Linux, macOS, and Unix ecosystems, can now be used from PowerShell in Cloud Shell as well.

Let's try something different this time: go to Mobile First and use the Azure app on your phone to launch the Cloud Shell:

At the time of writing this book, the PowerShell console you get on phones is Windows PowerShell (5.1) and not PowerShell. The remoting commands, as well as the protocols, are different on Windows PowerShell and PowerShell, and so we only use the mobile console to run the Linux commands.

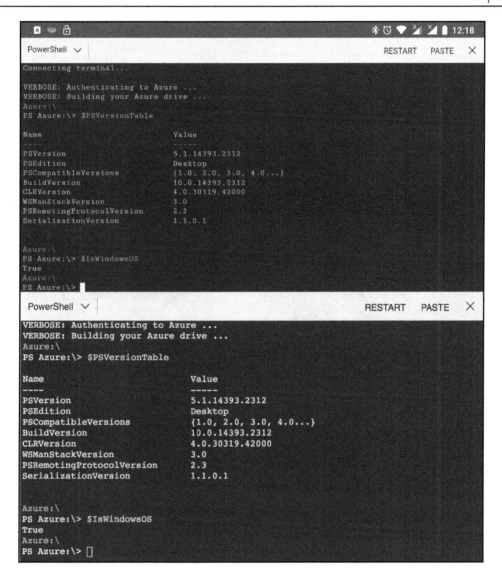

Getting ready

You will need a Linux computer set up on the cloud for this recipe. Go ahead and run the script that we wrote in the *Provisioning a Linux VM using a PowerShell Script* recipe to create all of the necessary resources, along with an Ubuntu VM.

How to do it...

Let's walk through the following steps to enable PowerShell remoting using OpenSSH:

1. SSH into the Ubuntu machine:

```
PS> ssh prashanth@40.117.213.80
```

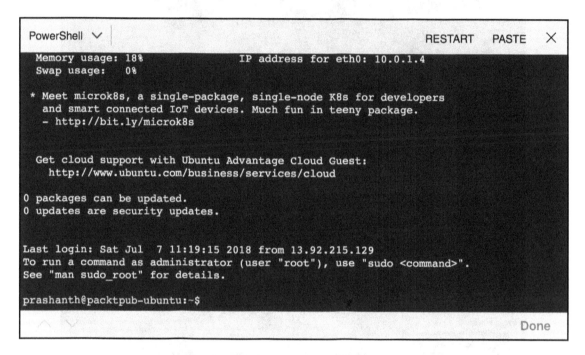

2. Register and download the PowerShell package repository:

```
# Import the public repository GPG keys
$ curl https://packages.microsoft.com/keys/microsoft.asc | sudo
apt-key add -

# Register the Microsoft Ubuntu repository
$ sudo curl -o /etc/apt/sources.list.d/microsoft.list
https://packages.microsoft.com/config/ubuntu/18.04/prod.list

# Update the list of products
$ sudo apt-get update
```

```
PowerShell ∨                                          RESTART   PASTE   ✕
prashanth@packtpub-ubuntu:~$ curl https://packages.microsoft.com/keys/microsoft.as
c | sudo apt-key add -
  % Total    % Received % Xferd  Average Speed   Time    Time     Time  Current
                                 Dload  Upload   Total   Spent    Left  Speed
100   983  100   983     0      0   9018       0 --:--:-- --:--:-- --:--:--   9018
OK
prashanth@packtpub-ubuntu:~$ sudo curl -o /etc/apt/sources.list.d/microsoft.list h
ttps://packages.microsoft.com/config/ubuntu/18.04/prod.list
  % Total    % Received % Xferd  Average Speed   Time    Time     Time  Current
                                 Dload  Upload   Total   Spent    Left  Speed
100    77  100    77     0      0    754       0 --:--:-- --:--:-- --:--:--    754
prashanth@packtpub-ubuntu:~$ sudo apt update
Get:1 https://packages.microsoft.com/ubuntu/18.04/prod bionic InRelease [2846 B]
Hit:2 http://azure.archive.ubuntu.com/ubuntu bionic InRelease
Get:3 http://azure.archive.ubuntu.com/ubuntu bionic-updates InRelease [88.7 kB]
Get:4 http://azure.archive.ubuntu.com/ubuntu bionic-backports InRelease [74.6 kB]
Get:5 http://security.ubuntu.com/ubuntu bionic-security InRelease [83.2 kB]
Get:6 https://packages.microsoft.com/ubuntu/18.04/prod bionic/main amd64 Packages
[14.3 kB]
Get:7 http://azure.archive.ubuntu.com/ubuntu bionic/main Sources [829 kB]
Get:8 http://azure.archive.ubuntu.com/ubuntu bionic/restricted Sources [5324 B]
Get:9 http://azure.archive.ubuntu.com/ubuntu bionic/multiverse Sources [181 kB]
```

3. Install PowerShell:

At the time of writing this book, PowerShell Preview is available for Ubuntu 18.04, hence the installation of powershell-preview and the use of pwsh-preview in the subsystem entry. PowerShell Preview should be considered the bleeding edge and must be tested before implementation outside of the lab environment.

```
$ # Install PowerShell
$ sudo apt install -y pwsh
```

4. Install the OpenSSH-Client and OpenSSH-Server packages. In Ubuntu 18.04 LTS, these packages are present by default:

```
$ sudo apt install openssh-client openssh-server
```

The aforementioned steps are not needed in most modern distributions.

5. Copy the `/etc/ssh/sshd_config` configuration file to `/etc/ssh/sshd_config_bakfile`:

    ```
    $ sudo -s
    # cp /etc/ssh/sshd_config /etc/ssh/sshd_config_bakfile
    ```

6. Edit the `/etc/ssh/sshd_config` configuration file using an editor of your choice:

> Switch to a more conventional Terminal emulator to do this; editing configuration files using `vi` on your phone may not be the best of experiences.

    ```
    # vi /etc/ssh/sshd_config
    ```

7. Ensure that password authentication is enabled; look for the following line:

    ```
    PasswordAuthentication yes
    ```

> SSH support multiple ways to authenticate users using the `sshd_config` file. The most common method is using a login and a password but you can also authenticate user with a login and a public key. If you set `PasswordAuthentication` to `no`, you will no longer be able to use a login and password to authenticate. And you must use a login and public key.

8. Add an entry for the PowerShell subsystem into the file. If you're using `pwsh` instead of `pwsh-preview`, change the entry accordingly:

    ```
    Subsystem powershell /usr/bin/pwsh -sshs -NoLogo -NoProfile
    ```

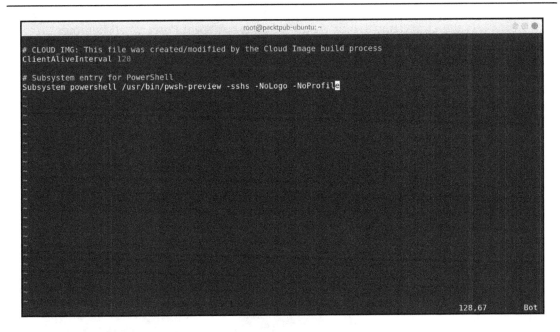

9. Restart the SSH service using the `systemctl` command:

```
# systemctl restart ssh
```

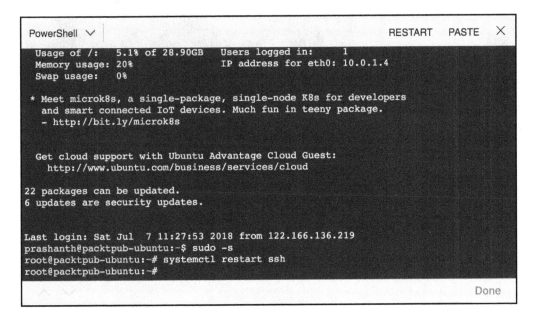

10. Now the Linux machine on Azure is ready to accept PowerShell Remote connections (in other words, without using the `ssh` command). Exit all SSH sessions you opened on the virtual machine (your phone, your desktop, and so on).

11. Open the Cloud Shell console and assign the IP address of your Linux virtual machine to a variable. If you so desire, you can use PowerShell on your local Linux computer instead:

    ```
    PS> $VmIp = (Get-AzureRmPublicIpAddress -ResourceGroupName
    packtpub-rg).IpAddress
    PS> New-PSSession -HostName $VmIp -UserName prashanth
    ```

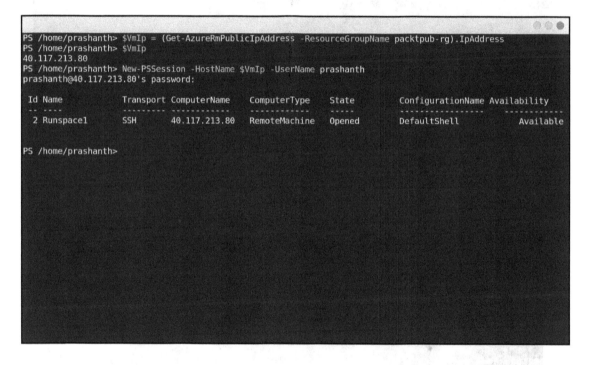

12. A connection has been built to the Linux machine. Next, get the session details using `Get-PSSession`:

    ```
    PS> Get-PSSession
    ```

13. Query the remote machine using `Invoke-Command`:

```
PS> $Session = Get-PSSession
PS> Invoke-Command -Session $Session -ScriptBlock { Get-Process }
```

```
PS /home/prashanth> Get-PSSession

Id Name        Transport ComputerName  ComputerType   State    ConfigurationName Availability
-- ----        --------- ------------  ------------   -----    ----------------- ------------
 2 Runspace1   SSH       40.117.213.80 RemoteMachine  Opened   DefaultShell         Available


PS /home/prashanth> $Session = Get-PSSession
PS /home/prashanth> Invoke-Command -Session $Session -ScriptBlock { Get-Process }

NPM(K)    PM(M)    WS(M)   CPU(s)     Id  SI ProcessName          PSComputerName
------    -----    -----   ------     --  -- -----------          --------------
     0     0.00     2.36     0.00   7128 127 (sd-pam)             40.117.213.80
     0     0.00     6.86     0.22   1066 066 accounts-daemon      40.117.213.80
     0     0.00     2.34     0.08   1150 150 agetty               40.117.213.80
     0     0.00     2.03     0.01   1164 164 agetty               40.117.213.80
     0     0.00     0.00     0.00     26   0 ata_sff              40.117.213.80
     0     0.00     2.45     0.00   1028 028 atd                  40.117.213.80
     0     0.00     0.00     0.00     12   0 cpuhp/0              40.117.213.80
     0     0.00     3.25     0.00   1072 072 cron                 40.117.213.80
     0     0.00     0.00     0.00     23   0 crypto               40.117.213.80
     0     0.00     4.34     0.07   1032 032 dbus-daemon          40.117.213.80
     0     0.00     0.00     0.00     33   0 devfreq_wq           40.117.213.80
     0     0.00     0.00     0.00     39   0 ecryptfs-kthrea      40.117.213.80
     0     0.00     0.00     0.00     28   0 edac-poller          40.117.213.80
     0     0.00     0.00     0.00    346   0 ext4-rsv-conver      40.117.213.80
     0     0.00     0.00     0.00    929   0 ext4-rsv-conver      40.117.213.80
     0     0.00     0.00     0.06    447   0 hv_balloon           40.117.213.80
     0     0.00     2.10     0.11   1031 031 hv_kvp_daemon        40.117.213.80
     0     0.00     0.00     0.00     32   0 hv_vmbus_con         40.117.213.80
```

How it works...

The easiest way to test remoting is to try it out on a single machine. In this recipe, we did the following:

1. We connected to the newly provisioned Ubuntu machine using the familiar `ssh` tool
2. We installed PowerShell on it
3. We then verified that the `ssh-server` and the `ssh-client` packages were installed on the Ubuntu machine
4. We configured SSH in a way that it would facilitate PowerShell remoting
5. We launched a PowerShell remote session using the same SSH protocol

We enabled password-based authentication in this recipe. Optionally, you can enable key-based authentication as well. PowerShell remote sessions are established over the SSH protocol and, once a session is connected to the remote PowerShell, the console will behave as if you are on the remote server. All of the commands that are run within the session will also run on the remote computer. This way, you can invoke commands and script blocks remotely.

Managing AWS credentials

Protecting and safeguarding data on the cloud has many unique challenges, especially if additional compliance regulations need to be met. Authentication always plays an important aspect in cloud computing. Credential management is key to the effective management of the cloud ecosystem.

In this recipe, we will discuss the process of generating the access key and managing profiles using AWS PowerShell cmdlets from a Linux machine.

Getting ready

This recipe requires that you have an AWS account. Go through the AWS documentation (`https://aws.amazon.com/premiumsupport/knowledge-center/create-and-activate-aws-account/`) to set yourself up with an AWS account.

How to do it...

In this section, we will discuss the steps to follow to obtain credentials and use the AWS tools for PowerShell:

1. Log on to the AWS Management console (`https://console.aws.amazon.com/iam/home`) portal.
2. Click on **Users** from the left-hand pane of the window.
3. Click on **Add User**.
4. Enter your username in the **Set user details** pane.

5. Select the **AWS access type** as **Programmatic access** and click the **Next: Permissions** button:

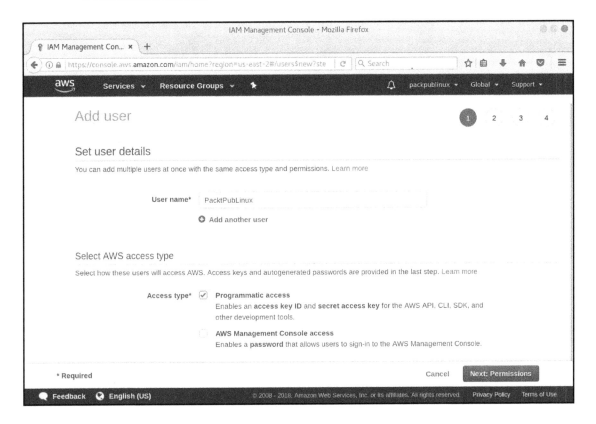

6. Choose the option to **Attach existing policies directly**. In the **Policy type** filter, check the **AdministratorAccess** box and click **Next**:

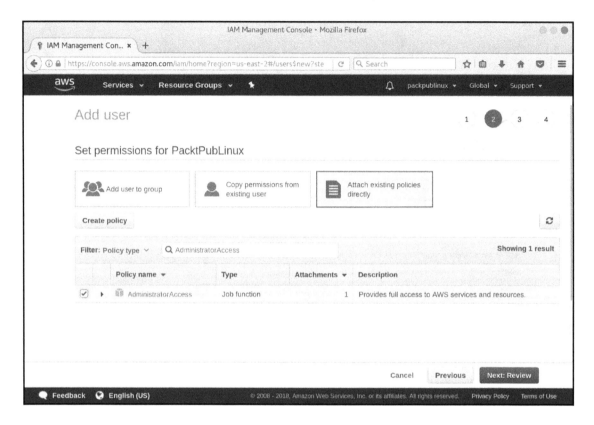

7. Click the **Create user** button.
8. The access key and the security key will be generated and ready to use.
9. Save the key in a secure location.

10. To build the session, you must use the necessary keys. The keys are used with
    `Initialize-AWSDefauultConfiguration`:

    PS> Initialize-AWSDefaultConfiguration

```
PS /home/prashanth> Initialize-AWSDefaultConfiguration

Credentials
Please enter your AWS Access and Secret Keys
AWS Access Key: AKIAJUJDK3UZAN7T2JLA
AWS Secret Key: doAfusJg5wsXmEXgy3KEHPizUQXiFPBQvlFpxIfa

Specify region
Please choose one of the following regions to use or specify one by system name
[] <Specify a different region>  [] ap-northeast-1  [] ap-northeast-2  [] ap-south-1  [] ap-southeast-1
[] ap-southeast-2[] ca-central-1  [] eu-central-1  [] eu-west-1  [] eu-west-2  [] eu-west-3  [] sa-east-1
[] us-east-1[] us-east-2  [] us-west-1  [] us-west-2  [] cn-north-1  [] cn-northwest-1  [] us-gov-west-1
[?] Help(default is "<Specify a different region>"): us-east-2
PS /home/prashanth>
```

11. To add the key to a new profile, run `Set-AWSCredential`:

    **PS> Set-AWSCredential –AccessKey AKIAIUR2HFYFHLHVYSCA –SecretKey
    ZPw8wkRqCBRKe7egbf/2MM5q2cV8WokwvajZou2L –StoreAs PackPubLinux**

12. To list the newly created profile, run `Get-AWSCredential`:

    **PS> Get-AWSCredential –ListProfileDetail
    ProfileName StoreTypeName ProfileLocation**
    ----------- ------------- ---------------
    PackPubLinux SharedCredentialsFile /root/.aws/credentials

13. To specify the profile for the PowerShell session, run `Initialize-AWSDefaultconfiguration`:

    PS> Initialize-AWSDefaultConfiguration –ProfileName PackPubLinux

How it works...

All AWS PowerShell Tools cmdlets expect a set of the Access Key and the Secret Key to authenticate with AWS. While it is possible to specify the credentials whenever you run a cmdlet or set the credentials at a session level, this recipe helps you create a profile to access these AWS resources. First, you initialize the AWS profile by entering the necessary credentials and then setting the geographic location. Next, you store the credentials within the PacktPubLinux profile and bind it to the default configuration.

This is one of the recommended ways to access AWS resources, since it strikes a nice balance between security and convenience.

There's more...

To remove the profile, use the Remove-AWSCredentialProfile cmdlet:

```
PS> Remove-AWSCredentialProfile -ProfileName MyProfileName
```

See also

- Refer to the AWS document for credentials management (https://docs.aws. amazon.com/powershell/latest/userguide/specifying-your-aws- credentials.html).

Connecting an EC2 Linux instance using SSH from PowerShell

In this recipe, we will look at how we can access an EC2 instance from a Linux machine using SSH.

Getting ready

Before you connect to the Linux instance, make sure that you complete the following steps:

1. Ensure that the OpenSSH client is installed on your computer. By default, most Linux distribution include an SSH client.
2. Launch PowerShell and load the AWS PowerShell Core module.
3. Get the launch information from the AWS Service Portal.

How to do it...

The following instructions explain how to connect to an AWS Linux instance using the SSH client from the PowerShell console:

1. To get the instance details, run the `Get-EC2Instance` command:

```
PS> Get-EC2Instance -Region us-east-2
```

```
Specify region
Please choose one of the following regions to use or specify one by system name
[] <Specify a different region>  [] ap-northeast-1  [] ap-northeast-2  [] ap-south-1  [] ap-southeast-1
[] ap-southeast-2[] ca-central-1  [] eu-central-1  [] eu-west-1  [] eu-west-2  [] eu-west-3  [] sa-east-1
[] us-east-1[] us-east-2  [] us-west-1  [] us-west-2  [] cn-north-1  [] cn-northwest-1  [] us-gov-west-1
[?] Help(default is "<Specify a different region>"): us-east-2
PS /home/prashanth> Set-AWSCredential -AccessKey AKIAJUJDK3UZAN7T2JLA -SecretKey doAfusJg5wsXmEXgy3KEHPizUQXiF
PBQv1FpxIfa -StoreAs PackPubLinux
PS /home/prashanth> Get-AWSCredential -ListProfileDetail

ProfileName  StoreTypeName         ProfileLocation
-----------  -------------         ---------------
PackPubLinux SharedCredentialsFile /home/prashanth/.aws/credentials


PS /home/prashanth> Initialize-AWSDefaultConfiguration -ProfileName PackPubLinux
PS /home/prashanth> Get-EC2Instance -Region us-east-2


GroupNames    : {}
Groups        : {}
Instances     : {packtpub-linux}
OwnerId       : 024287841517
RequesterId   :
ReservationId : r-040a7b7e30e524a78


PS /home/prashanth>
```

2. While launching the instance, download the private key file.

3. Use the `chmod` command to make the private key file publicly viewable:

```
# chmod 400 ./Downloads/linuxdemo.pem
```

4. Use the `ssh` command to connect to the instance. You must specify the private key (`linuxdemo.pem`) and that `ec2-user` is the default user to access the Linux machine:

```
# ssh -i "./Downloads/linuxdemo.pem" ec2-user@ec2-18-191-134-57.us-east-2.compute.amazonaws.com
```

5. You will see the following response:

```
The authenticity of host 'ec2-18-191-134-57.us-
east-2.compute.amazonaws.com (18.191.134.57)' can't be established.
ECDSA key fingerprint is
SHA256:Osf4nkGaPkHpsLuT73MUxcXCkWLXLOJHFWlc4UN1kgQ.
ECDSA key fingerprint is
MD5:0c:9a:f0:c8:1c:66:94:c5:02:4b:9b:95:b5:d0:c3:24.
Are you sure you want to continue connecting (yes/no)? yes
Warning: Permanently added 'ec2-18-191-134-57.us-
east-2.compute.amazonaws.com,18.191.134.57' (ECDSA) to the list of
known hosts.

      __|  __|_  )
      _|  (  /  Amazon Linux AMI
     ___|\___|___|

https://aws.amazon.com/amazon-linux-ami/2018.03-release-notes/
11 package(s) needed for security, out of 13 available
```

6. Now, connect to the superuser mode using `sudo -s` and run the `update` command:

```
[ec2-user@ip-172-31-35-255 ~]$ sudo -s
[root@ip-172-31-35-255 ec2-user]# yum update
Loaded plugins: priorities, update-motd, upgrade-helper
Resolving Dependencies
--> Running transaction check
---> Package cloud-init.noarch 0:0.7.6-2.15.amzn1 will be updated
---> Package cloud-init.noarch 0:0.7.6-2.16.amzn1 will be an update
---> Package dhclient.x86_64 12:4.1.1-53.P1.27.amzn1 will be
updated
---> Package dhclient.x86_64 12:4.1.1-53.P1.28.amzn1 will be an
update
---> Package dhcp-common.x86_64 12:4.1.1-53.P1.27.amzn1 will be
updated
---> Package dhcp-common.x86_64 12:4.1.1-53.P1.28.amzn1 will be an
```

```
update
---> Package gnupg2.x86_64 0:2.0.28-1.30.amzn1 will be updated
---> Package gnupg2.x86_64 0:2.0.28-2.31.amzn1 will be an update
---> Package kernel.x86_64 0:4.14.47-56.37.amzn1 will be installed
---> Package ntp.x86_64 0:4.2.6p5-44.36.amzn1 will be updated
---> Package ntp.x86_64 0:4.2.8p11-2.38.amzn1 will be an update
---> Package ntpdate.x86_64 0:4.2.6p5-44.36.amzn1 will be updated
```

How it works...

This recipe uses the Linux `ssh` tool to connect to the remote EC2 instance that we created on AWS. First, we download the key pair to connect to the EC2 instance so that the SSH agent can use it, and then we use the `ssh` command to connect to the remote computer.

 Save the private key file in a safe place. Amazon EC2 does not keep a copy of your private key; therefore, if you lose the private key, there is no way to recover it.

As with any cloud resource, release the resources when the lab exercise is complete in order to avoid wastage and save costs.

This concludes this chapter regarding the overview of cloud operations on Microsoft Azure and Amazon Web Services using PowerShell.

16
Using PowerShell for SQL Database Management

In this chapter, we will cover the following recipes:

- Introduction to PowerShell, SQL Server, and Python
- Installing .Net Core on Linux
- Installing PowerShell Core on CentOS
- Installing the `SqlServer` module
- Overview of SQL Server SMO
- Running cross-platform T-SQL queries
- Running cross-platform T-SQL queries on multiple servers
- Creating a repository for Get-Process in SQL database
- Data formatting examples with PowerShell
- Overview of PowerShell, Bash, and Python integration

Introduction to PowerShell, SQL Server, and Python

Today, Microsoft claims that Linux runs like a first-class citizen on Azure. .NET Core has been open sourced, and has been ported over to Linux, taking PowerShell along with it. PowerShell runs really well on Ubuntu, CentOS, Red Hat Linux, and even macOS. In the last decade, since its birth, PowerShell has propelled automation extensively due to several of its qualities such as flexibility, dynamism, remoting capabilities, and modularity, not to mention being baked into the operating system.

SQL Server is one of the greatest benefactors of PowerShell, having several database management and automation capabilities built in. Ever since PowerShell, we've found it a lot easier to load the related modules and invoke the respective cmdlets to take care of several day-to-day activities, from simple querying to complex maintenance.

The `SqlServer` module allows SQL Server administrators and developers to automate server administration.

PowerShell is the prime candidate when it comes to scripting and automation in the world of Windows systems that are based on one of the main benefits of PowerShell, which is the deep integration with Windows APIs, and its general extensibility. The flexibility of PowerShell addresses most of the challenges we've had for several years in managing Windows systems. Today, PowerShell is available for Linux as well. In my opinion, it helps both Windows and Linux administrators go cross-platform. Perhaps the day has come that we can use both systems as if they were one.

Python has been around for a long time and is known for its simplicity, among several other fortes, which makes it one of the go-to languages for deep learning and machine learning. Despite the current popularity of PowerShell, Python, for SQL Server, is still a matter of preference for some professionals, as it does offer some compelling features and advantages:

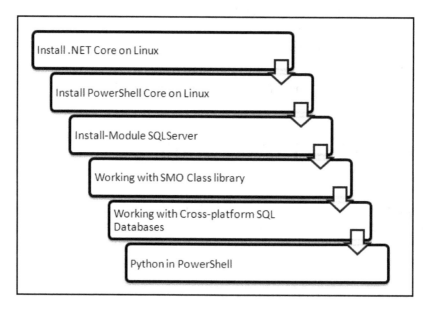

Technical requirements

Before getting into the recipes, let's understand the prerequisites and installation procedures that are required for the configuration of PowerShell Core and the SQL Server on Linux machines. You will need the following to complete this chapter:

- .Net Core
- PowerShell Core
- The `SqlServer` module for PowerShell
- Python

Installing .Net Core on Linux

The following installation procedures of .Net Core have been tested on the Linux distribution CentOS. This is a community-driven and supported free software platform, and the packages are compatible with its upstream **Red Hat Enterprise Linux (RHEL)** version.

First, let's install .Net Core before we configure PowerShell Core. PowerShell Core has an internal reference to the following components:

- It is dependent on .Net Core
- It relies on **.Net Core Runtime (.Net CR)**

Getting ready

Log in to the Linux machine and open the `sudo` console.

How to do it...

Follow these steps to install and configure .Net Core on Linux:

1. Register .NET Core. Before installing .NET, register the Microsoft signature key and add the Microsoft Product feed. This needs to be done once per machine.
2. Open a `sudo` Terminal and run the following commands:

```
# rpm --import https://packages.microsoft.com/keys/microsoft.asc
# sh -c 'echo -e "[packages-microsoft-com-prod]\nname=packages-
microsoft-com-prod \nbaseurl=
https://packages.microsoft.com/yumrepos/microsoft-rhel7.3-prod\nena
bled=1\ngpgcheck=1\ngpgkey=https://packages.microsoft.com/keys/micr
osoft.asc" > /etc/yum.repos.d/dotnetdev.repo'
```

3. Next, install the dependent components required by .Net by executing the following command:

```
# yum install libunwind libicu
```

4. Now, install .Net CR and .Net SDK by running the following command:

```
# yum install dotnet-runtime-2.0.6
# yum install dotnet-sdk-2.1.103
```

5. Verify the .Net metadata and installed version details by running the following command:

```
PS> dotnet --info
```

You should get an output similar to the following screenshot:

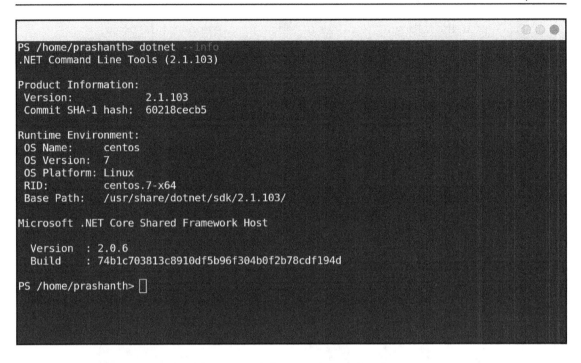

```
PS /home/prashanth> dotnet --info
.NET Command Line Tools (2.1.103)

Product Information:
 Version:           2.1.103
 Commit SHA-1 hash: 60218cecb5

Runtime Environment:
 OS Name:     centos
 OS Version:  7
 OS Platform: Linux
 RID:         centos.7-x64
 Base Path:   /usr/share/dotnet/sdk/2.1.103/

Microsoft .NET Core Shared Framework Host

  Version : 2.0.6
  Build   : 74b1c703813c8910df5b96f304b0f2b78cdf194d

PS /home/prashanth> []
```

5. Next, test .Net Core framework by running a simple test case.

6. Create a directory named PacktPub using the following mkdir command:

    # **mkdir PacktPub**

7. Change the pwd directory to PacktPub:

    # **cd PacktPub/**

8. Create a console application using the dotnet new console command:

    # **dotnet new console**

9. List the newly generated default programs using the ls command:

    # **ls**

10. Next, edit Program.cs using the available editors:

    # **nano Program.cs**

11. Type in the following few lines of code and save and exit the program:

```
using System;
namespace PacktPub
{
    class Program
    {
        static void Main(string[] args)
        {
            Console.WriteLine("Introduction to .Net Core on
Linux!");
        }
    }
}
```

12. Next, run the application using the `dotnet run` command:

```
# dotnet run
```

If you followed the preceding steps correctly, you will see the following output:

```
prashanth@packtpub:/home/prashanth/PacktPub

Running 'dotnet restore' on /home/prashanth/PacktPub/PacktPub.csproj...
  Restoring packages for /home/prashanth/PacktPub/PacktPub.csproj...
  Generating MSBuild file /home/prashanth/PacktPub/obj/PacktPub.csproj.nuget.g.props.
  Generating MSBuild file /home/prashanth/PacktPub/obj/PacktPub.csproj.nuget.g.targets.
  Restore completed in 165.84 ms for /home/prashanth/PacktPub/PacktPub.csproj.

Restore succeeded.

[root@packtpub PacktPub]# vim Program.cs
[root@packtpub PacktPub]# cat Program.cs
using System;
namespace PacktPub
{
    class Program
    {
        static void Main(string[] args)
        {
            Console.WriteLine("Introduction to .Net Core on Linux!");
        }
    }
}
[root@packtpub PacktPub]# dotnet run
Introduction to .Net Core on Linux!
[root@packtpub PacktPub]# []
```

How it works...

One of the main efforts that Microsoft has been working on is the development of .NET Core. .NET Core is a general-purpose development platform, maintained by Microsoft and the .NET community on GitHub. It is cross-platform, supports Windows, Mac iOS, and Linux, and is used in device, cloud, and **Internet of Things** (**IoT**) scenarios. One of the main characteristics of .NET Core is flexible deployment, that is, it can be included in your application, or installed side by side.

As mentioned previously, it's cross-platform. Therefore, it runs on Windows, macOS, and Linux, and it can be ported to other operating systems. As time goes on, there's going to be far more operating systems that support it. The command-line tools are much more powerful. All product scenarios can be exercised at the command-line level. There's also the compatibility factor. .NET Core is compatible with .NET Framework, Xamarin, Mono, and the .NET Standard Library, and lastly, it's open source.

The .NET Core platform uses the MIT and Apache 2 Licenses. To find out more about .NET Core, visit Microsoft's .NET Core page.

There's more...

The next step is to install PowerShell on your distribution. Refer to `Chapter 1`, *Introducing PowerShell Core,* for the steps to install PowerShell on your computer.

See also

To learn more about .Net code, visit Microsoft's .NET Core (`https://www.microsoft.com/net/learn/dotnet/hello-world-tutorial`) page. You can also refer to .NET core documentation (`https://docs.microsoft.com/en-us/dotnet/core/linux-prerequisites?tabs=netcore21`) for more details.

Installing the SqlServer module

This module allows SQL Server developers, administrators, and **business intelligence** (**BI**) professionals to automate database development and server administration, as well as both multidimensional and tabular cube processing.

There are two SQL Server PowerShell modules: SqlServer and SQLPS. The SQLPS module is included with the SQL Server installation (for backward compatibility), but is no longer being updated. The most up-to-date PowerShell module is the SqlServer module. The SqlServer module contains updated versions of the cmdlets in SQLPS, and also includes new cmdlets to support the latest SQL features. Previous versions of the SqlServer module were included with **SQL Server Management Studio** (**SSMS**), but only with the 16.x versions of SSMS. To use PowerShell with SSMS 17.0 and later, the SqlServer module must be installed from the PowerShell Gallery.

Getting ready

To install the SqlServer module, browse the PowerShell Gallery, which is the central repository for PowerShell content. Refer to the *Finding and installing PowerShell modules* recipe from Chapter 1, *Introducing PowerShell Core*, to find out more about modules.

How to do it...

To install modules, you will need to launch PowerShell with elevated privileges. Start PowerShell as a superuser, run the following script to install the module, and list out the cmdlets that are part of the module:

```
Set-PSRepository -Name PsGallery -InstallationPolicy Trusted

Install-Module SqlServer

if ((Get-Module -ListAvailable).Name -contains 'SqlServer') {
    Get-Command -CommandType Cmdlet | Where-Object Source -Match 'SQL' |
Group-Object Source
}
```

The SqlServer module should be installed and the cmdlets within the module should be shown, as follows:

```
PS /home/prashanth> Set-PSRepository -Name PsGallery -InstallationPolicy Trusted
PS /home/prashanth> Install-Module SqlServer
[]
 Installing package 'SqlServer'
    Downloaded 4.97 MB out of 24.78 MB.
    [oooooooooo                                                              ]
```

How it works...

This script is a simple one that sets `PsGallery` as a trusted source for modules, and installs the module.

Next, the script shows all of the cmdlets that are part of the `SqlServer` module.

There's more...

The goal of PowerShell Core is to remain as compatible as possible with Windows PowerShell. PowerShell Core uses .NET Standard 2.0 (`https://docs.microsoft.com/dotnet/standard/net-standard`) to provide binary compatibility with existing .NET assemblies. Many PowerShell modules depend on these assemblies (oftentimes DLLs), so .NET Standard allows them to continue working with .NET Core. PowerShell Core also includes a heuristic to look in well-known folders—such as where the **Global Assembly Cache** (**GAC**) typically resides on disk to find .NET Framework DLL dependencies.

See also

Refer to the PowerShell Gallery (`https://www.powershellgallery.com/packages/SqlServer/21.0.17199`) to find out more about the SQL Server package. You can also learn more about `Set-PSRepository` at `https://docs.microsoft.com/en-us/powershell/module/powershellget/set-psrepository?view=powershell-6`.

Overview of SQL Server SMO

SQL Server Management Objects (SMO) is a collection of objects that are designed for programming all aspects of managing Microsoft SQL Server. The SMO framework is a set of objects that have been designed for the programmatic management of **Microsoft SQL Server** and **Microsoft Azure SQL Database**.

SMO is further categorized into two classes: instance classes and utility classes.

SQL Server objects are represented by instance classes and explicit representation of tasks such as backup and restore, scripting, and object transfers. These are carried out by using the following utility classes:

- The `Microsoft.SqlServer.Management.Smo` namespace contains classes that represent the core SQL Server Database Engine objects. These include instances, databases, tables, stored procedures, and views.
- The `Microsoft.SqlServer.Management.Sdk.Sfc` namespace contains a set of classes that form an inheritance base for other SQL Server Management namespaces, such as `Microsoft.SqlServer.Management.Smo`. Do not reference this member directly in your code. It supports the SQL Server infrastructure.
- The `Microsoft.SqlServer.ConnectionInfo` namespace contains a set of classes that have support for connecting to an instance of SQL Server. This gets or sets the Boolean property (`https://docs.microsoft.com/en-us/dotnet/api/system.boolean?redirectedfrom=MSDNview=netframework-4.7.2`) that specifies whether the connection is established to the server by using Windows Authentication or SQL Server Authentication.
- Namespaces such as `Microsoft.SqlServer.SmoExtended` and `Microsoft.SqlServer.SqlEnum` contain the class libraries or APIs that support SMO classes.

- The `Microsoft.SqlServer.Management.PSProvider` namespace implements the SQL Server PowerShell provider and associated cmdlets such as `Encode-SqlName` and `Decode-SqlName`.
- The `Microsoft.SqlServer.Management.PSSnapin` namespace implements the `Invoke-Sqlcmd` and `Invoke-PolicyEvaluation` cmdlets.

The different stages of the SMO object creation and instantiation are as follows:

1. Create an instance of the object
2. Set the object properties
3. Create instances of the child objects
4. Set the child object properties
5. Create the object

How to do it...

1. Install and load the `SqlServer` modules on a Linux machine by following the *Finding and installing PowerShell modules* recipe from `Chapter 1`, *Introducing PowerShell Core*.
2. Import the module into the session using `Import-Module`.
3. To find out whether the installation went through, call the `AppDomain.GetAssemblies()` method. The `AppDomain.GetAssemblies` method gets the assemblies that have been loaded into the execution context of this application domain:

```
PS> [AppDomain]::CurrentDomain.GetAssemblies() | where FullName -
match "SQL" | sort-object -property fullname | format-table
fullname
PS> [AppDomain]::CurrentDomain.GetAssemblies() | where FullName -
match "SQL" | Select-Object -ExpandProperty Location
```

The output of the preceding PowerShell code is as follows:

```
PS /home/prashanth> [AppDomain]::CurrentDomain.GetAssemblies() | Where-Object FullName -Match 'sql' | Select-O
bject -ExpandProperty Location
/usr/local/share/powershell/Modules/SqlServer/21.0.17279/coreclr/Microsoft.SqlServer.Management.PSSnapins.dll
/usr/local/share/powershell/Modules/SqlServer/21.0.17279/coreclr/Microsoft.SqlServer.ConnectionInfo.dll
/usr/local/share/powershell/Modules/SqlServer/21.0.17279/coreclr/Microsoft.SqlServer.Management.Sdk.Sfc.dll
/usr/local/share/powershell/Modules/SqlServer/21.0.17279/coreclr/Microsoft.SqlServer.SmoExtended.dll
/usr/local/share/powershell/Modules/SqlServer/21.0.17279/coreclr/Microsoft.SqlServer.SqlEnum.dll
/usr/local/share/powershell/Modules/SqlServer/21.0.17279/coreclr/Microsoft.SqlServer.Smo.dll
/opt/microsoft/powershell/6/System.Data.SqlClient.dll
/usr/local/share/powershell/Modules/SqlServer/21.0.17279/coreclr/Microsoft.SqlServer.Management.PSProvider.dll
PS /home/prashanth>
```

See also

- Find out more about SMO (https://docs.microsoft.com/en-us/sql/
  relational-databases/server-management-objects-smo/overview-smo?view=
  sql-server-2017).

Running cross-platform T-SQL queries

Thus far, we've seen the steps for loading and configuring SQL Server SMO assembly.
Now, let's learn how to expand the cross-platform querying experience using PowerShell
Core.

Getting ready

Instantiate the `Microsoft.SqlServer.Management.Smo.Server` class by creating an object. You can create this object using the code:

```
PS> New-Object Microsoft.SqlServer.Management.Smo.Server <SQL InstanceName>
```

How to do it...

Let's connect to a SQL Server instance on a Windows machine from a Linux machine using the SMO object by performing the following steps:

1. Import the `SqlServer` module.
2. Assign an instance name to a variable called `$SQLServer`.
3. Initiate the SQL Server object's instantiation for the `Microsoft.SqlServer.Managament.Smo.Server` class.
4. Define the username and password using `Get-Credential` cmdlets.
5. Build the SQL Server connection.
6. Retrieve the properties of a Windows SQL instance on Linux.
7. Format the result set. The following script takes care of the aforementioned tasks:

```
$SQLServer='hqdbt01'
$SQLServerObject=New-Object
Microsoft.SqlServer.Management.Smo.Server $SQLServer
$SQLServerObject.ConnectionContext.LoginSecure=$false
$SQLServerObject.ConnectionContext.set_login("SA")
$SQLServerObject.ConnectionContext.set_Password("PackPub@2018")
$SQLServerObject.Information | Select-Object FullyQualifiedNetName,
Parent, Version, Edition | Format-Table -AutoSize
```

How it works...

The first database name is being assigned to a variable named `$SQLServer`. In this case, `hqdbt01` is assigned to the variable. Then, create an instance of the object using the `Microsoft.SqlServer.Management.Smo.Server` namespace. In the next step, set the object properties based on the authentication type. In this case, the Windows SQL instance is being accessed using mixed-mode authentication. So, set the `ConnectionContext.loginsecure` property of the Server object to `$false`. This enables the SQL Server to use mixed-mode authentication. This is creating child objects for the parent-object Server property. You'll need to explicitly specify the username and password to build the connection. After logging in using the username and password, the hardcoded values are passed to the `set_login` and `set_password` methods to build a successful connection.

Now, select specific columns from the information and format them into a table by using the `Select-Object` and `Format-Table` cmdlets.

Running cross-platform T-SQL queries on multiple servers

This recipe describes how to run a query on multiple instances of SQL Server on multiple platforms. Managing multiple servers on this cross-platform operating system has always had its own challenges.

Getting ready

Let's get started by capturing the server's details in an input CSV file:

1. Prepare the input file with instance and credentials details, separated by a comma:

   ```
   InstanceName,UserName,Password
   10.2.6.50,SA,whoVista@2018
   10.2.6.55,SA,whoVista@2019
   ```

2. Save the PowerShell script in a file and open the PowerShell Core console to execute the PowerShell script file.

How to do it...

In this recipe, we'll list all the SQL-Instances, along with the necessary credentials in a CSV file, by performing the following steps:

1. Explicitly load the `SqlServer` module.
2. Read the CSV fields using `Import-CSV` cmdlets.
3. Start the iteration using `Foreach-Object`.
4. Build a secure connection string with the `System.Management.Automation.PSCredential` class.
5. Instantiate the SQL Server `Microsoft.SqlServer.Management.Smo.Server` class library by creating an object.
6. Build the connection to the SQL instance.
7. Create a subobject for the main object to create a database named `PacktPub` on all the defined SQL instances.
8. Handle the exception using the `try`, `catch`, and `finally` clauses.
9. Close the connection.
10. Repeat the iteration until it reaches the end of the line. The following script takes care of the aforementioned tasks:

```
#Replace the path of the input file
$filepath ='./Input.csv'
#Import the SqlServer module
Import-Module -Name SqlServer

#Read the CSV file content using Import-CSV cmdlet
Import-Csv -Path $filepath|ForEach-Object {

#The Linux SQL Instance IP Address
$SQLServer=$_.InstanceName

#Define credential details
$User=$_.Username

#Convert password text to a secure string
$Pass=ConvertTo-SecureString $_.Password -AsPlainText -Force

#Build the credential using securing string
$cred=New-Object -TypeName
System.Management.Automation.PSCredential -ArgumentList $User,$Pass
$SQLServerObject=New-Object
Microsoft.SqlServer.Management.Smo.Server $SQLServer
$SQLServerObject.ConnectionContext.LoginSecure=$false
```

```
$SQLServerObject.ConnectionContext.set_login($cred.Username)
$SQLServerObject.ConnectionContext.set_SecurePassword($cred.Passwor
d)

#Handle the exceptions using Try and Catch method
try
    {    #Build connection to the Local SQL Instance
     $SQLServerObject.ConnectionContext.connect()
     $db=New-Object Microsoft.SqlServer.Management.Smo.Database
$SQLServerObject,'PacktPub'
     $db.Create()
     }
catch
     {
     #Write the exception message
     write-Error $_.Exception.message
     }
finally
     {
     #Close the connection
     $SQLServerObject.ConnectionContext.Disconnect()
     }
}
```

How it works...

In this topic, the database named PackPub is created on the entire listed instances of the CSV file. The CSV file provides the required data to build and manipulate the SQL instances. The reading of the CSV file is done through the Import-Csv cmdlet. The CSV file has Linux and Windows SQL instance IP addresses.

The Import-Csv cmdlet reads the text from the CSV file. To manipulate SQL Server instances and its objects programmatically, first, we need to instantiate the SMO class libraries by creating an object. The main object is created and referred for the instance type using the Microsoft.SqlServer.Management.Smo.Server namespace, like so:

```
$SQLServerObject=New-Object Microsoft.SqlServer.Management.Smo.Server
$SQLServer
```

The connection is built using a SQL login, and the credentials are managed via the System.Management.Automation.PSCredential class:

```
$cred=New-Object -TypeName System.Management.Automation.PSCredential -
ArgumentList $User,$Pass
```

After reading a CSV file, the text inputs are parsed to convert the password text into a secure string. The username is passed to the `set_Login` method and the password, a `SecureString` type, is passed to `set_SecurePassword`:

```
$SQLServerObject.ConnectionContext.LoginSecure=$false
$SQLServerObject.ConnectionContext.set_login($cred.Username)
$SQLServerObject.ConnectionContext.set_SecurePassword($cred.Password)
```

The `try`, `catch`, and `finally` clauses give you the flexibility to handle the error in an efficient manner. The trapping mechanism is used to catch any errors in the scope of the current script's execution.

The `try` block has some code that establishes the connection to an SQL instance and creates a database named `PacktPub` using the subobject, `$db`, which is created for the main object, `$SQLServerObject`.

To verify the output, connect to SQL instances using `sqlcmd`, or SSMS and query the database:

```
Select name from sys.databases where name='PacktPub'
```

See also

- `Get-Help about_Try_Catch_Finally`

- The *Overview of SQL Server SMO* recipe of this chapter

Creating a repository for Get-Process in the SQL database

In the real world, administrators store system metrics at regular intervals, since they are crucial for forensic reporting and troubleshooting. In this recipe, we'll discuss how to store the output of a cmdlet in a table.

Getting ready

Let's complete the following configuration to load the data into the table via the following steps:

1. Install the `SqlServer` module
2. Prepare the script using Visual Studio Code or nano, or any other available editors
3. Save the script by changing the instance and credential details

How to do it...

In this recipe, we will discuss the ways we can store the cmdlet data in the repository:

1. Import the `SqlServer` module. This module provides a platform to run and operate system-related cmdlets and stores the output directly in the database objects.
2. Define the target instance to the repository.
3. Specify the credentials to connect to the SQL instance.
4. Convert the plain password text into a `SecureString` type.
5. Build the secured connecting string using the `System.Management.Automation.PSCredential` assembly.
6. Use the pipe to pass the `Get-Process` cmdlet output as an object to the `Write-SqlTableData` cmdlet. The following script takes care of the aforementioned tasks.
7. Now, save the following content in the `DataLoading.PS1` file:

```
#Import the SqlServer Module
Import-Module -Name Sqlserver
#The Linux SQL Instance IP Address
$SQLServer='10.2.6.50'
#Define credential details
$User='SA'
#Convert password text to a secure string
$Pass=ConvertTo-SecureString 'thanVitha@2015' -AsPlainText -Force
#Build the credetial using securing string
$cred=New-Object -TypeName
System.Management.Automation.PSCredential -ArgumentList $User,$Pass
(Get-Process | Select-Object -Property `
Id,ProcessName,StartTime,UserProcessorTime,WorkingSet,Description)
| `
```

```
Write-SqlTableData -Credential $cred -ServerInstance "localhost" -
DatabaseName `
"PacktPub" -SchemaName "dbo" -TableName "TaskManagerDump" -Force
```

How it works...

This recipe gathers information about processes that run on a remote machine and writes it to a table. `Write-SqlTableData` writes the data into `PacktPub.dbo.TaskManagerDump` on a local instance of the Linux machine. In this case, `PacktPub` is the database name and `TaskManagerDump` is the name of the table.

On specifying the `force` parameter, it checks for the existence of the `TaskManagerDump` table on the `PacktPub` database. In the case of its absence, the table will be created.

The following script is executed to pull the data into the table:

```
$ /usr/bin/pwsh -c  'cd /tmp; ./DataLoading.PS1'
```

The same script can also be run on any tool, such as Azure Data Studio.

Data formatting examples with PowerShell

Before getting into the formatting examples, let's read a dataset from the table using .NET class libraries. PowerShell always works seamlessly with .NET integration. PowerShell has a set of cmdlets that allow you to control which properties are displayed for particular objects.

Getting ready

Let's get started with the following configuration:

1. Prepare the dataset using .NET class libraries
2. Run the script from the PowerShell console
3. Work with the output using format cmdlets

How to do it...

In this section, we'll discuss the steps to perform data formatting on the sample data:

1. Define the variables.
2. Prepare the database connection string.
3. Instantiate the `System.Data.SqlClient.SqlConnection` .NET class library.
4. Open the connection, and the instance will be ready to use.
5. Prepare the SQL query to run on the defined connection.
6. Create a subobject called `$cmd` for the main object `$ConnStr`.
7. Execute the SQL using the `ExecuteReader()` method.
8. Load the result set into the table variable.
9. Format the output with the formatting cmdlets.
10. The following script takes care of the aforementioned tasks. Now, save the following content in the `/tmp/DataFormatSample.ps1` file:

```
#Define Input variables
$dataSource = "10.2.6.50"
#Define the login credentials for SQL authentication
$user = "SA"
$pwd = "thanVitha@2015"
#Define the database name from which the data is going to be read
$database = "PacktPub"
#Build the connection string
$connStr = "Server=$dataSource;uid=$user;
pwd=$pwd;Database=$database;Integrated Security=False;"
#Prepare the query
$query = "SELECT * FROM TaskManagerDump"
#Instantiate the sqlConnection namespace
$Conn = New-Object System.Data.SqlClient.SqlConnection
$Conn.ConnectionString = $connStr
#Open the connection
$Conn.Open()
#Create sub-objects to the Main object $Conn
$cmd = $Conn.CreateCommand()
#Assign the Query text to a $command object
$cmd.CommandText = $query
#Execute the adapter
$resultset = $cmd.ExecuteReader()
#Create an object DataTable namespace
$table = new-object "System.Data.DataTable"
#Load the data to the table
$table.Load($resultset)
$table |Where-Object {$_.ProcessName -match "pwsh"}
```

```
#$table |Where-Object {$_.ProcessName -match "pwsh"} | format-table
-autosize
#$table |Where-Object {$_.ProcessName -match "pwsh"} | format-list
#$table |Where-Object {$_.ProcessName -match "pwsh"} | format-table
$format
#$table | Where-Object {$_.ProcessName -match "pwsh"}| format-table
$format | Out-File /tmp/output.txt
$Conn.Close()
```

How it works...

In this section, let's discuss the various available methods to format table output. .NET libraries are used to invoke SQL to read data from a SQL instance. The steps include building a connection string; preparing the T-SQL; creating the dataset; creating the `DataAdapter`, and filling the `DataAdapter`. Once data is in `DataTable`, you can transform the data in several ways by using PowerShell pipe concepts, along with the built-in cmdlets.

Let's dive deep into the .NET Class libraries to understand more about querying SQL Server. The class libraries are further divided into Connected classes and Disconnected classes. Let's look at these in detail:

- **Connected classes**: Using connected architecture, you can connect to the database, gather data, and close the connection:
    - `SqlConnection`: Connects to the SQL Server .NET data provider in order to establish and manage the connection to the target database.
    - `SqlCommand`: Contains the details necessary to issue a T-SQL command against a SQL Server database.
    - `SqlDataAdapter`: Provides a bridge between the connected classes and disconnected classes. This class includes the Fill and Update methods. Use the `Fill` method to populate a `DataSet` or `DataTable` object. Use the `Update` method to propagate the updated data in a `DataSet` or `DataTable` object to the database.
- **Disconnected classes**: Using disconnected architecture, you can build a connection to the database, get all the data into an object, and reuse the same connection, if needed:
    - `DataTable`: Stores the data returned by your query. The data is stored in rows and columns, similar to how data is stored in a database table.

The output of the Powershell script is stored in a variable called $table:

```
PS> $table=/tmp/DataFormatSample.PS1
PS> $table
```

Using the Format-Table option, the output is displayed as a table. When the number of properties increases, the output becomes nearly impossible to understand. In such a case, the output can be handled better using the Wrap parameter:

```
PS> $table=/tmp/DataFormatSample.PS1
PS> $table |Format-Table
PS> $table |Format-Table -AutoSize
```

In the following example, the columns are overridden with a custom value. Each column is defined with the definite width, and the values of the fields are displayed based on the defined property:

```
PS> $format = @{Expression={$_.Id};Label="ProcessId";width=5},
>> @{Expression={$_.ProcessName};Label="Name"; width=4},
>> @{l="WS";e={$_.WorkingSet/1024};width=10},
>> @{l="StartTime";e={$_.StartTime};width=20},
>> @{l="UserProcessorTime";e={$_.UserProcessorTime};width=20}
PS> $table|Format-Table $format
```

Using the Format-List clause, the output is displayed as a list of properties in which each property appears on a new line:

```
PS> $table=/tmp/DataFormatSample.PS1
PS> $table |Format-List
```

By using the sort-object cmdlet, the sort operation is based on the listed column's property value. In the following example, the WorkingSet column is sorted in descending order:

```
PS> /tmp/DataFormatSample.PS1|Sort-Object WorkingSet -Descending|Format-
Table -AutoSize
```

The Select-Object cmdlet creates new, custom objects that contain the properties from the objects you use to create them:

```
PS> /tmp/DataFormatSample.PS1|Select-Object -Last 2
PS> /tmp/DataFormatSample.PS1|Select-Object -First 2
```

Overview of PowerShell, Bash, and Python integration

Python has several strong points, which makes it worthy of attention. Apart from being a **Free and Open Source Software (FOSS)**, it is, far more significantly, easy to learn. It is also easy to read, even for people who are not Python programmers. Python is capable of being used to write full-scale applications and server software, but as database administrators, we'll find it more interesting that it is very handy when it comes to writing quick utility scripts.

PowerShell's love with the Microsoft community is significant and we use it every day, but there's an entirely new world out there in the open source land. Linux is also a thriving community with a great set of tools and products to manage things more efficiently. In Linux arenas, when it comes to scripting, PowerShell is the weakling on the block. The big boys of scripting in Linux are Python and Perl. Although PowerShell and these languages are all technically cross-platform, it's clear that each language has its dominant audience.

Of course, SQL database administrators have already been taking advantage of PowerShell to manage databases and database servers, and those non-SQL administrators might have an upper hand with Python. However, when there are multiple ways of managing SQL servers, it cannot hurt to know more than one way to achieve near-perfect administration via APIs.

PowerShell Core is not meant to replace Python or any other Linux technology. I feel that it is a good companion tool to use in combination with Python. It's just another efficient way to extract and manipulate data as objects using the available .NET libraries and when creating automation solutions.

Getting ready

To get started, open the Linux Terminal and type in the `pwsh` command to open the PowerShell console.

How to do it...

This recipe has a few samples so that you can understand PowerShell Core shell support for Python. The shell also supports any other programming languages such as Ruby, Perl, and so on.

In this case, let's look at a few Python script samples for beginners:

1. To execute a Python script from the PowerShell console, type in the following command:

```
PS> python -c "print('Welcome to PowerShell and Python!') "
```

2. In this sample, you'll see the use of expressions and the integration of Python output with Powershell. The firstPython.py file has the following content. It has two arguments, that is, first and second. The first argument is referred to by argv[1] and the second is referred to by argv[2]. The values will be passed to arguments during the runtime. The output is then integrated with PowerShell values:

```
#!/usr/bin/pythonimport
sysfirst=sys.argv[1]
second=sys.argv[2]
print(float(first)+float(second))
```

The output is then integrated with integer values:

```
PS> 3+ (python ./FirstPython.py 2 3) +5
8
```

3. This example is of a Python script using here-string and no-file-extension. here-string is used to declare a block of text. It is very helpful for making a string of text an executable command. The text is encoded in ASCII format so that it can be read by search programs such as Findstr and Grep:

```
PS> @">> #!/usr/bin/python
>> import sys
>> print(float(sys.argv[1])*float(sys.argv[2]))
>> "@|Out-File -Encoding ascii multiply
```

4. Change the file permission into an executable by using chmod +x:

```
PS>chmod +x ./multiply
```

5. Invoke the file in the PowerShell console by executing the following command:

```
PS> ./multiply 2 36
```

How it works...

In this recipe, you've seen very basic sample scripts for Python—things like printing text, passing arguments to a file and integrating output to a variable, and the use of `here-string`. You also saw how to put it all together in the PowerShell console. Python is an extremely powerful programming language. You can get started almost immediately, with minimal setup required. It is cross-platform, which means that it can run on most major operating systems including, of course, Linux, Windows, and macOS, since you don't have to modify your code at all. This is a beginner-friendly recipe. If you have at least some basic general programming knowledge, you can explore this option to greater heights.

Using PowerShell with Docker

17

In this chapter, we are going to cover the following recipes:

- Installation of Docker on Linux
- Getting and listing the Docker management cmdlets
- Overview of Docker Hub and its operations
- Building an image from a Dockerfile using PowerShell
- Pulling a Docker container image from the repository
- Listing Docker containers and the images
- Starting and stopping Docker containers
- Removing containers and container images
- Working with a container using miscellaneous Docker PowerShell cmdlets
- Running a PowerShell script to set up Docker containers
- Finding Docker tags using PowerShell cmdlets from the remote registry

Introduction to Docker

Containerization has become increasingly popular of late. It could be said that the concept came as a reaction to the it-works-on-my-machine issue, which is prevalent in every organization and deals with software development. Containerization aims at a few goals, such as the abstraction of libraries and the elimination of the hypervisor in order to improve application performance, scalability (scaling out), application portability, and so on. Docker popularized the concept of containerization.

Docker containers pack everything that is needed to run a project: services, libraries, networking, storage, and code… it even packs protocols that the system needs to run the application. In other words, all of the dependencies that are required for an application to run are bundled into a single container so that there is no external dependency. Docker uses images. These can be thought of as snapshots that contain the specifications of the aforementioned entities that are required to run an application. Metaphorically, we could think of the Docker image as classes, and a container as an object instantiation of a Docker image process that runs on the Docker host. It is isolated from other running processes on the machine—just like creating one or more objects for a class.

Docker has a social community platform that allows you to share your images with others, or use a container that's been built by someone else but that meets the requirements of your application. This makes the Docker containers highly portable—theoretically, they run no matter where you throw them.

Developers typically update the container images during every version upgrade.

PowerShell is available as a Docker image as well. It runs on every Linux distribution that PowerShell supports, and Docker runs on. The Docker image is available at `https://hub.docker.com/r/microsoft/powershell/`. This aids in testing PowerShell on any Linux distribution that supports Docker, without having to install PowerShell first. Also, now that PowerShell is cross-platform, you could run the Docker image on multiple computers running different operating systems, and test your PowerShell scripts on all of them!

Before we try out the recipes, let's look at the different definitions pertaining to Docker:

- A Docker image is the filesystem and application configuration used to create containers
- A Docker container is the running instance of a Docker image
- A Docker daemon is the background service running on the host machine that manages Docker containers
- A Docker client is the command-line interface that allows the user to interact with the Docker daemon
- A Docker Store is a registry of Docker images

Installation of Docker on Linux

On Linux, the installation procedures are simple and straightforward. This recipe will help you set up Docker on CentOS, using the latest Docker `.rpm` package, which will be installed using `yum`.

Getting ready

Getting ready to install Docker on the host machine is simple. You simply need a working Linux computer, and you must have the root user credentials.

How to do it...

To install the Docker engine on Linux, follow these steps:

1. Go to `https://download.docker.com/linux/centos/7/x86_64/stable/Packages/` to download the latest `.rpm` file for the version of Docker you want to install.
2. Save the `docker-ce*.rpm` file in a convenient location. In this case, the file is saved to the default Downloads directory.
3. Log in to the Terminal with a user with superuser privileges:

```
$ su
Password:
```

4. Install the RPM package using the `yum install` command. Specify the complete path to where the RPM file is:

```
# yum install /home/prashanth/Downloads/docker-
ce-18.03.1.ce-1.el7.centos.x86_64.rpm -y
```

```
                                    prashanth@galago:~
Total download size: 102 k
Installed size: 151 M
Downloading packages:
(1/2): pigz-2.3.3-1.el7.centos.x86_64.rpm                |  68 kB   00:00
(2/2): container-selinux-2.55-1.el7.noarch.rpm                          |  34 kB  00:00:10
---------------------------------------------------------------------------------
Total                                                    9.7 kB/s | 102 kB  00:00:10
Running transaction check
Running transaction test
Transaction test succeeded
Running transaction
  Installing : pigz-2.3.3-1.el7.centos.x86_64                                    1/3
  Installing : 2:container-selinux-2.55-1.el7.noarch                            2/3
  Installing : docker-ce-18.03.1.ce-1.el7.centos.x86_64                         3/3

  Verifying  : docker-ce-18.03.1.ce-1.el7.centos.x86_64                         1/3

  Verifying  : 2:container-selinux-2.55-1.el7.noarch                            2/3

  Verifying  : pigz-2.3.3-1.el7.centos.x86_64                                   3/3


Installed:
  docker-ce.x86_64 0:18.03.1.ce-1.el7.centos


Dependency Installed:
  container-selinux.noarch 2:2.55-1.el7              pigz.x86_64 0:2.3.3-1.el7.centos

Complete!
[root@packtpub ~]#
```

5. Once the installation is complete, verify the package information to ensure that the right package was installed:

   `# yum info docker`

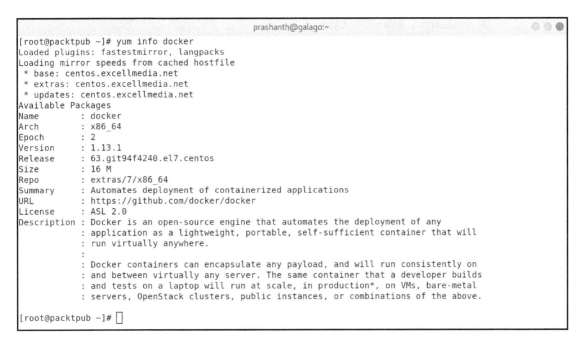

```
                              prashanth@galago:~

[root@packtpub ~]# yum info docker
Loaded plugins: fastestmirror, langpacks
Loading mirror speeds from cached hostfile
 * base: centos.excellmedia.net
 * extras: centos.excellmedia.net
 * updates: centos.excellmedia.net
Available Packages
Name        : docker
Arch        : x86_64
Epoch       : 2
Version     : 1.13.1
Release     : 63.git94f4240.el7.centos
Size        : 16 M
Repo        : extras/7/x86_64
Summary     : Automates deployment of containerized applications
URL         : https://github.com/docker/docker
License     : ASL 2.0
Description : Docker is an open-source engine that automates the deployment of any
            : application as a lightweight, portable, self-sufficient container that will
            : run virtually anywhere.
            :
            : Docker containers can encapsulate any payload, and will run consistently on
            : and between virtually any server. The same container that a developer builds
            : and tests on a laptop will run at scale, in production*, on VMs, bare-metal
            : servers, OpenStack clusters, public instances, or combinations of the above.

[root@packtpub ~]# 
```

6. Get the status of the Docker service using the `systemctl` command:

   `# systemctl status docker`

```
                              prashanth@galago:~

[root@packtpub ~]# systemctl status docker
● docker.service - Docker Application Container Engine
   Loaded: loaded (/usr/lib/systemd/system/docker.service; disabled; vendor preset: disabled)
   Active: inactive (dead)
     Docs: https://docs.docker.com
[root@packtpub ~]# ▌
```

7. The service is disabled. To enable and start the Docker service use the
`systemctl` command again, with the appropriate parameters, use the following
commands:

```
# systemctl enable docker
# systemctl start docker
# systemctl status docker
```

```
                              prashanth@galago:~                              ○ ○ ●
[root@packtpub ~]# systemctl status docker
● docker.service - Docker Application Container Engine
   Loaded: loaded (/usr/lib/systemd/system/docker.service; enabled; vendor preset: disabled)
   Active: active (running) since Tue 2018-06-12 11:59:08 IST; 18min ago
     Docs: https://docs.docker.com
 Main PID: 13411 (dockerd)
   CGroup: /system.slice/docker.service
           ├─13411 /usr/bin/dockerd
           └─13423 docker-containerd --config /var/run/docker/containerd/containerd.toml

Jun 12 11:59:08 packtpub dockerd[13411]: time="2018-06-12T11:59:08+05:30" level=info msg=serving... a...rp
c"
Jun 12 11:59:08 packtpub dockerd[13411]: time="2018-06-12T11:59:08+05:30" level=info msg="containerd ...ne
rd
Jun 12 11:59:08 packtpub dockerd[13411]: time="2018-06-12T11:59:08.197539053+05:30" level=info msg="G...nd
s"
Jun 12 11:59:08 packtpub dockerd[13411]: time="2018-06-12T11:59:08.198680128+05:30" level=info msg="L...rt
."
Jun 12 11:59:08 packtpub dockerd[13411]: time="2018-06-12T11:59:08.482780688+05:30" level=info msg="D...es
s"
Jun 12 11:59:08 packtpub dockerd[13411]: time="2018-06-12T11:59:08.685890880+05:30" level=info msg="L...ne
."
Jun 12 11:59:08 packtpub dockerd[13411]: time="2018-06-12T11:59:08.712025795+05:30" level=info msg="D...1-
ce
Jun 12 11:59:08 packtpub dockerd[13411]: time="2018-06-12T11:59:08.712191337+05:30" level=info msg="D...io
n"
Jun 12 11:59:08 packtpub dockerd[13411]: time="2018-06-12T11:59:08.719228572+05:30" level=info msg="A...oc
k"
Jun 12 11:59:08 packtpub systemd[1]: Started Docker Application Container Engine.
Hint: Some lines were ellipsized, use -l to show in full.
[root@packtpub ~]# ▮
```

8. Test the Docker engine services by running a container. To run a container, use
the `docker run` command. In this example, we'll use the `hello-world`
container image. If the image is not present on your computer, it will be
downloaded from the Docker library:

```
# docker run hello-world
```

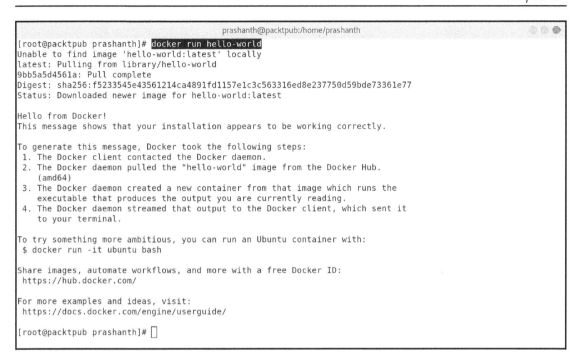

```
                              prashanth@packtpub:/home/prashanth
[root@packtpub prashanth]# docker run hello-world
Unable to find image 'hello-world:latest' locally
latest: Pulling from library/hello-world
9bb5a5d4561a: Pull complete
Digest: sha256:f5233545e43561214ca4891fd1157e1c3c563316ed8e237750d59bde73361e77
Status: Downloaded newer image for hello-world:latest

Hello from Docker!
This message shows that your installation appears to be working correctly.

To generate this message, Docker took the following steps:
 1. The Docker client contacted the Docker daemon.
 2. The Docker daemon pulled the "hello-world" image from the Docker Hub.
    (amd64)
 3. The Docker daemon created a new container from that image which runs the
    executable that produces the output you are currently reading.
 4. The Docker daemon streamed that output to the Docker client, which sent it
    to your terminal.

To try something more ambitious, you can run an Ubuntu container with:
 $ docker run -it ubuntu bash

Share images, automate workflows, and more with a free Docker ID:
 https://hub.docker.com/

For more examples and ideas, visit:
 https://docs.docker.com/engine/userguide/

[root@packtpub prashanth]# 
```

How it works...

Installing Docker directly on a Linux machine is comparatively easier than installing it on other platforms such as macOS or Windows because there's no need to set up a virtual toolbox or machine to run Docker on Linux; you can run it directly on your localhost. The Docker installation documentation page has several sections covering the installation procedure for various Linux distributions. In this recipe, though, we recommend installing Docker via the repository.

Once the installation is complete, we need to check the status of the Docker daemon. The `systemctl status` command provides required information about the status of the service/process, including the PID and the memory consumed. We use the `systemctl enable` and `systemctl start` commands to enable and start the Docker daemon. The status loaded indicates that the file unit has been loaded into memory. It also lists the path to the unit file and shows its state. The `systemctl enable` command enables the daemon to start at the boot of the machine.

Finally, we run the `hello-world` container image to test the Docker engine services. If the image is not locally present, `docker run` automatically downloads the image from the Docker library and runs the container. The message **Hello from Docker!** indicates that the Docker client did contact the Docker engine daemon to build a container using the downloaded image.

See also

- Installing Docker from a package (`https://docs.docker.com/install/linux/docker-ce/centos/#install-from-a-package`)

Getting and listing the Docker management cmdlets

Docker containers and the Docker engine itself can be managed using PowerShell. The Docker PowerShell module builds on top of the Docker Engine's REST API interface, enabling the user to choose between Docker CLI and PowerShell to manage their Docker operations. Administrators can even use a combination of the two.

This recipe shows you how to install the Docker module and list out its cmdlets. To know what each cmdlet does, follow the recipes in `Chapter 1`, *Introducing PowerShell Core*.

Getting ready

You must have PowerShell installed on your computer (which should be the case given that you are this far into the book). If you would like the module to be installed system-wide, you also need superuser access.

How to do it...

Let's now begin by installing the Docker module and getting its capabilities:

1. Open the Terminal. At the prompt, type `pwsh` to launch PowerShell. If you would like the module installed system-wide, launch `pwsh` with `sudo`.

2. At the PowerShell prompt, type in the following command:

```
PS> Find-Module Docker
```

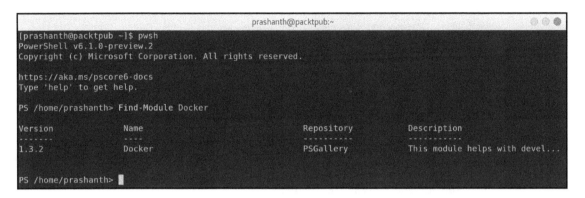

3. There's a module called `Docker` available in PSGallery. Let's get its description:

```
PS> (Find-Module Docker).Description
```

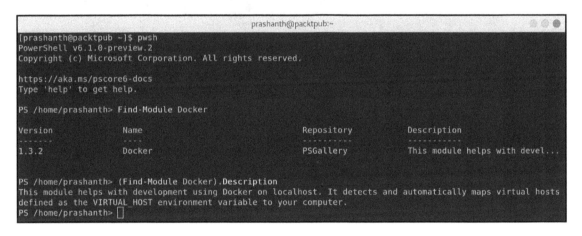

This is the module we want.

4. Go ahead and install the module:

   PS> Install-Module Docker

```
PS /home/prashanth> Install-Module Docker

Untrusted repository
You are installing the modules from an untrusted repository. If you trust this repository, change its
InstallationPolicy value by running the Set-PSRepository cmdlet. Are you sure you want to install the modules
from 'PSGallery'?
[Y] Yes  [A] Yes to All  [N] No  [L] No to All  [S] Suspend  [?] Help (default is "N"): Y
PS /home/prashanth> []
```

5. Once the installation completes, list out the cmdlets that are available in the Docker module:

   PS> Get-Command -Module Docker

```
PS /home/prashanth> Get-Command -Module Docker

CommandType     Name                          Version    Source
-----------     ----                          -------    ------
Function        Install-Docker                1.3.2      Docker
Function        Invoke-DockerCommand          1.3.2      Docker
Function        Invoke-DockerComposeCommand   1.3.2      Docker
Function        Set-ModuleDocker              1.3.2      Docker

PS /home/prashanth> []
```

This module currently has only four cmdlets. We need more capabilities than that. How about we go with the bleeding edge of the module?

 This project is no longer being actively developed because of low usage. Microsoft recommends using `Docker.DotNet` instead. However, given the capabilities available in the module, we should still explore them.

Follow these steps to install the Alpha build of the module:

1. Download the PowerShell Docker module from `https://github.com/Microsoft/Docker-PowerShell/releases`.
2. Download `Docker.0.1.0.zip` (`https://github.com/Microsoft/Docker-PowerShell/releases/download/v0.1.0/Docker.0.1.0.zip`).

3. Next, extract the ZIP file to the `/tmp/Docker` folder using the `unzip` command:

```
# mkdir /tmp/Docker
# unzip ./Downloads/Docker.0.1.0.zip -d /tmp/Docker/
```

```
root@packtpub:/home/prashanth/Downloads
[root@packtpub Downloads]# ls
Docker.0.1.0.zip  docker-ce-18.03.1.ce-1.el7.centos.x86_64.rpm
[root@packtpub Downloads]# mkdir /tmp/Docker
[root@packtpub Downloads]# unzip ./Docker.0.1.0.zip -d /tmp/Docker/
Archive:  ./Docker.0.1.0.zip
  inflating: /tmp/Docker/_rels/.rels
  inflating: /tmp/Docker/Docker.nuspec
  inflating: /tmp/Docker/en-US/Docker.PowerShell.dll-Help.xml
  inflating: /tmp/Docker/Docker.psd1
  inflating: /tmp/Docker/Docker.psm1
  inflating: /tmp/Docker/Docker.Format.ps1xml
  inflating: /tmp/Docker/clr/Docker.DotNet.dll
  inflating: /tmp/Docker/clr/Docker.DotNet.X509.dll
  inflating: /tmp/Docker/clr/Docker.PowerShell.dll
  inflating: /tmp/Docker/clr/Newtonsoft.Json.dll
  inflating: /tmp/Docker/clr/System.Buffers.dll
  inflating: /tmp/Docker/clr/Tar.dll
  inflating: /tmp/Docker/coreclr/Docker.DotNet.dll
  inflating: /tmp/Docker/coreclr/Docker.DotNet.X509.dll
  inflating: /tmp/Docker/coreclr/Docker.PowerShell.dll
  inflating: /tmp/Docker/coreclr/Tar.dll
  inflating: /tmp/Docker/[Content_Types].xml
  inflating: /tmp/Docker/package/services/metadata/core-properties/2b9ed1ff72af462cb6521b96eeaba1c9.psmdcp
[root@packtpub Downloads]#
```

4. Verify the existence of the `Docker.psd1` manifest file using the `ls -l` command:

```
# ls -l /tmp/Docker
```

```
root@packtpub:/home/prashanth/Downloads
[root@packtpub Downloads]# ls -l /tmp/Docker/
total 28
drwxr-xr-x. 2 root root  158 Jun 13 14:23 clr
-rw-r--r--. 1 root root  722 Aug 27  2016 [Content_Types].xml
drwxr-xr-x. 2 root root  105 Jun 13 14:23 coreclr
-rw-r--r--. 1 root root 4294 Aug 27  2016 Docker.Format.ps1xml
-rw-r--r--. 1 root root  721 Aug 27  2016 Docker.nuspec
-rw-r--r--. 1 root root 4350 Aug 27  2016 Docker.psd1
-rw-r--r--. 1 root root  799 Aug 27  2016 Docker.psm1
drwxr-xr-x. 2 root root   44 Jun 13 14:23 en-US
drwxr-xr-x. 3 root root   22 Jun 13 14:23 package
drwxr-xr-x. 2 root root   19 Jun 13 14:23 _rels
[root@packtpub Downloads]#
```

5. Next, open the `pwsh` console.
6. Import the `docker` module using the `Import-Module` cmdlet:

```
PS> Import-Module -Name /tmp/Docker/Docker.psd1
```

7. To list the modules that are registered with the current session scope, use the following command:

```
PS> Get-Module -Name Docker
```

```
PS /home/prashanth> Import-Module -Name /tmp/Docker/Docker.psd1
PS /home/prashanth> Get-Module Docker

ModuleType Version    Name        ExportedCommands
---------- -------    ----        ----------------
Script     0.1.0      Docker      {ConvertTo-ContainerImage, Copy-ContainerFile, E...

PS /home/prashanth>
```

8. List the PowerShell cmdlets for Docker using the `Get-Command` cmdlet:

```
PS> Get-Command -Module Docker
```

```
PS /home/prashanth> Get-Command -Module Docker


CommandType     Name                         Version    Source
-----------     ----                         -------    ------
Alias           Attach-Container             0.1.0      Docker
Alias           Build-ContainerImage         0.1.0      Docker
Alias           Commit-Container             0.1.0      Docker
Alias           Exec-Container               0.1.0      Docker
Alias           Load-ContainerImage          0.1.0      Docker
Alias           Pull-ContainerImage          0.1.0      Docker
Alias           Push-ContainerImage          0.1.0      Docker
Alias           Run-ContainerImage           0.1.0      Docker
Alias           Save-ContainerImage          0.1.0      Docker
Alias           Tag-ContainerImage           0.1.0      Docker
Cmdlet          ConvertTo-ContainerImage     0.1.0      Docker
Cmdlet          Copy-ContainerFile           0.1.0      Docker
Cmdlet          Enter-ContainerSession       0.1.0      Docker
Cmdlet          Export-ContainerImage        0.1.0      Docker
Cmdlet          Get-Container                0.1.0      Docker
Cmdlet          Get-ContainerDetail          0.1.0      Docker
Cmdlet          Get-ContainerImage           0.1.0      Docker
Cmdlet          Get-ContainerNet             0.1.0      Docker
Cmdlet          Get-ContainerNetDetail       0.1.0      Docker
Cmdlet          Import-ContainerImage        0.1.0      Docker
Cmdlet          Invoke-ContainerImage        0.1.0      Docker
Cmdlet          New-Container                0.1.0      Docker
Cmdlet          New-ContainerImage           0.1.0      Docker
Cmdlet          New-ContainerNet             0.1.0      Docker
Cmdlet          Remove-Container             0.1.0      Docker
```

How it works...

The PSGallery repository has a module called `Docker`, which is used to manage the Docker Engine. This module, however, has a very small number of cmdlets. The bleeding-edge `Docker` module for PowerShell contains more cmdlets to manage Docker, however, the cmdlets are in their alpha stage.

The alpha Docker PowerShell module contains more capabilities. However, this module needs to be installed from the GitHub repository.

Here are the PowerShell cmdlets, their aliases, and their CLI equivalents, which are available in the alpha Docker module:

PowerShell cmdlet	Alias	Docker command
ConvertTo-ContainerImage	Commit-Container	docker commit
Copy-ContainerFile		docker cp
Enter-ContainerSession	Attach-Container	docker attach
Export-ContainerImage	Save-ContainerImage	docker save
Get-Container		docker ps -a
Get-ContainerDetail		docker inspect
Get-ContainerImage		docker images
Get-ContainerNet		docker network ls
Get-ContainerNetDetail		docker network inspect
Import-ContainerImage	Load-ContainerImage	docker load
Invoke-containerImage	Run-ContainerImage	docker run
New-Container		docker create
New-ContainerImage	Build-ContainerImage	docker build
New-ContainerNet		docker network create
Remove-Container		docker rm
Remove-ContainerImage		docker rmi
Remove-ContainerNet		docker network rm
Request-ContainerImage	Pull-ContainerImage	docker pull
Set-ContainerImageTag	Tag-ContainerImage	docker tag
Start-Container		docker start
Start-ContainerProcess	Exec-Container	docker exec
Stop-Container		docker stop
Submit-ContainerImage	Push-ContainerImage	docker push

See also

- About PowerShell Module manifest (`https://docs.microsoft.com/en-in/powershell/developer/windows-powershell`)

Overview of Docker Hub and its operations

Docker Hub is an online repository for sharing Docker images. Docker Hub is a cloud-based registry service that allows you to link to code repositories, build your images, and test them. It also stores manually pushed images and links to Docker Cloud so that you can deploy images to your hosts. Organizations can even create workgroups to manage access to image repositories:

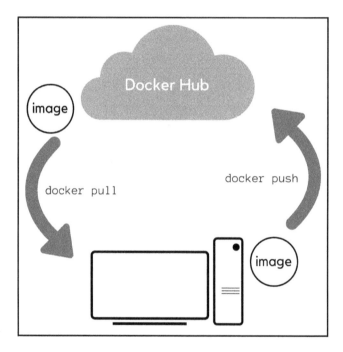

Getting ready

It is recommended that you have met the following prerequisites steps before you proceed:

1. Create a Docker ID at `https://hub.docker.com`.
2. PowerShell should be available on the host machine.
3. The Docker module manifest should be available and loaded into the session.
4. You must be logged in to the session as a user that has superuser privileges.

How to do it...

In this recipe, we are going to see the complete life cycle of a Docker image by using PowerShell Docker cmdlets in conjunction with Docker CLI commands:

1. Open a Terminal and enter root mode.
2. Launch PowerShell using `pwsh`.
3. Log in to the Docker registry using your Docker username and password credentials or using a standard file as an input for the password. The second option is not recommended, for security reasons:

   ```
   # docker login
   ```

```
PS /home/prashanth> docker login
Login with your Docker ID to push and pull images from Docker Hub. If you don't have a Docker ID, head over t
o https://hub.docker.com to create one.
Username: prashanthjayaram
Password:
Login Succeeded
PS /home/prashanth>
```

4. Now, pull the sample `hello-world:latest` image from the Docker Hub using the `Pull-ContainerImage` cmdlet:

```
PS> Pull-ContainerImage hello-world:latest
```

5. To run the container image, use the `Run-ContainerImage` cmdlet:

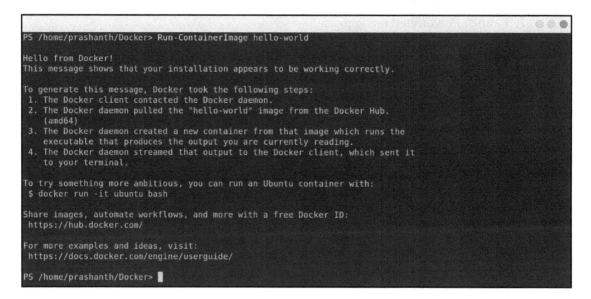

6. Let's find the container ID by using `Get-Container`:

```
PS> Get-Container
```

7. Let's pick just the container ID. We will use the `Select-Object` cmdlet to do this:

```
PS> Get-Container | Select-Object ID
```

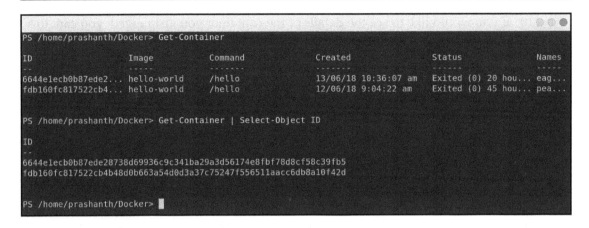

Make any changes you may want to (or not) to the Docker image. We want this customized image to be saved.

8. Save this as a new image using the `Commit-ContainerImage` cmdlet. This new image has all of the changes that we made to the base image:

    PS> Commit-Container <container ID>

As you can see, the container has no tags (`<none>:<none>`). Tags are unique identifiers for Docker images. Note the change in the container ID. You need this ID for the next step.

9. Now, let's add a tag (a unique identifier) to the image using `Tag-ContainerImage`. The ID is the SHA ID of the image. Just like in Git, where you can use the first seven characters of the ID, you can use the first three characters here, in this case, as follows:

    PS> Tag-ContainerImage –Id 840 –Repository
    prashanthjayaram/packtpubhelloworld

10. If you would like to see the details of the container you just tagged, you can do so by selecting all of the properties of the object:

```
PS /home/prashanth/Docker> Tag-ContainerImage -Id 840 -Repository prashanthjayaram/packtpubhelloworld
PS /home/prashanth/Docker> Get-ContainerImage

RepoTags                                ID                  Created              Size(MB)
--------                                --                  -------              --------
prashanthjayaram/packtpubhelloworld:l... sha256:840b6de1dc... 14/06/18 6:19:29 am    0.00
hello-world:latest                      sha256:e38bc07ac1... 11/04/18 6:11:49 pm    0.00


PS /home/prashanth/Docker>
```

10. Push the new image into the repository using the docker push command. We are using docker push because Submit-ContainerImage doesn't seem to work in this build:

```
PS> docker push prashanthjayaram/packtpubhelloworld
```

```
PS /home/prashanth/Docker> Submit-ContainerImage prashanthjayaram/packtpubhelloworld
The push refers to repository [docker.io/prashanthjayaram/packtpubhelloworld]
Submit-ContainerImage : errors:
denied: requested access to the resource is denied
unauthorized: authentication required
At line:1 char:1
+ Submit-ContainerImage prashanthjayaram/packtpubhelloworld
+ ~~~~~~~~~~~~~~~~~~~~~~~~~~~~~~~~~~~~~~~~~~~~~~~~~~~~~~~~~~~~
+ CategoryInfo          : OperationStopped: (:) [Submit-ContainerImage], Exception
+ FullyQualifiedErrorId : Docker.PowerShell.Cmdlets.SubmitContainerImage

PS /home/prashanth/Docker> docker push prashanthjayaram/packtpubhelloworld
The push refers to repository [docker.io/prashanthjayaram/packtpubhelloworld]
2b8cbd0846c5: Layer already exists
latest: digest: sha256:cf0d1eaf7ebe4ddad87b5aa05c1c34f1b17884ce6031698968f2d19d3cf5028a size: 524
PS /home/prashanth/Docker>
```

11. Log in to `https://hub.docker.com` to verify whether the image is available:

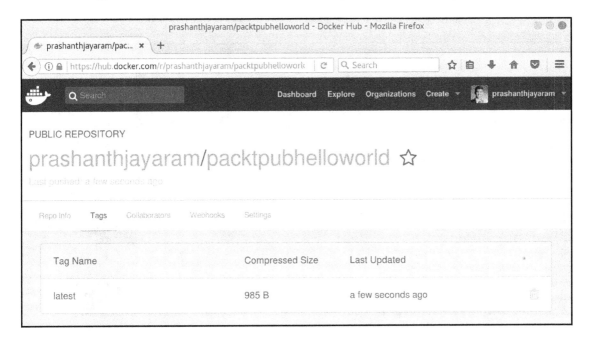

12. Now, validate the newly created image by pulling it from the remote Docker Hub registry:

```
PS> Pull-ContainerImage -Repository
prashanthjayaram/packtpubhelloworld
```

13. To run the newly downloaded image, use the `Run-ContainerImage` cmdlet:

PS> Run-ContainerImage prashanthjayaram/packtpubhelloworld

```
PS /home/prashanth/Docker> Run-ContainerImage prashanthjayaram/packtpubhelloworld

Hello from Docker!
This message shows that your installation appears to be working correctly.

To generate this message, Docker took the following steps:
 1. The Docker client contacted the Docker daemon.
 2. The Docker daemon pulled the "hello-world" image from the Docker Hub.
    (amd64)
 3. The Docker daemon created a new container from that image which runs the
    executable that produces the output you are currently reading.
 4. The Docker daemon streamed that output to the Docker client, which sent it
    to your terminal.

To try something more ambitious, you can run an Ubuntu container with:
 $ docker run -it ubuntu bash

Share images, automate workflows, and more with a free Docker ID:
 https://hub.docker.com/

For more examples and ideas, visit:
 https://docs.docker.com/engine/userguide/

PS /home/prashanth/Docker> 
```

How it works...

Docker Hub is an online central repository for sharing Docker images. To use Docker Hub, you need to register with the Hub. Once you sign up, it is simple to pull images shared by yourself or others.

To build a custom image, open a Terminal session with superuser privileges and launch PowerShell. Log in to the Docker Hub using your Docker login credentials.

In this recipe, we demonstrated a sample container life cycle, wherein we got a public image, made modifications to it, committed the image, tagged it so as to uniquely identify it in the repository, and pushed it to the Hub for others to use. We tested the pull as well, and showed that it worked. We used PowerShell cmdlets for all of the operations other than the container image submission. (At the time of writing this book, the current build of the cmdlet, `Submit-ContainerImage`, seems to have issues with authentication.)

The PowerShell module for Docker does not have any dependency on the Docker CLI that we installed on our Linux computer. Therefore, the PowerShell module can run without Docker CLI being installed. The cmdlets in the module are merely wrapper cmdlets, meaning that they run Docker cmdlets under the hood, based on how you call the cmdlets. While it does not provide us with additional capabilities, the benefit of using the Docker module is the uniformity, readability, and discoverability of PowerShell cmdlets.

See also

- Docker Hub documentation (`https://docs.docker.com/docker-hub/`)

Building an image from a Dockerfile using PowerShell

In the previous recipe, we took a sample image through a mini life cycle, which involved working with Docker Hub. In this recipe, we will look at building an image using a Dockerfile.

Getting ready

If you did not close the Terminal after the previous recipe, you can continue. If you did launch a Terminal session and, optionally, launch PowerShell.

How to do it...

To build a Docker image automatically with the instructions from a Dockerfile, follow these steps:

1. Use a text or code editor to create a Dockerfile. The name of the file is case-sensitive:

```
PS> vim Dockerfile
```

2. Add the following text to the Dockerfile. (You can use the base image of any distro; CentOS is not the only option.) Change the value for the MAINTAINER key to your email address:

```
FROM centos:latest
MAINTAINER powershellsql@gmail.com

RUN yum install wget -y
RUN wget --directory-prefix=/etc/yum.repos.d/
https://packages.microsoft.com/config/rhel/7/prod.repo
RUN yum install powershell -y

CMD /usr/bin/pwsh
```

3. Build the new Docker image, packtpubdemo, using the docker build command:

```
# docker build --tag packtpubdemo .
.
.
.
Successfully tagged packtpubdemo:latest
```

```
Userid       : "Microsoft (Release signing) <gpgsecurity@microsoft.com>"
Fingerprint: bc52 8686 b50d 79e3 39d3 721c eb3e 94ad be12 29cf
From         : https://packages.microsoft.com/keys/microsoft.asc
Running transaction check
Running transaction test
Transaction test succeeded
Running transaction
  Installing : 2:libunwind-1.2-2.el7.x86_64                         1/3
  Installing : libicu-50.1.2-15.el7.x86_64                          2/3
  Installing : powershell-6.1.0~preview.2-1.rhel.7.x86_64           3/3
  Verifying  : libicu-50.1.2-15.el7.x86_64                          1/3
  Verifying  : 2:libunwind-1.2-2.el7.x86_64                         2/3
  Verifying  : powershell-6.1.0~preview.2-1.rhel.7.x86_64           3/3

Installed:
  powershell.x86_64 0:6.1.0~preview.2-1.rhel.7

Dependency Installed:
  libicu.x86_64 0:50.1.2-15.el7          libunwind.x86_64 2:1.2-2.el7

Complete!
Removing intermediate container 5a3ce0e441cc
 ---> 2d8821f9ec66
Step 6/6 : CMD /usr/bin/pwsh
 ---> Running in 586b10b1c50a
Removing intermediate container 586b10b1c50a
 ---> 50eecb704824
Successfully built 50eecb704824
Successfully tagged packtpubdemo:latest
PS /home/prashanth/Docker>
```

4. Find the newly created images by using `docker images` with the `grep` command:

```
PS> docker images -a | grep packtpubdemo
packtpubdemo latest 4b5e7f30245d 53 seconds ago 450MB
```

5. Test and verify the Docker image using the `docker run` command. To make the result seem more pronounced, exit PowerShell and run the `docker run` command at the root prompt:

```
# docker run -it packtpubdemo
```

```
[root@packtpub Docker]# docker run -it packtpubdemo
PowerShell v6.1.0-preview.2
Copyright (c) Microsoft Corporation. All rights reserved.

https://aka.ms/pscore6-docs
Type 'help' to get help.

PS />
```

How it works...

A Dockerfile is a small configuration file, designed to describe how to build a Docker image. The file has several steps to create a new image. The first line indicates that the new image is created from the `centos:latest` image. If you see the output, the container ID is different for each step; these are intermediate containers. The output shows detailed information about what is being done.

You build the Docker image with the `docker build` command. You specify the tag for the Docker image. You also tell the command that you have the Dockerfile in the current directory, which you would like `docker build` to use. The `docker build` command looks in the current directory for the Dockerfile, and builds the image based on the information you provide in the Dockerfile:

- If the Dockerfile is created somewhere else, you replace that dot with the actual path to the directory containing the Dockerfile.
- When `docker build` finishes running the Dockerfile, an image will be created locally and registered in the local Docker registry. It is now ready to be run with the `docker run` command.

- Each step produces a new image. The file has six steps, therefore, six images are created. However, each of these intermediate images is deleted as the operation progresses.
- The steps are exactly the same as those for creating a new image manually, which we saw in the previous recipe. However, in this recipe, the same steps are done using a Dockerfile.

See also

- Refer to the instructions from a Dockerfile to build a Docker image (`https://docs.docker.com/engine/reference/builder/`).

Pulling a Docker container image from the repository

So far, we have learned that the Docker PowerShell cmdlets can be used along with Docker commands to manage the Docker container stack effectively. We've also discussed the basics of Docker containers and their implementation on Linux machines using PowerShell commands. However, the PowerShell package for Docker is still in the development stage and it has been made public as an open source project. PowerShell Docker cmdlets use the Docker Rest API to connect to the Docker service.

Starting with this recipe, we'll look at Docker PowerShell cmdlets to manage Docker containers.

Getting ready

If you did not close the session after the previous recipe, continue by entering PowerShell. If not, log in to the Terminal as root and launch PowerShell. Then, install the development build or download the Docker PowerShell module manifest. If you followed along with the previous recipes, this should already be set up for you. If not, refer to the *Introduction to Docker PowerShell cmdlets* recipe for more details.

How to do it...

We will start by identifying an image to pull. In this recipe, we will pull the PowerShell image that was created by Microsoft. It is available at `https://hub.docker.com/r/microsoft/powershell/`:

1. Pull the specified image from the Docker Hub registry using the following command:

   ```
   PS> Pull-ContainerImage -Repository microsoft/powershell:latest
   ```

2. Pull the repository with all of its images:

   ```
   PS> Pull-ContainerImage -Repository centos -ALL
   ```

To cancel a pull request, press the universal Linux abort combination, `Ctrl + C`.

How it works...

Pre-built Docker images are downloaded from the Docker Hub registry to create a layer on top of the host machine. The Docker images consist of layers of a filesystem and application configuration that are used to create containers. Docker Hub is a collection of many pre-built images that can be pulled and further customized.

To download a specific image (or set of images), use `Pull-ContainerImage`. If you don't specify a tag, the engine uses `:latest` as the default tag. The first cmdlet we ran pulls the `microsoft/powershell:latest` image from the repository.

By default, `Pull-ContainerImage` pulls a single image from the specified registry. However, a repository may consist of multiple images. To pull all image from a repository, use the `-All` switch parameter.

Listing Docker containers and the images

In this recipe, we will look at how you can use PowerShell cmdlets to view a list of images and containers (running instances of Docker images, which includes an application and all of its dependent pieces), which may be in different states.

We'll look at how to list the containers using conditional constructs in PowerShell, as well as how the PowerShell output can be integrated with the `grep` and `awk` utilities.

How to do it...

Let's start by listing all the containers in the system:

1. Use the `Get-Container` cmdlet to list out all of the available containers:

   PS> Get-Container

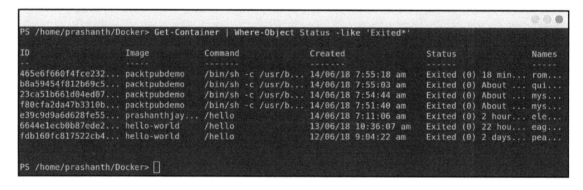

2. Next, list out only those containers that are in the `Exited` state:

   PS> Get-Container | Where-Object Status -like 'Exited*'

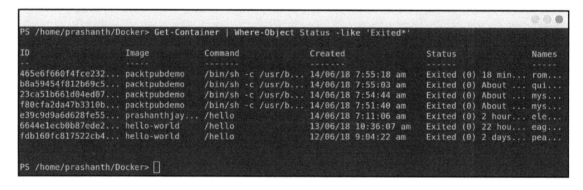

3. You could even narrow down the search results. For instance, you could find the containers that are running and were created in the last six hours:

   PS> Get-Container | Where-Object {$_.Status -like 'Up*' -and $_.Created -lt (Get-Date).AddHours(-6)}

```
PS /home/prashanth/Docker> Get-Container | Where-Object {$_.Status -like 'Up*' -and $_.Created -lt (Get-Date)
.AddHours(-6)}

ID                    Image          Command              Created             Status         Names
--                    -----          -------              -------             ------         -----
465e6f660f4fce232...  packtpubdemo   /bin/sh -c /usr/b...  14/06/18 7:55:18 am  Up 3 minutes   rom...

PS /home/prashanth/Docker> []
```

4. The output can also integrate with commands such as `grep` and `awk`:

   PS> Get-Container | grep bin | awk '{print $1}'

```
PS /home/prashanth/Docker> Get-Container | grep bin
465e6f660f4fce232...  packtpubdemo   /bin/sh -c /usr/b...  14/06/18 7:55:18 am  Up 5 minutes          roma...
b8a59454f812b69c5...  packtpubdemo   /bin/sh -c /usr/b...  14/06/18 7:55:03 am  Exited (0) About ...  quir...
23ca51b661d04ed07...  packtpubdemo   /bin/sh -c /usr/b...  14/06/18 7:54:44 am  Exited (0) About ...  myst...
f80cfa2da47b3310b...  packtpubdemo   /bin/sh -c /usr/b...  14/06/18 7:51:40 am  Exited (0) About ...  myst...
PS /home/prashanth/Docker> Get-Container | grep bin | awk '{print $1}'
465e6f660f4fce232...
b8a59454f812b69c5...
23ca51b661d04ed07...
f80cfa2da47b3310b...
PS /home/prashanth/Docker> []
```

5. Next, list out all of the container images:

   PS> Get-ContainerImage -All

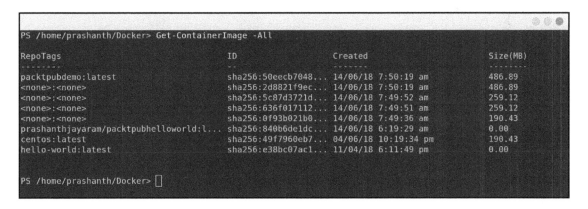

```
PS /home/prashanth/Docker> Get-ContainerImage -All

RepoTags                               ID                   Created             Size(MB)
--------                               --                   -------             --------
packtpubdemo:latest                    sha256:50eecb7048... 14/06/18 7:50:19 am  486.89
<none>:<none>                          sha256:2d8821f9ec... 14/06/18 7:50:19 am  486.89
<none>:<none>                          sha256:5c87d3721d... 14/06/18 7:49:52 am  259.12
<none>:<none>                          sha256:636f017112... 14/06/18 7:49:51 am  259.12
<none>:<none>                          sha256:0f93b021b0... 14/06/18 7:49:36 am  190.43
prashanthjayaram/packtpubhelloworld:l... sha256:840b6de1dc... 14/06/18 6:19:29 am  0.00
centos:latest                          sha256:49f7960eb7... 04/06/18 10:19:34 pm 190.43
hello-world:latest                     sha256:e38bc07ac1... 11/04/18 6:11:49 pm  0.00


PS /home/prashanth/Docker> []
```

6. Get all of the details about the first image in the output:

```
PS> Get-ContainerImage | Select-Object * -First 1
```

```
PS /home/prashanth/Docker> Get-ContainerImage | Select-Object * -First 1

ID          : sha256:50eecb70482400a16f1ac1ec7543f94927a5ec9bad9cb7554ebad08a99b919f1
ParentID    : sha256:2d8821f9ec669e608ab3b282510a8ce26a75a581f31a4849a8146de719472814
RepoTags    : {packtpubdemo:latest}
RepoDigests :
Created     : 14/06/18 7:50:19 am
Size        : 510539448
VirtualSize : 510539448
Labels      : {[org.label-schema.schema-version, = 1.0     org.label-schema.name=CentOS Base Image
              org.label-schema.vendor=CentOS     org.label-schema.license=GPLv2
              org.label-schema.build-date=20180531]}

PS /home/prashanth/Docker>
```

How it works...

To examine the state of Docker containers, we use the `Get-Container` cmdlet. The rest of the commands mentioned in this recipe are simple implementations of PowerShell filtration and selection.

Starting and stopping Docker containers

In this recipe, you'll find out how containers can be started and stopped using Docker cmdlets.

Getting ready

If you have been following along, you should be able to continue with the same state. Otherwise, follow these steps:

1. Open a PowerShell console with SU privileges
2. Load the Docker PowerShell module using the manifest
3. Create one or more containers, which should be in different states

How to do it...

To start and stop the Docker containers, follow these instructions:

1. Check the status of the containers in your system using Get-Container:

   PS> Get-Container

   ```
   ID                      Image          Command Created        Status
   Names
   --                      -----          ------- -------        ------
   -----
   3d8f26818889bbd58... microsoft/po... pwsh 6/4/18 8:46:12 PM Up 6
   seconds sleepy...
   b41c1cc5fe36eac65... microsoft/po... pwsh 6/4/18 7:44:09 PM Exited
   (0) 2 seco... upbeat...
   5ce6d3f9de452135e... microsoft/po... pwsh 6/4/18 7:44:05 PM Exited
   (0) 2 seco... sharp_...
   af771ace8d1ed692d... microsoft/po... bash 6/4/18 7:14:04 PM Up 3
   seconds quirky...
   ```

2. Get a list of running containers using a conditional Where-Object clause construct:

   PS> Get-Container |where-object {$_.Status -match 'up'}

   ```
   ID Image Command Created Status Names
   -- ----- ------- ------- ------ -----
   3d8f26818889bbd58... microsoft/po... pwsh 6/4/18 8:46:12 PM Up 3
   minutes sleepy...
   af771ace8d1ed692d... microsoft/po... bash 6/4/18 7:14:04 PM Up 2
   hours quirky...
   ```

3. Stop the running containers using the Stop-Container cmdlet. Use the pipe to pass the container objects to Stop-Container:

   PS> Get-Container | where-object {$_.Status -match 'up'}|Stop-
   Container
   PS> Get-Container

   ```
   ID Image Command Created Status Names
   -- ----- ------- ------- ------ -----
   3d8f26818889bbd58... microsoft/po... pwsh 6/4/18 8:46:12 PM Exited
   (0) 4 seco... sleepy...
   b41c1cc5fe36eac65... microsoft/po... pwsh 6/4/18 7:44:09 PM Exited
   (0) About ... upbeat...
   5ce6d3f9de452135e... microsoft/po... pwsh 6/4/18 7:44:05 PM Exited
   ```

```
(0) About ... sharp_...
af771ace8d1ed692d... microsoft/po... bash 6/4/18 7:14:04 PM Exited
(0) 4 seco... quirky...
```

4. Start the stopped containers:

```
PS> Get-Container | where-object {$_.Status -match 'exited'} |
Start-Container
PS> Get-Container

ID Image Command Created Status Names
-- ----- ------- ------- ------ -----
3d8f26818889bbd58... microsoft/po... pwsh 6/4/18 8:46:12 PM Up 6
seconds sleepy...
b41c1cc5fe36eac65... microsoft/po... pwsh 6/4/18 7:44:09 PM Exited
(0) 2 seco... upbeat...
5ce6d3f9de452135e... microsoft/po... pwsh 6/4/18 7:44:05 PM Exited
(0) 2 seco... sharp_...
af771ace8d1ed692d... microsoft/po... bash 6/4/18 7:14:04 PM Up 3
seconds quirky...
```

5. Stop the running containers by using the `grep` and `awk` commands in conjunction with Docker commands:

```
PS> docker ps -a | grep "Up" | awk '{print $1}' | xargs docker stop
```

5. Start the stopped containers using the `grep` and `awk` commands in conjunction with Docker commands:

```
PS> docker ps -a | grep "seconds" | awk '{print $1}' | xargs docker
start
```

How it works...

Starting and stopping containers is one of the basic tasks in any production Docker workflow. While these tasks can be achieved with Docker CLI commands, the fact that PowerShell has these wrapper functions brings the consistency and friendliness of PowerShell to the table.

`Start-Container`, as the name suggests, starts a container. A stopped container can be restarted with all its previous changes intact using `Start-Container`. Stopping is equally simply handled.

The use of conditional constructs, such as `Where-Object` in PowerShell, comes in very handy for filtering containers. The transparent mechanism of passing values as objects through the pipe has been demonstrated as well.

Removing containers and container images

Removing unused/obsolete containers is also part of a normal Docker workflow. In this recipe, we will discuss the process of removing Docker containers and Docker images.

How to do it...

You should have the PowerShell session open and have loaded the Docker module into the session by now.

Now, let's remove some containers and images. You can use the conditional construct to list specific containers, or we can remove all of the containers and images to start with a clean slate:

1. Get the list of all available containers:

   ```
   PS> Get-Container
   ```

2. Stop all of the running containers:

   ```
   PS> Get-Container | where-object {$_.Status -match 'up'} | Stop-
   Container
   ```

   If you would rather not filter, that's OK:

   ```
   PS> Get-Container | Stop-Container
   ```

3. Remove all of the containers:

   ```
   PS> Get-Container | Remove-Container
   ```

4. Remove all of the Docker images. It is important that the images are removed after the containers are:

   ```
   PS> Get-ContainerImage -All | Remove-ContainerImage
   ```

How it works...

This recipe is no different from what we saw in the previous recipes. As usual, the names of the `Remove-Container` and `Remove-ContainerImage` cmdlets are self-explanatory.

While working with Docker, many containers may get created and many images may be downloaded. Removing images helps us save disk space.

As Docker containers are the layer that's built on top of the Docker images, it is required that you stop the containers before removing the Docker images to avoid potential inconsistency in the system state.

We can also remove the image without stopping the containers by using the `-Force` inline argument on the `Remove-ContainerImage` cmdlet. However, we recommend against doing this because the `-Force` option is not a recommended solution for any tasks to remain complacent.

Working with a container using miscellaneous Docker PowerShell cmdlets

In this recipe, we will walk through some of the other cmdlets that are in use or in the development stage at the time of writing this chapter.

How to do it...

To understand the process of building a Docker image using the PowerShell cmdlets, follow these steps:

1. Create a container image from an existing repository or remote registry:

```
PS> New-Container microsoft/powershell -Name packtpub -Terminal
pwsh

ID Image Command Created Status Names
-- ----- ------- ------- ------ -----
a4e5c8f1f30c201d9... microsoft/po... pwsh 6/5/18 6:44:08 PM Created
packpu..
```

2. Start the newly created container, `packtpubdemo`:

```
PS> Start-Container packtpubdemo
```

3. Check the status of the newly started container:

```
PS /home/PacktPub/Docker> Get-Container packpubtdemo

ID Image Command Created Status Names
-- ----- ------- ------- ------ -----
a4e5c8f1f30c201d9... microsoft/po... pwsh 6/5/18 6:44:08 PM Up 8
seconds packpu...
```

4. Get the metadata of the newly started container:

```
PS> Get-ContainerDetail packtpubdemo

ID :
a4e5c8f1f30c201d9ab3b16b319e9b161bc7f09d2f0423fa26235e6ec920041a
Created : 6/5/18 6:52:18 PM
Path : pwsh
Args : {}
State : Docker.DotNet.Models.ContainerState
Image :
sha256:708fb186511e482523afd0f087a2ab656b7abf2512815eb8e4d765d64237
6a8a
ResolvConfPath :
/var/lib/docker/containers/a4e5c8f1f30c201d9ab3b16b319e9b161bc7f09d
2f0423fa26235e6ec920041a/resolv.conf
HostnamePath :
/var/lib/docker/containers/a4e5c8f1f30c201d9ab3b16b319e9b161bc7f09d
2f0423fa26235e6ec920041a/hostname
HostsPath :
/var/lib/docker/containers/a4e5c8f1f30c201d9ab3b16b319e9b161bc7f09d
2f0423fa26235e6ec920041a/hosts
LogPath :
/var/lib/docker/containers/a4e5c8f1f30c201d9ab3b16b319e9b161bc7f09d
2f0423fa26235e6ec920041a/a4e5c8f1f30c201d9ab3b16b319e9b161bc7f09d2f
0423fa26235e6ec920041a-json.log
Node :
Name : /packtpubdemo
RestartCount : 0
Driver : overlay2
MountLabel :
ProcessLabel :
AppArmorProfile :
ExecIDs :
{b3cc995121ba8a7ea8dd9f885a528c9ac656e2d6461bcc90fc54d1841c123524,
5499dbf5ae28757361cfddc51f2646ec7b48a3f5ea3dd04b26453169b7b3cee2}
HostConfig : Docker.DotNet.Models.HostConfig
GraphDriver : Docker.DotNet.Models.GraphDriverData
SizeRw : 0
```

```
SizeRootFs : 0
Mounts : {}
Config : Docker.DotNet.Models.Config
NetworkSettings : Docker.DotNet.Models.NetworkSettings
```

5. To view the details of the network and driver connecting the host machine and containers, use the `Get-ContainerNet` cmdlet:

   PS> Get-ContainerNet

   ```
   Id Name Driver
   -- ---- ------
   d4c71941fc31... bridge bridge
   fdf8108f964d... none null
   5619c84bc7b8... host host
   ```

6. Now, commit the container's changes into a new container image:

   PS> Commit-Container a4e5

   ```
   RepoTags ID Created
   -------- -- -------
   <none>:<none> sha256:f4ff9aaffd... 5/14/18 8:20:0...
   ```

7. Tag or label the newly created Docker image:

   PS> Tag-ContainerImage f4ff9a packpubposh

8. Save the container image locally using `Save-ContainerImage`:

   **PS /home/PacktPub/Docker> Save-ContainerImage packtpubposh -
   DestinationFilePath /tmp/Docker/packtpubposh.tar
   PS /home/PacktPub/Docker> ls -l /tmp/Docker/packtpubposh.tar**
   ```
   -rw-r--r--. 1 root root 324026368 Jun 5 15:26
   /tmp/Docker/packtpubposh.tar
   ```

9. Use `Import-ContainerImage` to create an image on the filesystem:

   PS> Import-ContainerImage -FilePath /tmp/Docker/packtpubposh.tar
   ```
   Loaded image: packtpubposh:latest

   RepoTags ID Created Size(MB)
   -------- -- ------- --------
   packtpubposh:latest sha256:d3a81499d6... 6/5/18 7:23:30 PM 303.36
   ```

10. Now, copy the files/folder between the container and host machine by using the `Copy-ContainerFile` cmdlet:

```
PS> Copy-ContainerFile -Path ./myfile.txt -Destination /tmp/ -
ToContainer packpubdemo
PS> docker exec -it packpubdemo bash
root@cdf58d38145f:/# ls /tmp/myfile.txt -l
-rw-r--r--. 1 root root 45 jun 05 17:59 /tmp/myfile.txt
root@cdf58d38145f:/#
```

11. Open a session with the running container by using the `Exec-Container` cmdlet:

```
PS> Exec-Container -Id d5a -Terminal bash
```

How it works...

In this recipe, we performed a series of activities on a container to demonstrate the use of all of the miscellaneous Docker cmdlets. This recipe is pretty self-explanatory; each of the actions is specified in the steps. Here is a rundown of the cmdlets we used in this recipe.

The `Get-ContainerDetail` cmdlet provides detailed information about the metadata and constructs controlled by Docker. The `Commit-Container` cmdlet commits the container's changes or settings into a new container image. (In general, though, it is recommended that you use the Dockerfile to manage the docker images.) The `Tag-ContainerImage` cmdlet is used to create a label or a unique identifier for the Docker container image. The `Save-ContainerImage` cmdlet generates a tarred repository to the standard output stream which contains all of the parent layers, tags, and versions. The `Import-ContainerImage` cmdlet is used to import the contents from a tarball to create a filesystem image. If you specify an individual file, you must specify the full path within the host.

To get network details, use the `Get-ContainerNet` cmdlet. The `Exec-Container` cmdlet will run the command mentioned in the parameters on the container. In this case, the `bash` command is invoked while running a `packtpubdemo` container. Copying of files between the containers and host machine can also be done. The `Copy-ContainerFile` cmdlet will copy files and directories between a container and the host machine filesystems.

See also

- A developmental build and PowerShell module for Docker engine reference (`https://www.diycode.cc/projects/Microsoft/Docker-PowerShell`).
- To create a file system image, refer to the tarball reference guide (`https://docs.docker.com/engine/reference/commandline/import/`).

Running a PowerShell script to set up Docker containers

Over the last few chapters, we saw how PowerShell scripts are powerful automation solutions. In this recipe, we are going to use a PowerShell script to manage Docker containers.

In this recipe, three SQL Server docker containers are created and tested within a span of 10–15 minutes. The sample script shows how easy it is to integrate Docker CLI commands with a PowerShell script.

How to do it...

To create a PowerShell script, follow these steps:

1. Create a PowerShell script file using a code editor:

   ```
   PS> vim SQLInstance.ps1
   ```

2. Define an array of elements [1,2,3] as input for the `Foreach-Object` loop cmdlet.
3. Prepare the SQL container names (such as PackPubDemo1, PackPubDemo2, and PackPubDemo3) using the concatenation operator +.
4. Assign the container name to a variable named $Name.
5. Integrate the variable with the Docker CLI command to create SQL Server 2017 Docker containers:

   ```
   #Define the array of elements [1,2,3]
   1,2,3|foreach-object {
   #Build the name of the servers.
   #Its going to be like PackPubDemo1,PackPubDemo2,PackPubDemo3
   $name='PackPubDemo'+$_
   ```

```
#print the name of docker containers
write-host $name
try
  {
#integrate the powershell variable with the docker cli command
docker run -e 'ACCEPT_EULA=Y' -e
'MSSQL_SA_PASSWORD=PacktPubDemo$2018' --name $name -d
microsoft/mssql-server-linux:2017-latest
  }
catch
  {
#Handle exception
  write-host $_.Exception.Message
  }
}
```

How it works...

Run the PowerShell script SQLInstance.PS1 on the pwsh console. Using the Foreach-Object looping construct, the name is prepared each time by appending the input value [1, 2, 3].

First, the image is searched for locally. In the case of its absence, the image is pulled from the specified central repository. Subsequent executions refer to the locally downloaded image.

Using the input values, the docker run command creates new SQL Server 2017 containers:

```
PS> pwsh ./SQLInstance.ps1
PackPubDemo1
Unable to find image 'microsoft/mssql-server-linux:2017-latest' locally
2017-latest: Pulling from microsoft/mssql-server-linux
f6fa9a861b90: Already exists
da7318603015: Already exists
6a8bd10c9278: Already exists
d5a40291440f: Already exists
bbdd8a83c0f1: Already exists
3a52205d40a6: Already exists
6192691706e8: Already exists
1a658a9035fb: Already exists
d057e89d8e94: Already exists
1ed0a0d4098f: Already exists
Digest:
sha256:b5d494d104394b8c1f451406f4062ab711add3032af52241140b7e27a01d8851
Status: Downloaded newer image for microsoft/mssql-server-linux:2017-latest
```

```
cd0faef05d5f93c29d9122c0b1583f536058012a79c017fcc3a4a0b20151c323
PackPubDemo2
cdf58d38145f39688270a95b30fda3c601db9406b3c71bd369bd44dd47d177f6
PackPubDemo3
09e7e5beee0f3d08cc7ad20958f6969503ff516f5ee13aa544356100d39722ef
PS>
```

If we run `docker ps -a` with the formatting option, we are shown the list of the images; note the names and the time they have been up for:

```
# docker ps -a --format
'table{{.Names}}\t{{.Image}}\t{{.Status}}\t{{.Ports}}'
NAMES IMAGE STATUS PORTS
PackPubDemo3 microsoft/mssql-server-linux:2017-latest Up 6 minutes 1433/tcp
PackPubDemo2 microsoft/mssql-server-linux:2017-latest Up 6 minutes 1433/tcp
PackPubDemo1 microsoft/mssql-server-linux:2017-latest Up 6 minutes 1433/tcp
```

Finding Docker tags using PowerShell cmdlets from the remote registry

There is no direct way to list all of the tags of the repository using Docker commands or using PowerShell cmdlets. In some cases, it is required to download the specific images. In this recipe, you'll find out how you can list all of the tags of the repository using PowerShell as well as using the `sed` and `awk` commands.

How to do it...

We will perform two activities in this recipe, one using PowerShell cmdlets and the other using Docker CLI commands:

1. Define a variable, called `repo`, which contains the repository names. This will become part of the repo URLs:

   ```
   PS> $repo='centos'
   ```

2. Use the `Invoke-WebRequest` cmdlet to extract useful information from a web page, and use the `ConvertFrom-Json` cmdlet to convert the web page data from JSON into a PowerShell object:

   ```
   PS> Invoke-WebRequest
   https://registry.hub.docker.com/v1/repositories/$repo/tags |
   ConvertFrom-Json | Select-Object -Property *
   ```

3. Assign the output to a variable, say, `$result`:

```
PS> $result = Invoke-WebRequest
https://registry.hub.docker.com/v1/repositories/$repo/tags |
ConvertFrom-Json | Select-Object -Property *
```

4. There is a lot of data that comes in. Initially, none of it seems useful. However, the `SyncRoot` property seems to have what we may need. Pick only the `SyncRoot` object, and select the `Name` property:

```
PS> $result.SyncRoot | Select-Object Name
        name
        latest
        5
        5.11
        6
        6.6
        6.7
        6.8
        6.9
        7
        7.0.1406
        7.1.1503
        7.2.1511
        7.3.1611
        7.4.1708
        centos5
        centos5.11
        centos6
        centos6.6
        centos6.7
        centos6.8
        centos6.9
        centos7
        centos7.0.1406
        centos7.1.1503
        centos7.2.1511
        centos7.3.1611
        centos7.4.1708
```

5. The entire command can be executed in a single line, as follows:

```
PS> (Invoke-WebRequest
https://registry.hub.docker.com/v1/repositories/$repo/tags | ConvertFrom-
Json | Select-Object -Property *).SyncRoot.Name
        latest
        5
        5.11
```

```
6
6.6
6.7
6.8
6.9
7
7.0.1406
7.1.1503
7.2.1511
7.3.1611
7.4.1708
centos5
centos5.11
centos6
centos6.6
centos6.7
centos6.8
centos6.9
centos7
centos7.0.1406
centos7.1.1503
centos7.2.1511
centos7.3.1611
centos7.4.1708
```

6. Let's wrap this into a simple function:

```
function Get-AllImages {
    param(
        # Get the base image name
        [Parameter(Mandatory=$true)]
        [string]
        $Repo
    )
    begin {
        $UriTest = Invoke-WebRequest
"https://registry.hub.docker.com/v1/repositories/$Repo/tags" -
DisableKeepAlive -UseBasicParsing
        if ($UriTest.StatusCode -eq 200) {
            # Just proceed
        }
        else {
            break
        }
    }
    process {
        (Invoke-WebRequest
"https://registry.hub.docker.com/v1/repositories/$Repo/tags" |
```

```
ConvertFrom-Json).SyncRoot.Name
    }
}

# Call the function as `Get-AllImages -Repo centos`
```

7. Now, let's look at how we can execute this in a Bash shell with the `sed` and `awk` programs:

```
# wget -q
https://registry.hub.docker.com/v1/repositories/centos/tags -O - |
sed -e 's/[][]//g' -e 's/"//g' -e 's/ //g' | tr '}' '\n' | awk -F:
'{print $3}'
latest
5
5.11
6
6.6
6.7
6.8
6.9
7
7.0.1406
7.1.1503
7.2.1511
7.3.1611
7.4.1708
centos5
centos5.11
centos6
centos6.6
centos6.7
centos6.8
centos6.9
centos7
centos7.0.1406
centos7.1.1503
centos7.2.1511
centos7.3.1611
centos7.4.1708
```

How it works...

As an example, use a JSON interface to query the `registry.hub.docker.com` web page. This permits the use of `Invoke-WebRequest` and returns a JSON-formatted string. The `invoke-WebRequest` cmdlet performs a lookup of the specified URL. In this case, it's the CentOS tag's web page and returns a name field. The query contains the website, the API, the name, and the format that's been requested. After execution, the data is converted from JSON using `ConvertFrom-Json`.

In the function, we create a simple `begin` block with a ping test to the URI. We look for the HTML status code (`200` stands for success). Once done, we fetch the JSON from the page, and then strip out only the `name` field to get a list of all of the tags that are available for CentOS.

Next, we will look at how we can pull the tags using the Docker CLI `sed` and `awk` commands. The `wget` download options, `-O` and `-`, are used to write the document to files.

`-` is used as file output. The web page tags are printed to standard output. The output is then processed to fetch the desired result using `sed`. You can see that the `sed` data selection process is not as easy to understand as PowerShell, and writing conditional logic requires effort.

This recipe shows how comfortable PowerShell is with structured data, and how, with very limited knowledge and after working with a few sample examples, PowerShell starts to seem much friendlier.

See also

- Try `Get-Help Invoke-WebRequest -Detailed` to learn more about its parameters.
- Check out more `wget` examples (`https://gist.github.com/bueckl/bd0a1e7a30bc8e2eeefd`).

Other Books You May Enjoy

If you enjoyed this book, you may be interested in these other books by Packt:

Learn PowerShell Core 6.0
David das Neves, Jan-Hendrik Peters

ISBN: 9781788838986

- Get to grips with Powershell Core 6.0
- Explore basic and advanced PowerShell scripting techniques
- Get to grips with Windows PowerShell Security
- Work with centralization and DevOps with PowerShell
- Implement PowerShell in your organization through real-life examples
- Learn to create GUIs and use DSC in production

Mastering Windows PowerShell Scripting - Second Edition
Chris Dent, Brenton J.W. Blawat

ISBN: 9781787126305

- Optimize code through the use of functions, switches, and looping structures
- Install PowerShell on your Linux system
- Utilize variables, hashes, and arrays to store data
- Work with Objects and Operators to test and manipulate data
- Parse and manipulate different data types
- Write .NET classes with ease within the PowerShell
- Create and implement regular expressions in PowerShell scripts
- Deploy applications and code with PowerShell's Package management modules
- Leverage session-based remote management
- Manage files, folders, and registries through the use of PowerShell

Leave a review - let other readers know what you think

Please share your thoughts on this book with others by leaving a review on the site that you bought it from. If you purchased the book from Amazon, please leave us an honest review on this book's Amazon page. This is vital so that other potential readers can see and use your unbiased opinion to make purchasing decisions, we can understand what our customers think about our products, and our authors can see your feedback on the title that they have worked with Packt to create. It will only take a few minutes of your time, but is valuable to other potential customers, our authors, and Packt. Thank you!

Index

B

base conversions
  performing 262, 263
Bash
  about 483
  output, comparing with PowerShell output 41,
    43, 45
binary numbers
  working with 260, 262
Boolean property
  reference 470
breakpoints
  using 365, 369
business intelligence (BI) 467

C

calculated properties
  working with 259, 260
calculations
  performing, on output 254, 257
cmdlets
  about 94, 96, 98, 100
  discovering 25, 26
  executing, on remote computers 401, 402
  executing, with minimal keystrokes 100, 103,
    105
  execution, recording on PowerShell console
    118, 120
  Linux admins note, writing 12
columns
  selecting, from output 148, 151, 153
Command-Line Interfaces (CLIs) 415
Common Language Infrastructure 10
complex loop
  writing, on predefined array 238, 240
conditional breakpoints
  using 370
connected classes 481
considerations, for complex script writing
  about 328
  functions, naming 330
  Host cmdlets, using 328
  objects, returning from functions 329
content

importing 172
searching for 297, 299
CronTab PowerShell module
  installing 138, 140
cross-platform T-SQL queries
  executing 472
  executing, on multiple series 474, 477
currently-running processes
  used, for measuring resource consumption 128,
    129
custom object
  creating, from returned object 186, 188, 189
custom type data
  removing 199, 200

D

date method
  working with 126, 127
date properties
  working with 122, 123, 125
DateTimeFormatInfo Class
  reference 125
debug output
  writing 360, 362
delays
  using 235, 237
dependencies
  adding 344
  handling 342
Desired State Configuration (DSC) 48
directory
  listing 305
  working with 303
disconnected classes 481
Docker container image
  pulling, from repository 510, 511
Docker containers
  listing 511, 514
  removing 517
  setting up, for PowerShell script execution 522
  starting 514, 516
  stopping 514, 516
  working with, using miscellaneous Docker
    PowerShell cmdlets 521
Docker Hub

working with 307, 310
Update-TypeData cmdlet
  reference 199
URI (Uniform Resource Identifier) 427

V

variables
  about 175
  used, for modifying shell behavior 68, 72, 74
Visual Studio Code
  Debug tab 360
  download link 65
  installing 64, 66
  reference 66

W

While loop construct
  using 243, 244
Windows PowerShell, comparison with PowerShell Core
  about 45
  convenience aliases 46
  Desired State Configuration (DSC) 48
  snap-ins 46
  workflow 47
Windows PowerShell
  comparing, with PowerShell Core 45
Windows
  OpenSSH configuration, sshd_config used 385, 387

www.ingramcontent.com/pod-product-compliance
Lightning Source LLC
Chambersburg PA
CBHW060637060326
40690CB00020B/4428